OASIS JOURNAL

2010

Stories

Poems

Essays

by New & Emerging Writers Over Fifty

Edited by Leila Joiner

Copyright © 2010 by Leila Joiner

All rights reserved. No part of this book may be reproduced or transmitted in any form or by any means, electronic or mechanical, including photocopying, recording, or by any information storage and retrieval system, without permission in writing from the publisher.

Published in the United States of America by:

Imago Press
3710 East Edison
Tucson AZ 85716

www.imagobooks.com

Names, characters, places, and incidents, unless otherwise specifically noted, are either the product of the author's imagination or are used fictitiously.

Cover Design and Book Design by Leila Joiner
Cover Photograph: Doorway at end of alley © FotoliaXIV

ISBN 978-1-935437-26-0
ISBN 1-935437-26-7

Printed in the United States of America on Acid-Free Paper

ACKNOWLEDGMENTS

I want to thank the OASIS Institute, all the judges who have generously volunteered their time to select our contest winners and comment on the work of our authors, and all the writers over fifty who continue to contribute their work to *OASIS Journal* every year.

May we all have many successful years ahead of us.

LIST OF ILLUSTRATIONS

"Blinded by Love," photograph © craetive, p. 20

"Enigma Wren," photograph courtesy of Margaret Francis, p. 96

"Tattoo," photograph courtesy of Trudy Campbell, p. 117

"Wild Thang," photograph by Suzanne Schmidt, p. 128

"Anziana signora seduta in solitudine," painting © carlacastagno, p 220

"Price of Bubbles," photograph courtesy of Mary Rose Durfee, p. 234

"The Mona Lisa Revisited," artwork by Sarah Bolek, p. 250

"Gently poppies on the canvas," artwork © Ivan Gulei, p. 264

"Nocturnal Dip," artwork courtesy of John J. Brennan, p. 266

"African Beauty," photo art © Yahya Idiz, p. 348

CONTENTS

EDITOR'S PREFACE	15

WINNER: BEST FICTION CONTEST
    SEARCHING FOR MR. MISTLETOE
    Janet E. Irvin
	21

WEDDING HIGH MASS IN TUCSON *Mary H. Ber*	32
BOUND *Tabinda Bashir*	33
LIFE INTERVENES *Tony Zurlo*	44
JAMAICA ROMANCE *Clare Selgin*	45
"AND ON THE SEVENTH DAY" *Teresa Civello*	57
CHOCOLATE COVERED GRAHAM CRACKERS *John Barbee*	59
A DATE TO REMEMBER *Michael B. Mossman*	61
SHE WAS LOST IN TIME *Manuel Torrez, Jr.*	64
THE PANHANDLER *Manuel Torrez, Jr.*	65

FINDING A PRISTINE FLOWER IN THE MAILBOX *Ruth Moon Kempher*	72
1st RUNNER-UP: BEST NON-FICTION CONTEST FLIRTING WITH FIASCO *Ruth Moon Kempher*	73
BELATED *Bobbie Jean Bishop*	77
LONG DARK NIGHT *Steve Snyder*	78
PRIZE FIGHTER *Ron Porter*	79
ONCE *Helen Benson*	80
THE WOUNDS OF A SISTER *Albert Russo*	81
A POEM AFTER AUSCHWITZ *Anthony Adrian Pino*	86
NIGHT TRAIN *Carol Poss*	87
WHERE IS HOPE, THERE IS LIFE *Jane Boruszewski*	88
AN ENIGMA WREN *Margaret Francis*	92
THE ROXBURY DIARY *Jack Campbell*	97
THE PEA COAT FIASCO *William Valitus*	103
CHRISTMAS 1944 *Martha J. Martin*	114
TATTOO *Trudy Campbell*	117

ORANGE AT DUSK *Tiina Heathcock*	118
A DATE WITH PAPA *Suse Marsh*	119
THE NIGHT MY FATHER DIED *Diana Griggs*	121
PLEA *Helen Benson*	122
LULLABY AND GOOD NIGHT *Marie Therese Gass*	123
AGE AIN'T NOTHIN' BUT A NUMBER *Suzanne Schmidt*	129
CONFUSION AT EDGEWATER MEMORY CARE *M. Clark Wilde*	133
SHE WAITS BESIDE MY BED *Anne Whitlock*	135
MRS. BUMBLE GOES TO TOWN *Ruth Turner*	136
A BUNCH OF DAFFODILS *Kathleen A. O'Brien*	138
INVISIBILITY *Kay Lesh*	139
MY BREATH *Carol Louise Christian*	141
CHOOSING BURIAL PLOTS *Maurice Hirsch*	142
IT ALL COMES DOWN TO THIS *Mary Lou Stafford*	143
CREATOR *Una Nichols Hynum*	144

TREASURED PLEASURE *Barbara M. Traynor*	145
NO SMALL GIFT *Evelyn Buretta*	147
1st RUNNER-UP: BEST POETRY CONTEST TODAY OUR TEACHER TAUGHT US HOW TO WRITE A LETTER *Tiina Heathcock*	148
ABANDONED *Nancy Sandweiss*	150
A CONVERSATION WITH AMY *Sarah Bolek*	151
ON BALDY *Jim Frisbie*	153
RUSHING THE GROWLER *Frederick J. Schubert*	154
THE DUMPSTER *David Ray*	155
MOTHERS TONGUE *Carol Louise Christian*	161
EARLY FAILURE *Mardy Stotsky*	162
INTROSPECTION *Tom Humphrey*	163
THE SANDALS *Jeanne Henderson*	171
VIGILANT *Natalie Gottlieb*	174
EXIT MY SOUL *Tina Mori*	175

ONLYNESS *Sarah Wellen*	180
UNDER THE PEAR TREE *Helena Frey*	181
COMING UPSTATE – THE IMMIGRANT EXPERIENCE *Adrienne Rogers*	185
THE QUALITY OF LIGHT *Judith K. Rose*	188
MOVING: *HELP WANTED* *Judy Ray*	189
CONTRAST IN HAIKU *Joan E. Zekas*	198
WHY DISTURB A WINNER? *Eleanor Whitney Nelson*	199
A PAINTED CLOCK *John Russell Webb*	202
A SECOND CHANCE *Sally Carper*	203
BENT TRUNKS *Sarah Wellen*	206
MIRACLES DO HAPPEN *Joan Harris*	207
HURRICANE 1938 *Una Nichols Hynum*	210
ROLLOVER *Fred K. Taylor*	211
HEARTLAND *Bobbie Jean Bishop*	214
A PLEASANT MEMORY *Paul E. Voeller*	215

EVENING LIGHT *Barbara Ponomareff*	216
CANCER *Joel Berman*	217
LLANA ESTACADO *Susan Cummins Miller*	221
FIRE *Mimi Moriarty*	222
SMALL MIRACLES *Ginger Galloway*	223
GOD DOESN'T MAKE MISTAKES *Mitzie Skrbin*	227
ACOUSTICS OF AUTUMN *Kathleen A. O'Brien*	228
THE DELIGHTFUL OBLIVION OF BEING FIVE *Sharon Laabs*	230
THE PRICE OF BUBBLES *Mary Rose Durfee*	231
POTTY CHAIR *Robert Brooks*	235
DINING ROOM CHAIR EPISODE *Sharon L. Voeller*	238
MESSAGES IN THE SAND *Dorothy Parcel*	239
COSMO DOG *Flora Gamez Grateron*	244
HANS *Eleanor Little*	246
DOG DAZE *Alfred J. Stumph*	248

LIFE WITH A CATERAN *Claudia Poquoc*	251
CHAT WITH A CAT *Anne Whitlock*	252
SPECIAL DELIVERY *Marilyn L. Kish Mason*	253
HARMONY *Kathleen Elliott-Gilroy*	255
SUMMER DREAM *Jean Chapman Snow*	256
TAKE-OUT DINNER *Barbara Ostrem*	257
ENCOUNTERS WITH CROWS *Ellaraine Lockie*	258
NOTE FROM A COBALT AZURE BUTTERFLY *Carrie Anne Howell*	260
FOR CREATION, BENEDICTION *Joan T. Doran*	262
LA SABANILLA DE SAN PASQUAL *Rita Ries*	265
THE UNEXPECTED GUEST AND HIS NOCTURNAL DIP *John J. Brennan*	267
WATERED DOWN MEMORIES *Phyllis J. Seltzer*	269
COMING OF AGE *Eileen M. Ward*	272
THE KNOTHOLE *Anne McKenrick*	273
WINNER: BEST NON-FICTION CONTEST BLINK *Tilya Gallay Helfield*	275

RUBY SLIPPERS *Bernadetter Blue*	286

2nd RUNNER-UP: BEST NON-FICTION CONTEST
    MOBIUS STRIP
        Janet K. Thompson
	287

A HAUNTING DREAM OF ANGELS *Seretta Martin*	291

WINNER: BEST POETRY CONTEST
    EVOLUTION
        Ellaraine Lockie
	292

CONIFER RESURRECTED *Evelyn Buretta*	293
OUTWARD BOUND *Lolene McFall*	294
STRATAGEMS *Neal Wilgus*	295
KILROY WAS HERE *Bill Alewyn*	301
ON THE LIP OF SUMMER *Irma Sheppard*	314
DYNAMITE *Andrew J. Hogan*	315
COMPUTERS ARE A GOOD THING *Nik Grant*	327
THE GORMLEY CURSE *Richard O'Donnell*	331
PINBALL *Esther Brudo*	340
SKINNY POST *Buck Dopp*	341

"IT'S NOT THE SAME!" *Alice Correll*	344
GOTTA GO *Susan Thompson*	345
HERE TO STAY *Jacqueline Hill*	347
CALLED HOME *Jacqueline Hill*	349
NEGOTIATING CULTURE *Tony Zurlo*	354
A FAKE ROLEX *Carl W. Snow*	355
THE SALAMI STORY *Howard Schuman*	359
AT THE SUPERMARKET THE OTHER DAY *Jean Marie Purcell*	362
2nd RUNNER-UP: BEST FICTION CONTEST FOOD FOR THOUGHT *Elisa Drachenberg*	363
2nd RUNNER-UP: BEST POETRY CONTEST WE DELIVER *William Killian*	376
A BLUE FUNK *Carol Poss*	378
WINDMILLS *Marlene Newman*	379
INVISIBLE *Gloria Salas-Jennings*	382
1st RUNNER-UP: BEST FICTION CONTEST SQUEEGEE *R. E. Hayes*	383

CURTAIN *William Killian*	391
CONTRIBUTORS' NOTES	393
ORDER INFORMATION	413

EDITOR'S PREFACE

This ninth annual edition of *OASIS Journal*, our biggest edition ever, contains the work of 112 writers over fifty from the U.S., Canada, and France. Why such a big book this year? Mainly because we had many more poems and short stories submitted than in previous years, while the nonfiction entries stayed about the same.

The most frequent themes in this year's entries seem to revolve around both positive and negative aspects of personal relationships, from family to friends to love and romance. Even animals get into the act. I received more entries involving pets and other non-domestic creatures than any other year.

As usual, our judges have provided helpful hints as to the reasons for their choices. I do recommend reading their comments after reading the winning entries, to see what attracted them to the work of these writers. The fiction judge, in particular, has shared general comments to all our readers, as well as submitting his list of honorable mentions.

L. J.

FICTION: Judge, Dan Gilmore, has published a novel, *A Howl for Mayflower* (Imago Press, 2006), and a collection of stories and poems, *Season Tickets* (Pima Press, 2003). He has received awards from the Raymond Carver Fiction Contest, the Martindale Fiction Award, and *Sandscript*. His poems have appeared in *Atlanta Review*, *Aethlon*, *Blue Collar Review*, *The Carolina Review*, *Rattle*, *Sandscript*, and *Still Crazy*. Several poems have been anthologized in *Loft and Range* (Pima Press, 2001). A book of collected and new poems, *Love Takes a Bow*, was published by Imago Press in April 2010.

As Raymond Carver said, "The next best thing to writing your own short story is to read someone else's short story." I had the pleasure of reading twenty of them sent to me by Leila Joiner, who founded *OASIS Journal* several years back as a place for older writers to show their work. She asked me to read the stories blind (without knowing the authors' names) and select the three I liked best. Before telling you my method and choices, a few words about Leila and *OASIS Journal*.

What a service Leila Joiner has done for all of us. Much of the material in past issues of *OASIS Journal* has been top notch, but, perhaps more importantly, the *Journal* has been a place where less experienced writers can show their work. John Gardner once said that the world does not need another bad story (or something to that effect). I disagree. Writing, especially writing by older folks, is not necessarily about producing a great story or poem or essay. Writing for us is a way to discover the wondrous richness of our lives and imagination. It helps us connect with ourselves and thus with the world. *OASIS Journal* is part of that world, and I am privileged to play a part in judging this year's short stories. First my biases.

I am drawn most to stories about real people in realistically detailed situations. I like stories that catch a character in dramatic situations that count: love, death, ambition, self-delusion, the struggle to survive in real human situations that bring out the best and worst. I want to be drug into a story. I want my mouth to fall open. I want surprise and tears and laughter. I want to learn something about people I'll never meet except on the page.

My method was to read all twenty stories straight through fairly quickly. Then I read them again more slowly and selected my favorites according to my biases. I ended up with six favorites. I read these six again and picked my favorite and two runners-up.

WINNER: "Searching for Mr. Mistletoe" [Janet E. Irvin]

This was my clear favorite. It's a seamless story that feels real, that feels as if the writer knows exactly what she is talking about. It has a memorable and likable narrator with a sense of humor who tells a heartbreaking story. This is a fine and moving piece of writing.

FIRST RUNNER-UP: "Squeegee" [R. E. Hayes]

This is a well-crafted, efficient exploration of the horrors faced by a cop convicted of murder who is now an ex-con trying to exist with the realities of a world that rejects him and a head filled with his own fear. This story feels as if the writer knows at a deep level what's going on in the protagonist's world.

SECOND RUNNER-UP: "Food for Thought" [Elisa Drachenberg]

This was more difficult to choose. I finally settled on "Food for Thought" because I was pulled into the bizarre world of a very unreliable narrator who, to put it lightly, likes things to go his way.

I can't leave it at that. Although Leila Joiner didn't ask me for honorable mentions, I feel compelled to recommend: "Introspection," "The Panhandler," "The Gormley Curse," "Exit My Soul," and "The Dumpster." I hope you read these stories with the same joy and excitement I experienced.

POETRY: Judge, Robert Longoni, has taught at the University of Arizona, directed the university's poetry center for one year and taught 23 years at Pima Community College, Tucson, retiring as faculty emeritus. His poems have appeared in periodicals, two anthologies, and his collection of work, *Woodpiles*. He also has edited two poetry volumes. Longoni is a resident of Chandler, Arizona and has conducted workshops for Phoenix College, the Writer's Voice and in western New Mexico, where he spends his summers.

It was difficult judging this contest because so many of the submissions held up well through several re-readings, resisting elimination and sometimes even growing in appeal. In the end I chose the three that held my interest the longest.

WINNER: "Evolution" [Ellaraine Lockie]
The winning poem stood out because of its arresting images, which account for much of the emotional impact. They combine with efficient language and form to sustain and heighten a sense of the prevalence of violence, both in the natural scheme of things and in acts of human depravity. The unexpected note of ambivalence at the end—a fittingly human response.

FIRST RUNNER-UP: "today our teacher taught us how to write a letter" [Tiina Heathcock]
The appeal of this poem begins with the disarmingly ordinary title, which becomes increasingly ironic as the child continues her petitions to her absent father. The epistolary form is the right vehicle for revealing character indirectly, as do most dramatic monologues, but in this case it isn't the speaker (or writer) whose secrets are exposed—the child's innocence is never in question—but the cruel surrogate father's and, to a lesser extent, the mother's, who is trapped in her own culpable submissiveness. Simultaneously, and significantly, we learn in the same way about the real father's sorely missed parental warmth. Finally, the balanced shape of the poem provides one more way of subtly pointing to the difference between appearance and underlying reality.

SECOND RUNNER-UP: "We Deliver" [William Killian]
One might expect that the unfolding of the tragic event at the center of "We Deliver" is what provides the principal impact of the narrative. But what interested me most about the poem was how that event is entangled with the story of the narrator's awakening to the fact that the amusement he found in trying to take advantage of a seemingly inconsequential misdialing of a telephone number is itself of no significance in the face of human suffering. Even the generosity he shows when he decides after all to deliver the pizza without thought to his own profit fades into insignificance when he discovers

the boundless generosity of the friends of the victim's family, which they extend even to him in the form of extravagant tips. In the end, it is their story that shapes his.

NON-FICTION: Judge, Allyson Latta, editor of award-winning literary fiction and non-fiction. Based in Toronto, Canada, she has for the past 14 years worked with authors of books such as *The Polished Hoe*, winner of the 2003 Commonwealth Writers Prize; *A Blade of Grass*, nominated for the 2004 Man Booker Prize; *Someone Knows My Name*, winner of the 2008 Commonwealth Writers Prize; and the memoir, *The Boy in the Moon*, this year's recipient of Canada's richest non-fiction award. Visit her site at: www.daysroadwriters.blogspot.com.

WINNER: "Blink" [Tilya Gallay Helfield]

At times humorous, at times poignant, this memoir stands out among the nonfiction finalists as a story told using some of the most effective elements of fiction. The opening piques the reader's curiosity: "It was snowing heavily the night Joan took me to see Harold ...." Who is this Harold, and how did he end up where he is? But "Blink" is more than a character sketch of an unusual boy and his tragic life. It explores along the way the writer's feelings about her childhood during the 1940s, and the differences she observes and experiences between her family and another Jewish family in the neighbourhood. As the narrative unfolds, even the minor characters come alive. The flow is seamless, from the "now" of the story back to the 1940s and forward again, the words chosen with care, the dialogue natural. The final words vibrate in the heart.

FIRST RUNNER-UP: "Flirting with Fiasco" [Ruth Moon Kempher]

The unique and appealing voice of the narrator, beleaguered by disappointment and yet with a resilient spirit, stands out in this short, moving memoir. The use of language is at times unusual, but somehow makes the story all the more fresh and striking. Skilfully crafted, the piece weaves together an older woman's observations of a young boy on a bicycle and bittersweet memories from her life. The ending is understated and achingly beautiful.

SECOND RUNNER-UP: "Mobius Strip" [Janet K. Thompson]

This deceptively simple story's originality is what strikes the reader. The language is spare, the narrator's voice familiar, as if she's chatting with us casually over a cup of tea at her kitchen table. She's recounting the stories of two friends, women whose life paths have been remarkably different. But the piece seduces and then surprises, its meaning far greater than the size of its canvas suggests.

OASIS JOURNAL
2010

Stories

Poems

Essays

Winner: Best Fiction Contest

Searching for Mr. Mistletoe

Janet E. Irvin

For twenty years my husband, Harlan, refused to go to the dentist. When he finally agreed to let Dr. Ellis examine his teeth, she discovered the rotten truth. Four appointments later, all those gleaming pearly whites were gone. And that was the end of our kissing. It about killed me to think no more mouth-to-mouth. I remembered the first time, walking home from Ohio University's Memorial Auditorium right before Christmas break. The snow fell in soft wet hunks and that halo effect around the streetlights turned Athens into a blanket of accumulated wonder. Harlan, scuffing his combat boots in the soft white flakes, shoulders hunched forward in the green Army jacket he wore home from Nam, asked could he walk with me. Halfway down Jeff Hill, he just put one arm around my shoulders, leaned down and planted one. My mouth tingled for a month.

This memory attacked me as I sat in the gynecologist's office, waiting for my yearly checkup and reading one of those women's magazines filled with articles about estrogen drying up and collagen treatments for your lips and how to spice up your sex life after fifty. That's when the idea came to me. A kissing contest to raise money for the food pantry. To find the best kisser in Pike County. A vicarious hunt for what had been rinsed out of my love life. I would call it "The Search for Mr. Mistletoe."

I felt a bit preoccupied as I walked into the November meeting of the Interdenominational Ladies Auxiliary at the Episcopalian Church on South Street, but I shook off the feeling as soon as I spied Yolanda Coomer setting up a CD show of her trip to the Australian Outback.

"Lord help us, it's another travelogue," I groaned to the statue of St. Francis. He declined to comment. Maybe he liked watching all those photographs of leaping kangaroos. I couldn't imagine why. All you ever saw was the back end of anything Yolanda video'd. Squirrels. Rabbits. Wild turkeys.

You name it, she snapped its picture a second later than precisely necessary for good coverage. I hoped it wasn't too late for me. The gynecologist told me I had to get a follow-up mammogram. Something about calcifications and cysts.

We were well past Yolanda's account of her two-week vacation Down Under before I found the courage to stand up and offer my suggestion for the contest.

"What's your ulterior motive, Carla?" Yolanda asked, slipping her designer frames two inches down her nose and giving me the stare over the top of the sparkly alligator-striped rims.

I flipped my hair back off my forehead, touched my index finger to my teeth and sighed. "Now, Yolie, you know the pantry needs supplies. I just thought this might liven up the fundraising." Behind me, the spinster Deutcher twins murmured their approval.

Sister Clementine folded her arms across her Santa belly and shook her head. "No can do, Carla," she said. "The Christmas Carnival is only three weeks away. How will we ever get out enough publicity?"

"You aren't really going to kiss anybody, are you?" Reverend Spicer's wife interrupted, sitting up straight in her folding chair and pursing her lips together in awkward imitation of a crow. The Presbyterians always wanted to know the nuts and bolts of things. We Catholics, on the other hand, didn't mind a little ambiguity.

"Well," I temporized, thinking fast. That had been my intention. Sort of. "Why not make it an essay contest? Write a nominating paragraph and tell why your mister is the best candidate."

"Good idea." Sister Clementine, English teacher syndrome rearing its head, had jumped on board. "We can encourage literacy at the same time." Heads nodded up and down the rows.

"Well," Yolanda spoke up, eyeing me once more down the ski slope of her snoz, "why not let Carla take charge of the entire project? I'm sure she's capable of handling her own idea."

I resented her emphasis of the word *entire*, but I did think I could do it, so I stuck my hand out and forced her to shake.

When I got home that night, Harlan had already received a phone call. "What's this about a kissing contest, Carla?" he asked, standing in front of the open refrigerator in his tighty whities, assessing the possibilities of a late night snack.

"You shouldn't be eating all that rich food right before bedtime," I said, taking the carrot cake out of his hand and setting it back on the shelf. "Have a glass of milk."

Harlan gave me one of those old married looks that meant *don't tell me what to do*, but he put down the fork, whispered *later* to the cake, and settled for a few slices of Swiss cheese on crackers.

"What'd Dr. Blair say?" he said, scooching his butt onto one of the counter stools and brushing crumbs off his stomach. I turned my back and ran water in the sink, scrubbing at the ink and marker stains on my fingers, leftovers from grading Spanish III quizzes. A snail trail of ice crystals zigzagged their way across the windowpane, warning of the storm to come.

"I have to go in for another test." I stared into the darkened window, clinging to the edge of the countertop and thinking about lumps and kisses and the meaning of life. When Harlan slipped his arms around me, I crept back to that memory of the snow falling and our first kiss, full of its own kind of wonder and the promise of new beginnings. Tomorrow I'd send an ad to the Personals column of the *Waverly Gazette*. That ought to flush out some potential candidates.

PUCKER UP!
Who's the BEST MALE KISSER in Pike County? Send a 100-word paragraph nominating your favorite smoocher to P.O. Box 135 Quarry, OH 44001 by Dec. 10. $100 prize awarded at the Quarry Christmas Carnival. Entry fee: $5 donation to the Pike County Food Pantry.

༄

"Señora," Tatiana called, "do I really have to wear reindeer ears?"

I looked up from the essay I was reading and stared at the group clustered around my desk. "If that's what it says in the directions," I said, crossing out an incorrect use of the verb *ser* and replacing it with *estar*. *Yo quiero estar en Hawaii*. I want to be in Hawaii. *Yo también*. I nodded in agreement with the writer.

"You'll make a great reindeer," Tyrell said, poking at her dimpled cheek. "I'm Santa." He puffed out his belly and waddled across the choir room. Practice for the traditional senior pageant began in ten minutes, but most of the students had already shuffled in, anxious to find out precisely which person each had drawn for a partner. The skit was built around the idea of hunting for the Jingle Bell rock and included a cameo performance by jolly old principal McCormick, he of the hairy nostrils and peppermint breath.

"Mrs. McNair." Paco Campbell leaned over my shoulder and fiddled with the egg timer I used to keep us on schedule. "I heard…" A hush crept over the room, just like that old securities' commercial on television. Paco always brought the juiciest rumors to practice. I lifted my head and sighed.

"You heard what?" I asked.

"I heard you were holding a kissing contest at the Carnival." A burst of excited laughter greeted this announcement.

"You heard…" I paused, too, just to drag out the suspense a little longer, "…right."

"Wow!" Paco straightened up, stroking the fuzz of beard that had recently taken over his chin. Then he looked straight at Margaret Kali, and I knew who would be practicing with whom tonight. I had to straighten out this misconception.

"The contest," I said, tapping my pencil for order, "is an essay contest. No real kissing is involved."

I watched their shoulders slump, their expectations deflated by reality. *Get used to it, kids*, I thought as I put down my pencil and smiled at Tina Albert and Patsy Tori, who were studying verb conjugations in the corner. Amid a general sigh of dismay, I moved to the middle of the room and called the rehearsal to order. We had almost reached the halfway point before Beryl Benjamin, all six feet two inches of feminine energy, pointed her long thin arm at me and thundered, "Mrs. Mac, who's going to be the judge?"

I hadn't thought of that.

The Post Office mailbox exploded into my waiting hands when I stopped by a week later to check on things.

"Lots of folks think they know who kisses best in this county," Martha Petee said, leaning around the end of the counter to see me better. She lifted a stack of envelopes and held them out for me to take. "Here's a few more."

"Thanks, Martha." I wrestled the stack into my backpack and roosted the bulging bag on the ledge. "I never dreamed so many people would want to talk about kissing." We shared a giggle.

"Well," Martha said, "good news for the food pantry, I think."

I agreed with her, took another deep breath and lifted my bag, preparing to leave, when she called my name again from the back room.

"Almost forgot." Gasping and out of breath from lugging her large bosom back and forth, Martha leaned on the counter. "This came certified for you, Carla. Didn't get around to delivering it earlier."

I reached for the envelope, hefting the slender contents. Good news. Bad news. They both weighed the same. I looked at the return address: Radiology Associates, 786 River Street, Chillicothe, Ohio. I stuffed the envelope into the bag along with all the kissing letters and hurried to the car. I needed to pick up our Thanksgiving turkey before five.

"Alexander says he really likes your class," Yolanda commented, the barest whiff of skepticism floating behind her words, as she passed me another plate to fill with green beans and fruit salad. The ladies of the Auxiliary stood behind the long tables, serving Thanksgiving dinner to the down and out of Pike County. Most of them—the ladies, I mean, not the down and out—had assigned their husbands to watch over the roasting turkeys in their ovens at home. I felt a bit nervous about Harlan's vigilance. He tended to fall asleep while watching one of the innumerable football games that marched across the channels on turkey day. Although the Spicers had invited us to dine with them, we elected to stay home. Neither of our boys could make it for dinner. Paul, stationed in Iraq, would call when he could, and Evan didn't have the energy between shifts at the hospital for more than a courtesy chat. Interns rarely got time off, and Chicago was far enough away to make travel difficult. Besides, with storms plowing their way across the heartland, flying turned into stress city. And I didn't want them to sense my unease. Those boys always read me better than Harlan did.

"That's nice," I said. I had taken a vow of politeness for the holiday and pressed my lips to guard against any untoward remarks. Hoping to forestall any further discussion of classroom activities, I plopped a large helping of stuffing on the plate and lifted it to Sister Clementine for gravy.

"So," Yolanda responded, clutching the plate I reached to take from her, "how's the contest coming along? Had many entries?"

I tugged at the dish, but Yolanda just tugged back, her face squished up in a frown. "A whole bagful," I said, nodding at my book bag sprawled in the corner by the kitchen door. "The biggest problem will be picking a winner."

Yolanda sniffed and let go of the plate. I rocked backward, windmilling a bit as I tried to regain my balance. Virginia Conn pushed me upward and whispered encouragement.

"Well, I'm sure you'll pick someone, you know, good at reading." Virginia brushed imaginary crumbs off my shoulder and returned to her station by the cranberries.

Yolanda sniffed again, louder, plunking a full helping of beans and fruit onto another plastic plate, and I realized with a shock that she thought I'd already selected the winner. I decided to change the subject.

"I think you'll be pleased with the pageant this year. Rolf's one of the Magi." I neglected to say that her son was one of the rocking Magi. He and George Swift and Hamilton Rudolph had been practicing their song and dance to the classic "Rock me gently, Rock me slowly" and were set to bring the house down with their can-can routine.

Monica Dipinski raised her head at my announcement and nodded. "Emily's one of the famous sports figures. They're singing Queen's 'We will rock you.'" She handed a full plate to one of our patrons and shook her head. "I don't know why, but she just loves that song."

General chatter gave over to concentration as the number of people waiting in line swelled out the door. I wiped my forehead on my sleeve and straightened my back. Only two hours more, and I could lie down for a nap. The chapter tests would just have to wait. But first I had to take care of Yolanda.

"Oh, Yolie." She lifted her head and stared straight at me, eyes unblinking and green in the light of the fluorescent bulbs hanging above the tables. "Since you're such a good reader…" I said, which was nothing more than the truth. Yolanda knew everything there was to know about all the best sellers on the New York Times Bestseller lists. Her summer reading material would sink the Titanic, if it hadn't already been downed by an iceberg. Come to think of it, Yolie reminded me of an iceberg herself, that jutting jaw and those steely eyes. Carla, I tutted, stay on track. "Don't forget to take my bag with you when you leave."

"Now, why ever would I do that, Carla McNair?" Yolanda smoothed her apron over her ski slope of a tummy and waited.

"Because, Yolie," I said, batting my eyes at her nervous stare, "you're going to judge the Mr. Mistletoe essays." I turned away before she could object and passed one more plate to Sister Clementine.

So much for diplomacy.

Sleet battered against the roof of the auditorium, punctuating each song with a tin drum solo. I thought Gene Krupa and sighed. No way Harlan and I would make it to dance class this week. He had agreed, after a fair amount of pouting on my part, to accompany me to tango and rumba lessons, a gift from the boys for my fiftieth birthday. I love to dance, and the only time I get to exercise my sense of rhythm is after Harlan has one too many at a wedding reception. Even then, we only do the shuffle and sway. Thinking of the unidentified lump bearing down on another of my favorite pastimes, I had hurried to sign us up for Wednesday nights in December. I just forgot about the dress rehearsal.

"Bobbie. Angel," I called, raising my voice to be heard above the rain symphony, "please don't fidget when you're in the manger." The faux Mary and Joseph managed to look chastised, but I saw the smiles creasing their downturned eyes. Bobbie was supplying the live animals for the nativity and, with her smooth, rosy complexion, was a perfect Madonna. The Magi trio lined up next to the Plymouth Rock boys. Berry, Parker, Albert, and Klem adjusted their pilgrim hats and hummed the chorus of "Rock of Ages." Guitar chords drifted out of the dressing room as Will introduced Ellie Morrison and Terry Banford in the first stanza of "Old Time Rock and Roll." Rafi Shujaat tugged my sleeve.

"Mrs. Mac, do I really have to wear this?" His ninja headscarf kept slipping every time he and Clark Donaldson danced to "Rock the Kasbah." I just nodded. The noise in my head sounded like a jet standing by for takeoff. I shooed everyone away, took a swallow from my water bottle and tried to breathe. Somewhere in the middle of my right breast a tumor grew—silent, grim, and potentially fatal. The thought threatened to spill out of my mouth in one long moan, but I clamped my lips against the tidal surge and looked at my watch.

"One more time, and then we'll call it a night."

Paco slumped down beside my deck chair and followed the script as the acts scrolled across the stage. Luke, Joe, and Chico Radigan had just finished their version of "Jailhouse Rock" when I felt him staring at me.

"What?" I barked, more crossly than I intended. Paco blinked but he didn't let my crabbiness stop him.

"Who'd you nominate, Señora?"

"Nominate?" I asked. It was a stupid question, but my mind didn't care.

"For Mr. Mistletoe," he said. "Did you nominate Mr. McNair?"

Tatiana waved at me. "How's my dress, Señora?" I gave her a thumbs up and turned in my seat to look at Paco. He avoided my eyes, but he didn't stop talking.

"Well, I just thought you'd write about Mr. Mac. You're always telling us stories about when you met. Like how you bumped heads in the bookstore reaching for the same copy of *Captains Courageous*. And how, the next time you met, you spilled a chocolate frosty all over his shoes."

Good thing the theater was dark. I felt a blush start up from my shoulders and settle across my cheeks. Had I really shared all those memories with my students? Had I forgotten what they meant? I hadn't once thought about submitting Harlan's name, even though it had been the memory of what a good kisser he used to be, about how much I liked his kisses, that had inspired the whole contest. "I guess I've been too busy, Paco," I said, swallowing down my embarrassment and my guilt.

"Never too late, Mrs. Mac," he said, unfolding his long legs and rising like a giant preying mantis wearing a sixties basketball uniform and a flowing Superman cape.

"You're right, Paco," I told him, but in my heart I didn't believe it. My fingers crept closer to my right breast, settled for the rib cage and clamped tight against my side. Maybe it was too late, after all.

By the time I packed up the last of the loose scripts and double-checked the locks on all the outside doors, the sullen skies had turned to full dark. Heavy clouds obscured the wan light of the moon and dripped snowflakes as I trudged my way to my car. Most of the students were gone, but silhouetted by the parking lot light a couple stood in close embrace, heads tilted forward, arms wrapped around each other. I didn't know who it was, and I didn't care. They seemed to embody all that promise and passion of youth and health that Harlan and I had held so long ago. I envied them their beginning.

I waited until they pulled away before I put the key in the ignition. Passing through the intersection two blocks from my house, I noticed the sanctuary light gleaming in the lobby of Community Baptist. Not my church, but I suspected God wasn't particular about where you worshipped. He just liked seeing your face now and then. Feeling the need of a little spiritual uplifting,

I coasted into the space next to the pastor's car. The snow made a more serious attempt to cover the lot, but I hugged my coat to my chest and plunged ahead.

No one was inside, although I could hear soft clinking sounds as John Hastings, Community's newest minister, worked in the office. Sliding onto one of the benches, I looked around, then hunched over and crossed myself. I didn't think John cared, but if one of the more conservative members of the congregation caught me doing that papist thing, there might be hell to pay at the next Auxiliary meeting. A carved mahogany cross hung slow and steady over the minister's chair. I wondered at the strength it took to open your arms and give yourself up to the moment. To know that pain crouched, a fierce and deadly animal, waiting for its moment to clamp your body in its terrible grip. I was afraid, and the words I recited offered no consolation. So I stared into the face of the greatest suffering, the greatest triumph over fear and death, and I cried.

Harlan was waiting at the kitchen table, his face pale but composed, his hand clutching a letter. "Why didn't you call them?"

"Nice to see you too, honey," I said, thumping my bag of papers and books on the floor and unwinding my scarf. "Call who?"

"Carla, don't tell me you didn't get the first letter." He was angry now, red and white splotches dotting his cheeks and forehead like a flashing neon sign.

I snatched the letter out of his hand and looked at the heading. Radiology Associates. "We have scheduled you for a biopsy..."

"There's a message from Dr. Blair's office, too." Harlan gestured at the answering machine, where the counter read 4.

"There are four messages," I said.

"They're all the same." He leaned on the table to stop the trembling in his arms. I had never seen him so upset. "How could you ignore this?"

I covered my ears to block out his shouting and thought about going to the post office for the letters and talking with Martha Petee, and it hit me. I had stuffed the letter in with all the Mr. Mistletoe entries. And I groaned. That first letter from Radiology Associates had been given into Yolanda Coomer's crocodile grasp. I sat down on the couch. I didn't look at Harlan.

"When do I have to go in?"

"The surgery's scheduled for Friday," he said.

"But I can't go then," I said. "That's the first night of the play." I thought of Tatiana and Rolf and George and Rafi and all the students, how hard they all had worked and how proud I was of this year's class, and I couldn't stand any of it one minute longer. Harlan caught me just before I swandived into the empty space between disappointment and fear.

I tried to ignore the IV in my hand, the one they'd used to calm me prior to rolling me down the hall and into uncertainty. Instead, I counted the holes in one of the ceiling tiles, multiplying my count by the number of tiles directly above my curtained square of pre-op heaven. I avoided thinking about Yolanda Coomer's cryptic message to "Just relax. I've got everything under control." I tried to recall the name of the patron saint of hopeless causes, but my mind kept skittering back to the Mr. Mistletoe contest and Yolanda's exuberant our-contest-raised-five-hundred-dollars-for-the-food-pantry announcement over the phone when she called last night. She didn't mention the letter from the radiology lab, but I knew in my heart she had seen it, read it, digested the information like a toad. *Oh, be kind, Carla*, I remonstrated, re-counting the ceiling tiles and releasing the balloon of my resentment. It floated upward and bobbed quietly next to the dance lessons I didn't get to take and the one holding all my unfinished cleaning chores.

"Carla?" Harlan tugged at my hand, the one he held next to his chest. I stopped looking up and blinked him into focus. I intended to say *what* but stopped short of the initial consonant sound. Whatever they were pumping into me blurred the edges of everything. All I heard clearly was Harlan's heart beating strong and steady against my hand.

"The kids are here."

I smiled. My sons had come to be with me. "Well, then, let me see 'em," I mumbled, struggling to inch my head higher on the pillow. But it wasn't Paul and Evan who crowded next to the gurney. It was Sophia and Beryl and Will and Ali and Emily and Rafi and Paco. All the players from the cast filled the small space, pushing up against the bed, belling out the privacy curtain. Now, I can't swear I saw all of them, but Harlan told me later. They had all skipped school to come cheer me on.

Paco stood next to me, shuffling his feet and clearing his throat. "How ya doing, Señora?"

A nurse peeked around the curtain and harrumphed. "It's almost time to go, Mrs. McNair."

Paco bit at his lower lip. "We just came by to wish you luck and give you this." He held out a small plaque. The light glared on the inscription, but I could just make out the letters that spelled WINNER.

"What did you win, Paco?" I asked, my eyes drifting to the ceiling tiles and those bobbing balloons of missed opportunity.

"Not me, Mrs. Mac," he said. "You. You won. Mr. Mac is Mr. Mistletoe for the Carnival." He set the engraved wooden tablet by my hand, the one Harlan wasn't holding anymore.

"But I didn't enter the contest," I said, my words slow but emphatic.

"No," he said, and the group behind him laughed.

"We entered for you," Tatiana said, stepping out from behind Paco.

And then the nurse closed in again and shooed them all away. Harlan tucked the plaque next to my head, leaned down and kissed me gently on the lips. "I changed the date for the lessons," he whispered. "You'll be dancing again by New Year's."

Some guy in a white mask appeared beside the bed to take my pulse. I felt the slip of time as he rolled me toward the door. The plaque scratched at my ear. Reaching over, Harlan shoved it under the pillow, touched my cheek and smiled, his new teeth gleaming in the bright overhead lights. Everything shifted to white then, and we were back in that first moment of promise and passion, walking downhill in the snow.

WEDDING HIGH MASS IN TUCSON
(to Don)

Mary H. Ber

Light the ocotillo candles.
Et introibo et altare Dei.
I want to marry under this blooming palo verde,
      thick as butter over coarse desert bread,
Give *Gloria* for a million golden chalices
      on the altar of Sonora.
Credo: I believe in breathing
      in fire on the tip of ocotillos,
      in the holiness of palo verde
Sanctus. Sanctus. Sanctus.
In this moment I marry everything:
      the strutting quail,
          saguaros, quiet and wise in centuries
              of witnessing,
         blue ocean of sky drenching arid earth.
I marry it all.
It becomes my body;
I become its soul.
Benedictus qui venit in nomine Domine.
May blessings rain
      on this great, round whole.
May the lambs of God
      have green enough to graze on
and the oil we pump
      be used for consecration.
May sons and daughters hold us
      deep in prayer
      in secula seculorum
Ite missa est.

Bound

Tabinda Bashir

Not of my liking, not at my insistence, not on my behalf, not at my request, and not with my agreement, I was born.

I was floating in a liquid dream of tranquility attached just by a cord to the source. My posture easy and comfortable with my head bent, eyes closed, arms and knees across the chest, I was in complete balance. I got nourishment from all around me in that surreal surrounding with some soothingly swishing and mild thumping sounds. Occasionally, I kicked and flailed my arms in joy as I celebrated my being. My abode had no boundaries and, if any, they were all subservient to me. I observed the milieu through closed eyes. Time did not exist. I was at peace. I wanted to be there…forever. That was exclusively my world.

I felt a slight pressure, like some soft pleasurable affectionate caress that brought sweet sleep, then invigorating arousal. I enjoyed those snuggles that siphoned life through me. My arms and legs undulated to the rhythm of that soft thumping music. I celebrated being. I thanked.

The soft pressure became frequent, and I loved it. I was being caressed. Then, a mild push. Oh yes, I was being cajoled, I was loved. Being was mine, the whole was mine, and I was the center.

The pressure became a push, a persistent push. It bothered me some. Unknown boundaries began pressing in. Then, with a sudden thrust, I was thrown out in a strange circumstance. I didn't know I had feet until I was held upside down, and I heard whispers, then loud words of worry. Someone gave me a sharp slap, and I gave a cry of agonizing pain and heard happiness, joy, congratulations. My eyes blinked in the dazzling lights of a sterile labor room.

"It's a girl."

"Tell those outside to offer a prayer of thanks and distribute food among the poor," said a voice I knew, one that would nurture me through life: Amma, my mother.

A long period of helplessness started after that. I was bathed and fed and carried from one place to the other by different hands. I felt ultimate peace in only one place, my mother's arms, where I had the same feeling of being nurtured. The hands that cared for me were not all gentle. I cried.

A few months later, my eyes learned to focus, and I saw a face smiling at me while I nuzzled around the breast: Amma, the source of my life. In the haze of colors and lights I grew familiar with people, things.

Little steps, but always guided. I could not do anything myself. Nourishment came more from the bottle and spoons and less from mother. I tried to run toward her but fell and heard loud laughter, which bothered me and I cried. I also cried when, dressed in fancy uncomfortable clothes, they asked me to blow out a candle. Hands, hands, hands, all alien. I resented the cuddles, the smiles of all except one, the one who had carried me in a sea of tranquility quite unlike the bath water I was thrust in. I longed for the quiet and peace of before. There was no escape. But, when Ginger the cat rubbed his furry head against my face, I squealed with delight. It reminded me of the warmth I had left far behind.

I walked to school, still guided. Life began to dictate norms, and all attempts at any other behavior were discouraged. Conformity was the rule. I read, played, and ate with others like me, all of us bewildered at what had happened. We were unable to comprehend where our paradise had gone, or if we had any. We laughed and clapped with the teacher, but our eyes betrayed the fact that we were looking for something that was not there. With time we learned that to follow was the only way to live. Some who tried otherwise were sent to the doctor or to special schools.

Lahore, Pakistan. Our extended family lived in a large compound spread over a couple of acres at the far end of the Canal Road, with separate houses for near relatives. They came and went freely with hardly a quiet moment. In that busy atmosphere, I conformed, smiled and frowned at the right moments, became a straight 'A' student; all in the hope of one day having my own space, which I could regulate myself.

One day, I rushed in from school, threw my bag on the floor and ran to the kitchen to get a glass of water. I wanted to show Amma my report card that had an A on every subject. Immediately, Uncle Basit said, "Steady, steady. What is the hurry? We are not supposed to pound the earth. A light step will not delay you for anything in life."

I froze in my step. I smiled and said, "Yes, Uncle." Then I proceeded to my room. I had lost interest in the report card. I resented being instructed at every step. Now I had to pay attention and look pleased. Why? Who was I? Why was I being molded? For what purpose? The question remained unanswered. I retreated to the family library and looked to Firdausi, Hafiz, Saadi, Ghalib for answers, half understanding what they said; I was too young. The void stayed.

Much to my inconvenience, I kept schedules, for I was a free spirit. Once in a while, I longed to be just by myself, away from the family and school, and often went into a room, closed the blinds, put the lights off and just sat. Peace, escape.

Amma took time from her household routine and talked with me. She encouraged me to face the facts of life. At times she took me to the nearby hamlet where she was helping to set up a girls' vocational center. She also helped people with their personal problems. Her face glowed when she visited the farmers' mud houses and told them about basic hygiene.

One such day we went to Zainab's house, a widow who had eked a meager living to bring up her two young sons out in the fields. Zainab had food ready for us and insisted we eat before we got to business. She said, "Guests bring God's blessings. We should eat something to solemnize the occasion."

Her simple meal of spicy mustard greens curry, flat corn *chapattis* with a dollop of fresh butter and a drink of *lassi* from freshly churned yoghurt was garnished with her affections. Zainab gave a toothless smile when she saw us enjoying the meal. Who said that poor people had a hard life? She looked perfectly happy to me. After the meal Zainab kissed me on my forehead, untied a ten paisa coin from the corner of her veil and gave it to me, saying, "This is my gift for you." That small coin could not buy anything but I kept it for a long time, as if she were with me.

Amma and Zainab then got down to business, checking her accounts. I looked at their tranquil faces, then drifted out to absorb the calm of the vast expanse of green fields, each leaf illuminated with bright sunlight lavished by the heavens. In that sea of green some squares stood out white with radish flowers, some yellow with mustard. I inhaled deeply to get that expansive coolness in me. I never wanted to leave.

Father told me about the books he was reading. He tried to make Rumi, Firdausi, and other philosophers easy for me to understand as he answered my questions. Those books were my refuge.

Auntie Halima said to Amma once, "Why does she turn only to you, when we are all here to help? This is the good thing about extended families. Is she insecure or a rebel? Her school report says she mostly looks out of the window with a faraway look in her eyes. And she excels in arts. That will not help her in setting up her own family."

"Yes, sometimes I wonder. But she will be fine if we just let her be. Education will surely help her find herself. I always wanted one. I think women are much more capable than we give them credit for. They should do a little more than just housework."

"In our Eastern culture? You know what happens if girls become too independent!"

"I leave it to God."

"As you wish! But I think the sooner you take care of it, the better." She rolled her eyes, raised her hands, and left.

End of school. Time for independence. I got a job, my own place, my own circle of friends who would let me be who I was, all in the hope of getting that elusive composure where I could do as I wanted. I could go anywhere or not go as I pleased. The office schedule, like that of the school, stayed with me. The pressure of work sometimes compelled me to stay overtime; no escape. I had to keep a decent relationship with colleagues and seniors or be branded strange.

Then it happened. I looked at him and forgot where I was. A hand came forward and a salaam, a smile like a million flowers, a thousand rainbows, the quickening of my heart—indescribable feelings. I quickly steadied myself and answered the greeting.

"I am new here. I will be thankful if you guide me in the first few days, as we shall be working together," he said.

I agreed, but I don't remember what I said. I glided back to my seat, sat down and put a hand on my chest to steady my heart. Had I made a spectacle of myself? What would my colleagues be thinking? From then on, I felt like he was always with me. I smiled at the most trivial things. I loved to be with him at the office. At home, I didn't mind the cacophony of people's chatter, clinking china, and blaring music. I was in heaven. He brought blitheness and left me speechless. Working with him required some effort, as I had to steady myself to look for the right words to say.

Would he reciprocate? I waited. I yearned to be alone with him, to just look at him and not say a word. Perhaps this was the presage of a world of equanimity that had eluded me so far. I looked for him even where he was not expected to be: in gatherings, in the glittering streets, in dark corners, in the far horizon, everywhere.

We were both sent on an assignment, just the two of us! It took longer than expected, and the day slipped into twilight. As we walked to an office building, it started pouring. He took out his handkerchief quickly and wiped my bare arm, then swung his jacket over my shoulders. I looked at him, dazed. As if in slow motion he embraced me tenderly, then let go, unsure. We had as yet not expressed our feelings for each other. He put his arm around my shoulders, held me close, and we ran to the building. That was it. I lost myself. I was him. He was me.

This led to a series of clandestine meetings, of avoiding company, even friends. We wanted to be alone. I had all the more reason because our office administration frowned at relationships between employees. So we escaped, we ran, we hid. Little actions became hugely important: his tucking a rosebud in my hair, cleaning the seat of a park bench with his handkerchief, always knowing if I desired ice cream or tea.

At home Auntie Halima's eyes followed me and judged me and pierced my core. Cousins wondered about my absent-mindedness. I saw shadows of worry on Amma's face. I would tell her sometime, I thought. She will understand.

"You are the most beautiful person I have ever met. I cannot imagine life without you," he said on a spring-scented evening.

"Come on, I am sure you have said this to others, too."

"To prove my love for you, I can bring the stars and the sky at your feet. You say it, and I will do it."

"Okay, let's see."

He swept his hand in the air, closed his fist and slowly opened it close to my face. "Here, I brought you the universe," he whispered with a glint in his eye.

"True to your name, Jameel, you are absolutely charming, fascinating, mind boggling. What *are* you?"

"I am *all* for you."

In that electrifying moment I thought I saw his soul. I believed him. I loved him so much. I was bound to him and he was bound to me.

Friends protested, grumbled, and accused us of neglecting them. But what did we care? Besides, we didn't think we neglected anyone.

I saw in him the future. A heaven promised to the earliest woman. My search for that world was about to be recompensed. But Jameel was just a mirage. I saw in him only what I wanted to see with complete disregard to the telling signs. Even his expression of love was cliché.

Friends informed me of his indiscretions, but I refused to listen. I believed it when he told me he was away on duty. We were in different departments by then. But when I saw him wrapping his jacket around Ruby's shoulders on a rainy evening and rushing to a restaurant, it hit me.

He couldn't do that to me. What sort of an imbecile moron was he? What were all those promises for? How convincing! Couldn't he see he was dealing with a sane, accomplished person? In my fury I didn't realize what I did or said.

The quizzical looks of the staff told me that something was amiss. There were whispers in the corridors.

Wink. "I see dark clouds gathering. God knows what is coming."

Suppressed laughter, rolling eyes. "Lightning and thunder…and a huuuge storm."

One day, I stopped Jameel as he came out of Ruby's office, wiping his lips. After some official talk I asked, "Where were you three days ago? I called."

"Oh, I was out of town. Maybe the signal was weak, and I didn't get the buzz."

"I wanted to ask you about our future plans. It may be better if we get engaged. We can inform the company when we have figured a way out."

"Yes, why not. Actually, I have been out of town for the past week. Let me finish this assignment, and then we can discuss."

"But I saw you at the Liberty Plaza with Ruby. You were right here in Lahore."

His color changed. With a little hesitation he said, "Oh, that. Her car had stalled, and I drove her home."

"Near Liberty? In *our* restaurant?"

I asked him to come clean, but he deferred. He could not refute my observation. That was the end for me. It shattered my dreams. I internalized my grief. I became steel. Regardless of all that, I continued as usual, with rigor and discipline. The search for my lost heaven spewed out with force, reminding me again that I was still tied and bound with strings of old traditions. Invisible strings, yet unbreakable. Suffocating. Oh, life. A burden. How could I break loose?

Auntie Halima gave knowing looks to Amma. Cousins began avoiding me, suddenly remembering something important to attend to.

Amma went quiet, worried, her movements slow; the shadows on her face grew darker. I looked for the smile but saw pursed lips. She was diagnosed with tuberculosis, probably from her social work, probably from worry. They came from the hamlet to wish her well, bringing fresh vegetables, home cooked pudding, chicken. Women sat on mats saying prayers for her recovery, giving her spirit an undefined strength.

She recovered, for she was a survivor. She pushed back the taunts and the rolling eyes for not being a good mother and slowly turned to her passion, the hamlet. I sat with her, read to her, fed her and saw her pale face get a glimmer of health. Her resolve and resilience gave me strength.

Never again was I going to be fooled by anyone. My solitude stayed with me with a tinge of pain. I worked harder, received accolades and got promoted. I resolved never to allow nearness to become an impediment to my vision again. Still, even a glimpse of Jameel disturbed me as I could feel his lips brushing mine, making me lose my composure momentarily. I wanted him out and was in a position to do so. And I did.

The monthly evaluation of staff performance brought many of Jameel's indiscretions to the fore. He could not produce any plausible explanation in his defense.

We had the customary farewell for him. I arrived late, dressed in a pale green ensemble in which he had said I "looked like spring." He smiled and advanced. I took a step instinctively then steeled, turned nonchalantly and mingled with other staff. He followed, and I avoided with mixed feelings of pain and elation, the past spinning through my head.

He did manage to squeeze in a word. "Please, please. Give me a chance. I promise you we will be the same again. You know you have always been the one for me. It was Ruby who tricked me into it. I swear I will make it up to you."

I gave him a hard, cold look. "Save your breath. Your transfer has nothing to do with me. The orders came from above. I am concerned with the output of our branch and the reputation of the company. You got a chance to explain and you did. End of discussion." Yes!

I made a formal speech, just what the head of department does, looking straight into his eyes. His eyes beseeched, implored, regretted. Suddenly, he looked older, drained of life, defeated. I tasted bitter victory.

Then I met Iqbal. We were both mature and well settled with no need to indulge in dreams and fantasy. We had respect for each other and could be together without uttering a single word. We complemented each other intellectually.

Marriage engulfed us in a realm of passionate intimacy. No one could interfere in this, despite the fact that we retained a large social circle and took part in community affairs. We covered each other like an impenetrable garb, nurtured each other spiritually, as well as in earthly pursuits. Both of us progressed and gained contentment.

Those were the days of utter happiness. We had our privacy even in company. After the hustle of a hectic day, we shared an intimacy that was far more than the physical, washing away all the stress. When he took me in his arms and I kissed the mole on his shoulder, when I touched the skin on his back, I forgot the here and the hereafter. When I buried my head in the soft down on his chest and inhaled his aroma, when our lips touched, we drank our fill of the eternal wine. Our ecstasy had no limits.

I had found a secure nest, sure of a buffer from the winds of despair and hurt. I knew Iqbal would always be there. He was a combination of intellect and selfless love, romance in a cruel world. He said, "You cannot imagine how much I love you." And I hid in the safety of his bosom.

Married life had its comical moments, too. The ever punctual Iqbal somehow always arrived late for social gatherings. He told me it was because of me that he came at all. Our friends had nicknamed him "Iqbal Last" or just "Last."

I clearly remember a day when, early in the morning, I started receiving anguished calls and e-mails from friends and relatives. They wanted to know if we were all right. Then it dawned on me that we had invited some friends for dinner the previous evening. But that day after lunch we just went out for a stroll. Sitting in a shady spot on the bank of the creek, we held hands and talked and forgot the dinner altogether. We got home late and went straight to bed.

The arrival of offspring brought back to me the primal bliss I knew when I was in the womb. Two girls and two boys. My children and I came from the only life source and surely were going back to the same pivotal point as if links in the chain of existence.

Life went on with its ups and downs, from the first baby steps through illnesses to graduation. Iqbal and I were overwhelmed with gratitude for what had been bestowed. We decided to take a cruise, just what empty nesters do. Driving to the port, Iqbal looked at me and said with a grin, "You and I at last."

As much as I try, I cannot remember anything except his laughing face, his salt and pepper hair falling in a wave over his forehead as he turned to look at me. "You and I at last." I get glimpses of the past without any structure.

They said that our car was hit head on by a truck. Iqbal died instantly, crushed beyond recognition. I was pulled out without any major external injuries. During the coma, they discovered I was paralyzed in the legs. They said I struggled to get back to the car, to pull him out to save him, shouting that only I could do it or else he would die. I passed out when I saw a rescuer pull out Iqbal's severed hand.

After gaining consciousness, I went through intensive physical therapy and medication for my nightmares. I don't remember, but they say I repeatedly called Iqbal to come out and save me from the darkness. It took a couple of years for me to become coherent. Doctors are happy with my progress. They don't know I am broken inside.

Now, at the tail end of my life, I have more than enough time to contemplate, to look at life gone by and to wonder about what is in store. How happy I was when I thought I had seen Jameel's soul, with all of life's secrets unfolded. I saw no need to look any further. I had stopped thinking, just handed myself over. Somehow, despite a scintilla of doubt somewhere in my mind, I told myself our union was eternal. I thought we celebrated togetherness. Yet it came to nothing. Why couldn't I see the obvious? Why didn't he see the intensity and seriousness of our relationship?

Shmaila from the office still visits me occasionally. She said the other day, "I am glad you are so much better. But poor Jameel had tough luck."

"Don't tell me about the past. What is the use?"

"Yes, but still I thought you would like to know."

"What is gone is gone. He is like a bad dream, no use remembering him."

"It may be better for you to know for some sort of closure. After his transfer he could not stick to any job. He became careless about his appearance. Remember how he used to take pains to look impressive? He started drinking heavily. He would just sit and stare in the distance. A few days ago he passed away—alone. He really had some special feelings for you."

"He only had feelings for himself. I am sorry he died this way. I have a headache. I better lie down a bit." Such a waste of a charming being. Kismet.

I can walk, but movement is difficult. I need assistance to get up and take baby steps with a walker. Otherwise, I remain in the chair. Sitting here on the patio in an armchair, I am not in any hurry. I sit here as long as I want—in fact, the longer the better. My family now have their own lives to tackle.

As I look at the sky with its changing colors, the clouds and the sunsets, my mind wanders back and forth without any pattern to my thoughts. Occasionally, a picture emerges. In the distant past, I have a vague impression of an event as if it happened to another person at another time. But it was I who went through it all. Neither wisdom nor compassion could have changed one iota of it. It was to be. Those colors come up for a second, then disperse. I try to reach out, but my hand comes back empty.

Immediately, one of my children comes out saying, "Well, well, Amma, is everything all right? It is such a pleasant day. There are no flies or mosquitoes out at this time."

"No, I am trying to catch—"

"Yes, I understand. Look, you are so much better. See the garden? Your favorite roses are in full bloom. If you just hold on for a while longer, we shall take you in for lunch. I am about to finish cooking. Or better still, why don't I send Ali to keep you company?"

"No, I don't want anyone."

"He loves to play with you."

Ali or some other child comes, and I try to talk with him about what one talks of with children. After a while, he looks confused and wanders off, and I am left in my own wilderness. My eyes roam skywards, looking for the unknown. The few clouds out there do have a silver lining, but what do they have inside? Longings? What are they searching for, wandering from place to place? They have been there forever, and yet they haven't found it?

My neck hurts. I have been looking up for too long. My eyes traipse around the garden, settling on the yellow spiky grass with bald patches or the withered bushes. These spikes bore into my soul. Where are the roses in full bloom that she was telling me about?

This is how life goes: sometimes in bloom, sometimes withered. This is also the story of my life. Some of what happened to me was due to my craziness, some of it karma. I was so intent on looking for my elusive heaven that I did not pause to think and weigh.

Now I am imprisoned within myself. How I had longed to be free—with Iqbal. We so complemented each other. I thought Iqbal and I could do this together. But he beat me to it. He broke free of all earthly restrictions in death. In this, he was "First," not "Last."

I think of death constantly. The yearning to go back and to break all bonds keeps me restless and sleepless. Only death can relieve me of this albatross. What happens next? Is there any escape from there? My mortal self will be in the grave. Where will I be? Will I have attained that elusive freedom at last? Or will I still be in my body? In that case, six feet under, I will be bound forever.

But perhaps, dear God, maybe I shall leave my earthly essence down here and be free forever.

Life Intervenes

Tony Zurlo

Far away you seem
Such tedious tasks intervene
A new job, a new time, a new place

This morning the eaves are silent
The daily dove calls diminished
The home you began for them unfinished

Their companion is missing
The one in baggy pants and oversized shirt
And wide-brimmed cloth hat to shade the sun

Your roses sag in the Texas heat
By noon your African violets are dry
Our aging border collie paces the floor

In the afternoon the answering machine
The cable man's incoherent mumbling
And a message from the Credit Bureau;

Dear Rescuer of Animals and Flowers
We regret to inform you that your application
For a loan for a home for your companions is denied.

In late afternoon we pass in opposite directions
I'm off to work at the same old time and place
While midnight memories of us together reassure me

Jamaica Romance

Clare Selgin

It's an hour and a half drive from the airport in Montego Bay to Negril, a sleepy Jamaican beach resort at the far west end of the island. The broad highway sweeps along the coast, through a couple of bustling market towns, finally passing Negril's famous seven-mile beach with its big hotels. At the bottom of the road is the scrappy town center, and then the narrow, seaside road heading to the "cliffs" side of town.

A friend had told me about the group going to Jamaica for Bob Marley's birthday in February. *Ya mon—it's all good!* But as the group turned out to be musicians, mostly drummers, and I'm a dance addict with no musical ability at all, I felt pretty much out of place.

In the five years since my marriage dissolved (with less fizz than an Alka-Seltzer), I hadn't traveled on my own except for work. But none of my girlfriends had been able to get away. And as for men friends—the truth is, I wasn't even dating anyone. Correction: I wasn't even *interested* in dating anyone. I regularly disappoint my friends with my lack of interest: not a spark, not a flicker, not a twinge of hormonal activity in the past five years.

So I will never know what made me say "okay"—emerging from the little supermarket into the dazzling sunshine of my very first morning in Jamaica—when the tallish, nice-looking guy with the baseball cap and the wide, solemn eyes offered to take me for a walk. Just an apologetic shrug and an almost-shy smile: "I can show you some t'ings.'"

Well, they are the most beautiful brown eyes.

Instead of politely brushing him off, I gave him a long appraising look, trying to figure out who he reminded me of. He gazed right back—no sales talk, just that open Jamaican smile.

So, "Okay" it was. The air was spectacularly clear and soft, California-plus. Walking up the road, we caught glimpses of the incredible glittering ocean in the gaps between the seaside properties. As we passed the last of the hotels, there was the ocean itself, framed between black cliffs: an infinite blue, damasked with steel. Darrin (as he introduced himself) ushered us through the large gates of the lighthouse and toward the seawall, with a gull's-eye view of the waves splintering on rocks. He pointed out the places where the local talent dives from the cliff edge, spectacularly, for admiring tourists.

I asked him where he had gone to school; his "proper English" was good. He told me about his mountain village and the primary school two miles down the hill. He told me about working in a hotel and later as a chef, and then (after Hurricane Ivan damaged the beachfront and the tourist industry) losing his restaurant job. And then he told me what a skilled chef earns in a week: "They pay me fifty dollars, and I work until eleven every night except Sunday."

'The place is screwed up," he added, with a bitterness that was out of place with the "tourist" routine. "I work hard, I do everything perfect, and I can't get anywhere." Or maybe that was the tourist routine. But Darrin could not have known that this was my song he was singing, the theme that has defined my entire working life. I serve as a cog in one of the smaller wheels of the international development business; I help manage staffing and budgets for development projects that are supposed to fix some little piece of some screwed-up system in some corner of the third world. We were definitely on the same page; to my ears, he was speaking poetry.

Walking back toward the hotel, Darrin kept a respectful distance. When he suggested we could be friends, I said okay, figuring this meant I should hire him to take me sightseeing. But then, still walking three feet from my side, Darrin announced—with a smile that managed to be shy and sly at the same time—"Maybe we can have some poom-poom." Keeping my voice as severe as possible, I told him I didn't think so. He quickly corrected himself, dropping the slyness: "Okay, just friends."

There was no doubt in my mind; poom-poom was out of the question, off the menu, not gonna happen. But "just friends" sounded good. Not understanding that it is nearly impossible to insult a Jamaican with cash, I came up with what I considered an appropriate thank you: I offered to buy Darrin a ticket to the Bob Marley's Birthday show, to be held on the beach that night.

And when he asked me, much later, whether I gave him that ticket because I wanted to see him again, I decided the answer was probably yes.

The concert took place in a large, fenced park on the beach, ringed with souvenir stands and dense with the sweetish smoke of the area's staple crop, known as ganja. Staged for locals as much as for tourists, it ran on Jamaica time. The tickets, adorned with that famously soulful long face, said 7 p.m., but our bus driver had assured us, correctly, that nothing would begin for hours. The classic Marley CDs began to spin exactly at eleven, and it was midnight before the first of the local bands began stomping around the stage.

As the DJ cranked up "Trench Town Rock," I asked Darrin for a dance lesson, unaware that no one danced to this music. Reggae was for singing and shouting, and a few stomping, striding, fist-waving moves that don't quite amount to a dance.

So I danced on my own to that mesmerizing reggae beat, with Darrin doing a sort of shuffle at my side, around my shoulders, and I was totally surprised to find the dance turning into a sweet sort of hug.

And then he bent to gently kiss my hair—and I'm here to tell you that those long-forgotten hormones made their comeback right on cue, emptied me out from the knees up. We spent that last hour barely swaying to the music, my head leaning into his chest, his long dark arms cradling mine.

I basically fed Darrin that entire week. We went to the little places owned by his friends, and we ate simply but well—red snapper caught the same morning, braised with slices of ginger and some coconut milk; Jamaican curried goat or conch; jerked chicken that parties in your mouth.

Darrin always thanked me for buying him dinner, but neither of us thought this was out of line. When he made a polite little speech of gratitude, I must have made a face. He protested, "Gail," (it sounds the same as "girl" in the Jamaican accent), "Gail, why don't you like me to thank you? I have to thank you for everything you do for me."

I'm not a complete idiot, and I didn't assume there was anything major to this relationship on Darrin's side. But for me, this was groundbreaking. I began to lose some serious sleep over this beautiful man.

Lying in bed alone and thinking about him—all of him—I felt my upper lip begin to quiver uncontrollably. It lasted a full minute, the tears trickling down into my ears, and then it was over. Something I no longer needed, something dug in deep, wasn't ever coming back.

On day three, Darrin asked me to come with him to meet his family in the country. That was enough to seal the deal for me—this guy actually *likes* his family. He spoke of his parents with gratitude and affection, of the enormous effort they'd made to send him to school. "I owe them *everything*, Gail."

Visiting Darrin's village felt almost like coming home. Jamaica was new to me, but my job had taken me to other countrysides, to third world villages too numerous to count. Manners are universal: smile, greet, remove shoes, appreciate whatever food and drink are offered.

But this visit was special. For Darrin, this was my introduction to what he insisted would be my own family. "My family already love you, Gail," he told me. "They are so happy for me!"

We had rented a car for a couple of days, and Darrin slid happily behind the wheel. Part of the driving experience, I learned, was the ritual of stopping whenever he spotted an acquaintance to shout out a greeting—"*Yo! Wa' gwaan?*"—throwing back his head with a delighted laugh when they realized just who this was, sitting in the driver's seat with his woman beside him. So now, climbing up his own dusty, rock-filled mountain road, we stopped every hundred feet to greet a shopkeeper or an old schoolmate—and his former teacher, who received a properly respectful greeting.

Up here, houses varied dramatically in size and condition. Front yards were nearly vertical, and the back yards either climbed the hill or dropped off steeply down a ravine (depending on the side of the street). Darrin's house was hidden behind a patched-together fence of boards and corrugated tin. As we stepped inside the yard, Darrin's mother rushed forward to give me a proper welcome, taking my outstretched hand in both of her own, with a broad smile. She looked younger than I expected, dignified and very straight. I soon decided that Darrin got his focused intelligence from her.

His dark skin came from his father, who was just coming up the road to meet us: a man still handsome, with a shy old-fashioned courtesy, but aged by physical labor and a diet heavy on rum and cigarettes.

I met Darrin's older sister and younger brothers, and nephews and nieces whose names I despaired of remembering. I wondered later where everyone slept; the house had only two small bedrooms and a smaller dining room, every surface covered with colorful crocheted doilies. The sliver of porch had just enough room for three small plastic chairs.

A visit from Darrin brought obvious pleasure to the family—not least to the boys. His mother treated us like visiting royalty, serving us our dinner before the rest of the family ate. I had no hope of following the conversation, in rapid Jamaican patois and full of names I didn't know. But the message was clear: a deeply loved son, the pride of his family, was home.

The week drew to an end, inevitably, and we both did a lot of thinking. Neither of us could be certain this wasn't standard operating procedure: meet a local (or tourist); have some fun; say goodbye. Shower and repeat.

For me, there were other questions. In Negril we weren't such an odd pairing, but back home? There was the language hurdle, the education gap, our different backgrounds. And did I mention that he's barely thirty-five? But heck, if you have to have a long-distance relationship, it's nice not to have to deal with his "performance anxiety" on top of it.

Not to mention race—but there, at least, we would get an automatic pass in my circle. Though, as I thought about sharing my photos, I had to wonder how uncomfortable some of my friends might be.

I knew I would come back if he asked me to, and not if he didn't. And that I wouldn't forget him for a very long time.

As for Darrin, he stopped talking on our last evening. We sat silently curled up together, listening to the performers at one of the beach dance places. He later told me he had never cried about anyone before.

In my "real" life I'm a well-educated professional woman, something of a fixture at the struggling non-profit I help to manage. My biggest asset is a great bunch of friends (plus the condo on Riverside Drive). My life is good. But—in Manhattan—Jamaica is just another stop on the Long Island Rail Road.

Traveling home, I had decided not to tell anyone about Darrin just yet. I needed to have some idea if this relationship was going anywhere before I laid it open for everyone to dissect. Projects have defined objectives and targets and scopes and contingencies—but this was no project. This was my heart.

That was the beginning of my double life. The next morning I drifted into the subway and showed up at my office; scrolled through a raft of e-mails, jotted down phone messages; ate a lunch of some sort; looked over an indecipherable proposal and some utterly pointless project reports.

Emerging from the office that evening, I met the frigid outdoors with a sense of indignation. Where, I wondered, was that glittering ocean?

As soon as I got in the door and fed my cat, I uploaded my Jamaica photos—and there was one shot of my beautiful man, leaning back in a chair with a thoughtful, unsmiling gaze as he watched me snap away. It was from the day before I left. I phoned him on his cell, and when his voice dropped to a murmur that matched the look in the photo, I was a goner.

Darrin and I talked on the phone almost every night for the next week. Two cheers for prepaid cell phones; before they came along, someone like Darrin would have had no phone at all. But several pieces had to be in place for him to phone me: not just motive and opportunity, but also sufficient battery and phone-card credit. Such occasions were infrequent, and I was guilty of a churlish lack of enthusiasm for my friends' calls, simply because they weren't his. My own cell phone took on a new and mischievous persona as it lay on my desk, unringing, flashing its sardonic green.

But when we did manage to talk, there was an unvarying theme to our conversations—"Book your ticket and come!"—in that crooning baritone of his.

I had to see him again. So, when the office closed for the long Easter weekend, I decided to add on a few days of leave time. I wasn't sure if it was crazy to go back or crazy not to go back—but there was only one way to find out.

So: Let's say, for argument's sake, you're a woman over fifty, and you're planning a trip to Jamaica to see the thirty-five-year-old stud-muffin you left behind. All of a sudden there aren't enough hours in the day to tend to all the body parts that need serious attention: waxing, brightening, hennaing, toning, not to mention some strategic shopping. It's like trying to get Senior Picture Day to coincide with a good hair day.

The problem was this: Jamaica had a kind of Dorian Gray effect on me. The combination of sun, sex, and sleep seemed to take about ten years off my religiously sunscreened face, and at least twenty off my attitude. Back in the city, however, the body went quickly downhill. I had to wonder, would this return visit be my unmasking? I envisioned myself trudging out of Montego Bay airport into the Jamaican sunshine, revealing the harried, haggard New Yorker I really am. Suntan in a bottle? Whiter teeth in seven days? Bring it on, bring it all on.

Here's to my sweet man, tall and loose-limbed. Here's to that long slim body and the fine slender hands, the ready smile and the dark eyes that take everything in and give it all back with interest. Here's to the irrepressible, laughing shout-out that lets you know the man has friends just about everywhere he goes.

There's no fat on this man, but he's no muscleman either, just pure strong Jamaica male, with skin like dark gingerbread.

I'd been gone just five weeks when I once again disembarked at the Montego Bay airport, lugging my laptop as penance. I was in high school all over again: how would he look, how would he look at me? What if the thrill was gone? Could I really stand to spend a week by myself, as a tourist on the beach?

Not to worry. The look was there, the thrill was there—and the man was all there.

Coming back to a place makes you more of a person than you were when you left. Not only Darrin's friends, but even some taxi drivers, street vendors, and shopkeepers expressed pleasure at seeing me back again so soon. As far as the neighborhood was concerned, we were as good as married. People who didn't know my name called me "Mrs. Darrin." He was proud of that, I knew. I heard him tell the friendly shopkeeper, "She's no girl, she's a *big woman*." Not just older—*bigger*, in the traditional African sense: someone with some property, achievements, position in society.

Bigger, and better. Sexuality, for Jamaicans, is thought to expand rather than contract with life experience. As my belly dance teacher once commented, only the mature dancer has lived enough to give the dance its meaning.

Darrin had by now become a major focus of my life. It was hard for me to imagine that he could doubt this. But he did have his doubts, just as I was constantly questioning his sincerity.

"Gail," he said, as we lay side by side in bed, "I can tell you don't love me the way I love you."

"You're joking, right?"

"When I put my leg on top of your leg, just now, I can feel it all the way up to here..." pointing to his chest. "It almost hurts, I love you so much. But I don't think you feel it at all."

I rolled toward him and gave him a long kiss, hoping this was a sufficient answer.

My life had developed a kind of rhythm: a week or a weekend in Negril (laptop in tow), followed by five, six, ten weeks in New York. Thanks to my well-known workaholic habits, I'd amassed weeks of accrued leave time.

At first I was simply commuting between Here and There. But it gradually became clear that this commute was between With and Not With. This was a real relationship, maybe even the relationship.

On the phone, Darrin sounded serious. "Gail, you know what I need? I need to have you next to me, not just on the phone. When can you come?"

"You have to be patient," I instructed, as if to a child.

"You don't even understand when someone loves you, that's why you can say that," he reproached me. "You know what it is to be lonely? I was happy before I met you, and now I'm sad. I'm in love, and I can't see my woman."

He was right, I didn't understand. It was impossible for me to believe that I could matter that much to someone. What about "out of sight, out of mind"? If it wasn't actually a law of physics, it seemed to hold true in my experience. But my mind was commuting constantly to Jamaica. What is the probability, I wondered, that two people would have the same feeling for one another, at the same time?

My own worries about this relationship centered on the undeniable youth deficit on my side. Talking on the phone after my third visit, he finally asked me my age, a question I would normally answer directly.

"I'm not telling you that."

"Why can't you tell me? I want to know."

"Because you might not want to be with me, because I'm too old for you."

"Gail," he sounded exasperated, "there's no way I would not want to be with you. I want to be with you my whole life!"

"Okay. I'm fifty-five."

"Ya mon," he chortled, "you know I got a big woman! I'm a big man, I can satisfy my woman!"

Who knew? My substantial years represent a real achievement, for him as much as for me. But, just between us, I intend to stay tight with my good buddies, yoga and henna.

Cherie, my only African-American girlfriend, is coming in from California for a few days. We used to hang out together after yoga class, before she moved away. The last time she came east, she stayed at my place, and we talked for hours. This time, we'll have a fabulous brunch at the same deli near the yoga studio.

And I'm nervous about what to wear! This makes no sense. Cherie does not care what people are wearing. She *does* have opinions about who they are dating, however. And I know I have no defenses against her direct questions.

As always, we quickly come around to bemoaning the lack of good men, especially (as Cherie complains) in her "demographic."

"Well, yeah," I tease her, "how many actual poets could there be in L.A.?"

"That is not the demographic I mean, as you well know."

And when Cherie asks about my love life, I lay those cards on the table. She stares at me, astonished—and the next minute she is laughing too hard to speak.

"You found yourself a Jamaican beach dude?" She breaks up laughing again, her shoulders shaking over the remains of her quiche. She finally dabs her eyes with her napkin, coughs to shift gears, and takes a long look at me.

"So my yoga buddy turns out to be—how shall I put this—an *Island Lady*!"

"Cherie, not everything is a *demographic*. It's not like I was out cruising for a Caribbean gigolo. I just met a sweet guy."

"Girl, aren't you the one always telling me not to just settle?"

"Actually, no, Cherie, you must be mixing me up with some *other* white girlfriend," I say frostily. "I never tell people whom they should be dating and not dating."

"Really? I do seem to remember a few words about Mr. Mitchell that time."

"Cherie, you wrote a whole poem about how bad he was for you!"

There was a bit of a strain as we sorted out the check, while I made a mental note not to share my secret life with my other friends. But then Cherie had the inspired idea that a good brunch needs a chaser, and off we went in search of a cappuccino ice cream soda.

It was important to Darrin to have me there for Sammy's wedding, even though it would have to be a short visit. Sammy, a bony-faced Rasta with a sweet smile—one of Darrin's first friends in Negril—was marrying a Jamaican-English girl.

The wedding took place on a day of perfect sunshine. Sprays of hibiscus and bougainvillea decorated the oceanside hotel terrace. Men showed up in colorful shiny tracksuits or crisp buttoned shirts and slacks. Women wore dresses in every color except black and white, with glittering shoes. Soon the pastor arrived, dignified in business suit with his graying, low-fade haircut and resonant voice.

There was no organ to herald the approach of the bride, but as the lively chatter fell to a murmur there was a swelling of other sounds—the wind coming over the water, waves spilling eternally over the rocks. Listening to the ancient phrases of the marriage ceremony in full view of the sea, I could almost believe that this sacred bond between two people would last for their natural lives. Our mingled voices, now resounding in upbeat and shouted hymns, affirmed this much at least: the circle of friends surely willed it so.

I knew that, for Darrin, attending the wedding was going to be bittersweet. Man's marriage shone a spotlight on his own relationship, with no ring in sight. Again and again he had told me, "I want to put a ring 'pon your finger!" And each time I would answer, "Darrin, I'm sorry, I am never getting married again." Sometimes I tried to talk about his options, as if discussing the design of some project: he's still young, he should find the right person to marry and start a family. "I won't come to your wedding," I summed up, "but I'll send you a nice wedding gift!" Sometimes that got a laugh, but not always.

So, as the wedding celebration became louder and more joyous, Darrin became quieter. Even when I squeezed his hand, I got no response. And afterward, as the entire party trooped to their cars and taxis to go to Sammy's house—where the music, food, and drink would last into the night—Darrin held back.

"Gail, let's just walk on the beach for a bit. I don't feel like a party."

It was still midday—not the ideal time for strolling on the beach—but we stowed our shoes under a thatch pavilion and walked slowly down to the harder sand, where the tide had recently turned away. Neither of us spoke for a quarter of a mile.

Finally Darrin said, "Gail, I don't need to get married."

"You don't want a family?"

"What I want is for you and me not to break up. Not ever."

"But Darrin, you know that marriages can break up, too! There are no guarantees in life."

"I can make you a guarantee. There's no way I will ever forget you or feel differently about you. My whole life is changed because of you. All I want in my life is to have you beside me."

Well, yes—that, *plus* a good job, and maybe a house of his own… By now, I think I know how to parse a simple statement. And I had learned a few things from my divorce: Steve didn't want to hang out with me, didn't want to be married anymore—but he actually hated losing me just the same.

We kissed on the beach and found our way to the wedding celebration, in the back yard of Sammy's little house. I had expected a good crowd, but this was huge. Most of our local friends, plus extended families from the countryside, and another contingent who came in from Montego Bay. Two of Sammy's friends had been cooking for two days, and there was plenty of liquid refreshment as well.

Rayna was there, of course. I had met her a couple of times before, and Darrin had finally admitted the obvious: they had once been a couple. To me it was obvious, too, that Rayna had not really gotten over him. Not that I could blame her for that.

And now, at the party, she was carefully avoiding Darrin altogether, talking loudly with some friends and even (I noticed) turning her back as we entered the yard. Not drama, exactly—but it had some potential.

I am never wrong about drama. The wedding party was still going on raggedly as we left, the DJ playing loudly to a few die-hards. Darrin and I got back to his place around midnight, after stopping by Shark's restaurant. At 3 a.m. I woke to his phone ringing. When I shook him awake, he glanced at the screen and shut it off without answering.

"They don't need to be bothering me," he said, turning his face into the pillow. But I didn't sleep so easily. Something made me pick up the phone and check the missed calls. That 3 a.m. call, as you may have guessed, was from Miss Rayna.

The drama that ensued took place in my own brain. Was this phone call merely Rayna getting a bit drunk? Or was it maybe a regular occurrence, and she just forgot that I'm on the scene right now? If I hadn't been there in the bed, wouldn't Darrin have answered that phone call?

I dropped into sleep around dawn with my brain in a muddle. I wasn't likely to get the answers to those questions, but I had to ask him. Darrin made us breakfast the next morning, before we left for the airport trip. As we ate our eggs and toast, I told him, "Your phone rang last night."

"Did you answer it? You can always answer my phone, I told you that."

"It was Rayna calling, don't you remember?"

"No, I don't remember anything." He looked at me and grinned widely. "My woman is jealous over me!" Then he turned serious. "Gail, Rayna doesn't matter. She has no manners, that's all."

But all the way to the airport I nursed a doubt that wouldn't go away—and a guilty thought. Would I wake up tomorrow smart enough not to come back?

"Bottom line is, you don't trust this guy." Cherie, as usual, was not pulling her punches. "Gail, you know you've been here before." I had phoned her for a reality check, and that's just what I got.

"Sort of," I mumbled. "But with Steve, I never felt that I came first, you know? Darrin wants me with him *all the time*. Anyway, that's how he makes me feel."

"So maybe that's enough. Maybe it doesn't matter to you what else the man has going on."

"Cherie, that makes no sense!"

"Think about it, Gail. Does *any* of this make any sense?"

I didn't have an answer for that.

"The truth is, life doesn't have to make sense. I've learned that it's actually *okay* if the thing you want doesn't make any sense. But you have to accept that it comes as a package; you don't get to mix and match."

"What do you mean?"

"I mean, your Darrin package comes with some uncertainties. You're the one who has to decide if the package is worth it."

Ending the call, I thought about the package. Looking at someone looking back at me, who can see me straight. Sinking into a deep hug and an even deeper kiss. Hearing that man's voice, even on the phone, that makes everything okay.

If wishes were airplanes, I'd be on my way back to Montego Bay.

"And on the Seventh Day"

Teresa Civello

He was arrested on his first-week wedding anniversary. Like many young couples, they'd married right after Pearl Harbor and moved directly into the apartment he'd shared with his brother and Buddy, the brother's Rottweiler. The brother moved out. Buddy stayed.

They were a handsome couple. People said she resembled a Mediterranean Ingrid Bergman. He had the dashing good looks of Clark Gable with a heavier mustache. He drove a taxi from noon to midnight. It was Buddy's job to protect the young wife, except the dog didn't know he was a Rottweiler. Buddy thought he was a Cocker Spaniel puppy.

Before going to work that day, the husband trimmed his mustache for the first time since he got married. He opened the zippered leather barber case his bride had given him as a wedding gift. The new scissors were very sharp, so sharp that his first cut to the left sliced away too much hair. As he attempted to even out both sides, his mustache became smaller and smaller until it was a black patch of hair centered over his upper lip. He looked like Adolf Hitler.

He'd worn a mustache since he was sixteen, and now he had to cut it off. In the mirror, a stranger stared back at him. He called to his wife, but she was out, so he left for work. He'd soften the surprise of his new look by bringing her chocolates when he returned home.

Later that evening, the wife was startled by someone banging on the door and men's voices in the hallway. Buddy, sleeping at her feet, transformed immediately from Spaniel to Rottweiler, and ran barking to the front door.

"Police! Open up."

She cracked open the door. Two policemen flanked a man in handcuffs. She held onto Buddy, who was snarling at the man. The cops asked if her husband was home. She said no, he was working late.

"Is anything wrong, officers?"

They explained that her husband's taxi might have been stolen. A passenger in the cab had signaled them because the driver didn't look like his hack photo displayed on the inside partition. They arrested the man when he couldn't produce photo ID. She didn't have a telephone, so the cops brought the man to the apartment for her identification.

"Ma'am, is this guy your husband?"

Buddy was still growling as she looked closely at the cuffed stranger. "No, my husband has a mustache and is very handsome."

"Honey, it's me. I forgot my wallet," said the cuffed man.

She stood back. "Is it really you?"

"Sweetheart, I accidentally cut off my mustache."

"Well, you're so ugly without it, I'm not sure I'd marry you again."

The cops, sensing a domestic situation brewing, quickly uncuffed the husband and left.

The husband tried to kiss his wife, but she pushed him away. "No lovey-dovey until your mustache grows back."

The next morning she awakened early and hid the scissors. There would be no mustache trimming for a while.

Chocolate Covered Graham Crackers

John Barbee

Words, glorious words—the English language has so many of them. On the back left-hand corner of my desk, looming high over the computer scanner, is a *Webster's New Twentieth Century Dictionary*, unabridged, of course. It contains well over 2000 pages with dozens and dozens of words per page. This book weighs four times as much as my cat, and I have a very large cat. There is a theory that the reason Methuselah lived 900 years was because he was learning the English language, one word a day.

Mine is a mathematical, engineering type mind. Two plus two always equals four, unless you have an MBA degree from Harvard; then it can equal anything you want. Just ask a banker, corporate CEO, or politician.

I find picking just the right words difficult; so many of them have almost the same meaning. If you don't believe me, pick up your Synonyms and Antonyms Dictionary and turn a few pages. I see so many words to choose from. Then, when I have to string a number of words together in a sentence to express a thought, there can be real problems.

When emotions are strong is when I have the most trouble. I'm always thinking of just the right thing to say, two hours later and a hundred miles down the road. I don't always say the wrong thing. When I got married, the words were already written, and "I do" isn't hard to memorize. I can never remarry because, nowadays, everyone writes their own vows and, even if I got help writing them, I couldn't memorize that many words. Maybe if the words were written on the bride's forehead, then I could just read them?

Sometimes, I get it right because I don't stop to think. Back when my first child was born, fathers were not allowed in the delivery room. You waited in the waiting room until the baby was cleaned up, dressed, and in the nursery for your first look. From a man's point of view, much is to be said for doing it this way. Our doctor was a friend and very forward thinking, so I was called in and handed my new daughter before she was even cleaned up.

(That takes a strong stomach.) As I stood holding this new life in my arms, love swelled my heart until I thought it would burst. For once, I got it right. I looked at her and said, "Thank you, Lord."

Then there was the time I got the words right by accident. We were sitting, holding hands and watching the stars in the night sky, when I told my future wife, "I love you!" There are many replies to a statement like that: "I love you, too," "Are you crazy?" and the ever popular, but meaningless, "Thank you." She just looked at me, and then said something totally different. "How much do you love me?" Time stood still. I felt like a deer caught in a car's headlights, unable to move, talk, or think. I wanted to declare my love in beautiful flowery phrases, I wanted to be Romeo, but my mind was blank. Finally, in desperation, words of nonsense poured from my mouth. "I love you more than chocolate covered graham crackers, and everyone knows I *really* love chocolate covered graham crackers." She smiled, kissed me and said, "I love you, too."

After we were married, from time to time she would leave me one or two chocolate covered graham crackers on my night stand, sometimes wrapped in tissue paper with a bow, other times with a romantic note. The fact that she would leave a gift that meant cracker crumbs in bed, or maybe chocolate stains on the sheets, showed me that she loved me. Sometimes, even the wrong words come out just right, and we lived happily ever after… Maybe the English language isn't so bad after all!

A Date to Remember

Michael B. Mossman

The leaves were falling as I was driving home through Alton, Illinois on my way back from the downtown post office. The route cut through the grounds of my old school, Southern Illinois University. I enjoyed glancing at some of the buildings as I drove along.

I noticed a group of children huddled around a large statue that had recently been erected in front of the old college administration building. I decided to pull over to take a look. I discovered that the iron statue was a likeness of Robert Wadlow, the famous Alton giant.

Robert Wadlow was said to have been the tallest man who ever lived. He stood almost nine feet tall and had grown up in the city of Alton. Although Robert died at an early age, he was a very good young man. His friends called him "The Gentle Giant."

While the interest of the crowd was on the statue, my focus was directed to the building behind it. I walked over to the big building and sat down on a bench in the patio area. I viewed the old limestone structure, and it looked just as majestic as it had in the past.

Stopping at the old college building was no accident. This was where I met the girl of my dreams. How long had it been? It had been exactly one year to the day since we first met. I felt that I had to return.

How could I ever forget that night? It was an early October evening when it happened. My buddies and I went to a dance that was being held in the big room on the first floor of the building. Upon arriving at the dance, I took a glass of punch and began to mingle with my friends. After a while, the band started to play. When a slow song came up, I asked a friend named Jane Stuart to dance.

While Jane and I were dancing, I noticed an attractive young girl looking my way. She was talking to another one of my friends named Barbara Johnson. I looked in the other direction and pretended not to notice. When I looked back at the girl, I found that her eyes had not left me.

After the song ended, I thanked Jane for the dance and went back to the punch bowl. The stranger who had been staring at me also came over to get a glass of punch.

"I haven't seen you here before," I stated.

"No, I attend Northwestern University in Chicago. I'm staying the weekend with my cousin, Barbara Johnson," she replied.

I noticed that the girl had sandy blond hair and was really quite beautiful. She was wearing a green skirt and a white blouse. Her blue eyes sparkled under the colored floodlights. We began to talk, and eventually made our way out to the patio in front of the building.

We walked along the patio wall and sat down on a nearby bench. We talked under the moon and stars in the crisp October night air. The girl and I seemed to draw closer together as we conversed. I felt I had known this girl all my life, and began to be fascinated by her. The beautiful blond told me her name was Kathleen O'Connell.

"But my friends call me Catty," she said.

Catty said she was majoring in French and planned to teach after graduation. I told her I also planned to teach, and we found we had much in common. Catty and I discovered we both enjoyed the same type of music, and we both liked to dance. In addition, we both loved dogs and kids.

Finally, Catty informed me that she had to go. "Barbara will be wanting to leave," she said.

"When can I see you again?" I asked.

"I can meet you here tomorrow night at seven, and we can take in a movie," she answered. Then she tenderly took me in her arms and kissed me on the lips. I eagerly returned the kiss. I knew I had found the girl of my dreams!

"Let's make the tenth of October our special day," I said. Catty agreed, and she suggested that we return to the administration building on the same date the following year. I laughed and said, "Okay."

I returned home and tossed in my bed all night. Never in my life had I been so passionately kissed. I couldn't wait to see Catty the following day.

I arrived at the administration building at seven o'clock the next evening. It was Saturday night and school was closed, so it was kind of lonely sitting there on the bench. I eagerly waited for Catty on the patio in front of the building. My wait began to turn into more than an hour's time. Finally, a car pulled up in a nearby driveway. It was Barbara Johnson.

"I'm sorry I'm late, Mike, but Catty told me to tell you she couldn't make it. Her ride decided to leave early and return to Chicago. She told me to tell you that she's sorry she was unable to keep the date. She said she would write, and I'll give you her address."

I thanked my friend, Barbara, and headed home. I was disappointed, but at least Barbara was there to explain why Catty couldn't show up. I wrote to Catty the very next day. I told her I couldn't wait to see her again. I waited a week and heard nothing. I wrote another letter, and then another. Still, I received no reply. The months went by, and then a year. Catty never responded to any of my letters.

I asked Barbara Johnson if she knew why Catty failed to write back. Barbara never seemed to know the answer. Dejected, I went on with my life. I graduated from college and began a new teaching position as a high school Social Studies teacher.

Now, a year later on the tenth of October, I found myself again sitting by the patio where Catty had given me my first real kiss. I wondered what had happened to her. "I hope she's alive and well," I said to myself.

I got up off the bench and started walking back towards my car. Suddenly, out of nowhere, Catty appeared! She was walking down the sidewalk toward me. She looked beautiful, and she was wearing a black velvet dress. We both began to cry as I took her into my arms. I embraced her warmly and kissed her on the lips.

"I prayed you would be here," exclaimed Catty.

"Where have you been? Why didn't you answer my letters?" I asked.

Catty said she had moved to New York in order to pursue a childhood dream of becoming a ballerina. But while she was in New York, she broke an ankle and was never able to find the satisfaction she had hoped for. She said my letters had not been forwarded to her, and she discovered them after she arrived home.

"I was truly committed to dancing. I didn't have time for a relationship. However, I grew to realize that love was more important. Discovering your letters was wonderful! It confirmed my decision," explained Catty.

Catty and I kissed passionately. Then we got into my car and drove off on the date we had planned on the year before. That's how I met my wife. And forty years later, she is still the girl of my dreams!

She Was Lost in Time

Manuel Torrez, Jr.

She was lost in time,
Beneath my book and song,
Almost gone her crimson smile
From a photo edge worn
And finger smudged.

I dodged searching—
Why stir I thought,

But then one rainy night,
I got a yearning itch,
Much like a fever rash,
So I began to pitch
To any God listening,
Just one more real look at her, please—
Then I'll stop annoying.

Soon the raindrop murmur
Lulled me to doze,
And like a new sprung rose
There she was beside me—

Tremendous thunder and I swear a mocking laugh
Shook me and I awoke
To find my pillow on the floor—
Queer it had a rose embroidered
On its case, stranger was,
The mesmerizing rain gave way
To rude awakening hailstones.

The Panhandler

Manuel Torrez, Jr.

The light at the intersection turned red, and Chris brought his pickup to a complete stop. The sun was beginning to set, and he closed his eyes. Immediately, his thoughts were on Gwen, the little brunette bombshell who had turned his world upside down since moving into the apartment next to his. It was too bad she'd brought her boyfriend, Joe, an ex-Army guy, along. It was too bad Joe had become his good friend, making his love affair with Gwen the double troublesome problem that it was, but he couldn't have known when he first met Gwen that they would fall for each other. He was determined, though, to do the right thing and explain the situation to Joe, tonight.

It was the Wednesday before Thanksgiving. Chris was twenty-eight, lived alone in a small apartment and worked at the neighborhood Home Depot. He'd stayed two hours extra to help get the store ready for Black Friday, the biggest business day of the year. He was beat. There wasn't a muscle in his body that didn't cry out for a therapeutic massage.

He opened his eyes and turned the car radio on, punching the tuner button 'til he got to the oldies station. George Gershwin's "Rhapsody in Blue" was playing. It was one of his favorites. He leaned back and closed his eyes again. He was looking forward to getting home. Joe had called him at work and asked him if they could drop by and watch a movie on his big flat-screen TV. He knew it had to have been Gwen's suggestion because he'd given her the idea in order to set up Joe for the bad news.

He heard tapping on his window. He ignored it. He figured it had to be one of the many panhandlers that worked the intersection. He'd been through it many times. The tapping got louder. He sighed heavily, frustrated at the continued annoyance. He opened his eyes and turned down the volume on the radio. He lowered the window. Immediately, he felt his blood pressure rise. Before him was a panhandler's mug, redder than a gulf coast lobster, with a sickly puffiness. Chris was certain that the owner of that ailing face was destined soon to be on a journey without a return ticket.

"Can you spare some change, man?" the panhandler barked, while displaying a front row of rotting teeth. He danced in place while he talked, as if he had ants inside his shoes.

Chris wrinkled his nose. The man reeked of wine. "No!" he cried out, then raised the window quickly and shut his eyes once more. He didn't want to be benefactor to a rough-talking binge bum who he knew was out to collect money for a bottle of wine and five more, if the opportunity presented itself. If he had the gumption to beg for money, he should have the gumption to ask for work, was his conclusion.

A loud smashing of glass interrupted his mental tirade. He opened his eyes just as debris from the blow to the window landed on his lap. Instinctively, he reached for the handle and flung the door open. He tried to jump out, but in his haste had forgotten to unbuckle his seatbelt.

Once out, he hurriedly scoured the area for the brazen culprit. The road was on a high embankment, and he spotted him running down to where a drainage ditch ran parallel to the road. Chris, eager to teach the guy a lesson, rushed down, too.

The vehicles stuck behind his truck began to honk. The light had changed. He took out his cell phone and called 9-1-1, but continued his pursuit. The man disappeared into a developing mist and the high brush that flanked the drainage ditch. Chris, in his eagerness to catch the vagrant vandal, took long strides into the murky brush and tripped on a large rock. His hands quickly explored the wet ground for anything that could help him get up. He heard the wailing siren of a cop's cruiser in the distance. He found a large stick and was getting ready to use it, when he felt a strong arm go around his neck and jerk him up with a vicious pull.

"Remember me, man?"

Chris recognized the gruff voice of the panhandler, who used his strong arm as a vise on his throat. A large Bowie knife in the man's other hand gleamed in filtered light from the street lamp above and kept him from struggling to free himself.

"How do you like my babe, huh?" he said, and flicked the knife several times. "This is my prize possession!"

"What d-do you want?" Chris stammered, while his heart drummed in his chest and the man pressed the cold steel blade of the knife against his cheek.

"The man wants to know what I want, Jesse." Chris's eyes were adjusting to the darkness. He could make out the figure of a young woman running toward them. "Should I cut him up now, and let the ditch rats start feasting? Huh, Jesse? What do you say?"

The woman kept quiet, but found Chris's wallet and yanked it out of his pants pocket. She shook the wallet in his face, then punched him in the mouth. He felt the pain from the blow vibrate all the way to the back of his head, then felt the blade sting as it sliced across his cheek. The man chuckled, let go his hold and pushed Chris's face into the slush in the ditch.

Chris raised his head slowly, his hand over the cut. Blood oozed over his fingers. He tilted his head up. The two had fled across the ditch to the other side. He could hear them rustle the brush as they weaved through it to escape.

Suddenly, Jesse's shouts cut through the night. "No, Frank! No!" Three pistol shots followed. One right after the other.

An eerie quiet blanketed the scene. He was cold and wet and scared, and he shook all over as a cop shined his flashlight on him.

In the morning, Gwen poured coffee into a mug for him. He was sitting at the kitchen table of his small apartment, still stunned from the night's ordeal. Joe had gone to McDonald's to get them breakfast. She sat down next to him. She was taking quick nervous drags on a cigarette. There was a newspaper on the table, and she picked it up.

"It's in the Metro section," he said. "Look in there."

She paged the paper 'til she got to that section, but lowered it to look at his trembling hands. He raised his cup to his lips; they were quivering, too.

"Poor, babe," she said, but she seemed just as jumpy. His eyes bulging, he stared at her intently, like a child frightened out of his wits looking at a friend experiencing the same ordeal.

Even though the Thanksgiving morning was cool and damp, Gwen had on shorts. She straddled one leg over the other and rocked it in a rapid, nervous manner. Her eyes darted. They had postponed the confrontation with Joe by one day, but the time had arrived.

"Read the article," he said quietly.

She put the back of her hand on the bandage on his cheek. "Does it hurt bad?"

He nodded. "Itches, too," he said and wrinkled his forehead. She leaned toward him and pecked him on his lips. "Will you read the article?"

"Why? You've already read it and told me what it says," she said and accidentally bumped his leg with her swinging foot. He jumped up from the chair with a start.

"What?" she said and rose in a hurry, too. He took backward steps 'til his back made contact with the wall.

"Chris! What's wrong?" she said. "Joe should be coming any minute. You are going to tell him about us—right?"

He didn't answer her.

"You gotta tell him! I already have some of my clothes in your closet."

After they got through eating their breakfast, Chris told Joe. Joe's eyes instantly watered and his face got red. He pushed himself away slowly from the table. His mouth froze halfway open, like he was trying to absorb what he had just been told. He glanced toward Gwen, but she had her head lowered and her arms folded against her body. Joe stood up. Chris rose, too, expecting a verbal barrage from Joe as a response. There was none. Instead, Joe doubled up his big right hand into a fist, drew it straight back as far as he could, and jabbed it forward with all his strength into Chris's midsection. Then he ran out the door in a rage, not even looking at Gwen.

Chris doubled up, dropped to the floor and gasped for air.

It was a week later, in the morning. Chris was standing in the kitchen, drinking coffee and reading again the article about his ordeal in the old newspaper that he'd saved. The reporter of the story quoted Jesse, the panhandler's accomplice. *It was all a ploy to get the sucker down to the ditch, rid him of his wallet, then beat him, so that he could remember the incident every time he hurt. I just wish Frank hadn't tried to show off his toothpick to those trigger happy cops. They killed him dead, quick.* Chris folded the paper and threw it on the kitchen table. He took a last sip of coffee and put the mug in the sink, then took a quick look in the bedroom. Gwen was asleep in her pajamas, lying on top of the sheets. He leaned over and kissed her cheek.

Outside, the early morning sky was red, and the redness seemed to be spread over everything. In his truck for the first time since the tragic Wednesday night, he lit a cigarette as he headed back to work. The red sky quickly gave way to dark storm clouds. The wind picked up paper debris

THE PANHANDLER

and empty cans and hurled them from one side of the road to the other. He turned on the truck's headlights. As he reached the intersection where it had all started, thunder shook his pickup and the sky opened up. The light turned red.

Stuck on the corner telephone pole across the street was a foam cross decorated with plastic yellow lilies. The kind of memorial some people leave at the site of a loved one's tragic death. A thin woman in jeans and a windbreaker with a hood was standing by it. He wondered if it was Jesse. His mouth started to hurt where she'd punched him. Not his stomach, from Joe's hard jab, or the cut from the panhandler's blade that had required stitches. He began to shake and sweat cold as the woman in the hoodie turned to look his way. She had a small tin box in her hand, and she pointed it at him and shook it in the wet air like Jesse had done with his wallet. With her other hand, she made a fist and waved it his way, too. He was sure it was her, but he couldn't see clearly because the rain was coming down in sheets. He turned the steering wheel around and peeled off in the slick blacktop; the friction dried the pavement under the tires instantly. Smoke and the smell of burning rubber filled the air as he sped back to his apartment.

Gwen was awake and sitting on the bed, her back against the headboard. She had her toes separated with bits of cotton, and she was painting them bright red. He got in bed next to her and clasped her head with his hands. He kissed her long and strong. She slid back and her head landed on the pillow. "What are you doing here?" she whispered and pecked his lips with hers several times. She pushed him back. "Weren't you going back to work today?"

He sat on the edge of the bed and lowered his eyes. "I got to the intersection where it all started. I saw a woman standing in front of a foam cross that was stuck to a telephone pole. I think it was Jesse."

"The woman that was with the panhandler?"

"I think it was her. It was raining hard. She had on a windbreaker with a hood."

"You really are spooked," she said and capped her toenail paint and put it away. "What if it was her—so what? She's probably out on bail—she'll do time. She took your wallet. She punched you. She'll do time."

Everything Gwen said was true, but he was still shaking. Still sweating cold. "She had a small box. She pointed it toward me and shook her fist at me, too. What do you make of that?"

Gwen was already out of bed and standing in front of her dresser mirror. She had a lipstick in her hand and was using it. She got through and pressed her lips.

"Where are you going, Gwen?"

She shook her head, but kept looking in the mirror. She picked up her hairbrush from on top of the dresser and started to brush her hair. "If it was Jesse, maybe that box contained Frank's ashes."

"What?" he said and got up. He stood next to her and looked at her reflection in the mirror.

"Yes. Why not? I read in the newspaper where this woman was in court for the trial of the man that had murdered her husband. It was the sentencing phase. She had a heart locket around her neck. Inside the locket were some of her husband's ashes."

There was a knocking at the door. "I didn't kill—I didn't kill anyone," Chris said. There was more knocking. Gwen discarded her pajamas in a hurry, leaving them on the carpeted floor while she hustled into the bathroom.

Chris poured himself some coffee in his mug, then went to the door. It was Joe. "What…what are you doing here?" Chris said and backpedaled, stunned to see Joe.

"I'm here to pick up Gwen."

"What?" Chris said.

"We're going out to have breakfast. We always used to go to McDonalds, before—"

"Before what?"

"Well, anyway, you were going to work today."

Gwen rushed out of the bathroom in shorts and a T-shirt. "Take an aspirin, babe, and lie down. I'll be right back. I'll bring you something." She said everything without looking at Chris. She closed the door behind them.

Gumption! The word popped into his head. The panhandler had it, when he asked for money. Gwen and Joe seemed to have it, now. He looked around. Her pajamas were still on the carpet. He picked them up, then washed his coffee mug thoroughly in the sink. He found that, when he had dried the mug and put it away in the cabinet, he'd stopped shaking.

The entrance door swung open. It was Gwen. She had a paper bag and two paper cups of coffee. She put everything down on the table, then clasped her hands behind his neck and kissed him.

THE PANHANDLER

"Joe?"

"Gone. He's gone away. He reenlisted in the Army."

"I don't understand."

"That's why he wanted to get together—to say goodbye."

"Are you over him, Gwen?"

She lowered her eyes. She took her hands away from him and walked to the window by the door. She drew the curtain.

"Well?" He pressed her for an answer.

"Isn't it enough that he's gone, Chris? I mean, we probably won't see him, ever." She let the curtain go, rushed to the door, stopped, turned around and stared briefly at him, then opened the door and was gone.

Chris, more puzzled than ever, approached the window, but before he could get his hand on the curtain, she rushed back in. She had the morning paper in her hand. "Let's eat before breakfast gets cold," she said.

He wanted to ask her why she hadn't eaten breakfast with Joe. Why she'd come back so soon, but he didn't. He took out his cell phone to call work. To let them know that he was going to be a little late.

Finding a Pristine Flower in the Mailbox

Ruth Moon Kempher

2 a.m. in the morning, at the 7th Street apartment, after somehow missing
an important wedding, told everybody I parked on a stuck-up pipe
otherwise unseen. Forget it.
Also almost hitting the garage wall. The mailbox sits
astraddle the palmettos, but when opened, there it was—
a blooming white flower, many green leaves, a branch

ripped untimely from some alien shrub; lovely, but
from whom did it come? some old student? an old love
passing by? its blossom bright white, a small sloppy star—
aura of past Christmases, but he couldn't. I know better.
Saw him last new moon, with his sly touch. He says
it's me that's crazy, but his eyes gave a gift, and that touch

extremely well known. Flowers are just not his style.
He leaves posies and such trash to his mother, gives you
bruises, that natural purple blush on flesh, Johnny-jump-up
or better, Forget-Me-Not, Bleeding-heart. This was
different. The whiteness stunned the shadows. Calico
red center. Who left it may not know who lives here, now.

First Runner-up: Best Non-fiction Contest

Flirting with Fiasco

Ruth Moon Kempher

The kid doing wheelies through rush-hour traffic down our once quietly deserted, once dirt road that somehow became a racetrack shortcut to the Interstate is not my son. He's way too young, and I'm way too old. But he touches my heart with some maternal conundrum sort of ambivalent emotion: I want to scream curses at him for worrying me and, at the same time, I want to dash out and drag him home into a fierce hug of safety. He reminds me of another.

Brash. A cover-up for vast sweating wonder at just being. I do remember being young. I think of my mother, whose brown eyes merge and melt into his, they were so alike in the soft-eyed expressions they'd shoot me down with, and I can hear her scolding, "O, Dolly, do be careful. You'll be the death of me, Dolly, if you end up in some ditch." And all the stuff she'd say about him. "He'll only use you and hurt you and off he'll go. It's what they all do. Men. O, Dolly, you need to be careful, listen to me."

Only years later did it occur to me that her name for me, "Dolly," signifies something fit to be manipulated, but back then I didn't ever really listen to her, and it certainly never occurred to me, in the glow of first love, that she might know what she was talking about. Surely, she couldn't be right. I was a self-willed child, and she wasn't particularly maternal. I'd have to admit, though, that I noticed how similar their eyes were, that sentimental mushy brown, and that I was as uncomfortable with him, sometimes, as I was with her.

The air trembles. The kid, hunched on his bike, and I, leaning on the fence, supposedly looking for Sadie—my hound friend who loves to wander—both hear the sirens shrilling closer and closer to us down the road from up by the new traffic lights. They put those lights in after the last crashing death. It took that, of course. It's the rescue truck or the fire engine, pounding closer with every howl. Drivers—my stupid neighbors in their four-wheel trucks—don't pull over. They only slow down for dumping beer cans and McDonald's wrappers. But the kid skids onto the sandy shoulder and tumbles off into scrub palmettos and stickers. I hope his jeans have good thick knees.

That other. The mocker. The tease. Under my breath, I'm saying "O, be careful," and I'm thinking how I must sound like my mother, suddenly all these years later, and probably that kid wouldn't listen any better than I ever did, I'd bet. Way back when I was his age, there was already a long history of struggle, of lies and recriminations between Mommy and me. That skirmishing seethed into open warfare, boiling up ferocious after those other brown eyes found me and kept finding me—on the school bus and into the algebra room and, Lord help us, biology—our famous school bus hurtling on under gold- and orange-leafed branches to the high school and on into history.

He had no mercy on the bus or elsewhere, later. Brown eyes, don't take me into your head like that, I said, a million or so times. Incredible, the hours and days and months and years gone by. But it was exactly what I wanted. What I thought I wanted. More fool, I.

It's the rescue truck. Not a fire this time, thank heavens. The woods are so dry from weeks without good rain. Danger signs. Lights and siren whirling past cut off my view of the boy fallen into the scrub palmettos and brush. Fire's a nightmare thought in the dry season, some years worse than others. This one hasn't been too bad, so far, but we haven't had the afternoon storms off the ocean, and cold fronts coming down from the north have stalled out before they reached us. My woods are dry as kindling, waiting for flame.

He liked this place. He pretended it meant nothing that I came home and looked for a property because I needed a place. My mother was alone and sick and needed me. She'd certainly never needed me before, but home I came, with the two German shepherds I had then, Bubba and Lily Belly. So much for the independence I thought I had to have. So much for being free. Well, it was my free choice, to tie myself up again.

They didn't either one of them like dogs. My mother never made a secret of thinking they were dirty creatures who would knock her over, and he never wanted to share my attention with anyone or anything. Maybe that was part of what Mommy didn't like, either. I never thought about that much, just had my dogs with me, looking for a place. A house in the trees, he said. It's what I always thought you'd have. A house in the trees, and dogs.

He had daughters. No sons, but daughters, and I had none. I was happy, blessed with the best dogs that ever came down the road, and one time that's what happened. Before the fence was built, good Jane—a still blind Beagle pup—came staggering up to the porch steps she was too little and weak to climb. Somebody'd dumped her out on the road, we guessed. Dogs who find you that way are the very best kind. They come to your hand, wonder-eyed.

The siren's dying, down the road, and the kid's whacking dust out of his jeans. Brown-eyed, I think, but I can't be certain. His bike's fallen all a-kilter. There were always bike parts in our kitchen. Gears and greasy pieces on the drain. Boat motors taken apart and waiting for some missing piece, waiting on my linoleum. He was hung up on anything speedy: boats and motorbikes, and cars, of course. Mostly, they were in the yard. Other houses, other times. He always wanted whatever it was to go faster. That's a greed. Dare me to go faster, and just watch my dust…

They liked each other in the end, the two brown-eyed eminences in my life. Uneasy with each other at first, the more they had to be together—they had to be for me—the more her practical optimism gave in to the inevitable. "Dolly," she'd sigh. "If you like him, he must have something. I trust your judgment. And you know I always say, if we have trust and faith enough, everything will be okay." Her hand tapping in the sweaty sheets. "Please be careful. But I do believe, if we have faith. Enough. It'll be okay."

The boy looks over, kind of waves. He knows I've been watching.

The dog of today is Sadie, and she's suddenly here, baying at the boy, her long, hoarse, hound dog bay that says stay away, we don't need you. It's also her way of letting me know she knows I've been looking for her and, wherever she was, she was busy, but now she's here, and I'm protected. It's a crazy game.

When I first moved in—awkward, like here I am, and I have to be because my mother needs me, who never needed me before—he showed up and gave his approval, not of the dogs, but the house and the trees, appearing one day with a load of insulation because it was an old house and the attic had no insulation, which he decided I'd need. He did that—sweating up there under the shingle roof, hauling up huge batts of pink fiberglass that prickled his skin. Maybe that was my payment for years of motor parts and grease in my sink. Sent him home to his wife for a shower. The showers have never worked well here. Wife and daughters. And a surrogate son, that was her child. A red-haired boy with freckles and a lopsided grin. A troubled child.

Surrogates, stand-ins, dogs and wonderful creatures. Boys on bikes.

I have a crazy thought, as I'm calling out to Sadie to shut up. I could just as easy call out to the boy, "Hey, kid, are you okay? Can I drive you to the hospital? Can I feed you biscuits and honey? Can I sew up the rip in your jeans? O, kid, do you mow lawns? Whack weeds?"

But he's back on his bike and flying away, that kid. Like the other, fast is forever the far best way to wheel away. "Good, Sadie," is what I say. She looks at me, uncertain. There's a little breeze, rustling leaves, a scent of rain. "You want a cookie?" and oddly, echoing my mother, "Don't worry. Everything'll be okay."

Belated

Bobbie Jean Bishop

…tearing open the plea that comes out of the blue from an address on Wilson Avenue, home of a woman I knew in 1964, I read—Help Me. How lost was this appeal before it arrived I can only imagine, a two word scrawl asking for support that hinges on old High German, *helfan*—to make more bearable, even change for the better. It rings of misguided optimism from someone dwelling on the outskirts of social relevance—era marked by assassinations, LSD, civil disobedience and Dylan's poetic harangues. Always the skeptic I ponder how anyone shapes another's fate with its door swinging from past to present. My memory forces me back to the duplex steeped in a ferocious inertia, its cheerless walls sporting photographs cheaply framed—a woman turns her bruised face from the camera's eye while a man leers near a crib's vague outline. Beyond these particulars lies a neighborhood littered with coupons and a working class struggle to survive. Speechless, I doodle a very large egg, place the woman inside wondering what I can add—rough puzzle of tools I sketch at her feet? In a morass of crude renderings, can she pick out hammer and chisel?

Long Dark Night

Steve Snyder

I am the water that freezes
in the cracks of rocks and splits them apart
yet listing the reasons why I miss you
is as useless as naming waves,
as useless as trying not to think
of you in the quiet of the long dark night.

Prize Fighter

Ron Porter

"Hector, you're not listening to me!"

The young couple sitting two tables over was getting loud again. Her accent was beautiful; it sounded something like Puerto Rican to me.

I like coming to the mall, especially on cold, rainy winter days like this one. And I enjoy sitting in the food court, watching and listening to the people. Today, Hector and his wife—I never did get her name—had a few things to discuss. I knew his name was Hector because she said it often, and when she did it was with contempt and loathing. I knew they were married because I could see his wedding band. And because of the way they talked to each other. Most of the conversation was in Spanish, so I didn't get it all. But anyone with an eye or ear would know. It flowed back and forth like the ocean's swell, approaching and receding. The last words I heard were in English.

"But I love you," said Hector.

"Well, I don't want you to love me anymore!" she said.

Something inside Hector crumpled. You could actually *see* it. He looked like a prize fighter who had just been punched in the face, very hard, his knees wobbly, no longer able to hold up his fists. No longer able to defend himself.

She sat back, knowing she had landed the final blow. Just like in the ring, I thought. Now the fighter will step back, confident and proud, and watch her defeated opponent go down, drop to the mat.

Once

Helen Benson

Once
There was a garden here,
Over there by the new paved area
A weeping willow swept the lawn
With its trembling branches;
An old iron bench stood in front
Overlooking the city.
Sometimes, my love and I
Would climb the hill and sit there
To watch the sunset.
The buildings of the city
Faded to shadows and the sky
Turned pink, then salmon, then gold,
And it all flared again
In the bend of the river.
Once,
We stayed so long the colors faded
And behind us a full moon rose.
We were caught between the soft yellow sky
And the warm silver moon. It was magic.
He turned to me and said,
"Do you think we should get married?"
I said, "I do," and we did.
The magic went on and on,
But his sunset came too soon.
Now I see the faint tinge of pink
In my own western sky.
I am climbing the hill
Where I know he will be waiting
On an old bench
Beside a willow tree.

The Wounds of a Sister

Albert Russo
(from his Eur-African novel, *And There Was David-Kanza*, which will appear in his own French version as *Exiles Africains - Et il y eut David-Kanza*, Ginkgo Editeur, Paris, March 2010)

During our stay in Riccione on the Adriatic coast of Italy, Massimo and his sister, Liliana, paid us a visit; they were my husband's first cousins. He had the litheness and the nobility of a Gregory Peck, and eyes that pierced through you to the soul, whereas she, a head shorter than he, could have seemed quite pretty if she hadn't frowned so much. Only later did I come to understand why such a young woman bore the wrinkled mask of a lady in her forties.

Unlike their parents, Massimo and Liliana had miraculously escaped from the concentration camp. Upon their return, they found their home in Pisa luckily untouched and unoccupied. Massimo resumed his medical studies at the city's reknowned university and became a pediatrician with a reputation for efficiency and great benevolence. Liliana taught junior high school, while at the same time taking care of the household. She doted on her brother like a mother hen. They had between them a tacit understanding that they should never speak of the horrors they suffered during the war, and especially not of the loss of their beloved parents.

What brought these young people to the Adriatic coast was not, like most holidaymakers, to have a good time at the sea, but to meet with their cousin. Considering Sandro like a family elder, they needed to hear his opinion on a serious and urgent matter that disturbed them profoundly.

At university, Massimo had met a young girl, Eva, with whom he had fallen passionately in love. She in turn reciprocated with the same intensity, to the point where they had decided to marry, once they had both completed their studies.

They had known each other for three years, but Massimo had always concealed their relationship from his sister, for Eva was Austrian. But after she returned home with her degree, to Massimo's distress, the young woman wrote him a long letter, telling him she had thought over their situation and, despite her strong feelings for him, she believed that the inhuman treatment he and his people had been subjected to during the war would sooner or later resurface. She feared that he would hold her, even if only subconsciously, responsible in part for that collective tragedy, and therefore it would be better if he forgot her.

Distraught, Massimo telephoned her several times, and seeing that she wasn't changing her mind, he took the train for Linz, where she lived. But even that visit didn't deter her. They were both heartbroken and cried in each other's arms. He rode back to Italy alone, wearing sunglasses even in the shade to hide the redness of his eyes.

After that sad and bitter experience, the young doctor had a few flings, but didn't want to hear about getting married, ever again. And he didn't hear from Eva thereafter.

The years went by; then, one day, by a stroke of fate, the two crossed paths in Florence, where Massimo was attending a medical congress. Their encounter was electrifying. Eva was recently divorced from her Viennese husband, but had conceived no children with him. This time the two lovers swore never to part again, though the young woman requested that he have a bit more patience, just a couple of months, until she could settle her affairs in Austria and rejoin him for good.

Came thus for Massimo the most crucial and difficult moment he had to confront: revealing to his sister his intention to get married. The latter received this news, which rekindled the accursed events of the past like the explosion of a dormant volcano, with shock and dismay, and she actually became physically ill. Sharing this heavy burden, brother and sister had asked to consult with their cousin.

They spent three days in Riccione, staying in a hotel near the pensione and, because of them, our vacation took another turn. Whether we were at the beach as early as 9:30 a.m., or eating lunch or dinner, or having a drink on the terrace of a café, or even before retiring to one of our bedrooms, from early morning until late at night the only subject to be discussed was Massimo, his Austrian fiancée, and the unbearable pain the situation was inflicting on Liliana, as it opened old wounds she had vowed to bury in the marshes of her mind. The wretched girl had become an insomniac and could hardly keep her eyes open, they hurt so much and were relentlessly moist; she had to wipe them every other minute or so. She also had to clutch the armrests of her chair with a firm grip, lest she break into new tears. The muscles of her neck were corded like those frightening creepers of the Cambodian jungle that seemed to enclose human bones, and her veins stood out so tensely that I was afraid they would spill over and burst at the slightest movement.

So as to avoid the inquisitive looks of strangers, especially since Liliana's shrill voice inevitably drew stares, the four of us would sidle into Massimo's room while I sent the children off to have some fun, sparing them this family drama. I had no desire for Massimo and his sister to spell out their problems in front of my daughters and Daviko, exposing them to events that reflected the darker side of the human soul, events they could never have imagined, since, growing up in Africa, they were spared details of the war even during their history classes. It was one thing to read that millions of people lost their lives during the two world conflicts, but another to face relatives who had suffered the consequences in the flesh, with all their sordid descriptions. People just didn't want to hear about it, and, even in Europe, those victims of the Holocaust who had escaped death did all they could to close their book of horrors.

Within the walls of our room, Liliana became hysterical and hurled verbal daggers at her brother, repeating them in long drawn-out wails like a wounded animal, so that the echo of her lament reverberated deep in one's marrow.

"What he intends to do is nothing less than blasphemous," she cried. "It is unacceptable! Why did our parents die, and with them millions of our folk? So that this massacre—the largest and most horrific mankind has ever experienced—could be so quickly forgotten, erased from memory? Pushed under the carpet, like dust? And, on top of it all, the father of that *Boche* was a nazi officer. My brother wants to marry a nazi!"

"Eva isn't a Boche—she's Austrian!" retorted her brother.

"Oh, a fat lot of a difference it makes!" Liliana snapped, brushing him off with another nerve-wracking tirade no one dared interrupt. "And, if that weren't enough, she bears the same name as Hitler's whore? Champion of the Aryan race—what a tragic farce! Remember how small he was and how disgusting he appeared, dressed like a clown, his hair the color of mud?

Beautiful, tall, and blond! Even the ugliest among the Jews was better looking than Hitler."

Then she would turn toward Sandro and reiterate her question: "Would you let one of your brothers marry the daughter of a nazi torturer? You see, it's as if they killed my parents a second time, with the difference that the crime, this time, would be committed by their own son."

Massimo was perspiring, his eyes downcast, shivers running up and down his spine. He let her blather on, so tangled up she was in her frantic verbiage, for five or ten minutes more, then, incapable of standing it any longer, he too began to holler.

"Stop it, stop it, will you! Didn't we both live through the same hell in Bergen Belsen? I loved our parents as much as you, and the image of their pleading stares will burn my heart until my last days, so don't play holier than thou with me, okay?" He was now out of breath, sweating profusely, and before she could resume her accusations, he stretched out his arm, determined to have the upper hand. Picking up strength, he addressed her this time with a more conciliatory tone.

"Do try to understand. Eva has always loathed the nazi regime, and she doesn't want anything to do anymore with the people who were involved with it, be they simple acquaintances, former friends of her parents, or even her own family. And, most important of all, we want to get married, start a family, and live—live normally, like millions of couples. Is there any sin in that?"

"You have the nerve to speak of sin!" Liliana bellowed, looking at me, the stranger, the Rhodesian Anglican. In her blind fury she forgot where I had come from, and, calling upon me as a witness, she said, "She will bear his children, and what will their faith be? Christian? Atheist? They might as well be bastards."

I didn't know where to put myself, and poor Sandro felt doubly insulted, for he had never demanded that I relinquish my faith to become Jewish, and, what's more, he allowed me to educate our girls in a Catholic school. Then, too, what could be said of Daviko, who was a half-caste?

"That's not how we intend it to be," countered Massimo, raising his voice again so he could be heard by all of us. "Eva wishes to convert to Judaism. She's the one who proposed it, not I, and she insists upon the fact that our future children should learn both Hebrew and the Torah, even if they go to

THE WOUNDS OF A SISTER

a lay school. Actually, she's against them frequenting a Christian institution, for she refuses to have them indoctrinated by some zealous priest or molded by pious sisters."

"So here we go again," exclaimed Liliana, "reverting to the abominable *Sippenschaft*, which the Boche concocted so they could hunt down the Jewish vermin! This time, though, it's the other way 'round, for even those Jews who had converted to the Christian faith were caught in their grip—like Sister Edith Stein, whom the Church will probably want to sanctify one day. The nazis traced suspects several generations back to search for a Jewish ancestor. An eighth of the so-called poisoned blood was enough to send you to a concentration camp."

These conversations weighed on me to such a point that, in order to avoid them, I pretended I had a splitting headache.

The day the cousins departed was a huge relief for our whole family, in spite of the fact that Sandro's long and compassionate interventions had no positive effect on their predicament. Brother and sister returned to Pisa, both exhausted and still at loggerheads with each other. I felt sad for them, for I could empathise with Liliana, for whom her brother's announced marriage had revived terrible memories. And yet I also understood Massimo's only too human desire to settle down with the woman he loved, no matter how torn he was between the two. Destiny sometimes can be so ironic you would think it is a farce, except that in this case it pulled a family—or what was left of a family—apart, with tragic consequences.

A Poem after Auschwitz

Anthony Adrian Pino

There are those who say that after Auschwitz
there can be no poetry; that

so near the shadow of death's unrivaled mastodon
there can be no succulent tongue or sweetness

no new hymns, lamentations, or psalms
only a stilled eternal trauma, a shudder, a cold chattering of teeth.

The orphans, forbidden to sing of their losses,
are like figures at Pompey,

frozen in grief. Testimony is silenced.
Motion pictures are stilled. Bells are muted. Gone, gone are the bells.

No rabbi, priest or cantor
may chant the invocation of him who has no name

but holds the secret sorrow and heart for such pain.
Vomit, dried blood and splintered bones

cover the rock from which there can be no calling-forth.
Silent, silent are the orphans

who move among their ancestors
like spirits in a ruined city.

      I hold differently.

The bone-chalk earth holds no solace
without song.

Children must come out of night
Names must be sung

The earth blessed
Incense burned, the cloud of precious smoke offered;

Lyric suffering liberated from its nocturnal cave.
Here are the children, ever-lost,

Eyes stretched with grief
Faces moon-wide with shock.

        (and Hiroshima too?
        Yes, yes, Hiroshima.)

Call the names, call them quickly.
Chant the life-giving names.

Never, never let them die
Call the sister, the brother, the laughing cousin.

Tokyo: remember: the woman with the burning hair
who threw her daughter into the river—the last memory: the saving river,
 the fire.

Remember her, that she should live.
Yes, remember her.

        (and Dresden too?
        Yes, Dresden too.)

Remember the girl falling out of her bunk to death.
Remember.

You must not hide it, must not forget: Chant!
Bring them out, their smiles, giggles and even their silly socks.

        (There's something in Somalia.
        Then call them here.)

They often loved strange things—pickles and dried meat, do you remember?
Yes: salted fish, old sweaters, nasty little pictures and secret prayer books.

They were stars! Yes, stars. Call out the stars
That they will live forever.

Night Train

Carol Poss

I've been away—away from home,
new places, far places—
on a train I'm coming home;
back to loved familiar faces,
        coming home, coming home.

Battle's over, war's no more,
back from far-flung foreign shore
over rails of shining steel.
Carry me homeward till I feel
the breezes of my native land
where I'll walk the grasses green
and run the purple moors again
        coming home, coming home.

The pulsing of each turning
of the black wheels sets me yearning
and I feel the rhythm of the churning
of the engine and the burning;
swaying as the rumbling of the
night train brings me closer
with each meted vibrant measure
        keeping time, keeping time.

Wheels swiftly turn for soon I'll see
those dearly loved who prayed for me;
Those I left so long ago—
Engine hiss and whistle blow
over mountain, vale and stream
through the long night's gathering dream
        coming home, coming home.

Where Is Hope, There Is Life

Jane Boruszewski
(submitted by her husband, Walter Boruszewski)

While lying on my blanket in an Uzbek's hut with other sick Polish children, I listen to a shepherd singing as he watches cattle grazing outside the mud walls. The walls are fencing our huts. His song is strange to me, as is his village located nearby. This is a hostile world we inhabit as we wait for the Caspian Sea crossing. The grownups tell us that trucks will come to pick us up and take us to the nearest train station, but weeks go by and they don't come. I know I'm dying of dysentery, but I'm not afraid any longer.

"Janina, you look like a skeleton," Mania says to me, holding out a container of boiled rice. She brings meals into the hut twice a day. "You have to eat to live."

I shake my head.

"Do you know the other children are afraid of you?"

I shake my head again.

"They're afraid because you look so awful."

I sit up with effort, spoon up rice into my mouth and force myself to swallow. I spoon out and spoon out, but when I look into the container, rice is still reaching the brim. I feel nauseated and don't want to throw up. Thus, I hand the container back to Mania, and she walks away with it. I'm sure she eats my food, for they never give us enough to fill up our stomachs. In fact, I'm glad not to have any appetite, for it hurts so to always feel hungry. Hunger drilled holes in my stomach before I became ill. I thought of nothing else but food all day and looked for any morsel to put into my mouth. I went to bed wanting food. In my sleep, I dreamed of eating delicious meals, but woke still hungry, hungry, hungry.

"Where is life, there's hope," I remember hearing people say. I have no hope. I don't want the slightest hope to enter my mind, so never to feel disappointment ever again. There's no sign of the trucks, and I've been bleeding for weeks now. Because I'm weak, I keep napping and dreaming of my family, from whom I was separated four months ago. How I miss not seeing them, especially my mother. If she only knew how sick I am now and how lonely.

In the afternoon, I hear a woman's voice and turn away from the wall to look. I see a lady standing in the doorway of the hut. She looks like an angel, a talking angel. "Children, trucks are coming, for sure this time. An official from our army, Anders' Army, has brought us this happy news. Get well, all of you, and be ready for the road."

Suddenly, I sit up and smile at the girl lying next to me. "I will get well," I tell her. "I will, you'll see." She gives me a small smile, but doesn't move. She dies an hour later.

But I eat half of the next meal, which is potato soup flavored with fried onions, and then I crunch a piece of dry bread and drink some water that's been boiled and cooled. Russians call it kipiatok. After some days in the hospital, I start walking around.

It's hope that brings my will to live back to me, hope and prayers that help me to recover and become healthy enough to cross the Russian border in 1942. I'm happy, so happy to be stepping down on the Iranian beach! Our crossing was very hard. We rode in trucks, in the train, did too much walking in between, and then traveled by boat. And now we plop down on the warm sand, breathing hard from exhaustion. Then they tell us it's too late in the afternoon for trucks to pick us up and take us to the nearest resting camp near Pahlevii. In the semi-darkness we children and a group of grownups settle down on our blankets to sleep.

As I stare at the stars twinkling up above the way I remember stars twinkling in Poland, I smile. The smile is not only on my face but it reaches my heart and my soul. "We're out of Russia," I say softly to myself. "We are, indeed, we are!" I want to get up and run about the beach and maybe dive into the waves, but it's too dark now. When I close my eyes, I hear the Caspian Sea, talking—no, singing—to me.

"Janina, you are finally free—free of Stalin, free from hunger and illness. Be happy."

And I smile the most joyful smile in the world and continue listening to the sea.

"All you need now is to be reunited with your family. Yes, you already have seen your sister, Marysia, in the group of lucky grownups on the beach.

And you will probably see your parents and two younger sisters at the very end of the traveling."

"Yes, I know I will, at least I hope and pray I will." I talk back to the sea as if I were a grownup, and not a child of ten.

"Your future will be good from now on," the waves say, sprinkling my face with salty drops. "You must be comfortable on the soft warm sands with all this space around you to stretch and turn to your heart's content."

I nod my head, remembering how crowded we were inside the vehicles, children squashed together. It hurts so to be forced to keep your arms plastered to your sides or hold them up above your head. Ach, how bad it is not to be able to move around!

"Janina," the sea calls my name again. "You're free now, free to laugh and to play all you want. Please, become a child again. Let your heart fill with hope and believe that you will have a good life, starting tonight."

Again, I nod while falling asleep with a smile on my face. Hope is important to have in one's life, I think. Life without Hope is not life, but mere existence.

An Enigma Wren

Margaret Francis

I was married in July, 1942, and my husband was posted to North Africa, where he served for almost three years in the North African and Italian campaigns. I decided to join the WRNS (Women's Royal Naval Service) because I felt I would be lonely while he was gone and would have lots of company in the service.

Basic training was at Mill Hill, London. We were supplied with awful dresses. I felt like a convict. Mine was way too long for me and, as they were just on loan, I couldn't cut any off, so just made an enormous hem in it.

I quickly made friends with three girls—Mary, Beryl, and Sheila—and we stayed together until the end of the war.

We had to get up at 5 a.m. and get breakfast laid for 450 wrens, then had to wash all the dishes on a terrible dishwasher, where the dishes traveled on a roller through very hot water and, when they came out the other end, the steam was terrible. It absolutely ruined my hair. Then we had to set up for another 450 wrens. I also developed a terrible cold with a runny nose. Anyway, we were told that we could leave after the two weeks, if we wanted to. I wanted to stay. I figured nothing could be much worse than what I had already been through.

We were then asked in what area we would like to work. PV (Pembroke V) was secret. If we volunteered for that, we had to sign the official secrets act and were not told what PV was. Funnily enough, the volunteers for this assignment were the only ones issued with Sou'westers (rain hats usually worn by fishermen). We definitely thought we would be working on the water. The first thing we did after getting our uniforms was go out and buy a different hat. The hats issued were terrible.

We were told to send our civilian clothes home prior to being sent to Eastcote for training, so were surprised to see Vera struggling to the bus loaded with hat boxes and suitcases. We said, "Vera, you were supposed to send all your civilian clothes home. Why do you have so much luggage?" She laughed and said, "My dear, I thought we would have a porter."

When we arrived at Eastcote, the officer who was going to train us was away on leave, so we had to work around the quarters. My friends and I were put to work cleaning windows with just soap and water, and there was fresh paint on the glass. Luckily, we had some one-sided razor blades and did quite a good job. We also had to put up our own bunks and, as we all wanted top bunks, we put up four. One of them collapsed in the night, but no one was hurt.

One of the strange things was that there were no bath plugs in the baths. If we wanted a bath, we had to buy a plug and keep it in our sponge bags.

We were very anxious to find out what we would be doing and to get on with our training. Finally, the training officer arrived and asked each wren her name. When she came to me, and I said my name was Margaret Francis, she said, "I'll remember you; you look like a Francis." The funny thing was my maiden name was Wilden, and I had only been a Francis for fourteen months. Unfortunately, she did remember my name and was constantly telling me to get my hair cut. I finally rolled it up in a nylon stocking when we had to go on parade. The officer said, "That looks much better, Francis." But it actually looked awful, and my hat stuck on the top of my head. As soon as I got away from the site, I would let it down.

We finally found out what we were going to be working on—one of the first computers, which was called a Bombe. (I think it was a Polish word, as they obtained the first enigma machine from the Germans.) This machine was invented by Alan Turing, a real genius, who unfortunately committed suicide after the war because he was caught in a homosexual situation and was too ashamed to appear in court. At that time, it was an offense.

Enigma was one of the best kept secrets of the war. Years later, the public was made aware of the program that enabled the Allies to decode all messages from the German army, air force, and navy. Sir Winston Churchill gave it the code name, ULTRA, and called it "the goose that laid the golden eggs, but never cackled."

One time, I lost my liberty pass. Petty Officer Bernstein, who knew me by sight, gave me a long lecture and said, "If you were a sailor, you could be put in irons for this."

After listening for awhile, I picked up my gas mask and started for the door.

P.O. Bernstein said, "Where are you going?"

I answered, "If you're not going to let me in, I'm going home." Of course, she let me in.

When we just had a sleeping out pass, we would take our gas mask out of its case and put in a clean collar, underpants, and our toiletries. Silly thing to do, but we were young!

We were asked where we would like to go. The three friends I had made at Mill Hill and I chose Gayhurst, and we were lucky to all be sent there.

I was on D watch. The watches did not mingle at all because one person was always on Day watch (8 a.m. to 4 p.m.), another on Evening watch (4 p.m. to Midnight), and another on Night watch (Midnight to 8 a.m.). The fourth watch was always on leave. After the 8 a.m. to 4 p.m. watch, we were given 24 hours off, and then started the 4 p.m. to Midnight watch. When we came off the Midnight watch, we went back again at 4 p.m. Then we had a five day leave and could get a pass to go away for that time.

I and my three friends were put in a room with five bunks that housed ten girls. We were able to change our bed linen once a week and put the top sheet to the bottom and a clean sheet on top. It is really quite astonishing how well we all got along. I never remember any controversy among us. We did not always do things together, but there was rapport among us.

After we came off day watch at 4 p.m., we were given the choice of doing squad drill or carting linen to the laundry room. We only had to make one visit, so we opted for that and never had to do squad drill except in the summer.

Sir Walter Carlyle (who lived with his wife in part of the house) allowed the boy scouts to camp on his property. Then, when they went to church on Sunday, if we were on the 4 p.m. to Midnight shift, we had to go, too.

We had all sent for our bicycles, so we could get around, as the bus service was not good. On the 4 p.m. to 8 p.m. watch, we used to go horseback riding at a fantastic riding school, where the owner was Irish and had beautiful horses. He taught us how to lead and not just follow the other horses. After our ride, we used to be booked into a lovely little inn and have a delicious home-cooked meal.

On Sundays, we cycled into Olney, a village five miles away where they had a WVS canteen, to enjoy a scrumptious tea very cheaply. We also cycled into Newport Pagnell, our closest small town about two miles away, to go to the cinema and do our shopping.

During the time leading up to D-Day, we were restricted to going only twenty-five miles from Gayhurst, and a notice appeared on the notice board stating that "All wren's clothing will be held up until the navy's needs are satisfied." The officer heard our laughter, came out of her office, ripped the notice down and replaced it with different wording.

One of our fellow wrens, Joann, who lived in Bedford, which was only ten miles away, invited us to go and stay with her mother. Joann kept geese in the river that ran past Gayhurst, and she was able to take eggs home to her mother, who made delicious scrambled eggs with them. It was a real treat, because we mostly had powdered eggs in the mess.

Also, when the ban came on about the distance we could travel, we got around that by having civilian clothes sent to us. We used to change in the restroom at Bletchley station, travel as a civilian, and change back when we returned. I had a really nice pageboy hairstyle and, in the damp weather, it often fell down to my collar, which was not allowed. I was hitching from Bletchley Station one time and got picked up by our 2nd Officer, who was a little peeved because she was the quarter's officer and did not know what we were doing. The first thing she said to me was "Get your hair cut!" I didn't, but, as I had had problems at Eastcote with my hair, I rolled it up in nylon whenever there was an officer around.

I think we must have been the only wrens who had stewards to clean our rooms, and all our washing was sent to the laundry. We were told we had such a stressful job that they tried to make things easy for us. I never felt it was that stressful.

However, one can get bored doing the same thing over and over. We would get a menu from Bletchley, set up the machines, start them up and, when they stopped, write down what appeared on a small strip at the side of the machine. Then we sent it into the checking room and, if it passed, it was teletyped to Bletchley. If it was a good match, Bletchley would call and tell us the code was broken, to strip the machine and get ready for another menu.

My friend, Mary, and I put in for a transfer to break the Japanese codes. The officer who interviewed us came the day after D-Day and told us how unpatriotic we were, requesting a transfer at such a crucial period in the war. Of course, we had no idea D-Day was going to happen on that particular day.

One of the things we were told was that we helped to sink the Scharnhorst. We broke the code giving its position, and we had to send a reconnaissance plane over before we could bomb, so the Germans would think the plane had spotted it.

We were also told we won the North African campaign, because Rommel was far superior to our generals, but we were able to break the code and find out when and where supplies were arriving by train and were able to stop any supplies getting through to him. Again, a reconnaissance plane had to be sent over.

After the war in Europe had ended, our machines were no longer needed, and we were given soldering irons to take them apart. They did not keep even one for a museum, but Bletchley is now an on-going museum, and a machine has finally been built and is running.

The Roxbury Diary

Jack Campbell

I am eighty-one years old and well into my retirement from a satisfying career. I served my country in various parts of the world and can say, with pride, that my generation did much to promote and sustain the freedom of my country and the world. Freedom has cost humanity more through the years than any other commodity necessary to survive. There can never be a bottom line to summarize, because we have never agreed on what a human life is worth, and human life, after all, is most of the price we pay for freedom. The journal I am about to present to you will document one soldier's contribution toward keeping his country free. Unfortunately, you will have to decide what must come next to sustain that freedom.

Before I get into the day-to-day pages of this diary, let me tell you how I came to acquire it, and define the man who wrote it. I was raised in a small southern Illinois town, population 2500. It was the mid-1930s and, during my eight years of grade school there, I became fast friends with Jimmy Glenn. He was in my class through graduation, and we were as close as brothers. I lived in town, and Jim lived on a rundown farm just outside of town. I spent my summers at his farm, serving as a water boy during the harvest. We would take turns riding Jim's pony out to where the men were threshing wheat. A jug of cool well water would be hung on each side of the saddle horn, a welcome sight to the men soaked in sweat from the midday toil.

Jim's dad worked from dawn till dusk to raise three girls and two boys. Jim's older brother, Orville, usually worked side by side with his dad, doing much for very little. When Pearl Harbor was bombed, Orville joined the Army Air Force, leaving Jim and his father to run the farm. Jim was deferred from the draft as "a farmer in residence," a common deferment back then. While many farmers migrated to the city to work for better wages, Jim stayed and worked the farm till the war ended.

It was a fond farewell the day I moved with my family to St. Louis, where I would attend high school and eventually enter the service myself. Jim and I stayed in touch right up until the war's end.

In May of 1944, I was a junior in high school, and I still remember my mother handing me a letter from Jim. I always looked forward to reading the news from my old hometown, but not this day. The news was daunting; Orville had been killed in the skies over Europe. There were no details in my letter, but I didn't need any. My great friend was gone forever. I remember I cried for days.

Orville had flown twenty missions earlier on, and was sent back to the states to instruct gunnery. He became bored with the routine and again requested combat duty, which was granted. I remember Orville as being a rather quiet and shy boy, who never complained about the work and loved playing pinochle at my father's Saturday night card parties. A flashback had the three of us naked in the back yard, tossing cold well water at each other after a sweaty day in the field. Our bodies were stark white except for our faces, necks, and arms, which were a dark and painful red. Grinning wide, Orville would pop our fannies with a wet towel and laugh like hell. Now, a part of my youth was gone forever. God rest you, Orville Glenn.

In the spring of 1947, I did indeed go back to visit my childhood friend, Jim. It appeared the war had hardly touched this quiet little town except for the silent reminders hanging in the windows of every other house. Banners with any number of blue stars would inform passersby which families had given up their sons or daughters to fight in the war. A gold star signified a life given.

An hour's drive from St. Louis found me winding my way up a familiar dirt road, the rocks and ruts still in the same places they had always been. I was soon parked in the chicken-filled front yard that belonged to Ira and Millie Glenn, who had lived there for years and years. Jim saw me coming up the road and was there to greet me with a bear hug as I stepped out of the car.

The reunion with Jim's family went on until late, then Jim took me to his room to share a bottle and feelings he might not have wanted his family to know about. He soon pulled out a tattered box from beneath his bed and proceeded to lay out Orville's belongings, which had been sent home from England after his death. He showed me the standard issue telegram, the kind the government usually sent, informing the recipient of a serviceman's demise. Each word I read stung me with a pain I did not expect. "We regret to inform you that your son, Orville—" I could read no further, so I folded the telegram and placed it back into its envelope. Jim then handed me a small notebook, about 3 by 6 inches, with the words, "Flight Log Roxbury," at the top and "Glenn" scribbled across the bottom.

"It's the log of the eight missions he flew on his last tour," Jim said, his voice a raspy whisper. I handled it with care, using gentle finger pressure against each page. Reading only a few of those pages convinced me to ask for its temporary custody. I wanted time in private to read Orville's words, absorb them, and try to feel as he did the day they were written.

"Dad would never let it out of the house that long," Jim offered. I told him I understood and put the idea to rest for the time being. The day we said goodbye, I knew I would eventually write a documentary worthy of this courageous soul; I just didn't know when.

In the summer of 1968, my childhood friend, Jimmy Glen, died of cancer, as had his father and mother before him. I visited him at his home two days before he died. It seemed to please him when he had his wife Ruth hand me the old tattered box containing Orville's effects, that same box I'd seen so many years ago. It came with a promise that I would write a plausible account of Orville's service to his country, an account that would make his family proud.

The years seemed to pile up as I followed a career in electronic design, never seeming to find the time to write my thoughts, but building up a great well to go to when time and circumstance permitted. In 2004, I did find myself enjoying retirement, and I knew it was time to start putting my life on paper, to write those short stories that seemed to burst forth without much effort. Although writing was now my passion, it was nearly a year before I thought my skills worthy of putting prose to Orville's diary with the dignity and acumen it deserved.

The time had come to read and understand this man's life and deeds, and then put them into words a fractured world might take to heart. We need to know now, as much as at any other time in history, just how thin the fabric of freedom can get, and what some people willingly face and endure to preserve it.

The day had come for me to lay the contents of that old shoe box out before me and crawl back into history, letting each item take me to the place I needed to be to give those days their due. The original items I'd seen years ago were there, plus an assortment of personal items: medals, ribbons, a scarf worn during his first twenty missions.

I placed the diary containing his flight log before me and let my desk light frame the dog-eared pages I was about to resurrect. I would search out every ounce of passion and dedication I felt was there and present it to a world that is deeply in need of such an example. I revered the person who had written this journal, and I was about to feel his day-to-day flirtation with death in every passage I read. My eyes went to the top of the journal, where the words immediately pulled me back into WWII.

Roxbury Airfield Flight Log

Sat. 1-7-44

We are down for the time being; fog too deep to fly in. Wrote to Mom today, was sorry to hear about Jumbo, good mules are hard to find. I like walking into the little town of Crosswell, sit by a small stream, reminds me of our creek. Weather is clearing.

Sun 1-8-44

Early fog, took off late, flack hits on both wings. Bad weather over target, turned back.

I flipped a few pages looking for an entry slightly more than just routine. I found it at:

Thur. 1-12-44

Me-109s shot up formation. Ed Owens, tail gunner killed, died at his station, his war is over, good guy. Lost hydraulic fluid, hand pumped gear down, landed o.k.

Fri. 1-20-44

Bombed Bremen, Me-109s everywhere. Mark Murphy waist gunner hit bad in leg. Pushed him out over Calais, hope he finds care, wouldn't have made it back.

The entry immediately reminded me that Orville had been wounded on two different occasions on his first tour; neither bad enough to send him home for good.

I was now determined to mentally project myself into that journal. I wanted to be on that airstrip and feel the chill that only a fog-shrouded English morning could impart. I wanted to hear the cough of those Pratt & Whitney engines as they struggled to reach the rpm necessary to climb to

25,000 feet over the skies of Europe. I wanted to stare into the faces of the men who were asked to look at nothing but sky for days on end and possibly die for their efforts. My fingers again searched the remaining pages for insights into the man who had written his last thoughts and deeds here. I was already feeling the dull resignation and fading hope it took to fly these planes into hell each day, so many years ago.

As the number of pages left to review dwindled, I leaned back, trying to summarize the journal to date. The grim facts were as follows: four pilots killed or wounded, two bombardiers killed, five gunners wounded or killed, and I was not yet to the end of the journal. Most entries were brief, but explicit, in listing the events of the day, so I was excited to find that the last three pages were filled with so much more detail. Since the day I had acquired Orville's diary, I could not remember ever reading it through. I could only recall flipping through it to get the feel of the moment.

Now, my journey with Orville Louis Glenn was near the end, and I leaned back in my office chair to prepare myself for re-living the last thoughts and observations of the man who had given the word "duty" a new meaning. He would indeed walk this land with me until I saw him again.

> Air Log; Wed 3-21-44
>
> The "Hun Hunter," my ship, is down for routine service. Our pilot, Capt. Lawson, has 20 missions, and is going to fly the Hun Hunter back to the States to sell war bonds, wants me to go with him, think I will. Wrote Mom I'm coming home.
>
> Air Log; Thur 3-22-44
>
> Re-assigned to fly waist-gunner for the "Nellie B" ship. Their gunner killed yesterday. Capt. Lawson flying The Hun Hunter home, I will be with him.

On the page opposite the last entry was a neatly folded envelope, secured to the cover. I freed it from the paper clip and took a single typewritten page from it, which read as follows:

My dear Mr. and Mrs. Glenn,

By now the war department has informed you that your son Orville died in combat in the skies over Europe. I am Captain Lawson, pilot of a plane we called the "Hun Hunter." Orville was one of our waist-gunners on our last eight missions. I flew my twentieth mission 3-20-44, and was ordered to return stateside, and fly the Hun Hunter ship back to help promote their bond drives. Orville had made up his mind to come with me, meanwhile he was assigned to another ship pending orders. That ship, the "Nellie B" was lost over Germany that same day, there were no survivors. Orville was credited with shooting down five enemy fighters during the twenty-eight missions he flew. You have a right to be so proud of this boy, who was an inspiration to us all. Please know that the sympathies of all who knew him are with you today, and always. Orville Louis Glenn served his country above and beyond all mortal expectations. He now shares that wild blue yonder with his God, he is home.

Respectfully,
Robert Lawson

Postscript

Orville Glenn was just one of over 26,000 airmen killed in the skies over Europe during World War II. Another 28,000 were captured and interned. The bombers they flew were cost effective; their lives were not.

The Pea Coat Fiasco

William Valitus

A month before my enlistment was up, the ship I was doing time on was programmed for an extended Mediterranean cruise. My discharge was scheduled to take place while the ship was in European waters. This would be inconvenient for the Navy, so they offered to transfer me to a ship home ported, stateside. Having had the dubious pleasure of visiting the Mediterranean twice in my Navy career, I immediately accepted the transfer. The transfer form listed a number of ships with billets for a 2nd class radar man, among which was a destroyer. My entire enlistment in the Navy was suffered on large ships where "spit and polish" was the order of the day. My choice was the destroyer (a small ship). They transferred me to the USS Mississippi, the oldest commissioned battleship in the Navy.

The Mississippi operated out of Norfolk, Virginia as a platform for testing a surface to air missile. The schedule had the ship out to sea five days a week, followed by spending the weekends in port. This meant that the crew would have liberty every weekend. Most of the ships allowed a portion of the crew to enjoy a liberty that permitted authorized absence from Friday to Monday morning. However, the Captain of the USS Mississippi did not. He held a Captain's inspection each and every Saturday morning at which all hands were to be in attendance. This cruel, inconsiderate mandate negated any possibility for long weekend liberty.

I had been wearing the same pea coat for close to four years, and it looked it. Other items of clothing were replaced when necessary. I was reluctant to replace the pea coat with a new one due to its somewhat high cost. Additionally, it is a rather useless garment in that the lower portion of the coat offers little protection from the elements. As a part of my future civilian wardrobe, it fell in the same class of uselessness as the white hat, neckerchief, and the thirteen-button trousers.

Being a new crewmember made it difficult to trade duties with shipmates to one that was exempt from attending Captain's inspection. This forced me to borrow a shipmate's coat on Saturday mornings, as my coat would never pass inspection. The elbows were threadbare and faded to gray, the button holes were frayed, and the pockets misshapen from four years of use.

The Chief radar man didn't appreciate my "short timers" attitude. Most of my conversations expressed my low opinion of Navy life, career men, the USS Mississippi, the food, the Captain, his liberty and mandatory inspection policy, and anything else of a sea-faring nature that came to mind. Somehow, he discovered that I was attending inspection wearing a borrowed pea coat. This practice was in violation of navy regulations.

The next Friday before inspection, I found it impossible to borrow a pea coat. The Chief told the radar gang that it was against the Uniform Code of Military Justice to borrow or lend clothing to a shipmate. He posted a notice to that effect in the radar room, with the added provision that anyone found guilty of violating that rule would be put on report and subject to punitive action at Captain's Mast. I found I couldn't even buy or rent a shipmate's pea coat, and I knew that, if I attended inspection wearing my war-torn pea coat, it would be found unacceptable. Some bad thing would result.

In desperation, I attempted to restore the coat to an acceptable state. I steam cleaned it, applied dark blue dye to the faded, threadbare elbows, and sewed up the buttonholes. The coat looked better, but still not too good. Buying a new coat was out of the question. This sailor would shortly be entering civilian life without much experience in the civilian work place, armed with only a high school education, very little savings, and with a wife and infant child to support. A useless pea coat was the last thing I needed to spend money on. I decided to wear my coat, as bad as it was, and hope for the best.

Saturday morning, before inspection, found me in the radar room drinking coffee. The Chief appeared on the scene with an evil grin on his face. He pointed to his notice on the bulletin board and asked if I had bought a new pea coat to wear to inspection.

"No."

"What you gonna wear to inspection?"

"A pea coat," I replied.

"What pea coat? It better not be someone else's."

"It won't be."

"You gonna wear that piece of crap you call a pea coat?"
"Aye, aye, sir."
"Your ass is gonna be had."
"Up yours, Chief."
"Up yours, too." The Chief and I understood each other.

Decked out in my unsuccessfully restored pea coat, I stood at attention waiting for the Captain and his entourage as they reviewed the ranks. The inspection party included the Executive officer, the Chief Master at Arms, and a Yeoman whose duty it was to record all discrepantly uniformed sailors. Yeomen were known to be able to write; Masters at Arms and some officers were not. The closer they came, the more I sweated. After what seemed like an eternity, the Captain came to me and passed by. Will miracles ever cease? I made it through inspection. I wouldn't be forced to buy a coat. Oh, unbounded joy and rapture!

My joy and rapture was short-lived. The Chief Master at Arms prompted the Captain to take another look at me. He did and frowned.

"Where did you get that coat?" he asked with raised brows.

"It was issued to me in boot camp, sir."

"That appears to be a long time ago."

"Yes, sir," I agreed.

"I think you need a new one. Take that coat to the incinerator and have the Master at Arms burn it." He gave me a hard look, then went on his merry way. Four years at the naval academy, countless years of experience as an officer, and here he was, seeing if the crew looked pretty. Didn't he have anything better to do?

He left so quickly I didn't have time to respond or in any way acknowledge his order. The Yeoman took my name, rank, and serial number with the Chief Master at Arms looking on, a smug expression of glee on his face. My offense was a matter of record and would have to be addressed. My ass had been had.

The order to burn the pea coat upset me. Did the Captain have the right to order me to destroy my personal property? I didn't think so. I decided that, whatever the consequence, I would not burn my coat or buy another.

After inspection I made my way below decks, headed for the radar room, being careful to avoid running into the radar Chief or any of the Masters at Arms gang. They might escort me directly to the incinerator and force me burn my coat, post haste. On the way, I hid my coat between the overhead and the top of an air-conditioning duct. It would be safe there for a while. Upon entering the radar room, I was confronted by my crafty Chief. He greeted me with a big smile. He was in his glory.

"Where the hell have you been?" he asked.

"I was hiding my pea coat."

"You were what?" I guess he didn't understand English.

"Hiding my pea coat." I repeated.

"The Chief Master at Arms is waiting for you at the incinerator."

"What for?" I responded.

"You were ordered to report to the incinerator to have the Master at Arms burn your damn coat."

"Let the bastard wait. He ain't got anything better to do. Anyway, I hid the coat."

"You ain't goin' burn it?"

"Nope."

"You could end up in the brig over this," he threatened.

"Maybe a bunch of us will end up in the brig over this," I countered.

"What are ya talkin' about?"

I informed the Chief that the first thing I was going to do was request an audience with the ship's Chaplain to ask for advice and guidance in this serious matter. I further told him I suspected a conspiracy between him and the Master at Arms to harass and nail me. It was too much of a coincidence that the Captain was prompted by the Chief Master at Arms to take another look at me after he had passed me by at Inspection. Additionally, the instruction to the radar gang about lending clothing and his posted notice in the radar room needed explaining. I informed him that I had a copy. The whole thing seemed fishy to me and would probably seem fishy to the Chaplain as well. In addition, I didn't think the Captain had the right to order me to burn my personal property. I further mentioned that the Chaplain would probably at least want to discuss this matter with him and his no good, goofy Master at Arms cohort.

The incinerator would enjoy carbonizing my coat if the good Chief would give me a written order endorsed by our Division Officer. With that document, my coat would be available for incineration. The document was needed for evidence if I pursued replacement of the coat through the process

THE PEA COAT FIASCO

of Courts Martial. I wouldn't mind burning the coat if they gave me a new one before the present one was disposed of. The Chief could call a stop to this whole thing right now if he gave me forty bucks, the price of a new coat. I also informed him that, if I didn't get satisfaction at Courts Martial, I would further pursue this matter in the civilian Appellate court with a civilian attorney at my side. I didn't know the significance of "Appellate" but neither did the Chief. I was enjoying this rhetoric, but the Chief wasn't. He was becoming confused, unsure of his involvement and the possible consequences of his nefarious plot.

Our conversation took place in the presence of about twenty radar men who had about as much use for the Chief and the Chief Master at Arms as I did. They were enjoying every bit of it. I was certain a number of them could be called upon to verify the facts in this matter. The Chief was aware of this also.

"Save yourself and your goofy, ape shit buddy a lot of trouble before you do anything else. It may not be too late," I suggested, and added, "You have pooped in your flat hat. You got a chance to empty it before you put it on your head. Think it over." There was a smattering of laughter from the spectators.

"Up your ass," was the Chief's parting comment as he left the radar room.

The radar room telephone rang. The caller asked for me. I answered the phone. "Who's calling, please?" I inquired.

"Dis is the Master at Arms. You the guy what 'posed to burn his pea coat?"

"You got that wrong. I'm not supposed to burn it. The Chief Master at Arms is the guy who's supposed to do the dastardly deed."

"I'm the duty Master at Arms. Get your ass down here. I been waiting for you."

"Did we have a date?"

"No! You some kinda wise ass?" he asked.

"Are you the Chief?"

"No, I ain't the Chief. He went ashore and told me to take care of burnin' the damn coat. Get it and your dumb ass down here."

"Hey. I already burned the coat with the Chief. Didn't he tell you?" A little white lie that went unquestioned. "Say, while you're on the phone. You wouldn't have a pea coat I could borrow or rent for the next inspection, do you?" I asked with tongue in cheek.

"No," he informed me.

"Maybe you got one that belongs to somebody what's in the brig. He ain't going to stand inspection. Or is he?"

The duty Master at Arms didn't appreciate the subtle humor in my comments and hung up with the expletive "Asshole." I guess he was satisfied, as he didn't call back.

I later heard that the radar Chief checked with the Master at Arms to find out if I had the coat burned. The duty Master at Arms told him that the Chief Master at Arms had taken care of burning the coat. This would keep him placated until he found out otherwise.

This pea coat thing was getting complicated. It was a convoluted mess. I became more determined not to burn my coat or buy another one. What could they do to me? My enlistment was almost up. My service conduct was good. My rank of 2nd class radar man spoke well of my proficiency in rate, which was not too bad a rank attained in four years. I decided I didn't have much to lose by continuing with this to the very end, as bitter as it might be. I figured about the worst that could happen is that I could get busted to a lower rank. I didn't need the 2nd class radar man status in civilian life.

If my last resort was to request a Captain's Mast, I doubted if the Executive Officer would let the request go beyond his pre-mast review. I figured he would get all of us together, find out what was going on, royally chew us out, and then send us on our way. The fact that I was a "sea lawyer" might influence his thinking. The "don't rock the boat" axiom might also be a factor in my favor.

This being Saturday afternoon, the ship was on holiday routine, and the crew was free to do whatever they wanted. I retired to my bunk to read a book for a while (Mickey Spillane's Zelda turned out to be a man). Having nothing better to do, I returned to the radar room, where I found the Chief. He greeted me with a victorious, "Hey, I thought you weren't gonna burn your coat."

"I guess you guys got me, Chief. I'm chicken to go up against you guys. You got me beat six ways to Sunday. Can't fight city hall. You guys are too clever for me. I guess I'll have to go to ship's stores next week and buy another coat."

THE PEA COAT FIASCO 109

This seemed to make him very happy. The grin on his face was evidence that he and his cohort had won some kind of glorious victory. I made his day.

"No hard feelings. Okay, Chief?" I volunteered.

"Nah," he condescended. "None at all."

"How 'bout a butt."

He handed me a cigarette with a big smile.

"Got a light?"

He gave me a light.

"Thanks, Chiefy."

He walked out of the radar room without his feet touching the deck and with his head in the clouds. He was in a state of ecstasy.

Later that evening, I hid the pea coat in a better place. I hit the sack wondering where this thing was going. I spent Sunday looking for someone who owned a pea coat that didn't have his name and serial number stenciled in it. My search was unsuccessful. Monday morning, we put to sea for another week of missile testing.

After breakfast, I had the radar watch. 10:00 found me relieved from scope duty, enjoying a cup of coffee and a cigarette. The off duty radar men were discussing the weekend adventures they claimed to have experienced. Most of it was BS, especially where the stories were centered on exploits with the opposite sex. We all knew the truth was stretched in these sea stories, but it was fun to hear the creative narratives. The Chief interrupted this interesting interlude by bursting through the hatch, his face as red as his neck, fairly screaming at me.

"I thought you said you gave the coat to the Master at Arms, and he burned it?"

"I did."

"He said he don't know nothin' about burnin' no coat."

"He's either got a short memory or he's pulling your anchor chain. I gave him the coat. He said he was gonna burn it right away. I felt too bad to stay and watch. I might have cried. I loved that coat." Then I added, "Got a smoke?"

He seemed to relax a bit. It was a reasonable assumption that the Chief Master at Arms was leading him on. He handed me a cigarette with the instruction, "Buy some."

I thanked him, but refrained from asking for a light.

Later that day, the Chief stormed into the Radar room again. Before he could say anything, I presented him with a written request chit to see the Chaplain.

"What the hell is this?"

"Read it, Chief. You can read, can't you?"

He read the request. I had filled out a chit to meet with the Chaplain, in private, to ask for advice on a pressing personal matter. I elected not to reveal the nature of the private matter at this time. I stated that I feared the consequences of it becoming public knowledge. The Chief didn't know what to do. He was compelled to either approve or disapprove my request.

"I want to talk to you about this," he stammered.

"Can't hardly wait, but can't talk now. I got the watch." It was time for me to go back to the radar repeater and do exciting radar things.

"I'll see you when you get relieved."

"Okay, Chief. Say, do you got a smoke?"

"No!" He was either out of cigarettes or he was upset about something.

We met upon my being relieved.

"The Chief Master at Arms told me he didn't get no coat from nobody to burn."

"Are you sure your goofy buddy isn't still rattling your cage?" I commented on what a splendid sense of humor his buddy had, and admired how cleverly he was putting it to use.

"If he got the coat from you, what do you want to see the Chaplain for?"

"Chiefy, that will have to be confidential for a while, but I'm sure you'll find out soon enough."

He left. This time he departed with his feet definitely touching the deck. He accented his departure by slamming the hatch.

Ten minutes later, the Chief Master at Arms called and directed me to see him in the Master at Arms shack "rat now." Taking my sweet time, I reported to him at the Master at Arms shack. He was alone and shut the door after I entered.

"What's this shit, you gave me your coat?"

"I did. Don't you remember?"

"You didn't give me no damn pea coat!"

"Sure I did. It must have slipped your mind. I can understand that. You're so busy with administering your important police duties," I suggested and followed with, "Didn't you burn it like the Captain told you to?"

"No, I didn't."

"You were supposed to. Did you keep it?"

"No."

"You must have lost it. Where is it? I might need it for inspection."

"I never had the damn thing. I don't know where it is."

He was really pissed now. I was enjoying myself. "Neither do I. You had it, and you lost it."

"Horse shit."

"I'm going to see the Chaplain."

"I know. What about?"

"It's a secret, and I don't have to tell you. Ha ha." This added to the flames of his anger. I was enjoying every minute.

"I'm putting you on report," he threatened.

"On report? What for? For you losing my pea coat?"

"For not burning your pea coat."

"I couldn't. You had it. Besides, you were supposed to burn it. Not me."

"Get the hell out of here. I'll see you later. Wise ass."

"Yes, sir. Say, do you got a smoke?"

"Get the $%&# out of my sight and watch your ass."

I retreated, elated and amused by the confusion of the two Chief Petty Officers. The situation was becoming increasingly complex. The Chief Master at Arms knew for certain that I did not give him the coat, while the radar Chief wasn't sure. Both Chiefs were troubled by my request to see the Chaplain. The Chief Master at Arms realized he was negligent for not putting me on report when I didn't bring him the coat to be burned, for which his superiors could subject him to punitive action for not doing so in a timely manner. He was also aware that I had threatened my Chief with legal action, both Military and civilian, in which he would be deeply involved. It was too late to put me on report without the benefit of a logical explanation for the delay at the Executive Officer's preliminary review prior to Captain's Mast. He was aware that I could, and would, make a number of serious and embarrassing accusations that would make him party and part of the conspiracy and harassment. The longer he waited, the worse it would get. His career was in jeopardy. My Chief wasn't sure of anything except that I never seemed to have any cigarettes.

The next time I saw my Chief, I asked him whatever happened to my chit to see the Chaplain.

"You don't need no damn chit to see the Chaplain."

"In this case I do."

"Why?"

"So it's a matter of record." Then I added, "Just disapprove the damn thing and give it back, so I can give it to the Division Officer and have him approve it. I'm sure he'll let me see the man."

"Are you going to see the Chaplain about this coat deal?" He was really worried that it was all about the coat.

"That's my secret, and I'm not telling you."

He approved the chit, which I put away. I asked him if he had an extra smoke. He gave me a dirty look and left.

It was now Thursday, past the middle of the week, closer to the imminent arrival of "Inspection Saturday" along with its impending, potentially dire consequences. A strange silence prevailed in which both Chiefs ignored me. I visited the Chaplain, who could hardly believe the evil plot these two Chiefs were instigating. He had never before been confronted with such a situation and didn't know how to handle it. I asked that he do nothing, but be aware of the situation and perhaps discuss it with the two Chiefs, indicating that I intended to take no vindictive action unless I was provoked. I didn't want them to put their careers on the line over such a stupid thing. If he did not talk to the Chiefs, I informed him that I feared for my well being. If anything further were done to me, I would be forced to request Courts Martial and subject a number of people to what, at present, were avoidable consequences. He must have talked to the Chiefs, telling them of his knowledge of the situation, which explained their strange silence.

My Chief asked me what I had told the Chaplain, so I said the same thing I had told him previously: it was Top Secret.

I refrained from asking him for a cigarette. I think this surprised him.

Friday found us entering Norfolk harbor, as was the ship's custom. As usual, there was a Captain's Inspection scheduled for Saturday morning. I was apprehensive about showing up for the gala affair sporting the pea coat that was ordered to be destroyed by fire. It was clear I could not borrow a

THE PEA COAT FIASCO

coat. I had not purchased a coat. I would wear the same threadbare, faded, war-torn mess and trust to the fickle finger of fate. If the Captain recognized the coat and me, I could be charged with disobeying a direct order, silent contempt, or conduct unbecoming a member of the armed forces, which are the Uniform Code of Military Justice catchalls. Then the fertilizer would impact the atmospheric impeller.

Saturday morning found me deeply concerned over what might transpire at inspection. All of my grandiose plans might backfire, the Chiefs might emerge without suffering any consequences, and I might go down the proverbial drain. I might get away with the garment at this inspection, but faced a couple more inspection sessions before the Navy gave me my walking papers. If I survived this inspection, I would buy a coat for the next one.

As usual, I stopped in the radar room before inspection for a cup of coffee and a much needed nicotine fix.

"Do you got a new coat?" inquired my Chief.

"Nope." I smiled.

"You gonna wear yer old one?"

"Yep. You got it," I responded bravely.

"The old Man is gonna hang your ass from the yard arm."

"So be it. If my ass is hung, a lot of asses will be hung. It will be one crowded yard arm," I threatened him.

"You got da watch."

I didn't have to stand Captain's Inspection. I won the contest.

"Aye, aye, sir. Got a smoke?"

I was off the hook. My anterior posterior would not be displayed, hanging from the yard arm, nor would I be keel hauled. I was given the watch for the subsequent inspections while I was aboard. I did burn the coat, but not until I was discharged and at home, in a pagan-like, eerie, moonlighted ceremony.

I guess they won the game after all. The coat went up in smoke.

Christmas 1944
Deming, New Mexico

Martha J. Martin

December 23rd, 1944
A package is delivered to my door.
Inside the box I take a peek.
There's one thing special that I seek.
Some presents wrapped with loving care
And things to eat are also there.
Sure enough, my wish comes true.
I see a string of lights or two.

I step outside and give a call
To my friend Bonnie down the hall.
"Whatever you're doing just let it be.
We're going to town to buy a tree!"
We'd been planning a big surprise
On Christmas Day for our two guys,
When they're allowed to leave the base
And spend the holiday at our place.

Our husbands are Air Cadets, you see,
And not too often are they free
To join their brides. It's been tough.
We 'weekend wives' do have it rough.
But now at last we'll have a chance,
If only one day, to enhance
Our joyless lives with a few thrills,
To decorate a tree with frills.

The sun is shining big and bright.
We head for town, our spirits light.
We'll make our room seem warm and gay,
So home won't seem so far away.
First stop at the grocery store.
The trees outside are pretty poor.
But we find one that's not too bad.
(Better than Charlie Brown has had!)

Next stop at the Five and Dime,
We're going to buy some balls this time.
But after looking all around
The balls are nowhere to be found!
"Sorry, ladies, don't you know?
Those were gone two years ago.
After all, there is a war.
Japan doesn't export anymore."

We look at each other in dismay.
How can our plans go so astray!
"Let's just buy us some balloons,
Use cranberries and popcorn for festoons."
"I'm afraid the balloons are just 'no-go'.
Uncle Sam got all the rubber, you know."
Back to the grocer for festoon stuff.
We guess it will have to be enough.

Heading home, we try not to mind,
As we drag our dear little tree behind,
Trying to picture how it will seem.
Will it look anything like our dream?
Once in my room we set up the tree,
Adorned with the lights, a real sight to see.
But Bonnie, not satisfied, wants to have more.
She gets an idea and runs out the door.

Down the hall to her room and back in a flash,
She's remembered and found the most perfect stash:
In the drawer of her nightstand, still wrapped in tissue,
An interesting packet marked "Government Issue"!
"So that's where the rubber went," I say with a smile,
And blow up 'balloons' for quite a long while.
Decorated with nail polish, some sequins glued on,
Our ornaments sparkle. We know that we've won!

Christmas Day soon arrives, and so do our fellows.
No one ever heard such earthshaking bellows
Of laughter as comes from our room on this day.
It was worth all the trouble, I'm happy to say.
But all things must end, and on New Year's Eve

Our husbands are transferred and we have to leave.
We go separate ways, lose touch with each other.
When we meet again, my friend is a mother!

At a party next Christmas, each other we spy.
We hug, oh so tightly, and laugh till we cry.
For there in a basket lies a three-month old girl,
With big bright blue eyes, blond hair in a curl.
Bonnie says, "On last Christmas, those balls did the trick.
Meet my daughter, Noelle, our gift from St. Nick!"

(Epilogue)
For sixty-five Christmases this story's been told,
Proof that a good tale never grows old.

Tattoo

Trudy Campbell

six-week-old baby girl, crying as we do, 22-year-old father,
home from Nazi Germany, married a year, never dated, life
was for work, work was for survival, survival was for suffering
for him, Mom, me; no praise, no smiles, hugs, kisses, even a new
baby girl was unwelcome,

marks on my tissue-soft bottom, not a rash or birthmark. Daddy's
telling Mom to shut me up, must not have worked out as his
handprint now mine forever, childhood tattoo for life.

ORANGE AT DUSK

Tiina Heathcock

sunset slants shard my lap
empty of
child, grandchild, womb

I reach into the cobalt bowl
for warmth of orange,
peel it father's way
all-in-one piece

tart citrus, pungent oils, waft memory…

rocker creak in firelight
father's lap
spirals of orange
fingers drenched in juice
"see, we can put it back together again"

now, alone
I separate each segment
careful not to rip the flesh
bite
chew
swallow the seeds

with gnarled, juice-scented fingers
I fumble
un-peel,
in trembling palms I cradle
empty weight,
tears
seal my sphere
back together again

A Date with Papa

Suse Marsh

Happy Birthday, Papa! This is a special day, and we have to celebrate. See, I brought you a gift, yes, it is a Sunday cigar. Let's relax, make some music on the piano and enjoy the day.

Papa gets his wooden box that holds the cigar cutter and extra long matches. He carefully unwraps the cigar, runs it under his nose, rolls it with his fingers and approves. He snips the end off and lights it. He smiles at me and carefully slips the band from the cigar. He hands me the band and I put it on, it is a perfect fit for my middle finger. He leans back and blows several rings into the air...

Then he walks over to the piano and asks: What will it be, Beizle?

I am sitting on a leather couch at the Leaf & Bean Company, a Cigar and Coffee House, sipping a cup of pumpkin spice coffee. The blackboard behind the coffee bar reads:

IT IS HARD TO BE IN LOVE AND WISE AT THE SAME TIME

I am the only woman here, and eight men are blowing cigar smoke into the air. Two younger guys are working on their laptops; five middle-aged men are sitting around a table, having a conversation. The owner keeps the guests happy with smokes and coffee. I need to find a way to get a cigar band. I muster my courage and approach one of the young men with a computer. Could I possibly have the band of your cigar? Certainly, he says, slipping the band off, and thereby spilling the ashes from his cigar all over his computer. Ouch! I thank him and put the band on my finger.

Next, I have a few questions for the owner. What is in the glass-encased part of the room? We keep most of the cigars in there; they need a special controlled climate with 70% humidity. Where do the cigars come from? Mostly from Honduras, Equator, the Dominican Republic, and Brazil; Cuban cigars are not allowed in this country.

Time passes, and my visit has to end. There is a tranquility in this smoke-filled room. Papa would have been 107 years old today.

Happy Birthday, Papa! I enjoyed my visit.

I miss you,

Love,

Beizle

The Night My Father Died

Diana Griggs

It rained
a steady drizzle forming the gray pallor
that drapes over trees and houses.

Each time I woke I was aware
of light taps on my window
fingers on the glass wanting entry
as though *they* had been called.

I left him that evening working
on his bank statement.
My kind of day he had said
content to watch raindrops bounce
on leaves & hit against the window.

When the nurse phoned she said
that when giving him night pills
he took her hand, held it tightly.
He had never done that before.

The night my Father died it rained.
I opened the window to let *them* in
saw the angels on his beloved cathedral
their faces drenched with tears.

Plea

Helen Benson

My child,
You sit beside me
And I see the caring in your eyes,
But your words have leather gloves
To protect your feelings from the cold.
I will not break
If you ask the tough questions;
I know my summers will not come again,
But I am not afraid.
My life has been a blessing
And you have helped to make it so.
It will not hurt me
To know you still need me.
Do you have any problems?
Do you need money? Are you well?
Do you know the secret of a good apple pie?
I am still the mother you had
At six and ten and eighteen.
I worry about the little things
But one has to face the big ones
And I am learning to handle this.
My life is more than pills and routine;
I still want to take on the world
And I can enjoy a good laugh.
I even have my dreams and make my plans
And think about one tomorrow
And then another.
So lay the gloves aside
And hold my hand.

Lullaby and Good Night

Marie Therese Gass

A pelting rain jags across my windshield this windy night, its irregular rat-tat-tat ceasing for seconds at the underpass. Dark hastening rivulets on each side of my car race down the windows like the thin icing my mother used to drizzle down the sides of cakes.

Mom has been dying for a week. Today, after work, I had a meeting about forty miles away and now all I want to do is go to my warm and safe home, but I know I should pull my strength together and visit Mom first. I don't want her to think she is alone, or to die without me, though probably nothing will happen tonight. Work was hell today. My exhausted self has been whispering Sleep! Sleep! so seductively that my mind is still not made up a few miles before the freeway turnoff. I could wait and see her tomorrow. Go home, my body urges. Mom will understand.

But what if tonight is your last chance to see her? The words are so strong that for a moment I wonder if Dad sent them. Nah! The voice in my head goes on: Then how will you feel tomorrow? Will getting home a few hours earlier tonight have been worth it? Doesn't matter where the message originates; it's something important to consider.

I used to think that communication with the dead was limited to saints and psychics until Dad's death a year ago. He was sick such a short time—three weeks from apparently healthy to the grave—we couldn't believe it. Mom had asked him toward the end, "Will you come back to visit me?" He no longer opened his eyes, but he murmured, "If they let me."

Having been scared of the dark and of anything unexpected, especially of visions like in the saints' stories we heard from the nuns in grade school, I certainly wasn't asking for any visitations, but, these days, every time I turned around it seemed like Dad was giving me advice again. Though I didn't listen to it much in my adult life when he was alive, it seemed harder to ignore him now.

The only time I was really certain that I heard Dad's voice after he died—out loud with decibels you could register on an oscilloscope—was a couple of days after his funeral, when Mom and I were talking on the phone. She'd said goodbye and hung up. Then Dad's voice said, very clearly and unexpectedly, Well, goodbye then, and there was another click like when they both used to get on the same line to talk to me before he died. I stood there staring at the receiver. Then I checked my reality, and yes, I swear it, I *did* hear him talk with my ears, not just in some general way in my memory.

As a matter of fact, I hadn't gone over to Mom's much after Dad died. Oh, I made a point of stopping by to take her along whenever we went out to eat, or to take her grocery shopping or to the craft store or sometimes a movie. And I had her over to our place a lot for dinner with the kids. But I wouldn't stay in her house, even though it took a long time for me to admit that Dad was still there. That evening when he died and the undertakers closed the hall door to the kitchen where we all sat around the table with Mom as they wheeled the body out—I was there, I saw that, and I know that, physically, Dad is gone. In some powerful way, though, he isn't. None of my siblings mentioned it, so one day I did, then they all said, Yeah, we thought the same thing. It was spooky.

Taillights on the double trailer rig in front of me waver sideways, and the stack of music slides off the back seat as I brake. Great...I was going to deliver that music to the organist in Portland tonight. That means a third trip unless I call her from Mom's and tell her I'll drop off the music on my lunch hour tomorrow.

The doctors said Mom was going to die last week. We had been sitting vigil at the hospital for ten days while she was in a deep coma, death rattles coming irregularly. It was 9 p.m., I was thinking about sleep again—all the sleep I would miss before work the next day—when the doctor came by. "What're you all hanging around for?" he asked, not too nicely. "She's never going to come out of this anyway."

"Well, what if she dies tonight?" I said, standing up and going over to his face. "I've heard that people in comas can still feel touch—we've been stroking her arms and forehead—and I'll bet they can even hear for a long time after it seems like they can't."

Part of the doctor's collar stuck up when he shrugged. He said nothing.

"So I want to be here when she dies," I went on. "What if she wakes up at the last minute? I don't want her to die alone."

The doctor hmmphed and picked up Mom's aluminum chart from where it hung on the foot rail. In a few seconds he clapped it shut and said,

"She's never coming out of that coma, so you don't have to worry about her dying awake and alone. That much cancer should have killed her weeks ago." Then he left the room.

We were stunned. I looked at my sister and her husband and my husband, and they looked at me. Even if that man is a pig, said Margo, he may be right.

So we went home.

The next morning on the way to the freeway, I felt a strong urge to call the hospital, so I drove into the convenience store lot and parked by the phone. The morning traffic was roaring so loudly I could hardly hear, but the nurse distinctly said, "Your mother is awake, talking, and we're feeding her Jello. You'd better get here fast!"

I called work and my brother. Then I raced to the hospital.

There was Mom, sitting up in bed, eating the little red cubes the nurse offered her on a spoon. It was Mom, but it wasn't Mom. The woman in bed had the same white curly hair, pale skin, and purple arms from all the blown veins, but her eyes were grey-blue. Mom's—heck, *all* of our eyes were deep brown. Most different of all, the woman in bed had this tremendous excitement in her eyes—not like, Hey, that's great! but about forty steps beyond that, into awesome and unfathomable joy, like

Whoa—that's *really* great!

I couldn't wait till the nurse left. "You saw him—you saw Dad!" I guessed, watching her expression. Mom nodded, started to speak, then held her throat. "I know, it's really sore from the tubes," I said, then took her hand. "You don't have to talk." Mom's eyes reminded me of those old stories of the saints, where they said that their eyes were "alight and shining." You could see just a little of the whites above the grey-blue part on top, and she had this serene, most joyful smile on her face as if she had been to heaven or something. Of all the times I had ever seen Mom excited or happy, this beat them all by far. A lot of times since then I have tried to describe how she looked, but I can't come close. All I can say is that I don't remember a single time in our lives together when she looked this jubilant.

Then Mom inched herself up farther, pointing to the foot end of the bed. Look! she whispered. I looked while the hairs on the back of my neck stood on end. I saw the steel traction bar hanging above the green rumpled spread and, beyond that, a bare white wall. Nothing else, not even a shadow.

Mom grabbed me with surprising strength, sweeping her other arm around the bed. Howww Manyyyy? she asked, her mouth sticking together.

I was embarrassed. I couldn't see anything, but she had convinced me that someone/something was there. I don't know, I mumbled, reaching for the ice chips and offering them to her.

Mom shoved the cup away and swept her arm painfully in a semicircle again, looking pleadingly into my eyes. I couldn't move; she was holding me tightly with her other arm. Count, she demanded in a surprisingly strong voice.

I looked back at the end of the bed. Ten? Thirty? I'm not sure, I said, this time avoiding her eyes. She seemed to require a better answer than that, so I added, You would know that better than I. Mom shook her head and dropped back onto the pillows. More! More! she whispered, her hand moving impatiently, leading me to believe my guess was considerably off.

Her grip swung me around to look at her. Right into my eyes, she said firmly, Two thousand. Two thousand? I repeated incredulously, not that I thought there wasn't room, but how did she know two thousand people who would come to greet her?

Then the nurse came in, and I got out of her way, walking around the foot end of the bed, stifling my impulse to say Excuse me to whoever might be there. Mom was already weaker, though she clutched my sleeve again as if she wanted to tell me one last very important thing. H-o-mme…she forced her mouth around the sounds her throat couldn't support. Then she held her throat with one hand and looked directly into my eyes. Home, she whispered, her voice nearly gone.

This is it, I thought. They always get better right before they die. Dad had wanted to die at home, too. I touched Mom's shoulder gently. All right, I said as the rest of my brothers and sisters filed into the room. Don't worry—we'll take you home. She relaxed then, right back into unconsciousness.

So that was were she was now. She could go at any time. My mother was lying on a hospital bed in her family room, back in a coma, her body swollen from edema, her arms yellow and purple, her friends, neighbors, and relatives coming and going, talking about her as if she weren't there or couldn't hear. Chances were, she could.

I sigh uncomfortably; the moments until the turnoff are few. Then this idea comes to me: Mom would love it if we would sing to her. I glance at the music on the floor of the back seat. All the old German Songs are there, plus some of the ones we girls learned in harmony while we did dishes on the farm. Mom loved music. When they started the Hit Parade, she had put a notebook on top of the icebox, and every time they played the Top 10 she wrote down a few more words so we could sing them together. In between times she taught us songs that would have made it in her day and her mother's day, had there been a Hit Parade then. We knew Whispering Hope in three-part harmony, Guten Abend Gute Nacht (Lullaby and Good Night), one about the shy little Indian maid, and some more—the girls would remember them.

I drive straight past my exit into Portland.

Every one of the visiting and in-town relatives is there in the living room: brothers and sisters and their spouses, as well as some of Dad's family from Canada. In the family room it is quiet except for Mom's deathly loud breathing. Her eyes are closed.

Margo, Popsie, Betty, and I stand around the bed sharing the sheet music, which is about ready to fall apart since some of it is from the 1920s. I stroke Mom's arm. We're going to sing to you, I say, and we begin. The more we get into the songs, the more words we remember of the ones for which we've lost the music.

Guten abend, gute nacht, mit roselein bedacht, I sing, wondering if those are the right words. It used to be that every time I sang "roselein," Mom corrected me: It's Englein…Roselein comes in the next line. Or was it the other way around? I watch Mom's face while I sing, but outside of looking relaxed and peaceful, she doesn't move a muscle.

We are on the second verse of Whispering Hope when Mom's right arm moves up into the air like there's a string around her wrist. Then it flops back down. Everybody stops singing.

She's trying to signal us, says Popsie. Yeah, right…you're off-key again, laughs Betty weakly. Don't worry, Mom, I won't let her drown us out!

We continue the second verse in a lighter mood, smiles on our faces. There is no longer any doubt that our mother can hear us. *Wait for the sunshine tomorrow, after the shower is gone*, we sing. *Whispering hope, O how welcome thy voice.*

Mom died in her sleep that night. I wonder how many children get to sing lullabies to their parents. I wonder if Mom has a singing group in heaven. Maybe the ones who came to the hospital.

Age Ain't Nothin' But a Number

Suzanne Schmidt

Tomorrow is Saturday again. I remember how hard it was sometimes to make the time every week, but throughout these last few years I vowed never to complain about being too tired or sick to go and see you. I think our weekly visits were as good for me as they were for you. I knew how lonely you were, especially this past year before you got sick and were given only two months to live. I guess that's what happens when you get older; you get sick and all your children are too busy with their own lives, but I made it a point to involve you in mine.

Looking back on our Saturday visits, I realize how important they were to us, not only for the counselling but for all the fun we had together. One Saturday in particular is my favourite story to remember.

It was a cold day in February; the sun wasn't shining, the temperature had dropped, and the snow was threatening to keep us apart. We decided I would bring my camera and take some funny pictures to send to Auntie Fern to cheer her up because the winters were so long for her, living way up in Sturgeon Falls. She wasn't able to come up and see you, and we wanted to do something extra special for her. The plan was to go to Zellers, our favourite stomping ground, try on hats, and take funny pictures to send to her.

I remember how we loved to go out for lunch, and this time I suggested we go to Montana's, because they have that great big birthday hat with the huge horns on it. When we got there, we convinced the waitress to let us take a picture with the hat, though it wasn't your birthday. She must have misunderstood me, because around the corner came the entire staff singing "Happy Birthday" and clapping loudly. They also brought you a cupcake with a candle on it, and I was killing myself laughing. As if that wasn't funny enough, you put one of those toothpicks with the ribbon on the end in your mouth, made a funny face, and I snapped the first picture.

When we went to the hat department at Zellers, I was a little disappointed with the selection, and suddenly a devious plan began to form in my head as I visualized not only hats, but a full wardrobe. You were pushing the cart as fast as you could to keep up while I threw in hot pink capris, slinky satin pyjamas, a bathing suit, earrings, bracelets, and even an umbrella. You kept saying, "But…but…we are not going to be allowed to take all these things into the change room." I told you not to worry, we would figure something out, and gradually you joined in the fun, started picking out things for yourself. I think your best pick was a pair of sparkling purple 6-inch heels that added to the glamour we were about to create.

When we reached the dressing room, there was a shy young girl attending the rooms. I took her aside and told her about our crazy plan. She looked in the cart, let out a slight gasp of shock and disbelief, and asked me how many items we had. I looked down at the hoards of items we had collected, put my hand on my chin and, giving her the most reasonable number I could think of, I said, "Hmmm…25?" I raised my shoulders and eyebrows and tried to look as innocent as I could, even though we must have collected well over 50 items.

She looked at us, smiled, probably thought 'how cute is this' and led us to this huge dressing room with a handicapped sign on it. It never occurred to me that you were almost 80, and my idea may have been a little over-ambitious. The first ensemble was the hot pink t-shirt and capris with a matching purple scarf. The pink glasses were a children's size, but we squeezed them on you, anyway. The little pink cap tilted to the side, 6-inch sparkly purple sandals and a huge bright orange and fuchsia purse added the finishing touches. I tried to stand you up, but you were very wobbly on those spiked heels. We had to think fast, but the giggles took over. I told you to brace yourself against the wall and left you teetering while I ran to the corner, holding myself and laughing so hard that I wet my pants down to my knees.

We couldn't let this little mishap ruin our plans, so I told you to sit down and cross your legs. Now, it had been a while since you had any reason to cross your legs, and it was no easy feat. I asked, "Can you possibly take that look of pain out of your face for a few seconds while I take the picture, and try to smile like you're having fun?" You quickly smiled, but if you look closely at the picture, you can see that your teeth are gnashed.

During the next pose, you were beginning to look a little tired, so I swung your legs up on the bench and told you to lean back. We tried to bend one leg, but your heel kept slipping. In the picture, you can see your hand grasping your knee so tightly in an attempt to keep it in place. After a few minor adjustments, you looked up and, thus, the dreamy "What's life all about" look.

I decided we had to make more use of the bench, so I asked if you could possibly lie on your stomach, and you said, "Sure." I told you to put one leg up, and you didn't know what to do with the other one, so I said, "Just cross them." By this time you were really getting into it, and you put your hand under your chin and made a cute smile. Even though you were grasping the bench for dear life with the other hand, we decided to put this picture in one of those yearly calendars and called it "Calendar Girl."

Before we changed outfits again, I was bound I was going to get one picture of you standing on those 6-inch heels, and it had been awhile since "the accident." Again, I told you to brace yourself on the wall with your elbow and butt and try to stick out one hip. I noted that body parts don't move as easily as you would think when you are almost 80. I said, "You look like a hitchhiker," so you stuck your thumb out and made this weird face. Your t-shirt read, "I'm in love with a beach bum," and the effect was too funny for words.

Next was the most challenging outfit of all, "The bathing suit." It was a size 24, and we all know you have been a size 14 for years. You refused to buy anything unless it was a size 14, but I assured you I would make it work. We had to use some of the accessories to stuff the bra of the bathing suit. Then we needed a hat and realized it was used for the stuffing, so we took the hat out of the left side and covered the deflated boob with a pink shawl. The hat was a skater's hat and looked a little mannish, so we put a big blue flower on the side to soften things up. We were running out of poses, so I told you to stretch out your arms in the air and, when you did, all the price tags popped out. We had changed your shoes to a low pump that was a little too small, but when I said, "Smile," you threw your head back and put on the biggest smile anyway. I laughed until my sides hurt because I knew all the price tags were showing, but the picture was "priceless!"

We wanted to get a few more shots with the bathing suit, so back to the corner you went, and this time we popped open a colourful umbrella. You were beginning to look very professional at modelling, and you were getting better at swinging that hip, even though the shoes were still pinching you. The result: "Age Ain't Nothin' But a Number."

I think you enjoyed the last few outfits the most—the lingerie. You liked the feel of the satiny material, and we came to the realization that you looked pretty good in hot pink. The first number was a long-sleeved pink satin shirt nightie that had two slits up the side, and your support hose really made your legs look good. The only problem was that, when you sat down, it was too tight and the buttons wouldn't stay closed, so I told you to put your knees up. We put on the pink sunglasses with black rims, and you had this naughty looking smile on your face. So what if you could see a little more than you wanted to see; your expression made up for it.

We tried a few more poses on the bench, and then I tried to get you to lie on your side. My thinking was to get you to lie on your back first, and that way it would be easier to get you to turn on your side. Wrong. You were on your back, all right, but you couldn't move because the nightie was too slippery. I started to laugh so hard that I had to run to the corner and yes, I wet myself again. You said, "I can't stay like this much longer." I was worried I wouldn't be able to move you because you were so heavy and slippery. Tears of laughter were streaming down my face, and I had nothing left to pee, but after a great deal of struggle I got you into a sitting position again and ready for the next shot.

The final outfit was a three-piece lounging set. The pants were a leopard print, and the tank top and little jacket had leopard trim around it. You didn't need much direction at that point, and you put one hand on your hip and the other behind your head and managed one more sexy smile. We called it "Wild Thang." You were a quick study for sure, and I think you liked that ensemble so much you wanted to buy it.

After several hours of fun, we packed everything up and walked out of the dressing room as if nothing had happened. We thanked the girl again, and I gave her a wink and a thumbs up. Luckily, my pants were black and quick drying. You made me put everything back in its place, of course. You were such a good sport about it all. This little adventure will always remind me that you are "The Best Mom on Earth," and you were always willing to do anything for fun. By the way, the apple obviously doesn't fall far from the tree. I miss those crazy times we had together. Now I have to make some memories with my daughters to pass on this legacy.

Confusion at Edgewater Memory Care

M. Clark Wilde

"*Mother!*" As he snapped on the overhead brights of the common room, Louis was shaken to see his mother there again with that man.

Louise Lovelace and Mr. Harold Baines were facing each other, wheels side to side, with only the mute flicker of the television lighting their communion. As Harold held her hand, occasionally gently stroking her hair or cheek, Louise told again the fears and joys of her debutante Cotillion.

Louis strode across the room. "I've been searching everywhere." He grabbed the handles of his mother's chair and wheeled her quickly away. "I'm taking you right back to bed. You'll catch your death of cold out here!"

Harold wheeled his chair quietly behind them as they hurried down the hall. He heard Louis scold Louise.

"He can't even speak. Why do you sneak off to see him?"

Glancing back, Louise replied, "Harry listens."

"Mr. Baines, haven't Staff and I asked you time after time to obey our Edgewater policies? Now look what you have done—our best account lost to Riverend. All because you can't follow a few reasonable rules. Listen to what Mr. Lovelace wrote in this Termination:

"'When I found them sitting in the dark, he had grabbed one arm and was reaching for my mother's throat. I'm afraid to think of what would have happened had I not come in time.'

"Mr. Baines, you know in these difficult times we are short-handed evenings. I am saddened that you took advantage and cost us that valuable account. It's such a shame, too. Mrs. Lovelace was making such surprising progress with us here at Edgewater.

"Mr. Baines, I shall have to ask Staff to see that you don't leave your room after recreation hours henceforth."

Mrs. Louise Lovelace
Riverend Care
Cisco, CA 94701

Sweet Lou,

    Thank you for saving me the last dance at the Cotillion.

    Your gown was glorious; your hair, perfect. I hope I didn't muss it as I held you close. You were light as a dream in my arms. I'll always remember the warmth of your words in my ear.

All my love,

Harry

She waits beside my bed

Anne Whitlock

veiled in morning light,
vintage wine uncorked,
virgin skin untouched
by my waking fingers;
ominous in her importance,
in her pure potentiality,
the new day waits for me.

Children's days are trinkets,
colored sparklers bursting in the sun,
copper pennies tossed in play.
My day is honey slowly dripping
from a spoon—old gold,
misered by a restless moon.

Mrs. Bumble Goes to Town

Ruth Turner

Mrs. Bumble walked all over town
Wearing her slippers and flannel nightgown.
She ambled along without a care
Quite unaware of her tousled hair.

Some children giggled and stopped their play
As the little old lady went on her way.
"I think she's asleep," said one to the others
And they hurried off to tell their mothers.

There's Mrs. Bumble, mused Mr. Skeptical.
Lordy me! She's quite a spectacle.

Haughty Harriet said not a word…
Just passed her by and muttered, "ABSURD!"

Mr. McFussy did a double take.
She's not properly dressed! For Goodness sake!

"Just taking a stroll?" asked the diplomat.
She kept on going, so he tipped his hat.

She passed some ladies and one of them said,
"I think she is lost. She's dressed for bed.
She saunters along at a steady pace;
We'd better follow her just in case."

Old Mr. Cranky took hold of her arm
And told her gruffly (with all of his charm),
"Wake up, Mrs. Bumble! Where are you going?
You look a fright and it's quite annoying."

She quickly stopped and opened her eyes,
Looked all around, then shrieked in surprise,
"Oh me! Oh my! Have I lost my head?
It's plain to see…I'm ready for bed."

The children rushed back with their mothers in tow,
The ladies she passed stood all in a row
And some curious people gathered and gawked
At the little old lady who slept while she walked.

"I'm so embarrassed…I'm such a disgrace.
How in the world did I get to this place?
I need to go home and comb my hair."
So she turned around and walked back there.

A Bunch of Daffodils

Kathleen A. O'Brien

An old woman, strong of heart,
    pushed a green grocery cart
    up a littered city hill
toward her public housing home—
    herself, alone.

I idled at a traffic light,
    taking notice of this sight.
    Peeking from one paper bag,
a bunch of yellow daffodils.

Invisibility

Kay Lesh

I have a childhood memory of sitting on the floor of my grandparents' living room, enthralled by a radio program called *The Shadow*. I was fascinated by the premise of the show. The hero, Lamont Cranston, had somehow acquired the ability to cloud men's minds so they couldn't see him. Using this amazing skill, Cranston went about solving crimes and righting many wrongs.

I wasn't sure how you would go about clouding men's minds, but the idea of invisibility had great appeal for a shy child like me. I figured it would be wonderful to pass unnoticed at family gatherings. When relatives cornered me to ask what I was learning in school or what I wanted to be when I grew up, I could just cloud their minds and disappear. And if I could learn to make a book invisible as well, I'd be able to sit around and read all day without hearing, "Close that damn book and find something useful to do."

What fun it would be to slip around unseen. I'd be able to hear other kids' conversations and find out what they really thought. If I listened carefully, I perhaps could learn how to be like them. Then I could be one of the cool kids. That would be great! When my parents fought, I'd become invisible. I wasn't sure invisibility would shut out the hateful words, but I figured it would be worth a try. Invisibility seemed like it could change my life.

Now that I am an older woman, I am surprised to find that I have achieved invisibility, and I didn't even have to learn how to cloud men's minds. My gray hair and aging flesh appear to have their own magical powers. I know I am invisible because I can stand at a counter in the store and be passed over for younger customers. I can browse through clothing racks unnoticed by any salesperson. I can sit in a restaurant without anyone coming by to take my order. I can pass a group of men without earning a single glance.

Being invisible is annoying, but there are advantages. They aren't the ones I envisioned as a child, but they are almost as good. I can go to the park to exercise without worrying about how I look. If I have clean sweat pants, a comfortable tee shirt, and a pair of well-fitting athletic shoes, I am good to go. New styles in workout gear are irrelevant to someone who is invisible. I huff and puff around the track and nobody sees me. All eyes are on the young things with their toned bodies and flashy spandex, instead of on the gray-haired granny struggling to last through one more lap.

As an invisible woman, I wear the same clothes to work for two days in a row if I choose, and it is not the big deal it was when I was younger. I can't believe the time I used to spend planning my wardrobe to make sure everything was coordinated and that I never wore the same outfit twice in one week. Now I just grab something comfortable from the closet and put it on. If I wore the same outfit yesterday, who cares?

My choice of colors has broadened, too. I wear shades that I used to pass by because they didn't suit me. Oh, I don't wear anything blatantly awful, but if I feel like wearing a hue that doesn't work so well with my skin tone, I just go ahead and do it.

Fashion is no longer important to an invisible woman. When I read that spike heels are making a comeback, I shook my head in wonder. Why would anyone voluntarily wear those things? I sometimes wonder if there are other women who wish they were invisible, too, so they wouldn't have to consider tottering around on those foot-constricting torture devices.

Invisible women don't need to worry about covering gray hair. A low maintenance cut is my aim, and if the gray shows, so be it. I don't have the patience to sit for hours in the stylist's chair trying to make my hair look like it isn't aging along with the rest of me.

Cosmetic surgery is not something an invisible woman needs, either. The thought of someone nipping and tucking my various body parts scares me. Botox injections have to be painful, and why would I want to numb my nerves, anyway? I can't see that these procedures have any purpose in my life. So I use sunscreen on my skin and let it go at that. Being invisible saves a lot of time and money.

I am pleased to have achieved invisibility. It is freeing in a way I never dreamed it would be. I'm not solving crimes or righting the wrongs of the world, like Lamont Cranston, but my kind of invisibility is useful, too.

And I expect that the popularity of the Harry Potter books has gotten a new generation of kids thinking about the advantages of becoming invisible. I would like to tell them, "Don't worry. Invisibility will happen when you get older."

But I'll just let them find that out for themselves.

My Breath

Carol Louise Christian

My breath is to be cherished as more
Valuable than any sum.

    Life flies in with each windy
Woeful puff of air I gratefully

Move in and out of my impoverished chest.

    I have seen death
        When the faint breeze stops.

Here within our world the loved one is
        Labored though the breathing be.
    When it quits the silence bursts and life like a weary light is gone.

So then as precious as my wheezing breaths
    I will do most any bidding.

Lay low, take horrible medications
    Stay on hold, with the phone against
        My heart, beating fast, both with effort and fear

Relief is to celebrate
With lung love and profound peace!

However air comes easily again,
    I will dance with the fire
        Of my renewed life.

Choosing Burial Plots

Maurice Hirsch

I visit New Mt. Sinai. The smartly-dressed,
over-perfumed saleswoman explains
its urban location a result of Jewish society
in the nineteenth century. As she drones on,
my eyes flutter closed. Her voice rises,
I snap awake, she uses a wine-red fingernail to point out
possible sites on the map on her wall,
speaks of their virtues
as if she were selling me a building site.
Here's one near a prominent family.
Another is next to a road — on rainy days
there's no need to walk around other graves: just park and visit.
A third has a spigot nearby to water pots of geraniums,
an oak at its edge, is
across from the maintenance building,
the outer boundary chain-link fence,
1950s ranch house subdivision beyond.

I visit each site in order,
lie down on my back
as if I'm testing mattresses,
close my eyes, listen.
The last is my favorite,
near men who will weed the perpetual-care ivy,
trim overhanging branches.
I put my hands behind my head,
say to the breeze, *Perfect.*

It All Comes Down to This

Mary Lou Stafford

He's just a lad from Mallory,
It all comes down to this.

Now living on one calorie,
It all comes down to this.

The final days of one man's life,
his daughter and his doting wife.
He weakens, sleeps and weakens more,
fading from the years of yore.

The years of books and trips and talks,
of pleasant meals and nature walks,
of laughter, poems, and generous care,
his gentle smile with love to share,
his intellect and humorous wit,
his grasp of knowledge and tidbit.

So now we sit, just holding hands;
he's drifting toward that far off land.

Our hearts are full
of life's great treasure,
richer by far
than any pleasure.

For as my father ends his run,
Love cradles him 'til he is done.

Love, it turns out,
is the gift.
And now we know,
it comes down to this.

Creator

Una Nichols Hynum

Not everyone has a father who created an island
but we did. Our father dumped the sludge
left over from a kelp factory after the good
part was taken out to make ice cream, he told us.
We never looked at ice cream quite the same
as other kids. My older brothers put themselves
through college driving the kelp run.
The rest of us considered it an honor
to get to ride along, perched on the seat
like the boy on the edge of a goldfish bowl.

There was no conversation. The truck was big,
noisy and dirty. We couldn't see out the windshield
but we loved to see Father jump down from
the driver's seat, pull the magic lever
that upturned the bed, dumped still-steaming sludge
with a swoosh, smelling faintly of low tide.
When hardened the sludge sat in grey cones
like craters in a lunar landscape as far as we could see.

When the island was finished architects built
an expensive restaurant overlooking the harbor,
planted oleander and palm trees.
Tonight after dinner, I caught up with my Dad
to thank him and whispered,
"Not everyone has a father who created an island."

Treasured Pleasure

Barbara M. Traynor

I hear my daughter calling to me from the bedroom downstairs. "Mom… come see this!" Silence. Then, again. "Mom!…there's more!" I pause in the midst of my attic rummaging to listen to her description of treasure discovered.

The contents of cabinets and dresser drawers, what we choose to keep or discard, speak to our personality as much as the jewelry we wear or the dates circled on our calendars.

My aunt was a dynamic lady, intelligent, and fiercely independent. Chipping away at the glass ceiling, she inched up from the steno pool at a prominent Wall Street stockbroker firm to a corner office as a portfolio analyst, earning a degree from NYU at age forty, the first woman to have her education fully subsidized by maintaining a B+ average—while working full time.

"I'm coming," I reply, stalling, lost in recollection.

Childhood should be joyful—at least, sometimes. In the days when you could travel without a security escort, my father would entrust his three under-age-ten daughters to a conductor on the New Haven railroad, destination Grand Central Station, our summer refuge. Our aunt would be waiting on the platform, and we would be off to the Automat for lunch, then ice cream sundaes for dessert. It was exciting!

The row house in Brooklyn that she and her husband shared with my paternal grandparents had a postage stamp back yard, streetlights, and clamoring garbage trucks that devoured trash by scooping and crushing. We had two sets of friends, the usual small town neighborhood kind that we saw on a daily basis, plus *big city* acquaintances renewed each year on "the stoop."

My Connecticut grandmother scoffed. "Nobody goes to New York City in the summer!" Actually, I think she was more jealous than appalled. We basked in the notoriety.

"Mom!"

My daughter appears in the doorway clutching a small, yellowed box. Tissue paper disintegrates as she lifts a pair of baby shoes, black and brown leather scuffed where toes would totter, four shiny buttons still intact. Tucked underneath is one soft, pink and white crocheted bootie with a pink satin ribbon tie. My fingers caress the silky threads of the bootie, my mind a carousel of elevated trains and Roy Rogers galloping across the 10" black and white TV screen.

"Is this a real fox?" With adolescent drama she grabs the fur from the closet shelf, swirls it around her neck, fluffy tail flying, beady eyes flashing, before she dashes downstairs, anxious to find more treasures. Items retrieved to be revered by future generations.

I sneeze.

Glancing around, I imagine my aunt and uncle dancing to "Peg O'My Heart," smell the Chicken Cacciatore he made in huge batches. She didn't cook, he did; she had *a career!* From downstairs, I hear a clatter of something being dropped, along with a quick, "Whoops! Nothing broke." I latch the closet doors, blow dust from the hatbox containing the feathered cloche with veil, and scoop pictures into shopping bags, envisioning a collage of faces, places, and styles.

"Look at all this stuff!" my daughter's voice exclaims as I descend the stairs. Peering over the railing, I smile at the jumble of silver and gold bracelets, chains, and earrings spilling out from her lap onto the floor. An eeriness causes me to shudder and peer over my shoulder. Is someone watching? Am I intruding?

Then, I know. It is not that something or someone is here. Rather, something is missing. A presence removed. A presence that encouraged and consoled. A presence provoking us to poke and discover and enjoy as if surprises were purposely tucked in each drawer, on every closet shelf. I sense a smug sigh. A presence treasured.

No Small Gift

Evelyn Buretta

He trudged in at dusk, hands grimy and dirty
from field dust and oily machinery
he hitched to his red tractor,
his constant daily companion.
We tip-toed around him at night,
did our chores to avoid his yell,
the threat of an outburst
enough to keep us in line.
Then Joey fell off a chair. My cup of milk
splashed onto the kitchen floor.
"Now you're both going to get it!"
Dad gave us lessons to be more careful.

Too shy to call out B-39 or I-25
for Bingo at church fundraisers,
he shoved his hands into iced tubs for hours
and pulled out cold bottles of beer to sell.
I dared to ask, "Dad, can you win me a teddy bear?"
He laid down hard-earned dimes. My heart beat
with the clicking of the spinning wheel,
circling fast, then the clapper slowing
to a stop, but never on his numbers.
I didn't believe he would even try.

On my pillow the next day a stuffed elephant
with a long nose nudged me and said "Hello."
I smiled and hugged the furry grey body.
"Better than an ol' teddy bear." My only gift
from Dad roamed with me through life,
greeted me every morning and night.
I kept him safe from smudgy little hands.
Time passed like the first turns
of the wheel in that booth years ago.
With the last kid gone, the pace slowed.
I took Dumbo from my cedar chest
to listen to him trumpet again.

First Runner-up: Best Poetry Contest

Today Our Teacher Taught Us How to Write a Letter

Tiina Heathcock

    I'm not allowed to say
    your name in the new
    house mommy calls our home
    but the teacher said we could
    write a letter to anybody we wanted to

    how are you
    do you hear me every night
    when I call you as quietly as I can
    why did you leave
    what did I do wrong
    I promise to be very
    very good
    here is my news

    I hide in my room
    so I won't make him mad
    when he shouts
    "come down now"
    I get so scared
    I hurry and sometimes I slip and
    fall on the stairs
    I don't look at his eyes or
    his big hands
    I don't scream
    "go away I want
    my daddy back"

    I curtsey and say "yeses"
    like mommy told me to
    I *never* call him daddy

    at suppertime there are no
    funny stories, we don't have
    roast pork, sauerkraut or brown gravy
    mommy has a new pressure-

cooker so that his food is
not too hard to chew
we have to be quiet when
we eat or he throws
spoons and even plates

if we make a noise
when he has a headache
he really yells
mommy gets very white
the baby cries

he sometimes smiles
at the baby

every time when mommy and I are locked in
the bathroom after he gets
a real red face
I tell her what you told me
about how we left Estonia
and grandma and grandpa because
bad people would hurt us
I tell mommy
"let's go away"
mommy whispers
"you're just a child you don't…"

I'm a child
your child
I'm not so little now
I can read books
in books people run away from
a bad place too

I know soon you'll
wake up
come and take me
in your arms
waltz me around in circles
till I fall asleep
please hurry

yours truly
Anna   oooxxx

Abandoned

Nancy Sandweiss

I must have forgotten my four-year-old self
weeping into sleep on long summer nights at camp,
clinging to my older sister as our parents drove off
after visitors' day. I must have forgotten my shame,
waking up in a wet bed; the embarrassment
of daily roll call on the functioning of our bowels.

I must have forgotten; how else could I have entrusted
our two-year-old son to a babysitter while my husband
and I followed his brother to India in search of miracles?
We'd set aside reason to check out his guru. It was a lark,
not a pilgrimage; we returned light-hearted, still skeptics.

David was toilet-trained in our two-week absence;
I never thought to ask how it was done, considered
the outcome a pleasant boon. I still can see him dressed
in red and blue, racing to greet us, arms flung wide.
I'd rather not remember how after that he reverted to tears
whenever the sitter appeared at our door.

Now here I am babysitting nearly 40 years later,
wrestling our two-year-old grandson into his carseat.
His good nature is strained after four days without
mommy; he flails, shrieks his impotence.
I'm disoriented by his pain, my helpless love;
accidentally hit the emergency blinker.
Beeping and crying fill my head all the way home.

A Conversation with Amy

Sarah Bolek

Going from Chicago to Los Angeles. She has just left her father and stepmother waving goodbye at the airport. She settles into her seat and fastens her seat belt. She carries a small plastic bag containing some chocolate chip cookies, a moth-eaten teddy bear, and a pink plastic wallet with pictures of her mother, stepfather, and the new baby. She is on her way home to L.A. in the care of the steward. She looks like Tatum O'Neal in "Paper Moon."

She says to me, "Push the button and call that man. I want a pillow, a blanket, and a drink of water."

"You will have to wait until we get in the air; he is very busy right now. Anyway, I didn't hear the magic word," I say.

"What's that?" she asks.

"When you say PLEASE, it gets you what you want a lot faster."

"I Don't Have To Say That," says Amy.

Searching out the window for the face of her daddy, she says, "My daddy said he would cry when I left, but I have to go because my mom would send the Police after him if he didn't send me home."

Amy starts humming a tune, then sings, with a western lilt to her voice, "You left a hole in my heart, Daddy…"

"Did you make that up?" I ask.

"Yes," she says, "and I sang it in a contest and I won a Barbie doll."

"Why don't you write a song about your daddy like 'you'll always be in my heart, Daddy'?"

"I'd rather write about clouds." After a pause, Amy starts singing again. "I dreamed I saw you in the clouds, Daddy, kissing me, mommy, and my new little brother."

She abruptly changes the subject. "You know, my daddy has a new wife, and she already has a grown-up daughter. My nana says she did that gross thing, and she is going to have a baby."

"What did you do on your vacation with your daddy?"

"Watched TV, went to the mall, and like that…"

"Well," I say, "I guess you'll be happy to see your mommy. She must love you a lot, and she will be waiting for you."

Amy starts singing again. "You left a hole in my heart, Daddy…"

To myself, I add, *Please, Daddy, make my heart whole again.*

On Baldy

Jim Frisbie

There is a sense
of victory
in skiing
with my sons.

To watch
them stretch
like fledglings
full of laughter.

Bound, yet free,
they call,
"Come on Dad!
Don't be so slow!"

I smile, knowing
it won't be long,
before they cease
to look back.

I have shown
them how to fly.
I dare not have regrets,
when I see them
disappear.

Rushing the Growler

Frederick J. Schubert

Thirty-four, prohibition's gone.
Wet your whistle, legal-like.
Mike's open again,
pulling draft on South Pearl,
one step above Second.
Same place like always,

"It's a warm night boy!
Get the bucket, there on the shelf."
Squat, tin, with lid, quart size.

"Here's four bits. Go to Mike's and
lager fill it. Quick now, I've a thirst!"

With whistle and skip, bucket swinging,
up the street and through the doors.
Dim, smoke hazed, babble of voices.

"Please sir, pap says fill, lager draft."
"Fifty cents, my lad, else no beer this night."
"Yes sir, right here, four bits, like papa gave me."

Filled to the brim, with foam overrunning.
Our growler has snaps, hold fast the lid.
Back on the run, no spill going home.
In the door, to the kitchen.

"There you are, boy, 'bout time
mouth as dry as the old Sahara!"

In the glass and down the hatch,
white foam mustache frames the lips.
Sigh of satisfaction.

Rushed the growler this night. Tomorrow?
Well maybe, if heat holds, thirst rises
and pap has fifty cents.

The Dumpster

David Ray

When Gabe was in the first grade, he was old enough to be sent to fetch his father from the tavern. One night, as he waited in a booth, now and then approaching his father to plead his mother's case, a burly man bent down, his breath strong enough to make Gabe slide away. He stared up into a red and wrinkled face. The man knew Gabe's name.

"I'll give you a dollar to dance for us," he whispered.

"A whole dollar?"

"Sure. Just give us a dance."

"I don't know how to dance."

"Just jump around then and clap your hands," the man said. "You can act crazy if you want to."

As Gabe jumped and whirled around, leaping and cavorting, some of the men at the bar stomped and whooped. When Gabe began to feel dizzy, he stopped. The man pressed a crumpled dollar bill into his hand and winked. "You did good, real good," he said. "You danced us a real jig." But Gabe did not get to keep the dollar. His father needed it for a final drink of the evening.

"Give us another," someone shouted, but the bartender spoke up. "Aw, leave the kid alone." The boy looked around, his blue eyes large with fear, but the group of men included his father, and the faces were friendly.

Thus was born a business. While waiting for his father to glug his fill, glass after glass, hour after hour, Gabe would jump up and down and clap his hands and look around with his eyes goggling loose, acting the way the men wanted. But they always wanted more. "Hey, Kid, why don't you learn to tap dance like a nigger?"

Sometimes the fear came back, for the rowdy drinkers, women as well as men, sounded like they wanted to hurt somebody. Even when they approached to give Gabe tips, they would wave cigarettes and blow smoke in his face, laughing all the while as if this were the funniest thing in the world.

But before long Gabe learned to endure the torture and acted up just as they wanted. A quick glance around, and he knew how he was doing. The customers liked him to jump and kick and spin around, his rear end bouncing, his arms flapping like wings. The crowd applauded, shouted encouragement and tried to outdo one another in buying him drinks, usually Coca-Cola. They threw money at him, and he would fall to his knees to gather the bills and coins when he finished. Soon he had perfected his own unique sequence of dances and antics, returning to his booth between acts. Sometimes he brought homework and huddled over arithmetic problems in the dim light.

Gabe's father strongly approved. Gabe shared his dollars and felt manly for reversing their roles, becoming the provider. Before long, much to the satisfaction of his friends, his father welcomed Gabe's initiation into the drinking life, and none of the bartenders ever seemed to mind. After a few sessions of feeling nauseated and dizzy from downing a bottle or glass of beer, Gabe began to feel proud that he stayed on his feet and managed to perform his prancing antics, dancing without his eyes getting heavy or his speech slurring the way his father's did.

When he helped the stumbling man home, steadying him by the elbow or tugging at his belt, Gabe felt like a father himself. He excelled at handling the problem of getting home and dealing with his mother, who was always waiting up, pinching her pink terry cloth robe as she confronted them from halfway up the carpeted stairs. But she ceased complaining, as if Gabe's sharing his money had silenced her. Her husband would stand aside, letting the boy speak for him. Gabe knew his father had to work hard not to tip over as he held onto the stair rail and waited until his wife turned and led the way back upstairs.

Gabe's mother would still go through periods when she complained mightily, but she often neglected this duty. At breakfast she would look as if she might complain, but then seemed to think better of it. She concentrated on cooking the pancakes or eggs and sausage, and when she sensed that her son, as well as her husband, needed coffee, she filled and refilled Gabe's cup, too.

In the taverns the boy got used to the smells that had made him sick at first—spilled beer, rising like mist, mingled with the effluvia of urine and vomit and rot of ancient flooring. In the toilets Gabe held his arm over his face. But he grew ever more fond of the amber brew. Men who had once held glasses down and invited Gabe to lick the foam off their beer now handed him a full glass for himself. Gabe began to love beer so much that he even loved the odor as he stood at a urinal, feeling the fluid flowing out of his body.

One night, a man standing at the next urinal leaned over and grabbed at Gabe, fumbling around. Gabe jumped back, wriggling loose, and slapped at the hand as best he could, but the man only laughed and whispered, "You tell anyone about this and I'll kill you." He reached into his wallet and offered a ten dollar bill. "This is to keep your mouth shut."

He made a motion of slicing his own throat, then turned and left the room. Gabe never saw him again, though his eyes would suspiciously roam crowds when he danced. He thought of the man as a monstrous giant, to be avoided at any cost.

Fifteen years later, Gabe was in a U.S. Navy holding tank, a jail cell. He had been arrested for being drunk and disorderly, though he had merely passed out in a ditch and awakened in the bright sunlight of mid-morning with two Shore Patrol sailors standing over him, caressing their billy clubs and discussing whether to bounce them off Gabe's head.

By the time he left the navy with his dishonorable discharge, Gabe thought himself worthy of no better housing than a tunnel or crawl space under a bridge, where he sometimes had to share space with other homeless men and women. He learned to use newspapers and cardboard for covers, and found food in green trash barrels.

"It's amazing what you find in these places," he told himself as he leaned into or crawled into a Dumpster. He was sure some people left food as donations, for he now and then found half or more of a sandwich neatly rewrapped in its foil. His favorite Dumpsters around the farmer's market were good sources of nearly fresh produce.

Yet there were times when nothing turned up, and Gabe had to carve teeth marks out of apples or rot from tomatoes and mildewed oranges with his pocket knife before biting into them. If he had had a few drinks, he didn't care enough to bother. He decided it didn't matter if he shared an apple or a sandwich with a rat, and he figured that alcohol killed the germs as good as any medicine.

One evening, the police arrested Gabe for vagrancy. It wasn't the first time, and he knew what he had to look forward to—a night or two in a bunk bed of woven iron slats with rust showing through the flaking aluminum paint. The lidless toilet was an open pipe in the corner, its porcelain so discolored that it looked like copper.

But the sergeant on duty that night was unusually curious, and he discovered that Gabe—or at least his widowed mother—had a home in the city. Stepping out of Gabe's hearing, he made a phone call, chatting a few minutes as he kept his eyes on the prisoner. When he returned to the booking counter, the sergeant spoke to the arresting officer. "She'll take him back," he said. "And it's not a bad address, either." He studied Gabe's face, seeking to solve a mystery there.

"I don't want no ride home," Gabe said. "I ain't seen my mother in a hell of a long time. No need to see her now, that's for sure."

"Get going. This good lady's willing to take you back. I hope she won't regret it. You've wasted enough of our time."

When the squad car drew up at a two-story brick house with a front porch that reminded Gabe of the White House, he blurted out, "Hey, that's not the right place."

"That's it, all right," the driver said, looking over his shoulder. "Maybe your ma moved up in the world."

"Yeah, buddy, you must've been away a long time," said the other officer, as he unlocked the handcuffs.

Gabe's mother opened the front door and dolefully agreed that the apologetic fool they had brought to her door was her son. Looking at Gabe with near disgust, she shook her head as if tempted to apologize for his behavior, or perhaps his existence. Gabe held his baseball cap crumpled in his trembling hands the way he had years before with his white seaman's cap.

"Madam, we can take him back down to the lockup for the night while you think it over."

For a long moment his mother seemed to consider the suggestion, then said, "Oh, he might as well stay, but, believe me, I have not seen this person in thirteen years. I thought he was in California."

"How long you been back in town?" the policeman who was clenching Gabe's arm said, squeezing it to force a statement.

"Maybe a year, maybe a couple or three," Gabe said.

He noticed that his mother's hair had turned grey. When he left home, her hair had been auburn and her cheeks not so hollowed, her eyes not so deeply inset. He did not remember wrinkles, but now her face reminded him of someone's fingerprint. Her gray-blue eyes bored through him with even more unfriendly intensity than when he was a boy.

"Gee, I'm sorry, Mom," he mumbled.

She looked at him in silence, seemingly uncertain whether she should hug or slap him. But she did neither. "We'll have to get you cleaned up," she said. "We'll get you some clothes down at Penney's tomorrow."

When he woke in clean sheets the next morning, Gabe pondered the mystery of why he had come home. No comfort could outweigh the pain of seeing his mother's face so uncertain of whether she had admitted a stranger into her home. When he asked about his father, she only shrugged and said, "He had some insurance from the army I didn't know about."

"He never talked about that. When was he in the army?"

"Before you were born. He never was the same after that."

"He tried to be a good dad," Gabe said, and looked around, seeking the canary he remembered from childhood. "Did Fanny die?" he said.

"Fanny?"

"Our canary."

"Oh, long ago. Funny you should remember that when you forgot all about me."

Each room of the house looked like a window display for a furniture store. Gabe's mother had a yellow-uniformed maid now, a black girl who cooked breakfast and handed Gabe his orange juice and coffee. He was aware that she watched him, as if ordered to do so. And, whatever Gabe did, his mother mostly just sat and watched him. When he suggested that he could mow the lawn and do some yard work, she said, "I have a man under contract. It wouldn't be right to deprive him of the work, now, would it?"

In a dresser drawer in the guest room Gabe found a pair of his father's suspenders, bright and red as new. His mother threw him an unpleasant look when she noticed them on him, but said nothing.

"You don't mind, do you?" Gabe said with a smile, pulling one of the straps out with his thumb and letting it snap against his chest.

"I guess not. I don't care," she said. "I could have saved you one of his hats, but I threw everything out, or thought I did."

"Maybe I remind you too much of him."

"I don't care about that either," she said. "You don't look much like him."

"Maybe I should find myself a place. I don't want to be a bother."

"I guess you can stay if you want," she said, without enthusiasm. The words seemed to cause her pain. She rubbed the gnarled, arthritic bones of her hands together, preferring to look at them rather than at her son.

Gabe didn't venture outside for a few days, then realized with a startling clarity that, for the first time in years, he was sober. "I've got an important decision to make," he told himself as he peered into the guest room mirror and wondered how many ghosts were trapped inside. He decided not to stay around to live his life out as a dutiful son.

His mother didn't seem surprised when he told her. "You can take your father's old suitcase from the closet." she said, "and you can keep his suspenders. He would have wanted you to have them."

When Gabe left with the suitcase no heavier than a sack of groceries, his mother stood in the doorway. "Goodbye, son," she said in a flat voice, barely moving her lips, and shut the door behind him. Gabe could hear her lock it before he reached the front gate. He had left the red suspenders behind on the guest room floor.

On the sidewalk he encountered the maid, arriving for work. She glanced at Gabe as she passed, and said nothing. But then he heard her voice behind him. "Y'all take care now, ya hear?" she called out in a tone Gabe thought was very sweet, although in the house she had been studiously rude to him.

Gabe smelled salt in the early morning air and strolled toward the beach. First, he'd sleep out under the stars, then find himself a job. And he could always count on the Dumpsters.

Mothers Tongue

Carol Louise Christian

Out of my Mother's mouth
Came feathers of her Truth
Disguising razor blades.

I twirl and duck away
With practiced
Fear and awe.

Still her words cut into my flesh.
I bleed without notice,
As my mind races to protect us.

I twist away, with my blood splattering,
Protesting with my silence
"No more of your honesty.
                      I don't have the blood for it!"

Early Failure

Mardy Stotsky

It was a Saturday and the flowerbed
was freshly turned, mixed with
peat moss and cottonseed meal

My job was planting, according to
my father's instruction: two rows of
lobelia, on either side of the walkway
leading to our brilliant orange door

I'd rather have slept, please it's Saturday,
but my father wanted me to be good
for something. Lobelia are low flowering
intensely blue and fairly touchy

On my knees, respectful of pinching
the soil just firmly enough, I planted
then watered two rows of royal blue

Later diagnosis was said to be too much
cottonseed meal for their tender selves

Instead of straightening up and growing
which was their job, they
thumbed their petals at me, curled their
little backs to all and died

Funny why I remember the vivid blue
that might have flowered

Introspection

Tom Humphrey

Richie's body lay on the snow-covered weeds in the Boston vacant lot for several days before it was discovered. Then it lay in the morgue for two more days before it had thawed enough for the coroner to examine it.

Margaret and Charles Carlson had been expecting their son to arrive any day at their home on Long Island to share Christmas with them. Richie had operated a one-man automobile repair shop during the day. At night, he attended college to become a draftsman. One afternoon, Charles received a phone call at his office in Manhattan.

"Hello, Mr. Carlson," the voice said. "This is Sergeant Detective O'Reilly of the Boston Police Department."

"Yes?" Charles said. "How may I help you, Sergeant?"

"I'm sorry to have to tell you this, Mr. Carlson. But your son's body was recently found. He was murdered."

Silence.

"Hello. Mr. Carlson? Are you there?"

Charles tried to pull himself together. This couldn't be true. But it must be. No one would joke about something like this. If true, how would he tell Margaret?

"Okay, Sergeant," Charles said. "I'm here. What happened?"

"Your son's body was found near the Boston airport. He was shot. I'm in charge of the investigation. I suggest you come to Boston so we can talk. And you can claim the body."

Charles moaned. The body. Not Richie or Richard. Not even Richie's body. Just "the body." But Sergeant O'Reilly probably saw dozens of bodies every year. To him, this was just the current body.

"All right, Sergeant, " Charles said. "My wife and I will fly up to Boston tomorrow. Thank you for the call."

Charles sat there behind his desk, stupefied, emotionally numb. Again, how was he going to tell Margaret? He couldn't do it over the phone. She would collapse. He had to tell her in person, so he would be there to support her as best he could. And he could not wait for the scheduled commuter train. He had to leave immediately. He picked up the phone and called a taxi service for a cab to pick him up.

The drive from Manhattan to his house on Long Island took almost two hours. It was the most agonizing two hours Charles had ever experienced. He sat on the back seat with his mind frozen on one thought. When he told Margaret that her only son was dead, she would become hysterical. But he knew of no easy way to say it. There was no easy way to say it. Their son was dead. Richie was dead.

The bad news was received exactly as Charles had feared. Margaret screamed and fell to the floor, moaning. He tried to calm her, and as soon as she was able to walk he drove her to their doctor's office. The doctor immediately gave her a sedative and a prescription. The next day, they flew to Boston.

"We know who did it," Sergeant O'Reilly told them. "His name is Victor Scarlini. The next day, he bragged about it at the local bar. Afterwards, we received a dozen telephone calls from people who heard him. Your son must have been very well liked."

"Have you arrested him yet?" Charles asked. Margaret sat silently beside him. Her eyes were red from crying. Her face was furrowed in sorrow.

"No, we haven't," the sergeant said. "All the calls were anonymous. Everyone is afraid of him. He's the neighborhood tough, and nobody wants to be known as a witness. But since we know who did it, we can focus our investigation on him."

"But you questioned him," Charles said.

"Well, no, we can't do that."

"Why not?" Charles was incredulous.

"Because it would prejudice the trial. If we question him without his lawyer present, then his responses wouldn't be admitted as evidence. And if his lawyer is present, he's not going to say anything. We're talking about a streetwise, experienced thug here, and he wouldn't say anything even without his lawyer."

"What kind of experience?" Charles asked.

"He robs drug dealers," the sergeant said.

"Has he killed before?"

"Yes," the sergeant said.

Charles did not ask for details. "So what can you do about Richie's case?" Charles' tone was flat. He was still too numb to feel emotion.

"We need forensic evidence. Your son was shot in Scarlini's car. When we find that car, we will find evidence…blood splatters, fingerprints, whatever."

"But why was he killed?" Charles asked. "What was the motive?"

"We don't know. Your son still had his wallet with a few dollars in it, so it wasn't robbery. All we know is that he left the Marriott Lounge alone at midnight, and three days later his body was found. We investigated his background, but he had no drug connections, no gang or criminal connections, nothing to indicate any motive."

Sergeant O'Reilly opened a desk drawer and pulled out a photograph. "Would you like to see what his killer looks like?"

Charles nodded and the sergeant handed him the photo. Victor Scarlini was young, in his twenties, and looked big and burly, with black hair. His most prominent feature was a receding chin. He had no chin at all.

The sergeant took back the photo. "He has recently grown a beard."

Margaret and Charles had a full schedule during their time in Boston. First, they had to identify the body. Margaret's anguish at that ordeal was too heartrending to describe. Then they had to make arrangements for Richie to be shipped to Long Island. They retrieved his effects from his apartment. They sold his car. They visited his garage and sold his tools. They discovered that he had a safety deposit box. That required them to go to court to get a judge's order, so the bank would open the box for them. Sergeant O'Reilly accompanied them, hoping to find useful evidence. He was disappointed. The only item worthy of note was a small bag of coins that Richie apparently was collecting. None of them had significant value.

The funeral on Long Island was closed casket. Richie had been shot three times in the back of his head, and the exit wounds in his face were a gruesome sight. The Carlson's Christmas, of course, was ruined. They never opened the presents under the tree. Eventually, they just threw them away unopened. Margaret made continuous use of her doctor's sedative prescription. Charles was self-anesthetized, emotionally numb. He went to the office every day, did his work chores automatically, then returned home to sit until bedtime. There was not a drop of joy in the house.

Then the death threats began.

One evening, the telephone rang. An unidentified male voice said, "You're going to die." Then he hung up. A week later, it happened again. "Stop it or you're going to die." By now, Charles suspected that the calls were connected with what had happened to Richie. A third call came. "Your whole family is going to die." Charles called Sergeant O'Reilly in Boston.

"I'm sorry, Mr. Carlson," the sergeant said. "Long Island is out of my jurisdiction. You should notify your local police."

Charles went to the local police headquarters. He told the officer who took his complaint everything about Richie's murder, the threatening telephone calls, and his suspicion that they were connected.

"We'll look into it," the officer said.

"Are you going to trace the phone calls?" Charles asked.

"No, we don't have either the equipment nor the authority to do that," the officer said. "I suggest you talk to the telephone company."

"But in the movies you do it all the time," Charles protested.

"That's the movies," the officer said. "In the movies they can do anything."

Charles called the telephone company. After multiple tries, well larded with persistence, he was finally connected to a real live person. He explained the situation.

"Can you trace the next threatening calls I receive?" he asked.

"I'm sorry, sir," the unctuous voice said. "We don't trace calls. We can't do that every time someone is unhappy over something."

No help from the phone company. The local police never contacted him. So he called Sergeant O'Reilly again. "Have you found Scarlini's car yet, Sergeant?" Charles asked.

"Not yet," O'Reilly said. "We have a complete description of the car, but it has disappeared, probably under water. Remember, Boston is on a large bay, next to a large ocean, fed by a large river. And a few miles away are the hills. The car could be anywhere. But we're still looking."

On their first trip to Boston, Margaret and Charles had met Larry, a good friend of Richie's. They had occasionally called each other since to maintain contact. Now, Larry called Charles and passed on some news. Another friend of Richie's, who happened to be a private detective, was going around the neighborhood asking questions about the murder. Suddenly, Charles realized the reason for the death threats. Scarlini, upon hearing that a private detective was snooping around, assumed Charles had hired him. The threats were an attempt to scare Charles off. This was ironic since he had never heard of the private detective before. But the threats were not amusing, because they were being made by a multiple killer.

And then a written death threat was left in the Carlsons' mail box in front of their house.

It was written on a torn piece of brown paper bag. "Death comes." As soon as he saw the message, Charles began handling the paper scrap with tweezers and carefully placed it in a clear plastic bag. He hoped he had not smeared any latent fingerprints that might be on it. Then he immediately took it to police headquarters. The officer there received it politely, but had no comment. Charles never heard anything from the police department regarding that or the other threats. Or anything else.

Charles thought about his situation. Scarlini obviously knew his address, as well as his telephone number. He, or his minion, had traveled all the way down from Boston to leave a death threat in his mailbox. That was a definite escalation in the danger level. And the police were no help. They would investigate his or his wife's death, but they would take no steps to prevent it. And he could not afford to hire a bodyguard. He was on his own.

Charles had no gun. In high school, he had received some firearms training from the R.O.T.C. and had acquired a .22 caliber rifle. He used to drive out into the Arizona desert for plinking. But as an adult working in New York, he had no interest in guns. Suddenly, now, he did.

Charles drove to the nearest gun shop and asked to see some pistols.

"Certainly, sir," the clerk said. "May I see your pistol permit?"

"What?" Charles said. "I don't have a pistol permit." He had never heard of such a thing.

"This is New York," the clerk said. "I can't show you a pistol unless you have a pistol permit."

"Well, where do I get a pistol permit and how long will it take?"

"The Police Department," said the clerk. "And it will take at least four months, probably six."

Frustrated, Charles drove home. Four to six months. Maybe he should send Scarlini a letter, asking him to hold off for a few months. By the time he got home, he had an idea. His friend, Nick, was a hunter and knew something about guns. He would ask Nick for advice.

Nick took him to the gun shop. "What you need is a shotgun," Nick said, as they looked over the displays. "No permit is needed, and it's more decisive than a pistol. A rifle is too penetrative. A rifle bullet would go through your wall and your neighbor's wall. Why get him involved? A shotgun is safer. Its pellets will only go through one wall at the most."

Nick reached up and pulled down a short-barreled pump shotgun.

"This will do it," he said. "Look, the barrel is short, which means it will be more difficult for an intruder to grab it and yank the gun out of your hands. And, when you rack the action, the sound is as intimidating as you can get without going military. When the bad guy sees that big bore staring at him, he's going to shit in his pants."

Charles bought the pump gun. He started going to the range every weekend to shoot skeet. It was an easy way to obtain proficiency in shooting his new shotgun. Soon, he was hitting more than he was missing. And that was encouraging because Scarlini would be a much bigger, closer, and slower moving target than the flying clays. At all other times, his pump gun was kept under the bed, loaded with buckshot.

Things were now quiet. There were no more death threats. Larry did not call again. Charles called Sergeant O'Reilly and learned that they still had not found Scarlini's car. It was probably rusting at the bottom of the bay. So the investigation of Richie's murder had gone stagnant.

Charles's grief gradually turned to hatred. That scumbag, Scarlini, had murdered Richie, his son, for no reason. The police knew who did it but were afraid to even question him. Margaret, Richie's mother, once a bright, effervescent woman, had become a morose lump of melancholia. And he had done nothing about it. He was no man, he was a mouse!

Then Charles had an idea. A short while before, he had been afraid that Scarlini would come down from Boston and kill him. What about turning the tables? Why couldn't he go up to Boston and kill Scarlini? He knew what the scumbag looked like. He knew what bar he frequented. He even knew where he lived. Scarlini still lived with his parents, and Charles had looked up the address in the telephone book. It would be so easy. And revenge so tempting.

Charles prepared some salami sandwiches, put his shotgun in its carrying case, and started driving north. It was late afternoon when he reached Boston. But he had to spend some time driving around unfamiliar streets, searching, so it was evening before he was satisfied that he had found both the bar and the parents' house. Now, which should it be? The house was on a dark residential street. A stranger sitting in a car for maybe hours would be noticed. The bar was on a lighted, active street, with people coming and going. A waiting man would not be so obvious. So the bar it was. Charles prayed silently that Scarlini would show up this evening.

He didn't have long to wait. The bar's door opened, and Scarlini came out with two companions. The beard was gone, but the receding chin was unmistakable. Charles started the car's engine and began creeping forward. Scarlini laughed and slapped one of his fellows on the back. Charles lowered the passenger side window and, with his right hand, moved the shotgun closer to the window. Charles stopped the car right in front of his target. He picked up the gun with both hands, poked the barrel out the window, and shouted, "Hey, Scarlini!" As Scarlini looked towards him, Charles pulled the trigger.

Scarlini did not fly into the air, smash through a window, and fall thirty feet into a swimming pool the way they always did in the movies. He merely crumpled and fell forward onto the sidewalk. He lay there, unmoving, in a pool of his own blood.

Charles sat up in bed, shaking and sweating. It took a moment before he realized where he was. God, what a dream! he thought. Then he got up and went into the bathroom to empty his bladder.

As time passed, Margaret's health continued to decline. She had an ulcer for a long time, so there were certain foods she couldn't eat. Then she developed high cholesterol. More foods were denied. Finally, she was diagnosed with diabetes. The doctor said it was triggered by the stress of losing her son. She did not have to take insulin, but her diet was further restricted. Charles felt so sorry for her. He was amazed she was able to live on such a restricted diet. And there was nothing he could do to help. Nothing.

Charles found himself unable to stop his self-analysis. Why didn't he drive up to Boston and terminate Victor Scarlini? Well, it wasn't that easy. He couldn't take a gun on an airliner without leaving a paper trail, so he would have to drive. He would probably be gone at least two days. How would he explain his absence? He would have no alibi. But he had a motive, so he would be the police's prime suspect. And would Scarlini just stand there and let him shoot him? Maybe he would shoot first. He would be with friends. They would swarm all over him before he could do anything. And, if he were successful, he would be convicted and sent to prison. Then what would happen to Margaret? He would still be alive, so she couldn't collect his life insurance. In her emotional condition, how could she find a job and support herself?

But the bottom line was simple. He was no hero. He was a coward.

"Smile when you say that, stranger."

"Do you feel lucky, punk?"

"Fill your hands, you son of a bitch!"

"Make my day!"

"Hello. My name is Inigo Montoya. You killed my father. Prepare to die."

Those were fine for the movies. But that was not him, not even remotely. He was supposed to be a man, but somehow he could not make the grade. He was a failure as a man. The world would be better off without him. Margaret would be better off without him. She would have the chance to find the man she deserved.

Charles walked into the bedroom. He reached under the bed and pulled out the shotgun. He put his mouth around the barrel. Then he reached down and pulled the trigger.

Maybe that was just another dream.

Or maybe not.

The Sandals

Jeanne Henderson

Too many things had gone wrong in too short a time. And now I was alone. Mercifully, I'd shut down, wrapped in soft spun cotton for a while, but it was beginning to unravel, leaving me to feel the gaping hole in the center of my being. People shouldn't die in the summertime. But they do. And now summer was coming to an end.

I'd decided to visit Gulls Beach one more time—maybe to say another goodbye. We'd spent so many happy hours there watching the gulls soar and dive and work little patterns in the wet sand with their feet. The ceaseless, steady crash and hiss of the ocean was a friend, and I had nowhere else to go.

My eyes blurred as I walked along, my tennis shoes barely making little prints on the damp sand to show no one that I had been this way. Occasional seashell fragments broke up the monotony of the endless tan crystals. My eye caught something moving with the seaweed near the water's edge. I walked over. Only a sandal. Just as I turned away, the dipping sun glinted sharply on the brass buckle. I looked closer. It was really a good sandal. Heavy duty. Thick leather. Obviously expensive—not the sort of sandal I would buy for myself. I picked it up and carried it with me. It was too nice a sandal to be swept out to sea. A few more steps, and there was the other one. I picked it up, too. A pair. They should be together, I thought, so I carried them along, one in each hand, unwanted burdens. Perhaps the owner had been desolate like me, had walked along the beach until she finally cast aside her sandals and walked into the ocean, the eternally embracing water. The choppy sea was beginning to show sparkles of russet gold from the lowering sun, and I found myself scanning the surface. Even now she might be slipping beneath a wave, all care and pain forever diluted in the endless sea.

The water swirled around my ankles, the froth hissing softly as it slipped back into the ocean. I took one step toward the waves and closed my eyes, letting warm tears slide down my cheeks. The next wave came higher, splashing up to my knees, wetting the cuffs of my white cotton shorts. I didn't care, only felt the orange light from the sun burning through my eyelids as my tears fell to be lost in the sea.

Startled, I heard, "Ma'am! Ma'am!" above the crashing of the surf. I turned away from the sea and saw a young girl and her dog standing beyond the reach of the waves. I made my way toward her, the sand and sea sucking and tugging at my feet, unwilling to let me go. The wind whipped her auburn ponytail in wild circles. Her mouth was a bit too wide and her nose a little too big, but her face was attractively dusted with auburn freckles that danced around it and under her eyes, which were the color of the sea with flecks of gold reflecting the setting sun.

"You found them!" she said.

"Who?" I said stupidly.

"My sandals." She pointed at my hands. "My mom saved a long time to get them for my birthday. Today's my birthday. I'm fourteen. I can't believe you found them! I thought they'd be washed away by now." She grinned as I handed them to her, her mouth an upturned quarter-moon spreading her freckles elfishly across her face. "And this is my birthday puppy. I got him yesterday. His name is Bouncer because he jumps around so much. My mom says he bounces off the walls."

As if to prove he deserved his name, the little brown ball of fluff that had been wiggling on his back in the sand began jumping up and down in a futile attempt to get the sandals.

"Hey! You got your shoes wet," she said, pointing at my feet.

Bouncer immediately began to sniff at my ankles, tail wagging in affirmation that my shoes were indeed wet.

"I…I guess I didn't realize how close I got," I stammered, trying to sidestep Bouncer's cool wet nose.

"Come on!" the girl said. "Let's go get an ice cream cone at Benny's. My treat—to thank you for finding my sandals. It's Wednesday. Benny always brings out a new flavor of the week on Wednesday."

She turned briskly, never doubting I could not refuse Benny's, and headed towards the ice cream stand across Gulls Beach Road. As we slogged through the sand, she regaled me with an endless list of possibilities that might be ours at Benny's.

"I can't believe it!" she squealed, looking at the red and white sign. "Pecan praline! My favorite ice cream on my actual birthday! We're getting

THE SANDALS

doubles," she said, as she pulled a ten-dollar bill from her red wallet and slapped it down on the counter. "Birthday money," she explained.

We sat at one of the white plastic tables in front of Benny's, watching the sun slip lower while we savored the ice cream, sweet with buttery pecans and small chunks of brown-sugared perfection.

"Isn't this the best day ever!" she said, smiling and willing me to nod my head in agreement. "Well, gotta go! My head will roll if I'm not home before sunset." She jumped up and dropped the cone wrapper in a trash can. "Bye!" she said, then added, "Come next Wednesday. You never know what it's gonna be."

"Okay," I said.

She began to jog up the street, her ponytail swinging from side to side. Bouncer bounced along beside her, making valiant efforts to snatch the sandals. She stopped and turned to wave, sandals in the air.

"Thanks again! I'm glad you found my sandals," she called.

I waved back. "So am I."

After she left, I stayed to enjoy the last of my cone, licking a little bit at a time, making it last. Lines from a Robert Frost poem wound their way though my head: "I have promises to keep, and miles to go before I sleep." By the time I finished my ice cream, the sun had spilled the last of its fire into the sea. I threw the wrapper into the trash can as I walked away and found myself wondering what the flavor of the week would be next Wednesday.

Vigilant

Natalie Gottlieb

Too late to capture lost wishes
That haunt my troubled world.
The jester knocks twice at my door.
He mocks me in my plight.
I answer, draped in misery
And let him stay the night.

I wake when daylight bakes the room
But warmth resists my reach.
The jester sheds me from his grip,
Escapes from crippling fears
And I am left submerged in grief
To weep my foreign tears.

My past is shaded by the night.
Ghosts permeate the room.
Memories, long gone, seduce me
In a dance to gain control
And I'm provoked to vigilance
Before I'm swallowed whole.

Too late to free the bonds' firm grip
And yet, hope still prevails.
I'll wait inside time's safety net
And pray that things will shift.

Is life just a useless vigil?
Will I always be adrift?

Exit My Soul
(Two excerpts from a work in progress)

Tina Mori

For the past two years since my mother was claimed by the hideous disease known as Alzheimer's, I have been visited in my dreams by her beautiful spirit-like countenance. She has asked me to tell her story. Each time she comes, she gives me the words to write. She wants me to tell it from her perspective, in her words, as though I was the one battling for escape from the Prison-like clutches of this wretched mind-thief. I hope I can do her justice.

> On one of her first visits, she wanted me to understand and relay her first moments of realization that something had shifted in her head. It was in the first few weeks after my father passed away that she knew she was damaged forever...

Written from a visit on 9-10-2009:

She was not born bad, in fact she was born very good. Too good...so good that the sins of the world would well up inside her and sling her bleeding heart to the careless moon...

I hold on by a thread. A tiny slim piece of string tethers me to the earth. Holds my crazy soul together. The string is taut...one more pluck from the well of life's eternal fuck ups and it will snap. I will plummet into OBLIVION.

Let it come. OBLIVION... Let it come and take me now, it may be easier. Just sit back letting the night creatures carry me away. Vultures and thieves... Let them have their way with my empty soul. There's nothing left for me to do but surrender to the madness. Fall prey to the swirling mist. Inside my tomb I live. Death is easy, it's living that rocks me back on my heels, sets my belly on fire with fear and empties the bowels of my existence.

Before the stranger stole my soul I was ensconced in a world filled with possibilities...but I could never see them. I never wanted to see them. *HE* was gone, the twin of my heart's beat. I found no peace in my life after he floated off and let go of my hand. I was alone; fear does not name the place where I dwelled... Drifting so far from myself.

The day I felt again, I knew my world was wrecked beyond repair. The alley behind my mind was littered now with bits and pieces of memories, ticket stubs, whiskey bottles, party dresses, and grainy smelling shards of *Him*... His essence, his smell, his seed... The tunnel to earth was so cold and moist with the deep dark remembrance, so jelled with roots and stems from our years together.

When they put him into the ground I held my head high, the keening in my brain was so loud, I know that's when it started... My slow decline into OBLIVION. I broke the sound barrier in my brain, and the waves of earth calling him home stole through my grey matter and collected bits of my sanity as it tore through. When the keening stopped echoing in my spirit on the day I felt again, the substance it left behind began to steal my mind.

It was dark and smelled of rotted fish, fermented dreams, and day old sex. Sometimes late at night I would feel the slow creep of the substance congealing in the creases between my brain cells and my heart... Alone in my bed, no male essence to hold me... No rough hands to grasp my spiral downwards and stop the destruction of a human being.

Gone were the sandpaper stubble of his chin and the hot velvet softness of his cock. The stillness would haunt me and alone in our bed I would surrender to the mold in my soul. Bacteria grew thick and multiplied like a fungus that came and went—remission of my disease was temporary at best. The light of day brought another spore to my failing. The light of day brought that wretched sunshine and birds singing and flowers blooming and children playing and the bane of my solitude would be given new birth. Fertile soil that cradled his body now stood in piles on my bedroom floor and I would be forced into action that day knowing I had to shovel it out and make nice for everyone else. Should they choose to stop by...the way I saw it, my job was to go on living when my journey was ended.

Time travel from living to existing every moment on this flimsy planet with war and crime and love and lust piling up around me and cluttering the alley behind my mind with its emptiness... *HE* felt none of my descent into madness. *HE* floated in loamy soil and excavated heaven's fields and orchards. *I* was left to root out a life and keep the faith we shared. But that was just it... *WE* was no more.

That silly insignificant word, *WE*, had left my vocabulary and when it went, it pulled a thread in my sweater coat of life. As it gained momentum, it pilfered the *WE-ness* of US. Ricocheting from my life, like the tiny thread of this dreaded disease, *WE* was attached…as the *WE* strolled out the door the thread pulled and unraveled the stitches that held me together. They pulled out slowly at first and then they too gathered momentum and the years stacked up like finely wound cashmere blend…softened, frayed, then melted away.

I was unraveling. *I* was disappearing. Dust mite by dust mite. Just a few chain stitches a day… A lifetime undone by a word that defined my space in time… *WE*… *I* is not warm… *I* is cold and stands apart from the crowd… *I* is not grateful nor passionate… It is not possessed of control…only the illusion of control…the crux of the matter of *I-ness* is solitude. Not peace, mind you, but solitude. Fragile and wafer-thin air permeates *I*, makes it transparent. Cellophane existence waiting for opaque reality…

I is where *I* stood while dirt crept in as *I* clawed into the ground to find *HIM*. Again, and again, alone at night, alone in our bed, where the soil piled up ever more; when the fear crept in… *I* is who asked *WE* to leave, taking that damned thread of my life's sweater coat with it.

I is a dictator of realism. No shelter from yourself in *I*. No soul searching in *I* is complete without the keyhole view of what *WE* might have been.

So let them come now. The time robbers… Age… Decay… Social Security fraud… Let them take my sanity. For without the *WE* of my Frank, *I* have no dawn. Let the grave robbers and vultures pick at my brain cells. *I* don't really have the strength to fight, because *I* is a coward at heart.

She tried so hard one day in the care facility to remember a word that described a time of peace, love, and joy. The word was there but her clarity was not…until a small window opened and the snatch of a memory filtered in…bringing with it the sought after word…and the emotions it embodied.

Written from a dream-visit on 6-1-2010:

Was a word that describes a peaceful, calm, nearly heavenly time. It escapes me memory now, but my know that there was a time when we knew that word, lived in that space, built life around the know that those days would never end…

Inside her prison me look out on my world now…days are not clearly defined with sharp edges and abrupt alarms. Only now, mark time by visits of persons who drift into her room and offer a word, a touch, a hard nugget to wash down with water. Meaningless gestures. No sense of time. No sense of anything, just drifting movements and stuttering phrases. Are alone in this prison. Tortured and afraid, my heart lying in my main part beats, but I don't know why.

When a curtain in front of the shiny window shifts by a touch or a breezey some unknown spirit, I sense the shifting light in motes that float before my eyes. When her can master what thoughts and the light seeps in, we search for the word we used for this light time? It is there, it is in my mouth, parched and dry with the effort to define this brightness…strain my throat trying to form sounds, croak them out to meaning…what?

Prison, am in prison. Choking on each own effort, pulling at the covers and shift my legs, impatient with herself. The sounds that form the words struggle against teeth to escape. Want the word for what? What am she looking for? We lose the thread and lay back against padding. Defeated again by this cloud around own soul, shroud of floating phrases and disjointed ramblings in me head. Adrift again, lost on mere sea of oblivion. No direction to our journey now, no word is not coming, the lightness has no formal moniker, no label is clear in me for the lovely seeping glow with the window. Some used to know the meaning of the fluffy essence billowing in… me mumble my way to nothing…no valuable sounds, organized into neat tidy meanings.

Shrouded thoughts trapped in here beckoning to mine to give them release…most words and knowing locked away, hovering just beyond own grasp, teasing and tormenting as unrequited lust. Can seek no form for movements; grasp no hand when lonely in we's prison, was there a hand to hold? So am sure there was, but when? What was the touch, the soft sandy bottom of the sea is home now…am sucked down into the quicksand under the ocean. Body laden most heaviness as water seeps into the being, pulling mine under and under and under…

There it are again, flicker of downy essence in head…a thought…a phrase perched on the brink of me's foggy ocean. It tickles the nose and so swipe at this face…it pulses in my cranial and I crave the publish, the issue, the let loose of it to the now…must burble a sound to stir juices…let the need to relive simmer in me core. Sort it out...slow my breath...touch me head...eyes opened to the glow from the pane...

Musty rapture at the thread of recall...heat, feel heat on my's face...green branches wave in the gentle wind. Voices, little bodies calling me mother...me? Mother? White dresses and satin hair with crystal glowing warmth float on the gust of vision before me...laughter as light as raindrops filtering into my senses while the shimmering memory slides into focus.

I hold my breath and see my life before the fog set in. The farm, the house the children...my children!

I have them, I love them, I see them...boys, girls, and sunshine! My life, my family, I see them in my mind crystal clear and vibrant with life's juiciness. We are all together and the hand holding mine is strong and tanned...calluses smooth and hard against my palm. I feel safe, and secure. I know this place, I lived this time. I have a filament of consciousness running through this being...it is sharp and clear, the honesty of my history real. The word, I know the word! *Halcyon*... I long for the *Halcyon* days. That's where I begin, where I end, where I pour myself over the ones who love me. I reach out for the sparkling scene hovering before me...arms grasping to hold it close before it fades again. I will always have this, always reside in the center of the *Halcyon* days I am channeling in this window of remember...

Onlyness

Sarah Wellen

My life-long love has left
And I linger on in loneliness.
Family and friends sustain me,
But onlyness is a palpable presence.
One cup of coffee,
Half a slept-in bed,
Solitary nights,
A silent house.

A steel ball,
I ricochet from wall to wall
In my arcade machine life.
He was the star that steered me,
The sun that warmed me,
The moon that comforted me.
Without him, darkness descends
And I am lost………

Under the Pear Tree

Helena Frey

Eleanor takes the wheel for our drive to my mother-in-law's house. We are returning to Detroit from Eleanor and Martha's country home, where I have spent the weekend. Louise, my mother-in-law, suggested that, when the three of us arrive back in town, we join her for dinner at her home. I know Louise will treat my guests to a splendid meal and enliven the conversation with stories about her years spent in Europe and the Far East. I expect our afternoon to come together seamlessly.

Eleanor and Martha keep up a running flow of conversation, which they continually interrupt to condemn yet another driver. "Look at him going through that yellow light! He thinks he doesn't have to obey the law like the rest of us," scolds Martha. Her darting brown eyes give her face a sharpness unmitigated by the sallow hue of her skin. Eleanor's face is all pinkness. Her intelligent blue eyes take in everything she sees and rest kindly on anyone who commands her attention. This reproving of other drivers takes place behind closed windows. It is as close as these refined women ever come to swearing.

Eleanor turns into my street and drives her car under an elaborate metalwork archway. The weeping willow overhanging the bridge, the bridge crossing the waterway, and the glistening stream beside Louise's house all converge to give the house its fairytale quality. In the '20s, an architect designed and built three contiguous houses to enhance the neighborhood. The archway at the entrance to my street and a small bridge at the end of our block were to set the tone for the entire neighborhood. But it was the Depression and its aftermath that set the tone. The neighborhood never fully recovered.

Eleanor slows the car and heads up the driveway between Louise's house and the house I rent from Louise. "Pull in under the pear tree, Eleanor." Behind the three houses the frozen stream can now support skaters, but none are in view as we exit the car.

Standing under the pear tree, I am reminded of the conversation Louise and I shared the previous week. "Do you know," Louise asked me, "that the man who has been working on his car behind your house wants to rent the space?"

"The space under the pear tree?" I ask.

"Yes. He wants to park his car there, and that might necessitate cutting down the pear tree."

The man Louise was referring to rented a basement room in one of the small houses across the street. Unshaven, he looks like he never sleeps or sleeps all too often in the clothes he's wearing. Louise gave him permission to work on his car in my back yard. On a number of occasions I had come home late at night to find him working on his car by a light plugged into an outside socket. When I parked my car under the pear tree, he never acknowledged my presence, which sent a chill through me.

"He gives me the creeps every time I come home late at night and find him in my back yard. Are you going to rent the space to him?" I asked.

"Well, dear, I didn't know you disliked him so much," Louise replied. "If his presence disturbs you, I'll tell him he cannot rent the space."

"Good," I said as I released the tightness in my throat.

Then she hesitated. "I'm never averse to making a little extra money."

"Louise, I *won't feel safe* with him behind my house."

"Don't give it another thought, dear. He'll have to find another place to park his car. I'll tell him today."

In a much calmer voice, I said, "Thank you, Louise. Thank you ever so much."

Now, as Eleanor and Martha walk beside me down the driveway to Louise's front door, I am pleased that our creepy neighbor is no longer a bone of contention between Louise and me.

Louise moved back to the United States after her husband died. Louise met Henry in the Far East. After his retirement from an English export firm in Hong Kong, they settled in an apartment in San Remo overlooking the Mediterranean. In her 60s, Louise is still a good-looking woman. Her beauty is on a par with Ingrid Bergman or Greta Garbo, and her elegance and wit add excitement to any party. As she welcomes my friends into her home, the smells from the kitchen alert them to her culinary skills.

Louise makes brief sojourns to the kitchen to check on the tempting delights she has prepared for us. The warmth of the fireplace, the high polish of the oak wainscoting, and the oversized, comfortable couches all contribute to the beauty of the living room. The wallpaper does not distract from the original paintings on the walls, but affords them a muted backdrop. In her free-flowing velvet caftan, Louise escorts us into the dining room.

"When I was in Czechoslovakia," she says, turning graciously to Martha and Eleanor, "I purchased crystal identical to that photographed in a toast when Khrushchev and Nixon had their 'Kitchen debate.' Do you remember the photograph?" Louise asks.

"Yes," Eleanor replies, and Martha nods in agreement.

"Let's toast to the "Kitchen debate!" Louise exclaims.

The steaming soup tureen draws us readily toward the table. The botanical pattern on the bright cranberry Spode dinner plates is repeated on the Francis I silverware, heavily embellished with fruits and vines. How inviting on a cold winter's day. Louise has not let my guests down.

Louise leans conspiratorially in my direction as Eleanor and Martha move to the other side of the table. "Helena," she says, "you know Ralph?"

I hesitate. "No," I say, shaking my head.

Peevishly, Louise says, "The man who lives across the street."

"Oh, *that* man," I reply. "I just didn't know his name."

Louise looks directly at me and in a low but level tone says, "I'm going to rent the parking space to him."

I am stunned. I am blindsided.

Eleanor is gracefully easing herself into her chair. Martha, too, is lowering herself onto a cushioned chair.

"Eleanor, Martha," I say, interrupting their descent, "we won't be staying."

Nonplussed, they both hang in midair. They look from me to Louise.

"Of course, you'll be staying," Louise says, without any trace of dismay. (She knows no one will depart the magnificence of her table.) "Helena, dear, I've worked slavishly to prepare this dinner for you and your guests. Everything will go to waste if you leave." Turning to Eleanor and Martha she motions them to sit down. "Naturally, you'll be staying," she intones.

"I'm sorry I've put everyone to such an unhappy inconvenience, but we can't stay. Louise, where did you put our coats?"

Under the pear tree, I make my apologies to Eleanor and Martha. "I regret that you were caught in the middle of something between my mother-in-law and me."

Still confused, Eleanor says, "Give us a call."

I appreciate their discreet silence in light of my aberrant behavior. Eleanor backs the car out from under the pear tree and waves to me as the car heads down the driveway. Once out of sight, I turn my attention to the first item on my agenda: Find a new place to live.

Coming Upstate – The Immigrant Experience

Adrienne Rogers

I "immigrated" to Troy, New York from New York City in the summer of 1960, following my husband, who was to begin his career as an English professor at Rensselaer Polytechnic Institute. It started as a harrowing adventure that all but exhausted our very limited resources. We had bought a used car for $800 (at a time when a new car cost $2000, but was out of our range). On the way up the Thruway with all our possessions, which included two cats and a fish tank whose fish were temporarily housed in a large plastic bag, the car abruptly went dead. We later learned a rod had gone through the block, and the car was essentially useless for several months. We called a friend in Poestenkill (a town outside of Troy) to come to our assistance, and he came in a pickup truck with a semi-rotted rope to be used for towing; he had taken it from a tree around which it had been wrapped for we knew not how many seasons. Not surprisingly, three attempts to use the rope to tow the car failed. So we abandoned the car less than halfway up the Thruway in Saugerties and piled into the pickup truck: people, fish, cats, bag and baggage. The cats yowled constantly, and their anxiety translated itself into a continuous shedding of fur. It felt like being in a Conestoga wagon in ninety degree heat, with the added attraction of clumps of cat hair clinging to our sweaty faces and arms. We did make it to our friend's house, where we spent what was left of the night before meeting the movers in Lansingburg (a section of North Troy, where we were to live) in the morning.

For months we were without a car, having to arrange, in my case, a five-day-a-week commute to Schenectady, where I had a part-time job teaching French. (One of my helpful colleagues drove me one-way in the morning, and I had to try to find my way back using various bus routes.) For one year, I taught at what was then Mont Pleasant High School. Circumstances quickly enlightened me about the state of the economy and the class divisions between employees or executives of General Motors (which gave Schenectady its nickname: The Electric City). Working class employees' children were represented at Mont Pleasant; the middle management or higher executives' children went to school in Niskayuna (a more upscale community) or elsewhere. Many of my students had Italian surnames, which I would try to pronounce appropriately. My pronunciation of "Castiglione" [kastileonay], keeping the final vowel, was promptly corrected to Castiglion [kastigleon], rhyming with "upon." This was a time when these students and their families wished to downplay immigrant status and be "all-American"—a tendency that was completely reversed a few decades later, when ethnic identities suddenly became fashionable.

The students thought my accent was foreign. (I am American-born and New York City bred.) If I teased them because they pronounced "Larry" as "Leery" or "Eric" as "Airic," they would come back with, "Ya wanna cuppa kawfee?" These exchanges were immaterial as far as our work was concerned, because I could model good French pronunciation, and, at least while they were with me, they did not have an alternate model.

After one year, I got a full-time assignment at Linton High School, where other events contributed to my feeling like an outsider. A new method of teaching French was being introduced at the time, and I wished to try it because Linton had good lab facilities in the classrooms. I offered an after-school lab. After one or two days, I had a visit from the principal informing me that my lab was interfering with "something important."

"Like what?" I asked in my habitual respectful-of-authority New York-ese, "the basketball team?"

"Yes," he confirmed.

And that is how it came about that I lost the opportunity to teach French to Schenectady's outstanding basketball player of the century and future nationally renowned coach, Pat Riley. It also gave me some perspective on the scale of cultural values in our society.

Perhaps the greatest shock came in a full faculty meeting at which the principal, choosing to open with "humor," told a blatantly racist joke. I don't know whether anyone heard me gasp, but as far as I could tell I was the only person in the room who didn't laugh. I asked myself whether the others were laughing just to brown-nose or whether they simply were indulging shared racism. I learned in the faculty lounge that it was not only blacks who were the objects of disdain: my married name disarmed people into thinking they could freely express anti-Semitism in my presence. I didn't disabuse them because I felt I could be more effective contradicting them if they didn't think I was defending myself. (That issue culminated in one teacher punching a "pushy" Jewish teacher in the nose.)

On the home front, I was a little surprised to find that I really liked being upstate despite the dire predictions of friends "down home," who could not visualize us as "homeowners" as opposed to life-long apartment dwellers. Despite our inexperience with home repairs and maintenance, we learned (at some expense and, admittedly, with some anxiety) to cope and overcome. And, in spite of hardships and disadvantages, there were compensations. Now, though we had not really thought about it before, it was not enough to have a few trees along a sidewalk, or a public park available if one wanted to take a nature walk. Even modest homes here had lawns and flower gardens. Another big advantage was that the cost of living was so much lower than in The City that it was possible to get by with less money (which there certainly was—less money, that is), but what I could never get over was the elegiac joy I felt every time I drove to the supermarket and, on the way, passed cows grazing in a large meadow next to the road. That era passed with the coming of Walmart and supermarkets that displaced silos, meadow, and cows. However, beautiful views of farms, silos, and livestock are still close by. I always take the route past them to go to my favorite post office just a few minutes away by car, "in the country."

Now, after almost five decades, I still sometimes feel like an outsider, or a "downstater." Certain habits and attitudes that are all but inherent in me because of education and training and, perhaps, also personality, sometimes seem to grate on, irritate, or even enrage others. Independent, self-assertive women are still not universally approved or liked, even though we are decades past "Women's Lib." But, much as everything else around has changed and will continue to change, I probably will keep my New York (City) identity to the extent of not giving in or giving up my own principles in order to be "accepted."

The Quality of Light

Judith K. Rose

Oh, how I wish he could hear
How much I felt
When I couldn't find him
A 30-year friendship
Limited Edition
Him downstairs   me up

Leaves and vines covered his windows
letting in only a yellow/brown light
My view   180 degrees   Mountains
Moons and Sunrises   took me by surprise

The 'Ellis Act' ending our long stay
at 638 Hill Street   a year or so ago
Still so uncomfortable
The unsettling of old dust

He gave away his books   where he could
Libraries, family, friends
So many 'histories of the world'

Now he had a living room window
A tree   was there   to be seen
He even got into buying new lamps

We never shared a meal   just our concerns
for the world   and new owners   and possibly
having to move

I came to see his new place
Just up Pico   away from the bustle
His only concern met

He would say, "I'll come to see you
            when you're settled."

But he never took the bus ride
Down Pico   straight to the beach

Moving: *Help Wanted*

Judy Ray

My husband, David, and I are preoccupied with an irony common to those about to sell their houses and move. We take on repairs and improvements, plans we have thought about and put aside as not being high priority in an old house of idiosyncratic design. Some of the repairs are necessary, some are undertaken only to make the place more appealing—maybe—to a prospective buyer. We get obsessed with practicalities, but try to stay calm in the hive of activity. If we were to set up a video camera, we could make our own segments of "This Old House" or "A Year in Provence" (with appropriate change of local color). Our cast of characters would be ideal for such a project.

Gene is a brisk, down-to-earth professional. We had called him as a plumber, but we discover he does all kinds of work—carpentry, electrical. He puts in a new window jamb and sill on the west side, moves a window from the cedar room to the east side, takes out a wallboard divider in the kitchen, puts in a new stove. He is efficient with time and skill, philosophical in conversation.

Glenn, with his hearing-impaired assistant, Pat, is upstairs and downstairs on his allotted days, putting an air conditioning unit in the attic, installing vents upstairs and in the landing. An air conditioning unit? We have lived here for twenty-four hot and humid Missouri summers with one window unit in the living room, another in the bedroom, and—most importantly—a powerful fan in the attic, which draws air through the house when the chain beside the trap door is pulled and louvers open to the fan's whirring. But the real estate agent says, You'll never sell this house in summer without air conditioning. (Yes, I say to myself under my breath, and we will never sell this house in winter when the kitchen stays cold even though the furnace is droning like the World War II doodlebugs that I remember from my English childhood. Those flying bombs had buzzing engines that cut out when the bomb was falling into eerie, anxious silence.)

The glass of the sliding patio door in the small "cedar room," which had once been a side porch, became cloudy years ago as the seal gave way. Thomas puts in a new door, but, as with all the tasks he has done, some mousehole-sized corner is left unfinished—a board not trimmed, a patch not painted, some nails rusting. I wonder if the unfinished detail represents a spiritual or cultural statement, or if it is merely negligence. Outside the new sliding door the huge oak tree's roots are making pleats of the bricked area around which dark and variegated hostas thrive. David buys more shrubs and flowers for the back patio and yard.

Adam dances his way onto the scene. He did odd jobs here years ago and still appears to be the same, zany, fast-talking, energetic young person whirlwinding around a cleanup job to earn a few dollars. He will probably spend it on beer, since the odor wafts around him even in the afternoon.

More workers join the procession moving through the house. An electrician, Tim, fixes a short and replaces some light fixtures. A plumber fixes toilet seatings. And each time after the visits something else goes wrong—another outlet does not work, the sink drain stops up. The house is deconstructing around us, but we speed up our efforts to outpace entropy. Thomas and Gene and Glenn and Patrick and Larry and Joe and Tim and Jack and Jamie and Adam…the litany of laborers grows long.

Someone on the radio wants to know how fast we are traveling—around the sun, the sun in the galaxy, the galaxy itself in the universe. We cannot comprehend the spinning speeds and magnifications. Yet the concept of staying still while spinning begins to make some sense as we contemplate moving our lives over to settle into a different space.

When the property is listed with the real estate agency and FOR SALE signs go up in the yard, our mandate is to keep things tidy, turn on the lights, and leave when the house is shown. That is fine by me. I do not want to answer questions or feel the scrutiny of assessing eyes. Here we sit, says David, like spiders in a web—an old web in which charm lies in irregularity.

I get up in the middle of the night and go downstairs. When I come back up, David asks, "Were you journaling?"

"No, I just went to turn the light off."

And he says sleepily, "Oh, yes, I left it on in case someone came to view the house."

Later that night (or should I say early that morning) I hear Radar barking outside in the front yard. I go downstairs again and open the front door

MOVING: *HELP WANTED*

to heavy, soaking rain. Radar is sheltering under the juniper bushes. I put him in the back room, the library, and think of his predecessor, Archie, who used to run away and turn up unpredictably in the middle of the night, barking on the front lawn to announce his return. Radar does not run away. He is a homebody, only coming around to the front door to let us know that the back gate is open.

I wonder if Radar will go with us when we make our big move to Arizona. He is limping badly, trying to walk on three legs, avoiding weight on the right front. The vet takes x-rays, making beautiful works of art, thin bones stretched out like a wing, the ball nestled in the cup of the joint, indicating that there is no dislocation. Another view from above shows the ribs as a frame of coiled light, tracery around the power packs of heart and lungs. But where the so-thin leg bones fly off there is a cloud in an otherwise clear sky, a thin swirl of grease on clear glass. A cloud of unknowing with heavy name, a cloud that can be explored only through the tunnel of the knife.

We decide not to go for the operation. Radar is already into the creaking time, the old dog days. The anesthesia, the cutting, the recovery would be a heavy assault. It is our responsibility to make this decision for him, and if he is up to it he can travel on with us when we leave. We discuss this as he sits on the patio licking his foreleg—he has always done that, even when young, and where he licks there is a rusty sheen to the otherwise black/grey shagginess. David has often recited Robert Frost's lines:

> The old dog barks backward without getting up.
> I can remember when he was a pup.

I have immediate sympathy now when I hear that a friend or relative is moving. The plan is often a joyful one—new beginnings, new spaces—but there will be some version of these chores and rituals to go through. I have come slowly to this experience, for when I was growing up in Sussex, England, I did not know anyone who moved. It seemed that everyone in our village and on the surrounding farms had lived there since their families' names were entered in the Domesday Book in the eleventh century. And my own first moves were from continent to continent to continent, with confines of suitcases rather than moving trucks.

If we want to sell the house quickly, a friend now recommends, we should buy a statue of St. Joseph and bury it upside down in the yard, facing the street. When David calls a church supply store, they know at once why he is asking about a St. Joseph statue, for this is now a popular item, a fad turning a profit. There are little kits made up with a small plastic statuette of St. Joseph and the baby Jesus, and a card on which is printed the prayer to St. Joseph, which must be said for nine mornings to expedite the selling transaction.

With a garden trowel we dig a hole under the front yard sumacs that flame to brilliant orange-red in fall. In the flowerbed where the center of an old furnace still sits as a "found sculpture," a heavy tiara of pipes, we bury the statue and read the prayer, placing personal interests and desires in the hands of a protector. We make a place for ritual, though not with faith. Still, the house has been on the market a while, the price dropping like a barometer.

The walnut tree over the back patio has grown tall and, this year, has a bountiful harvest. From morning until night there is a steady crunching and crackling as squirrels tear open the hard shells and drop pieces all over the patio, driveway, and lawn. I sweep up every day so the way will be smooth and clear for visitors. The black shells carry dark stain onto the laundry I foolishly hang below the tree. Then, suddenly it seems, the walnut feasting is over. A few yellow leaves fall instead. And the cicadas rev up their insistent chirring, a drilling that portends the end of their season. Are we ourselves ready for a switch of season?

Along with patching up the house goes de-cluttering. When we made the move to this city twenty-some years ago, we drove a VW van and left behind in Ohio anything that would not fit inside, a guideline that neighbors in the small town we were leaving found profitable as they stood around watching us pack the vehicle, waiting to see what would be discarded.

Admittedly, we mailed a few boxes of books, but up to the last minute essential choices were made. The heavy thirty-gallon pickle crock I had grown fond of claimed a central stand in the van, displacing other items, such as a fine oak file cabinet and a television. "Simplicity" is a concept, an ideal we and a number of friends talk of and strive for, but few of us manage to shed ourselves of possessions and their auras. Even when we think we have pared down to frugal essentials, we may need several trips with a pickup truck just to move across town.

We have become acquainted with a woman who has begun a business as a de-cluttering assistant. She accompanies people through their personal inventory and impedimenta, helping them make those dithery decisions about organization and disposition of property. I imagine her absent voice questioning me about the nature of each item. Is it essential and irreplaceable? Is it valuable in monetary terms, as an heirloom, or as nostalgia (or all three or none of the above)? Is it destined to be a gift for a specific person? If so, would this be an appropriate time to make the gift? Is it a candidate for a sale (and if not sold, for contribution to a charity—"Goodwill" becomes the generic term)? Is it—let's face it—junk?

Separate everything by such categories is the advice—but don't take too long with each item. You don't have to read all the old letters you come across, or the high school certificates, autograph books, and ten-year-old bills. You don't have to try on every piece of clothing. Sometimes snapshots of objects can be kept instead of the objects themselves, just as snapshots from travels provide souvenirs of place. Cameras will gain immeasurable value as they accumulate shadow memories.

The sale! Yes, of course we have a sale. In the West there are Yard Sales. In the East there are Tag Sales. In England there are Jumble Sales. Institutions hold Rummage Sales. We are in the Midwest, where there are Garage Sales, though rarely held in garages, and Moving Sales—the people are moving, not the sales—which seem likely places for bargains because one assumes the sellers will be under pressure to get rid of things. If the move is to a smaller space, there will be much to dispose of; if to a different climate, there will be clothing or products not suitable. We are moving from the Midwest to the Southwest and can thus discard wool coats and snow shovels, at least.

We gather up a great assortment of items, and go around affixing price labels. David gets fired up playing salesman, willing to take offers, discuss bargains. Furniture, tools, and household bric-a-brac roll away at a good pace as neighbors, friends, readers of classified ads, and followers of signs come by.

The day ends up as a dance around a small man called Harold who has been hanging around, persistently pestering us for more. He is clearly a dealer, pressing, "You don't have any other dressers? How about the bookcases? Let me know if you change your mind about those." He watches when others make offers. He buys some of the larger items, peeling off bills from a fat wad in his pocket, turning aside discreetly as if to hide the action. In late afternoon he sits with David in the driveway. He is waiting something out. He is timing his day, just as David is timing his. Buyer and seller are engaged in a pas de deux. We will not sell bookcases, since the books spilling over everywhere will need to be housed in the new place, too. But maybe something else has been overlooked?

Yes, there are rugs. We will keep our Oriental rugs, even though they might not be suitable in our new home. But we have Navajo rugs rolled up. They are old and valuable. They are rolled up because they are old and valuable, and we do not want to wear them out. We unfurl their classic red and brown and grey geometry of authentic threads. We take pictures. Is it right to let them go, to sell them? Harold is more than interested. He is hooked. I think we know this is one of the things we will look back upon with regret. There will always be regrets for something sacrificed.

The moving truck we rent and pack to its roof rides well on the trip. But in our new city of Tucson, in our new back yard, we need help unloading. We do not have friends to rally round, as they did in helping with our sale, with loading, and with last-minute chores. We do not have our list of handymen to call on. We wish Adam would dance down this alley, looking for another casual job.

David, living up to the "resourceful" label he has always carried, approaches two young men on the street and asks if they want a job. They look strong. In fact, they look like weight lifters. And so Quentin and Angel unload box after box, bookcases, and even the big file cabinets. It turns out that these two young men are in the Job Corps Program, so when we need more help a few days later, we call and ask them to come back.

While we were hiring the trail of workers to fix up our old house, it is possible that the previous owners of our new home were doing something similar. The carpet seems to be newly installed (though we do not want wall-to-wall carpeting and eventually will replace it with tile). The sprinkler system in the front yard has been fixed (though we do not want to use precious water to sprinkle a desert yard). But there are still tasks we decide need to be done. Utility lines droop across the back yard at a dangerously low level, affixed to the house in an ugly tangle above the meter boxes. We can have the lines laid underground, but we must get the ditch dug to power company specifications. Who better than the strong young men at the Job Corps?

Quentin is willing to earn some more dollars and brings along a couple of his buddies. These two are from the Navajo Reservation to the north.

MOVING: *HELP WANTED*

Elroy returns the following day, but the other is replaced by Mike, a tall, very skinny white boy with a ponytail. Each of the young men—they are aged about seventeen or so—already has a complicated life story of which we gather only glancing facets. If they can hang in with the program they are on, they will get vocational training—in auto repair or plumbing or electronics or carpentry. Over the next couple of weeks we have a new litany of laborers—Angel and Quentin and Nathan and Elroy and Mike and Brendan and Will and Jésus…

In the dazzling heat they sweat it out with their shovels along the laid-out lines across our back yard. But this desert is not just sandy. Below the surface is the rock-like caliche, which cannot be dug with a shovel. It must be pickaxed or poleaxed or cut through with a (rented) pneumatic drill. The trench must go underneath a cement slab of pathway and must avoid the water lines and gas line, which we have marked on a little chart, precious as a treasure map. Of course, one of the shovels hits the water pipe. But Brendan has been studying plumbing and is proud of his hasty repair of the line.

Before all this activity in the new back yard, which reminds me of photographed vistas of gold mines with workers crawling all over slopes and ledges, we said goodbye to old shaggy Radar, relieving him of too much pain. Soon a black-and-white ten-month-old puppy plays in the trench and clambers over stacks of paving bricks.

After the trench is finished and approved, and the electricians and power company have laid the lines, and all has been covered again, a man from the gas company turns up. He needs to check out the meter because the dial is moving too fast. Thus we discover that the line has been damaged with the trench digging and tests show there is gas drifting around the whole back yard. We are thankful no one lit a cigarette. The gas is shut off. A big decision: we will go all electric.

There are still more tasks, but the young men from the Job Corps are not very reliable in keeping their promises to turn up. They seem to take the "casual labor" label too literally, though they get paid in timely fashion if they do work. However, when we decide to add security/screen doors, Mike comes back to assist, an eager, fast worker. He seems to like talking with David and asks for help with his studies, since he had been a school dropout and is trying to catch up. But one day we arrive home via the back gate and, looking across the yard, I see a movement at our bedroom window. In one of those instantaneous overlays I see the snapshot of David from years before, when he was climbing in a window of our old house after painting the roof, the year he slid off and got green latex paint ingrained in a stigmata on his forehead. Here, too, are angled soles of feet framed in a window. I step back, go around to the side, and call out. By the time we get up to the door, Mike has appeared and seems to be sizing up the screen door he was going to work on. But I know that he has just scrambled out of the window. His footprints step their way across the carpet inside and lead down the hall. He has broken a trust.

And trust will be broken several more times in the next few weeks as we employ other casual labor for fix-up jobs. The man who arrives early in the mornings, has breakfast with us on the back porch and works hard if wildly for a few hours before heading out in the noonday sun blast with the cash earned for the day, also walks away with tools one weekend and, we suspect, with some books that he and David have been discussing. They are philosophers, these betrayers of trust. But this one, we realize as he disappears on us, is a drug addict with a severe problem. He is not a runaway teenager. We guess he is in his late thirties, a Harrison Ford look-alike. His mother and sister come from another city to search for him, We make calls, go looking, inquire of his neighbors, but cannot find him again. I do not use his name because he changed it even during the time he was around us, and I would guess that he has changed it several times since.

Another worker, who talks too much and too loudly, goes along to keep David company on trips to hardware stores to buy supplies. While David is looking for a light fixture, Richard returns on our behalf a roll-down screen for the porch and exchanges it for a different style. But his personal troubles begin to unravel around us, and David finds himself lending Richard transport and giving him a place to park his van in which he is temporarily staying together with his odorous pet ferret. Then comes my credit card bill with phone and service issued in this person's name to the level of $250, not authorized by me. I still have possession of my card, but he must have got the information when he made returns at the hardware store. So much for all the conversational exchange over cups of coffee and sandwiches on our porch.

For a while, it seems we have moved to a twilight zone, where the fringe is moving in on us. We need to gather new friends, trustworthy acquaintances, and reliable workers. We need to compose a sequel to the incantatory litany of names that we still recite with gratitude: Gene and Glenn and Patrick and Thomas and Larry and Adam and…

Contrast in Haiku

Joan E. Zekas

City Scenes

Plastic bags, puffed voids
Scud along in the wild wind
Urban tumble weeds

Tiny, feathered bird
In the lion's marble mouth
Sleeps there, soft and safe

Nature Scenes

Sun/Shade/Sun/Shade/Sun
While driving through sunlit trees
Strobe light   stac ca to

Crisp, crushed colored leaves
Our feet, the mortar's pestle:
Impressionist art

Why Disturb a Winner?

Eleanor Whitney Nelson

Frank stood next to me in the front yard and studied our house. "I have two weeks vacation—that should be enough."

"It's agreed then? No more changes?" I glanced down at the rough sketch in my hands.

"Agreed," he said, putting his arm around my shoulder. We both looked back at the white frame stucco house. Trimmed with redwood and fronted by a huge covered porch, it nestled between the mesquite trees and cactus of the Arizona desert.

"All we have to do is punch a hole in the wall over there, seal up the doorway, remove the window, and enclose the two open sides of the carport." He snapped his fingers. "Just like that—a new kitchen, twice as big as the old one."

I nodded. "And we'll move the dining room into the present kitchen, which will give us extra space in the living room."

"Good plan." Frank grinned. "I'll start getting supplies together, and we can begin this weekend."

"I'll clear out the cabinets. Using them and the old appliances for the new kitchen was a great suggestion. It'll keep our costs way down."

"The only major thing we have to build is a counter for the sink."

"I'd love to have it by the window," I said.

"I'm afraid that's not possible. We don't have any choice where it goes because we can't change the location of the main drain. It's built into the wall about a foot below the bottom of the present sink. We'll have to run a pipe from the new sink to that same spot."

"So what's the problem?"

"The carport where we're building the new kitchen is a foot lower than the rest of the house. That means the bottom of the sink will only be an inch or two higher than the main drain. If we get more than a few feet away from the connection, there won't be enough slope for water to flow."

"It sounds a little iffy. You're sure it'll work?"

"I've eyeballed the angle, and it should be enough…just."

I turned away. What did I know about construction? If Frank said it would work, it would work.

Ten years earlier, when we bought the house, it seemed to have all the room in the world. In fact, it swallowed up our few mismatched pieces of furniture. I reveled in the spacious kitchen. Little by little, we added new furniture, paintings, and knickknacks. Just as we became comfortable with our new home, our company sent us overseas. As exploration geologists, we expected this, and we looked forward to our time in Australia. Then a second posting took us to Indonesia. When we returned, we happily settled back into our familiar surroundings. But the house seemed to have shrunk, and soon we began to feel the itch of the remodeling bug.

Now, with our plans finalized, we plunged into the project, knowing that before long we might be asked to leave on another assignment. To our dismay, when Frank's vacation drew to an end, there were still gaping holes in the exterior wall. Only partially framed in, the new room was wide open to the elements.

Construction crawled along at a frustrating pace. The old cabinets and counters looked shabby in their new surroundings. Rather than purchase custom-made units, Frank decided to make his own. Because his job often took him out of town for weeks at a time, building slowed even further; and because we had torn out the sink I had nowhere to wash fruits and vegetables, pots, pans, and dishes except for a small washbasin in the guest bathroom.

Weeks, then months passed. A year went by and still the house was a construction zone. Rumors of exciting new assignments buzzed around the office. We wanted to be chosen, but because our house was unrentable in its present condition we were becoming increasingly agitated. Nights were often sleepless, and daytime hours filled with tension.

Two years after we finalized our plans for what we believed would be a simple two-week undertaking, everything was completed except the counter for the sink. Frank worked late, night after night, framing it in. Once done, I laid the ceramic tile countertop. Finally, we set the new sink in place, and Frank hooked up the plumbing. The project was finished. The kitchen was every bit as beautiful as I had imagined. The dining room was elegant, and the living room, spacious.

Long since, I had ceased to voice my concern about the kitchen drain, although my worry remained. Thus, when Frank reached toward the faucet for the first time, I held my breath. Water gushed out of the spout; the sink began to fill. Frank turned off the faucet, and we stared at the basin of water. He checked the stopper. It was open. Without a word, he reached under the counter and tapped the pipe. A faint shimmer rippled across the surface of the water. He pressed on the hole and pumped with his hand. Nothing changed. His face grim, he went to find a plunger. Again and again, he pumped. The sink remained full.

I watched as sweat trickled down his face. After hours of tapping, pumping, cursing, he set the plunger on the Saltillo tile floor and plopped down on a stool beside me. Suddenly, he said, "Get the small axle jack from the car."

Without asking why, I brought it back and handed it to him. Carefully, he placed the jack under the pipe just below the sink. Slowly, he began to crank, one twist, then another, each time pushing the pipe upward a fraction of an inch. I prayed the slight change in angle would allow gravity to work before the increasing pressure thrust the pipe through the ceramic sink.

Suddenly, a faintly audible rumble emanated from the drain, followed by a noisy belch of air that ballooned through the water. A swirl formed as the liquid flowed down the hole.

One month later, the new appointment came through. This time it was Chile. The house was ready for its new occupants. That was almost thirty years ago and, for all those years, the axle jack has sat under the pipe, pressing upward. The water drains—why should we disturb a winner?

A Painted Clock

John Russell Webb

Long before I bought this place
whose craftsmanship I did embrace
someone painted a clock on the wall
I touch it each time I go down the hall

To paint a clock seems so sublime
why would someone take the time
to still the hour at half past four
and the moment forevermore

What event carried such import
to bring one's living up so short
or was it simply to rein in time
to capture a life while still in prime

and were those hours stored away
for time on earth
on another day.

A Second Chance

Sally Carper

The river water was icy cold in Portland, Oregon, and the time was drawing near for the colorful dragon boat races that form a part of the annual Rose Festival season. The Willamette River, which runs north and south and divides the city, is conveniently spanned in over twelve areas by bridges designed in every shape and form, providing an aesthetic array of architecture and technology.

Dragon boat racing features brightly painted boats with a distinctive Chinese dragon head at the bow and a flamboyant tail at the rear. The canoe-style boats are manned by a crew that faces forward, paddling in cadence to a beat provided by the drummer or caller.

Among the racers was a group of women breast cancer survivors. These women, between the ages of 30 and 60, had survived chemotherapy, mastectomies, and reconstructive surgeries. They had looked death in the face. Then they came together to form a strong support system, sharing a love for the exercise of paddling and a joy in living.

One morning, prior to the actual race, eight of these women gathered to practice. At first, they thought they would have to cancel, as they did not have the requisite ten people needed for their forty-eight-foot boat, but the team doctor and a volunteer offered to join them. As they set out that early morning, wearing their matching pink life vests, they decided to change their normal practice route and stay close to the marina. Paddling steadily, but not in rhythm, they headed toward the Ross Island Bridge.

As the crew worked at getting their paddles moving in harmony, they saw what appeared to be a body plummet from the top of the bridge. With sudden energy they began to paddle as fast as they could, falling into perfect cadence while they raced to reach what looked like a red jacket bobbing in the rushing current. When they reached the jacket, they discovered it was a man. They threw a line and pulled him alongside. Not having enough room to pull him on board the narrow boat, several women reached under his arms and held him above the water. A nearby fishing boat rushed to their aide, transferred the body and the team doctor to their boat, and sped for the shore. Exhausted and in shock, the team prayed the young man would live.

    Georgia lay in the hospital bed, gazing at the small person cradled in her arms. This was her fifth child, and it was a boy. She had previously given birth to four beautiful girls, and now her son lay sleeping soundly. He had the start of what she was sure would be dark brown hair, but she could not yet determine whether he looked more like her or like his father. She named him Jason.

    At home, he was the center of attention, and his older sisters would fight over whose turn it was to hold him. Jason remained the perfect little boy and beloved little brother till the day he was old enough to start a life on his own.

    After marrying a lovely girl, he traveled overseas with her to finish his tour of duty in the Air Force. What happened next was a mystery to all who loved him. Did his drug abuse start before he returned home, before his wife divorced him and moved to another state, taking his newborn daughter with her? Only one fact was clearly apparent: Jason had found his drug of choice and embraced it with a passion. His tall good looks, charming personality, and the ability to get a job to support his habit kept him going for many years.

    But what started out as "good times" turned into a wasted life. After failing several attempts at rehab, losing job after job, and hurting and misusing people, the drug life finally caught up with him. He was thirty-two.

    Jason developed a plan. He bought new clothes, including a red parka, and stopped all drug use for twenty days. He did not want his mother to feel the shame of being told he was on drugs when they found his body. The fact that he was able to stay off drugs for twenty days in order to die, but not for twenty days in order to live never occurred to him.

    As he walked up onto the bridge, he felt suicide was his only option. Climbing over the railing and dangling his legs over the side, Jason remained confident in his decision until he pushed off. Then, in that instant, he knew he had made a mistake.

    As the women helped Jason into the fishing boat, all he could say was, "I'm sorry! I'm sorry! I'm sorry!"

A SECOND CHANCE

Three days after the rescue, the eight team members met at the hospital. Though not sure how Jason would react to their visit, they knew they had to see him. He needed to know the miracle of the events that had led to their saving his life.

The team had almost canceled pushing off because they lacked two paddlers. Because of that, the doctor was on board, and he later said that Jason would not have survived another minute.

Changing their route, they had headed toward the Ross Island Bridge instead of away from it, as was their normal practice.

The red, fiber-filled jacket that caught their attention also kept Jason afloat just long enough for them to reach him.

These courageous cancer survivors knew they had been put in the right place at the right time for a reason, giving them the opportunity to fight for someone else who was facing death. He needed them, and they intended to become a part of his life.

As they filed into the hospital room, they were greeted with a huge smile. Like mother hens, they surrounded Jason, laughing and hugging this man, who, like them, had been given a second chance.

Bent Trunks

Sarah Wellen

A crooked tree stands
Along the banks
Of the Charles River in Boston,
A testament to the lost lives
Of three talented college youths
Whose skidding car crashed into it
One icy night.

The revelers traveled
From a good time,
To no time,
In no time at all…

Along with the bent trunks
Of three grieving mothers,
The bent tree casts
Its long shadow of death,
Like a pall,
Upon the river of life…

Miracles Do Happen

Joan Harris

Several years ago my husband, Duke, and I were on our way to see our kids in Louisiana. Driving the back roads in our Class C motor home, we were looking forward to a pleasant visit. We were about an hour outside of Baton Rouge when mother nature decided to play with us. The sky opened up and the rains came, gentle at first, but then more intense. We were on a narrow road with nowhere to pull over. I didn't want the bed to get wet, so I unbuckled my seat belt and climbed up to the cab over bed and closed the little windows on each side. Somehow, I managed not to disturb our dog, Max, who was sleeping on the couch, or our cat, Molly, who was sleeping up on the bed.

Making my way back down and into my seat, I was looking forward to a leisurely drive while listening to the summer rain. Instead, what the next few minutes brought is a memory I will never forget. I barely had time to get back into my seat when a red mini-truck came racing past us on the driver's side. Driving like that in the rain was bad enough, but then the driver of the truck suddenly stopped at the entrance to a narrow country road to make a left turn. We don't know if he was drunk, or if he just didn't realize he was so close to where he needed to turn. It didn't matter. In an instant we were sure we were going to be involved in a fatal collision. Duke reacted quickly, though, and was able to swerve, barely missing the truck. If I had been driving, we would have hit it for sure. There was no time to rejoice in an accident avoided, however, as we were immediately put into another life or death situation.

It seems that a man on a bicycle—not a regular bike, mind you, but one of those low to the ground ones where the rider lies back almost parallel to the road—was riding to the right of the red truck. The bike hadn't been in front of us before the red truck passed us, so the cyclist must have been passing us on our right side while we were watching the truck on our left. I thought for sure we were going to hit him, but then miracle number two happened, and my husband was able to swerve again, barely missing him.

As I hung on to the dashboard, I could hear the dog crashing to the floor, then sliding back over and hitting the couch. Somewhere overhead, the cat was flying through the air, but eventually grabbed the curtain, shredding it to pieces on her way down.

In his attempt to avoid hitting the man on the bike, my husband ended up driving us onto the edge of a deep ditch alongside the road. He floored it and somehow kept us from turning over. I don't know how he managed that with the angle we were on as we drove for what seemed like an eternity before we were able to get back onto the road. When we looked back, the cyclist was nowhere in sight.

It was a few minutes before Duke was able to find a spot for us to pull over and stop. I don't know how long we sat there, going over what had just happened. Each individual incident could have been devastating in its own right, but to have all three happen, one right after the other in mere seconds, was unbelievable.

After checking on Max and Molly and getting them calmed down, we continued on our way to Baton Rouge. This time, I was able to fasten my seat belt. When we arrived at our son's house, I suggested that we park in his driveway. My husband didn't agree, though, and instead parked on the street in front of their house.

My daughter-in-law and three grandchildren immediately ran out to greet us. We invited them in to see our fairly new motor home and were having a pleasant conversation while waiting for our son to get home from work. I was telling everyone about our near misses in the rain when, all of a sudden, we felt a thud on the street side of the rig and were jolted out of our seats. My youngest granddaughter had been climbing up the ladder to the bed. I managed to catch her as she fell off, then we all ran out of the rig to see what had happened.

Our motor home had been run into by a teenage girl who had backed out of the driveway across the street. I don't know how she didn't see us, but perhaps the fact that she was on her cell phone at the time might have been a bit of a distraction. As we stood there, not believing the day's events, the girl decided to drive away rather than face us. Bad decision.

Fortunately for us, a teenage neighbor washing his truck in his driveway had seen the whole thing. He quickly drove over, picked up our daughter-in-law, and the chase was on. They ended up finding the hit and run driver in the mall parking lot. While my daughter-in-law called the police, her friend made sure the teenage girl didn't get away. After she was taken to the police station, they contacted her mother, but we never did find out if she had her cell phone or license taken away.

Nobody was injured in the incident, so we didn't press any charges. We just wanted our motor home repaired, which our insurance company took care of. When my son arrived home, we relayed the day's events while inside his house.

We have not forgotten any of that day's events, and even now, as I recount those moments, I marvel at how we were protected from hurting that man on the bike or the men in the truck, or turning our rig over in that ditch. One thing we did learn: when bad things happen, don't talk about them. Put the thoughts aside and talk about something pleasant. Maybe if we had been discussing something else, the accident that finally did happen might not have. Or, then again, if my husband had parked in the driveway…

Needless to say, we went to bed that night counting our blessings. My husband is a very good driver, but there is no doubt in our minds that he had help that day driving down the back roads of Louisiana in the rain.

Hurricane, 1938
Lebanon, Connecticut

Una Nichols Hynum

I remember the absence of sound
in the eye like a lid on the world.
All of nature froze.
The storm gathered up its skirts,

sprinted between silo and milk house
where we lay on the wind,
light as paper lanterns.
The farm began to come apart

and fly around us. We fled
to the veranda, watched the apple orchard
lie down in slow motion.
Next morning places where we played

were scattered in the fields,
silage plastered everywhere
glittering in the reborn sun.
Fallen trees barricaded houses.

Cows hung in stanchions
where the barn blew from under them.
The steeple fell into the body of the church.
The village was changed forever.

What I remember is exhilaration.
I was still a child.

Rollover

—excerpt from *Ask No Questions: Poems & Stories*

Fred K. Taylor

Everything was so very clear. I saw the world in vivid color and detail. I felt the ground, the bumps and the rough spots. I smelled the grass, and I believe I remember even feeling the texture of the grass. As I lay there thinking of my next move, I was aware of the movement of the tractor in my direction. I was very focused on the movement of the Ford 8N Tractor and only that point of time. If I did not take care of business in that second, there would be no more time for me.

My haymaking experience was only in the second or third year, and that was limited to a four-acre flat field. Those four acres were at our seven-acre Deerfield Road farm. Our new property on Oak Park Road was seventy-two acres with fifty in hay. Over half of that land had slopes, some fairly steep. Sol would say inexperience was going to play a role in moving the hay from the hilltop field. This was the first time I made hay from this field.

My equipment was undersized for this farm, both for the size of the fields and for the slopes. Bob Klubertanz was the farmer who had cut the hay on this hilltop field in the past. He had a large enough tractor. When baling the hay, his tractor pulled the baler, and the hay wagon was attached to the baler. At one place he had to start turning a tight turn while still on the slope. He got away with it through good equipment and farm experience. His tractor was 105 horsepower; the tractor I had was a 1950 Ford 8N 25 HP. I would not even begin to try to pull a baler with a hay wagon attached using the Ford 8N. What I did was bale the hay with my old red International 46 baler, dropping the bales on the ground. Also, there weren't any tight turns on the slopes. This seemed to work as, without the weight of the hay wagon, the little tractor did the job of baling. A hay wagon with a full load weighs about 7100 pounds. Then came the job of picking up the hay bales; a loaded wagon is what the 8N was moving around the field.

As I drove the tractor, a friend, Jim Valeria, and my wife, Faye, lifted the bales on the wagon. This is hard work; the dust pollen, the dirt, and the heat plus walking up and down a hill loading bales of hay made for a long day. We had been working for hours, and the last load was in the wagon. It was very full as Jim and I finished up. Faye left to get us drinks from our house on Deerfield Road.

I was driving off the field with the tractor in low gear. The incline was getting steep. With effort, I steered to keep the tractor and wagon lined up straight. But then the weight of the wagon was too much for the tractor. The tractor was being pushed down the hill, sliding over the grass; I was unable to steer. Then the tractor was at a sharp angle in relationship to the wagon. No, it hadn't jackknifed yet, but was ready to at any time. The tractor was still being pushed over the grass. Then it happened. The 8N started to roll over, with the large right rear wheel leaving the ground. I felt my best chance was to jump off the tractor. It had to be a clean jump; that is, without getting caught or blocked by any part of the tractor when I leapt. I had to leap far enough to clear the tractor. This was so I had time to get out of its downhill roll. The first jump got me off. The second would get me out of the path.

How did I feel? Other than being very aware and focused, I felt nothing emotionally for I believe panic or fear would have done me in. They are a luxury, a luxury someone trying to save themselves can't afford to indulge. I felt that way in Vietnam, and I guess in some form or another, most of my life.

Time seemed to be slowing down. I jumped in the only direction available to me downhill from the 8N. I jumped far enough and hit the ground hard, seeing the tractor still rolling towards me. I decided in a quarter of a second to roll on the ground at a 90-degree angle. This would put me out of the path of the tractor. I was able again to move my body fast enough and avoid getting smashed, with the tractor just brushing my leg.

Then I noticed the hay wagon had been disconnected from the 8N and, for some reason, stayed in place on the hillside while the tractor was taking its shots at me, again finding myself in a bad spot downhill from the wagon. In another quarter of a second, the wagon took off like a freight train directly at me. Again, I rolled and pushed myself out of danger. Not having the time to stand, I must have looked like a fish out of water; flopping for all it's worth, trying to save itself. I watched as the wagon roared 200 feet downhill until it tipped over.

I was breathing hard. Time started to return to normal as my body shook. Jim uphill had watched the entire event. He could not believe I was alive. He came running to me shouting, "I didn't know what I was going to say to your wife. I thought it was all over for you. I can't believe you made it." I just sat on the ground, shaking and coming back to normal time.

In a few minutes, Faye drove up the drive. She walked up to us and asked, "What happened? You look like you've seen a ghost." She wasn't one for seeing the big view. I pointed to the upside down tractor, then downhill to the wrecked hay wagon. She had some quick questions and soon realized that I had escaped death once again.

Heartland

Bobbie Jean Bishop

My father grasped the wheel as we drove state by state following the numbers—route this and route that—we played the game of maps leading us from one highway to the next, counting incomprehensible

miles on various cross country trips, the rush of two nights and three days with my nose pressed out of shape against the back window, we raced against time and my father's lean paycheck, barely arriving

before we'd have to start back—roadsides wild with asparagus, the last tiny unpaved leg lumbering along past stockyards and alfalfa fields, our trips fueled by my mother's desire to touch home, leading to that

curved dirt drive shadowed by elms, branches looped with tire swings above thick grass. By the shade of orchards, a cluster of sheds and ramshackle barn behind the farmhouse, ditches drifted around us like

moats churning with water for crops. As he parked next to the sloping stoop, my father sounded the horn. We all stepped out into the sunlit yard where my grandparents appeared spry and short as gnomes who

tended this acreage as if their lives depended on it. I had to conceal my eagerness to rush by them into the sitting room where the player piano waited just for me, stacked with dozens of boxed rolls.

Gleefully, I loaded one into the heart of the beast. Legs stretched to distant pedals, my feet pumped out notes of a thunderous march. Even now, our family airwaves resound with "Stars and Stripes Forever."

A Pleasant Memory

Paul E. Voeller

It was summertime in southern Oregon, and I was working for my grandfather on his farm near Winston. The South Umpqua River served as the western boundary to his property. Since I was a city boy, all the farm work was new and interesting from hand-milking the cows to cleaning out the barn to bailing hay and gathering eggs.

It had been warm and dry for several days, and the alfalfa hay was ready to bale. Fred, a neighbor boy, my grandfather, and myself would bale hay that day. Grandfather would drive the tractor that pulled the hay baler. Fred's job on one side of the machine was to poke two wire ends through the hay. One end had a loop, while the other end was straight.

My job on the other side of the machine, facing Fred, was to put the straight wires through the loop wires, cinch up, and twist the "pigtail" around the base wire two times.

Grandfather wore his wide-brimmed hat, a long-sleeved shirt buttoned at the top, long pants, and boots. Fred and I wore shorts, sneakers, and no hat. We all wore semi-fingerless tight-fitting gloves.

Most of the time things went smoothly. However, Fred and I began sweating profusely on this hot day and were slowly being covered from head to toe with chaff and dust that swirled about the baler. This, in turn, caused us to scratch, scratch, and scratch some more. We couldn't stop scratching. Finally, unable to resist, I yelled at grandfather, who was driving the tractor, *"Can we go swimming now?"*

Grandfather immediately turned the tractor and hay-baler off and said, "Boys! Let's go swimming."

The next day aboard the hay baler, the weather was hot and dusty again, but this time Fred and I were wearing clothes similar to what grandfather was wearing: long pants, long-sleeved shirts, hats, boots, and bandanas.

Hay baling that day went off without a hitch. "You boys did a good job today," said grandfather, as we all began walking toward the river.

Evening Light

Barbara Ponomareff

The field has been stripped.
Stipple it ochre.

Furrow its canvas
with your broad strokes;
catch the sun before dying
and conjure up
the chalk-white breasts
of the chorus of seagulls
facing west, as if
salvation was near.

Soon darkness
will sink to its knees
here in the field—
gather up colour and texture,
hope and despair.

Cancer

—excerpt from *Fifty-two Pieces: short stories*

Joel Berman

Mrs. Burton is dying. Seven months ago, she had a segment of her descending colon removed for cancer. The tumor had extended beyond the wall of the bowel and into the surrounding lymph node drainage from that segment of the intestine. It was read by the pathologist and by the surgeon as a Duke's C classification, with a relatively poor prognosis.

Somehow, I always lean heavily towards the hope that there might be a cure, even though I know deep inside how slim the chances are. It is hard to picture death in the face of life. As I looked at the vibrant Mrs. Burton several months ago, eating her meal in the morning several days after her surgery, I had no picture of how she would look when her body began to deteriorate under the grasp of the cancer. She was so willing to go through the pain of surgery and the recovery period, but she wanted some small assurance from me that all this was behind her. She wanted so much to look forward to the future, to her children and grandchildren. Her unspoken desire is to live for the comedies and the tragedies of the future.

"Just don't place any final statement in the story. Don't make a finite story out of one that now is unrealistically, but so humanly, unending."

The liver scan had been negative, and the metastatic surveys had all been negative. Damn all the high scientific technology that imbues us with false hope. Damn the x-rays and blood tests, the computerized scans and erring examinations. The disgusting cancer cells smile at us in their omnipotence and defy our scientific tomfoolery. Like the pendulum that never stops moving, the growth continues until it destroys the source of its own sustenance.

Four months ago, I had seen her in the office, wearing a new dress, the results of her examination completely negative. She was eating well and gaining weight. Her wounds had healed nicely, and she was telling me about a recent trip to Santa Barbara with her daughter and son-in-law and her two grandchildren. There was no end to her vibrancy; her total love of life was invigorating.

The following month, she noticed mild nausea and began to lose weight. She unconsciously fought the signs and symptoms and was almost apologetic when she casually mentioned the changes. She had been getting chemotherapy and tried to attribute her symptoms to the treatments. But there was no clinical correlation, and the picture was one I had seen so many times before. I have become a master of euphemism and have learned how to couch the truth in phrases so ambiguous that the words came out gently. The total truth, too often, is crushing and leaves no room for hope, like the words in Markandaya's book:

Life without hope
Draws nectar in a sieve
And hope without an object
Cannot live.

The words often come back to me. They were used in that context to depict the hopelessness of the starving Indian in a poverty-ridden India. But the Indian had, at least, the prospect of life, and the chance, however small, to improve the human condition. I have learned never to deprive a patient, no matter how sick, of that last hope. Someone in my training once told me, "Never close the door completely. Always leave it a little ajar, even in the most moribund last moments, so that the suffering individual can look out towards the future, and his mind can believe what his physical body knows can never be."

There is a hackneyed expression that the doctor so often uses when the patient states, "I'm dying, doctor, aren't I?" and that is a callous, "But we're all dying!" It is, of course, no comfort, because, although we all recognize our mortality, we believe it to be far off in the future, bearing no relation to our everyday living. How often we hear the middle-aged man after his first heart attack state, "But it can't be. Not me!"

Mrs. Burton is dying. Her family knows it and wants to know when. I have heard the question so many times, I have sometimes said to myself, "Yes, yes, she will die at exactly 07:23:40 next Thursday evening." But no,

I just reaffirm that no one knows when (in my religious moments, I add, "but God"). I have told Mrs. Burton that the tumor has grown back, and she will require more therapy. After much bandying with words, she finally asks me if she is dying. I respond, without directly answering her, that we will continue to treat her. She asks the question again, and I say, "Yes, but..." My voice seems to face an implacable obstruction in mellowing the truth with supportive encouragement to help her continue on in the days or weeks that remain. We seem to develop a keen understanding of one another, and she welcomes me twice a day in the hospital as I make my visits. She seems relieved to know that she and I share this big "secret" that her family cannot quite bring themselves to discuss with her.

I grow too attached. I think about her at lunch and while standing at the scrub sink in surgery. I see her in the tissues during lapses in the flow of cases, and I momentarily think about her in bed before I doze off. She has given herself to my care, and I cannot let her down. The ebb of life is sad, and only now do I think about the course of evolution, with birth and death and rebirth and death again. How insignificant is Mrs. Burton, and yet how important. In one moment, she represents the pinnacle of a long, long line of genetic transfers over a million years of evolution. And here she lies, abdomen distended and partially obstructed, liver riddled with cannonball metastases, and the body screaming for a few minutes more. In the last moment of her life, she still maintains a magnificence of structure and function that man cannot hope to even approach. The sickest kidney, the least-functioning liver or pancreas still excels at performing functions that we shall not fully understand for a millenium.

In her last moments, she drifts into a semicomatose state and, after a few shallow respirations, ceases to exist as a human being, lying in bed as a complex accumulation of matter whose function is now only to return to its elements. I touch her briefly, fulfill my medical duties and leave the room, saddened, yet reassured by the magnificence of life and death, and more eager to cherish the hours, the days, or the years that I have left.

Llano Estacado (The Staked Plain)

Susan Cummins Miller

In the season of nightmares
the woman waits
like a threadbare cabin
with nobody home, standing
in a canyon furrowed
by rillwash, dwarfed
by brutal sky.

The wailing wind searches
ceaselessly, moans in her ears,
drives dust through split skin, whistles
between grave mounds
on the Caprock, strips away
what's left
of the topsoil.

Under the planting moon
she waits, binding wounds
with hardscrabble hope, handknit
scarves, and barbed-wire fencing—she waits,
watching drift-clouds plough the night sky
like clumsy drunks,
lurching, falling,

staggering on   until, one dawn,
La Llorona rests. Hailstones crash
on the old tin roof. Water soothes, then erases,
the polygonal cracks that grieve the cotton fields.
The woman kneels, fingers kneading ochre mud
as one arrow of sunlight steals between
the shafts of rain.

Fire

Mimi Moriarty

Someone yesterday confirmed your fate.
She opened her mouth into a forest
and the trees trembled, then shed leaves.
I grabbed a rake, gathered them into piles
set them ablaze.

Someone yesterday uttered *ovarian*
a wreck of a word, it felt like rushing
empty-handed into a burning church
searching the aisles for penitents still
on their knees, you plead with them
to leave with you.

Someone yesterday pressed
her hand into mine, relieving
me of earth, wind, water,
leaving the singed taste
of months wasted,
ashes to ashes, dust.

I now know how much time
we ought to have left.

Someone shared one last word,
but I could not hear it,
lost in the smoldering piles.

Small Miracles

Ginger Galloway

I knew all about miracles, or at least I thought I did. Miracles were awesome, unexplainable. For instance, Christmas was all about miracles… religious traditions, families and friends bonding, babies being born, children laughing and playing, all were miracles. I lay in bed thinking about miracles, that first day after Christmas. I'd celebrated a little the night before, so it wasn't unusual to feel a strange gripping sensation in the pit of my stomach when I woke up. I knew deep down inside something awful would happen that day, but I quickly dismissed the idea. Hurriedly, but carefully, I drove to work in a very light snow, whipped my car into a parking space in the employee's garage, then ran through the dark tunnel to the time clock. I made it, out of breath, on time to the very minute, just like always.

Upstairs, the atmosphere was normally chaotic, everyone bustling about getting ready for the day's excitement. We checked the schedule, all of us still tying the ropes to our pants, the sashes to our dresses. Our paper shoes with conductive strips made flopping noises on the tile floor as we shuffled quickly to our areas. We all stood at the big sink, our knees pressed firmly against the regulator bars. Energetically, we carefully and meticulously scrubbed from fingertips to elbows, never retracing our paths, careful not to contaminate, lest we had to start the 10-minute scrub all over again.

As we talked through our masks, the adrenaline began to pump. For me, there was nothing like a simple little "D and C" to start the day. The bigger, more challenging cases would come later. It was like being in a symphony. We'd start out soft and slow, then finish off the day with a big blasting forte. A heart transplant was the most awesome—ah, the privilege of being in that room with Dr. Lancing.

Still dreaming, I moved away from the sink, swishing backwards through the swinging doors, floating gracefully into the arms of my gown.

My circulating nurse, John, took pride in dressing me just as elegantly as when he dressed the doctors. He had the routine down pat. As I walked toward my instrument table, I surveyed the room again. I'd helped or assisted with this procedure many times before. It looked like a typical "D and C" to me. No big deal. Piece o' cake. The suction machine always sat idle in the corner—a waste of money, as we never used it. "Just there in case of an emergency," they told me.

Dr. Levine soon burst through the door in his usual jovial manner, singing loudly. You'd think he was auditioning for a part in a Broadway musical. I liked working with Larry's Uncle Ron. Just last week I had ridden with Dr. Levine in his Cutlass, when he was pulled over for speeding, then escorted by two police cars, one in front, one in back, all the way across town to Methodist Hospital. What a ride! Ninety m.p.h. through downtown Louisville. Oh, were those cops pissed—told Dr. Levine to ride with the ambulance driver next time—not ever to drive like that again or they'd ticket him for sure—then send him to driving school!

I assisted the OB-GYN staff the day of the big race—I was a nursing student, and they invited me to help deliver twins. When the first twin slipped out, Dr. Levine cut the cord and handed "Mary" to me. I was ecstatic, holding that baby in my arms. What a guy! Everyone loved to work with Dr. Levine. It was an honor. We all felt so proud walking alongside of him, whether we wore our white coats or those drab green O.R. scrubs. With Dr. Levine, we witnessed miracles as he helped bring new life into this world.

"So…how was your weekend, Ginger? How's school?" he asked me as I handed him the speculum with one hand, the #4 dilator with the other. He didn't really have to tell me which instrument he needed. I was trained to anticipate.

In the O.R. background, the circulating nurse was writing on the patient's chart. Suddenly, Dr. Levine's voice went up an octave. "Uh, oh, John, better bring out the tube—fast."

John plopped the sterile tubing onto my tray. I froze, then moved like a robot. Dr. Levine fed the tube into the uterus. The next thing I saw was the big machine moving in like a bulldozer. "Okay…turn her on…"

Never in my life had I heard such a bloodcurdling sound as the sound of the suction in that tube. It did not sound like the other suction devices we used in other surgeries. I glanced over at the jar, and that's when I stopped breathing. My throat went dry; tears welled up in my eyes. My stomach began to turn, and soon saliva rose in my throat.

I saw the thin tube spitting out a tiny arm with a hand and fingers attached. On the bottom, inside that quart jar, an ugly mass of tissue and blood accumulated. It was bright red, not a blood-like color. Then I saw a tiny foot swirling around—didn't see a leg, though. All I saw were the toes. My head began to swim...I was speechless...Oh, my God...what was I witnessing...what had I done? Was I really seeing human fragments, or was I just imagining this nightmare?

I broke scrub and threw my gloves on the ground. I plunged through the swinging doors toward the hopper, a huge sink we generally use to clean our instruments. I ripped off my mask, gripped the hopper on both sides, and threw up all the evil things I felt inside of me. Weak and pale, I was shaking and crying all at once. I flushed the hopper over and over and over. I vaguely remember Tada, a fellow technician, coming in and escorting me out of there and into the women's dressing room. He sat with me for a long time, holding me in silence. Even Dr. Levine came in to see about me.

No one had bothered to brief me about that case. No one informed me that Dr. Levine "might" be doing an abortion. All the other nurses knew, and they had refused to take the case. "Give it to Ginger—she's just a kid—it won't bother her." I felt betrayed. How could they be so heartless? Not even to ask me if I minded—doing-an-abortion!

I was so upset, I remember yelling at my supervisor and creating an awful scene at the front desk before leaving the premises. I returned to the room, picked up the jar, and I gently handed it to the head nurse, Salinas. I cried, "You dream about these little arms and fingers. Damn you!" Then I went home and took the phone off the hook.

Assisting with an abortion is not just part of a job description; it's a moral issue. I, too, should have had a choice. This was not in my contract. I was not hired to do elective abortions. I joined the medical staff because I wanted to help 'save' people's lives, their limbs, their arms, their hands, their fingers. I could not voluntarily assist in the destruction of any living thing, nor watch a fetus being ripped apart with no compassion for its little soul.

I learned something very important that day...that I needed to take a deeper look at myself and start standing up for the issues and ideas in which I believed. I learned I needed to stand up for what I believed, no matter what the cost, and to always pursue those beliefs.

For many weeks after that incident, Dr. Levine did his abortions without a scrub nurse, or else he took his patients to another hospital. A technician or a nurse could not be tricked or forced into assisting with an abortion. Abortions could not be camouflaged as "D and C's." The word "abortion" had to be written on the schedule. Eventually, Salinas hired one scrub nurse whose sole job was to assist on abortions. And all abortion cases were restricted to Room 5. Our original staff of nurses and technicians continued to stand up against scheduled abortions, and no one was fired.

I still dream about the contents in that suction jar, even though thirty years have passed. I will never forget the devastating experience that opened my eyes: the little arm, the hand, the fingers swirling out of the thin plastic tube into that glass jar, agonizing helplessly in silence. I have experienced many miracles in my lifetime, but the most precious memory—the little miracle that didn't make it—has emphatically filled my heart with compassion and empathy.

God Doesn't Make Mistakes

Mitzie Skrbin

"You're pregnant," said the doctor,
"There is no doubt about it."
But this was baby number six;
I didn't want to shout it.
I didn't want to celebrate;
I just wanted to cry.
And in distress I sought the Lord,
"Why, please tell me why?
I'm older, tired, I've done my part;
I don't have what it takes."
But the Lord just smiled and answered,
"God doesn't make mistakes."

And so this brand new little life
grew more real by the minute
and as he grew beneath my heart,
he also grew within it.
He was born on Easter Sunday
and this funny little boy,
like the season of his birth,
filled our hearts and lives with joy.
He never caused a moment's pain—
not even teenage heartaches,
and I often heard God chuckle,
"See, God doesn't make mistakes."

And now, too soon, he's been called home
before he's reached his prime.
But this is wrong! There's some mistake;
this cannot be his time!
Again I sought the Lord in tears
to ask, "How can I bear it?"
"My child, your grief's not yours alone;
you must know that I share it.
Remember that he's my child too,
and though your heart now breaks,
you'll meet again and understand:
God doesn't make mistakes!"

Acoustics of Autumn

Kathleen A. O'Brien

No longer needs an afternoon nap,
    four-year-old dressed in orange knit cap
walking with grandmother hand-in-hand;
    generations spanned.

Pace is slow, stride is short;
    he tests himself on the rough asphalt,
scaling the curb that's a balance beam,
    future member of Olympic team.

"King of the Mountain" played on stumps;
    elevated from the world, he jumps
clear from a trunk low to the ground,
    roaring a beastly sound.

Kneels down; digs his fingers in dirt,
    fills the pockets of his blue sweatshirt
with acorns saying, "I can plant a tree."
    Change of clothes will be necessity.

We stroll beside the town roadway
    on this rain-washed, sun-ablaze day.
He drops acorns through the sewer grate,
    listening to the "ker-plunk" they make.

Squirrel overhead in red oak tree
    twitters displeasure at grandson and me.
October knows to jostle trees
    with whisking wind and stiffened breeze.

A pile of leaves on a lawn, he spies,
    wide smile and brightened eyes;
stomps the colored harvest gold.
    Crunching recalls adventures old

when my delight was much the same.
    Repeated discovery, new memory to frame.
He sees his mother; he's off on a run.
    Thank you, daughter, for loaning your son.

The Delightful Oblivion of Being Five

Sharon Laabs

The mamas aren't paying any attention.
They're around the corner sitting in the shade,
sipping on tall cool drinks of iced tea.
But we're going out to explore for awhile.
You see, being five…that's what we do.

The barnyard is hot like the witch's oven
so we decide it's time for a swim,
slipping into the waters of the horse trough
where the moss feels like fairy finery.
Well…of course we get into trouble,
but some of these things are so hard to understand
when you're five.

Then we're off to the dusty granary,
where cousin Chad makes circles with his pee-pee
on the mountains of golden wheat,
while I'm quite disappointed with my little puddle.
Some of these things are so hard to understand
when you're five.

We run and run 'til there's no breath left in us,
throwing ourselves wildly down on the grass
listening to the poplar trees gossip with the wind.
This is where we live…right here.
Maybe it's an empty place, maybe we're poor
but nobody really cares…when you're five.

The Price of Bubbles

Mary Rose Durfee

By the early 1920s, Henry Ford had surpassed his competitors and become the largest automobile producer in the world. He could not keep up with the demand for his most famous automobile, the Model T, until he created his "moving industrial production line." As the popularity and affordability of his motor cars improved, there was the need for hard-surfaced roads. The construction of new roads began expanding into the countryside even out as far as the small town of Waterville, New York, which according to the 1920 U.S. Census had a population of 1,050.

If you are questioning why dirt roads in such a small town were being paved in the early 1920s, perhaps it was because in 1875 Waterville (about 53 miles from Syracuse, New York) became known as the "Hop Capital of the World." Hops are grown extensively for the brewing of beer. Additionally, dairy trucks needed to pick up milk from the dairy farmers and take the milk to be processed in the city.

Paving was done in several stages, and the first stage was to grade the dirt road or prepare the road bed surface. The gravel wagon followed, dropping its load of crushed stones evenly across the expanse of the road. What came next was a sight to behold! A huge roller made of iron and steel moved ever so slowly, packing and crushing the gravel tightly onto the road. The roller went forward, and then backward. One man used a large tin can to dip water from a pail, and he would wet that hot roller every so often. How it would belch steam then! It kept the stones from sticking to the roller.

Hot tar was then poured on top of the crushed gravel. The boiler wagon held all of the tar, and workers kept the tar hot by stoking the fire with wood. The boiler wagon emitted a strange odor that lasted for days; some people thought the smell was offensive, and others thought it pleasant. Finally, an asphalt composite was dumped from a truck onto the hot tar, and men used rakes and shovels to spread this mixture evenly over the road bed. Close behind the asphalt truck was another roller that compacted all of the road materials into one finished paved road. A tent-like cab was erected over the front part of the roller, and it looked like a small house with no sides. Standing at the edge of their hop farm, watching the new road being paved, was a family with two small children. The parents watched for a while, but they had chores to attend to, so they left Mary and Fatti at the edge of their farm next to the almost completed road. The parents cautioned the two children, in no uncertain terms, to stay back from the road. It could spell danger to two little tots ages five and six.

"Wow! Look at that roller, Mary! It's almost as big as our house," exclaimed Fatti. Just then, the huge roller backed up closer to the farm's driveway, pressing out hot tar onto the drive and over the edge, forming huge bubbles that sparkled in the sunlight. Mary and Fatti were fascinated by the glistening, colorful reflections in the tar bubbles; however, their train of thought was interrupted by the man at the steering wheel of the huge roller as he looked down at the two children standing there and yelled, "Hey, there! Don't get too close. Stay back! Ya hear now!" With that, the driver moved the roller up the road while spitting a cud of tobacco onto the new pavement.

Mary and Fatti inched backwards little by little; at the same time they shouted out to the driver, "Bye, bye." Mary and Fatti waved to the man, but they were focusing on the tar left in the driveway.

"What big bubbles! I know what we can do," Fatti declared. "Let's build our own roller and make a nice driveway for Papa and Mama."

"Oh, that's a good idea," Mary answered excitedly, as they both ran to the edge of the road. The tar stuck to their shoes, so they took them off. Using their toes, they broke the bubbles, creating pops delightful to their ears and letting the warm tar ooze between their tiny toes.

"Ooh! It feels so good," the children exclaimed as they looked around their yard for something to use for a giant roller. They spied a small, sled-like skid or platform where goods were placed for ease in moving, and they also spied an empty milk can near the mailbox. This 24-inch tall milk can was used to haul the milk from the barn to the edge of their yard for daily pickup by the dairy or to haul a chunk of ice to the milk house for the cooling process. They tipped the milk can on its side and rolled it in front of the skid. To build the cab of the huge roller, the children gathered an assortment of sticks. They smeared them with tar and stacked them on the skid, one on top of the other, but they just wouldn't stick.

"I don't want to play no more," Mary declared. "I'm thirsty. I'm going in and get a drink of water."

"Me too," said Fatti.

They ran up the porch steps to the screen door, barely aware their feet were sticking slightly to the steps, leaving telling signs for Mama and Papa to discover. They could barely open the door as their hands were covered with tar. In fact, they had tar all over themselves—in their hair, on their faces, on their clothes, but mostly between their toes where the tar had congealed.

"Let's wash before Mama sees us," said Mary. "She might get mad."

"Yeah," said Fatti. "But I want a drink first."

The sink was too high for them to reach, so they brought chairs from around the kitchen table and placed them in front of the sink. They found two empty jelly jars nearby and filled these with water to quench their thirst. Fatti helped himself to an extra glassful of water. Mary then poured water into the wash basin, and they both put their hands into the water, thinking the tar would come off as quickly as mud does. As the tar didn't budge, the children then thought of what Mama used when she bathed them, so off to the back porch they went, where Mama had hung the towels from last night's bath. But the washcloths were of no help, and neither were the towels. The tar just stuck solidly.

"I'll go get Papa's shaving soap and brush," declared Fatti. "If it takes off his whiskers, it should take off this tar."

"Okay, Fatti. Stay there. I can reach it better'n you. Mama's comb is there, too. I bet it'll take the tar out of my hair," exclaimed Mary.

Mary and Fatti heard the terrifying sound of footsteps on the porch, which is not what they wanted to hear at that moment. "Uh-oh! We better get out of here. Let's go hide under the bed," Mary and Fatti whispered in unison and quickly clambered off the chairs and ran through the dining room and living room, leaving a telltale trail of destruction behind them.

"Mary! Fatti! Where are you?" Mama's shrieks resounded throughout the house.

Papa mumbled some indistinguishable words under his breath as he took down the leather strop from its hook and headed for the bedroom. The two small children were dragged out from under the bed, crying and hollering, because they knew they were in serious trouble. Mary and Fatti lay on their stomachs across the bed. Fatti turned and stretched out his little arms for his mother to comfort him as tears streamed down his little red face.

However, Mama did not console Fatti, but held both children down on the bed while Papa stropped them.

Author's Note:

I am Mary, and Fatti was my younger brother. I don't remember any pain from that walloping—the only one I ever received. By today's standards, it would be called abuse.

I was always afraid of my mother the rest of my life.

I often wondered how two small children could trash a house the way we did in such a short time! Kerosene cleaned up the mess and us two kids. This happened approximately 90 years ago. I like the smell of fresh tar to this day.

Potty Chair

Robert Brooks

There was really nothing special about it; it was just your classic chair—all in right angles. It had arms, of course, to keep one from falling out, and a hinged seat that, when lifted, revealed an enameled potty—white, with a black rim. When the potty was no longer required, the chair was designed to serve as an ordinary chair for a small child.

But, to my knowledge, mine never served in that capacity. It was already quite old when it appeared at our house. Its white paint was almost completely worn off by then. Where had it served before then? I suppose at my cousin Evelyn's house. And it had probably done duty (excuse the pun) at our own house, when my older sister was a toddler, and may very well have served under (another pun) my cousin Julie, even before that. Chances are very good that my little cousin Sonny inherited it from me, but by then I had lost all interest in it. How could I have been so cavalier about an accessory that meant so much to me and played such an intimate role in my life?

Left alone on that chair for what seemed to me an eternity, I had been forced to occupy my leisure. I remember singing the songs I had often heard my mother sing while she did her housework. And, if she happened to be working in a room nearby, I would engage my mother in conversation. If not, I would play with my two dogs. They were not real dogs, of course, but, by contorting my fingers, I could create play-dogs to keep me company until such time as my mother would deem fit to come for me.

Ah, how well I remember the circumstances that first forced me to contemplate a life without a potty-chair! In Indianapolis, my mother had a brother and sister-in-law to whom she was devoted. They were much older than she, and they had raised her with their own three girls after her father died. Since they were unable to come see us in Cleveland, our family went to see them in Indianapolis. Not often, however. The trip over badly paved country roads in a broken-down second-hand car was a daunting one. My parents had made it once, years before I was born, to show my sister off to them when she was little, and now it was my turn.

The trip had seemed endless to me, but I had been too carsick to be bored. Once there, however, I found Auntie Dubbie and Uncle Simkhe well worth the effort. They both adored my mother and made a great fuss over me. They lived in a dark, musty old house with—imagine!—the bedrooms upstairs. And, best of all, they had a hen house! Every morning, Auntie Dubbie took me with her when she went to collect the eggs. Who knew that it was chickens who made eggs?

But there was a fly in the ointment. When Nature called, my mother took me upstairs to the bathroom, of course. But there was no potty-chair to be seen. What was I to do? My mother seemed unaware of the seriousness of the situation.

"Auntie Dubbie doesn't have any little children," she explained. Indeed, she didn't. She had four grandchildren by then, and every one of them was older than I. "I guess you will just have to sit on the toilet, like Mommy and Daddy."

In those days, toilets were chest high, and the hole in the middle yawned like the jaws of a hungry shark. "No! I can't!" I wailed. "I'll fall in!"

"Nonsense," comforted my mother. "I'm right here. I will hold you. Don't be scared."

Hmm. No solitude. No songs. No dogs. What a concept! And could my mother really be trusted not to let me fall in?

Mother conducted herself like a trouper. It was the first time for me, but she behaved like a woman with prior experience. The next day, I made less of a fuss. By the time we returned home, my potty-chair had been replaced by a sturdy wooden stool, which enabled me to climb up and down by myself. It also served as a footrest when I played with my dogs. It had a slot in the top to permit easy carrying. I thought it had been made just for me, but it had really been designed to help housewives hang out their wash in those places where the clothesline was out of their reach. Like the potty-chair before it, my stool had seen years of service in that capacity before being promoted to its present position. It was just the right height for a toddler to sit on, and I very quickly became even more attached to it than I had been to the potty-chair, probably because, by slipping my fingers through the slot in the top, I could carry it with me everywhere—indoors and out. It quickly became known, by both family and neighbors alike, as "Bobby's Chair."

Strangely enough, I didn't even notice when, during one of our many changes of address, it got left behind. Ah, fickle child that I was! Forever looking forward, never looking back! I guess I'm still doing that. I can forget how to drive while I learn to go up and down the stairs with my new cane. I can forget how to dial a number on my rotary phone while I learn to master the amplifier on my computerized telephone. I can forget about many of my favorite foods (well, most of the time) while I learn how to manage the purchase, dosage, and timing of dozens of pills every day. Yes, my attention is constantly being called forward. But, today, looking backward is just a little exception.

Dining Room Chair Episode

Sharon L. Voeller

We had purchased some new chairs for sitting by our dining room table. They had aluminum frames and padded seats. Some years later, the chairs were getting old, and the aluminum frames would slowly bend easily when we sat in them. I mentioned to Paul that we ought to get new chairs. Paul's comment was, "Let's wait until they give up totally."

We had Thanksgiving dinner that year at our house. I was concerned that our daughter-in-law, who was pregnant, would sit in that particular chair, and the chair would give way. I forgot to take that chair away from the table. We all sat down to a wonderful Thanksgiving dinner and were eating when, all of a sudden, Paul seemed to be disappearing. Paul had gotten the faulty chair and was sinking to the floor slowly.

Everyone started laughing while Paul was disappearing. He didn't stop eating or look surprised as he sank to the floor. Paul commented, "I didn't spill a drop!"

Messages in the Sand

Dorothy Parcel

...Lessons

When I was a kid, we lived in the dust bowl of Oklahoma. My mother spent the days sweeping dust and getting sheets ready to dunk in water to hang over doors and windows. She worked on a very short fuse, so my sisters and I spent as much time with Dad as we could.

My dad owned the local garage, where he put tractor pistons in cars in hope of making them run a few miles more. Cars, trucks, and farm machinery that no longer worked was stored behind the garage. There's no place greater for kids to play than a junk yard.

The garage smell was a combination of rubber tires, gasoline, grease, and, I guess, dust from far-off Canada. My sisters and I loved hanging around the garage. Sometimes, Dad gave us pennies for candy. He let us play with the tools and pretend to fix things. It was at the garage that we learned to cuss.

Unlike my sisters, I sometimes let my talent get out of hand. One day, my dad was discussing the preacher's car with him. Dad, the Reverend, and his son were hunched over the motor. I was perched on the front bumper, ready to help out.

"We can't imagine what went wrong," the preacher said. "It was going along fine, and it started coughing."

"Well," I said, "I think it's this son-of-a-bitch right here."

My dad snatched me up with the speed of light, swatted my butt, and aimed me toward home.

Despite all that, I'd always had a soft spot for auto repair shops—until last week, when our savings got creamed to fix our old clunker.

...Sick Days

My regular doctor was out that day, and I was sick enough to go to urgent care, so I had to take pot-luck. Luckily, I got a doctor who was very thorough. The first thing I learned in this adventure was that every step needs patience. Not on my part. No. I'm always reasonable.

The nurse weighed me, measured my temperature, and took my blood pressure. Then she did the blood pressure again on another machine. Then she did it a third time. I began to wonder if I had died and hadn't noticed.

Then they sent me to the lab. First, they drew enough blood to measure every possible parameter, including the distance to the moon. After that, they handed me a tiny cup and told me to pee in it. This torture was invented by a man, I feel sure. For women, it's a major and messy operation.

After that, they let me see the doctor. He was at a computer, frowning at my lab results. Finally, he turned away from the computer and greeted me. He was a nice young man, and I knew he'd spent his time in doctor school, learning important things, for the first thing he did was rinse his hands in ice water before he began his examination.

When he had finished, he ordered the nurse to put two pints of joy juice in my vein. It worked so well, I asked for some to take home, but he said, "No." Sometimes, doctors are so selfish.

Anyway, he did the best he could with what he had to work with. I couldn't ask for more.

…Babies

Babies tackle life the way we all would—if we had the nerve. When they see something interesting, they stare at it, often without blinking, for long periods of time. In a restaurant the other day, a year-old boy decided I was the most fascinating thing he'd ever seen. He twisted around in his high chair until he was almost sitting backward. I had long ago figured out why babies were interested in me: it's the white hair. No one in their family has that, and they feel it deserves all their attention.

Anything babies feel like doing, they do, and manners be damned. If they want to blow spit bubbles, they do. If they want to poop in their diaper, in public, with sound effects, they do. If they want something, they bawl as loudly as they can, so everyone snaps to attention.

They do all these things where they have the greatest effect. Restaurants are a good place, and so is church. The very best place is at three in the morning, after the parents have been out partying.

Mommies like to dress their little ones in fancy clothes: ruffles for girls, manly suits for boys. I have seen babies spit up on these fancy creations, but they often save that for special occasions. A good time to lose the last meal is upon being handed to Grandma, who is wearing her new black dress. Daddies are a good target, too, and if Daddy is in his best suit, old milk makes a nice contrast.

This uninhibited behavior is interesting to watch from a distance of space and time. My own children were born well before the end of the last century, and so I enjoy other people's children.

All this may be humiliating to their parents now. Just wait until the babies become teenagers.

…Words

After many years of dealing with the male sex, it has finally penetrated that, although we speak the same language, words mean different things to men and women.

When my sons were young, they sometimes came home muddy, bloody, and wearing torn clothes.

"What happened?"

"Nothing."

"Where have you been?"

"Nowhere."

"What were you doing?"

"Playing."

If the police didn't come, we left it at that.

I've found that the word "party" means different things to men and women. To women, it means dressing up, seeing friends, and possibly meeting new people. Men look on the word the way they do "torture" or "shopping." They cluster in a corner and mutter among themselves. "Mingle" and "converse" mean nothing to them. We were watching a football game on television, and at half time a tiny blond girl interviewed an enormous steaming lineman. I listened for a while, trying to understand what the man was saying.

"Is he speaking a foreign language?" I asked.

"He's sweating," himself answered.

Well, I could see that! In that moment, I had an epiphany. The reason men and women don't understand each other has to be genetic.

...Room Mates

Dogs are interesting in that they don't mind showing their likes and dislikes. For instance, they don't see anything wrong in peeing on the floor, if they get mad at me. Naturally, they don't do this often, because it makes the boss (me) shriek and flail around with a mop, and the language could strip paint.

Dogs are conservative, for they have their own place to eat and sleep, and they resent any change. And yet, if they get a chance, they climb on my bed and roll around, moaning with pleasure. They know I won't sleep in a bed that smells of dog.

I'm not good at training dogs (or kids), but I did teach the family Airedale to smile. This is not a sight you want to witness unless there is a good stout fence between you.

Our oldest dog is Boots, a Manchester Terrier mix. He is sixteen years old now and, because of his vast age, I give him a little treat in the evening. I don't give it to him too early, or he'll forget. He starts prancing, his ears straight up, his eyes popping.

"You forgot my treat," he says. "You're getting that old-timers disease, aren't you?"

"Yes," I answer. "But I remember feeding you, you tiny con-dog."

I like dogs because they don't judge. They don't mind if I go around in a ragged tee shirt and tennis shoes while doing the chores. Sometimes, they allow me to sit on my own couch.

...Charlie

Charlie waited at our gate for hours before we noticed that he had been dumped by some fine monster. After being invited in, he came slowly, modestly. After a few days, to bring his weight up, we visited the vet, for which he never blamed us. But on his annual visits to the dog hospital, he rolls his eyes and dispenses massive amounts of drool on the floor, the weight table, and our shoes.

On his first visit, the vet pronounced Charlie a black lab mix. I have never been able to guess what "mix" meant, except that he is large, 90 pounds now, so possibly one of his forebears was a Great Dane, or maybe a moose.

We live in area where, if we don't have big dogs, we get robbed a lot. We haven't been robbed since Charlie took up guardianship of our house and yard. Not that there haven't been some tries. One cold night, some unfortunate male lost his pants, shoes, and, likely, some of his hide on an invasion try.

I don't mean to infer that Charlie is perfect. No! He has his little crotchets, as do we all. He doesn't like strangers, crows, or hot air balloons. Strangers aren't a problem, if they're with us. He's always ready to make new friends, but he lets us know that, if they begin to act funny, he'd be willing to eat them. I've been told that, if we're not home, he hurls himself at the gate and threatens all kinds of dire consequences if they don't go away.

Crows sit in the trees and shriek curses at Charlie, then they fly away, laughing. This behavior offends Charlie deeply. He runs around barking threats until they're out of sight. He thinks cursing is very low class.

Hot air balloons leave from the local airport in the cool early morning hours, and the wind usually blows them near our house. The pilots have learned not to come too close, for we have a thermal, and if they get captured they go around and around until they give up and land. The crew sometimes come over and thank Charlie for getting them down safely. I thank them for exercising my dog. The whole drama makes Charlie stiff-legged with pride.

Charlie is eight years old now and has grown a white moustache and goatee, which makes him look very dapper. It's a sign that age has crept up on both of us. I don't care. We are both getting older, even if we're no wiser.

Cosmo Dog

Flora Gamez Grateron

We were a young family when he arrived
the kids spun him on the floor like a dust mop,
used him as a personal ottoman to rest their feet
blew on his face to watch him run madly in circles
and displayed him in show-and-tell at school.

He never protested, just went along with the game
was undaunted when he fell into the pool, leash and all
protested at javelinas invading his space, and
could challenge a jackrabbit's jumping
record if he felt like it.

He knew how to be a gentleman, polite
and respectful, never pushy or forward
and had manners that most teens lack,
he learned to adjust to stages of age
as the kids grew older and busier.

He calmed one with anxiety issues as
she struggled to quiet the demons inside,
consoled another when her first boyfriend
broke her heart, and watched the parade of
friends and family coming and going.

Soon the eldest left home and the family grew
smaller. The next two left for college and became
roommates and best friends. Finally, it was time
for the youngest to leave. By then, he could barely
see her clearly but knew she was leaving.

Arthritis set in and he suffered the ache of
painful joints. The running had stopped,
jumping became intolerable, and he kept
bumping into walls, but he persisted, intent
on reaching two decades of life.

Hands caressed his crooked joints when they
came home to visit. Their words of encouragement
went unheard. He searched for familiar faces but
saw only blurry images. He recognized them by
scent alone.

They threw a family party for him, tossed confetti,
wore fancy party hats and placed one on his bowed
head, blew out the candles for him, and took
lots of pictures. He was too tired to care.

One day he moved in with the eldest who was
willing to care for him in his old age, and
his friend's puppy moved in with them; a
ball of energy who ran circles around him.

Suddenly the sands shifted.

New surroundings, a new friend, isolated no longer
and in closer proximity to the college girls who live close by,
a rejuvenation that was unfathomable has begun;
he enters his golden years with dignity, and his grace
has returned; he resides in an essence of contentment.

Cosmo slips effortlessly into his twilight years,
but the paw print he leaves in our hearts remains forever.

Hans
   —for my cousin, Herman

Eleanor Little

My best friend
lies on a steel table
at the Veterinary E.R.
He lights the room,
tawny satin fur the
color of a Hershey bar.

Paws and legs relaxed,
noble head at ease,
muscles at rest—
and he's gone.

They said he'd come home in
a day or two. But
he crossed the rainbow bridge
today.

> *Gone!*
> *I want him back.*
> *I beg you,*
> *raise him like Lazarus.*

 We went everywhere together
the bank, post office,
a park where he ran with joy,
played ball for hours.

He bounded across grass
in snow, sun, or rain,
muscles taut,
long legs like wind.

> *No more can I touch him,*
> *a comfort in the night*
> *next to my bed,*
> *watch TV, he on my couch.*

He waited as I cooked
fresh chicken, vegetables, steak,
to savor big mouthfuls
and lick his bowl clean.

There is no click of toenails
on the stairs;
no elegant head
to lay my hand on.

> *Hans, when I die*
> *we'll be together again.*
> *I'll join you in Heaven—*
> *please run to me then.*

Dog Daze

Albert J. Stumph

Although I must have grown attached to her, and considerable evidence supports that she had become attached to me, I never counted myself among the fans of our family dog. Now I'm questioning that. After nearly fifteen years of complaining about her, we had her put down a couple of weeks ago, and I miss having Haley around.

That's not the reaction I expected. And I've been wondering why I have been using the rather curious phrase, "had her put down," to speak about our decision to end her life. What actually happened was that Kathy drove her to the vet, who administered euthanasia and cremated her. Nonetheless, when someone asks me, "Where's Haley?" I usually reply, "We had her put down. She was old, in pain, and not eating."

The euphemisms we Americans employ to avoid saying "died" are legion. We might say, "Mom passed on." "Sue fell asleep in the Lord." " Dad was called home." And on and on.

I suppose this is all part of our avoidance of any discussion of death and dying, or even of the aging process. I recall the occasional assignment to meditate on my own death during the thirteen years I prepared for the priesthood. What I don't recall was any serious attempt on my part to do so. After all, I was young during those years, so denial of my own death was as natural as my curiosity about girls. And girls were definitely a more enjoyable focus for meditation.

Since those days of theology studies, I've added a few years to my experience with both death and girls. I probably don't understand girls much better than I did many years ago, but I think I have learned from my varied encounters with death, including those occasions when my own mortality has been made obvious to me.

Here are two things I've learned:

- Death happens.

- I'm within striking distance of seventy years, so by actuarial tables my death is more imminent than it used to be.

Because I've gained this knowledge, I've made these decisions:

- I want to enjoy the aging process, so I'm postponing my death for a few more years.
- If that does not work, well, I'll just enjoy being alive in the present, because that's what life is.

Haley made her final trip to the vet after the equivalent of ninety years of human life. Not a bad deal for someone whose primary lifelong interests were food and affection, coupled with an astounding ability to sleep. She had lost interest in the opposite sex following an operation early in her life. And on that final ride to the vet she struggled, but eventually managed to stand up. She put her head out the car's window and enjoyed the wind in her face.

Life with a Cateran[1]

Claudia Poquoc

I live with a meddler, a plunderer—
a Catalan from Catalonia.
Not exactly a blood relative but
kin just the same—
a marauder with Scottish roots,
red hair and freckles.

He brings catastrophy in his wake.
Occupies my bed, my chair.
Expects to be fed on demand.
He acts like a breadwinner;
brings home morsels to share—
always fresh and often bloody.

I've contracted catalepsy
lasting for hours,
especially when I see him
catapult toward a lizard
he's marked for our table.

I try to thwart him, lock him inside,
deaf to his pleas,
pussyfooting to protect his feelings.
Has it helped? Has it stopped him?
Categorically, NO!

We're both animals with
willful natures. I curtail
his antics while advancing his guile.
As for myself, I'm learning
to let nature take its course. It is either
that or end up in a catacomb. GRRRR!

---

[1] cateran - a Scottish Highland's robber

Chat with a Cat

Anne Whitlock

It was a typical Tuesday evening with the cat
draped over my lap. We were watching Judge
Judy. An irate landlord was ranting on and on
about his trashy tenant when I heard the defendant
say, "Rub the other ear." I killed the remote.

"Oh Tiger," I cried, "how did you learn English?"
"Do you know how many hours of TV I've
listened to?" he answered. "You precious darling,"
I blurted, "is there a God? Is there life after death?"
"How should I know," he said. "I'm just a cat."

"But this is a miracle—" "A miracle," he said,
"is when they invented Whiskas Temptations."
"Do you know what this means?" I told him.
"We'll be on Fox News, on CNN, on Larry King,
on Animal Planet— We'll tour the world!"

"Speak for yourself," he said. "I'm staying right
here." He looked at me, his moonstone eyes swimming
out of their galaxies, right into my soul. "Tiger," I risked,
"Do you love me?" "If you don't know that by now,
you're as stupid as a mouse. Shut up and rub the other ear."

Special Delivery

Marilyn L. Kish Mason

Rusty was not happy being stuffed in a cardboard box and taken for a ride in the minivan. His little nose and paws kept poking out through the closed flaps as he tried to make his escape. His meowing was pitiful. He did not know it, but he was being "catnapped" for a noble purpose.

Hours had gone into the planning of this "kitty caper;" now we just needed to pull it off. Awkwardly, we carried our hostage from the parking structure to the elevator. Afraid of detection and expulsion from the building, we sneaked through the heavy metal doors on the third floor. There was no one in sight. Our accomplices were late, and timing was everything. "No pets allowed." We could soon be in big trouble.

We heard the echo down the long hallway before we spied our partners in crime. At last, they rounded the corner and were in sight. It was slow going for Dad, who was pushing Danica in the wheelchair. Wheeling along behind was an IV line attached to her arm. You see, she was receiving treatment on the Oncology ward of The Children's Hospital in Denver, Colorado. Danica was recovering from her second operation in four months for a malignant brain tumor that was now growing again.

Danica was weak and fragile from the ravages of the operations and radiation and chemotherapy treatments. She was very withdrawn and had not been eating. Her once sunny disposition had deteriorated since this latest surgery. We had not seen that precious smile in days. She seemed to be increasingly giving in to the pain.

We were desperate to break through the wall that Danica had built around herself. Our family tried everything we could think of to cheer her, but to no avail. Thus, our little conspiracy began to hatch. We knew it was impossible to get permission to bring Rusty to her room, so we decided to take matters into our own hands. Nine-year-old Danica always had a love for animals. Rusty, a beautiful yellow tabby, had been her favorite pet ever since he came to the family as a kitten.

As Danica approached, she appeared too weak to look up. She slumped in her wheelchair. Her mother removed Rusty from the box and placed him on Danica's lap. For a split second, there was no reaction, and then a look of pure joy spread across her pale face. Her incredible topaz eyes were once again shining brightly. As Rusty began to play, delighted giggles erupted from the once silent little girl. Rusty nestled in her lap, and she cradled him in arms bruised and swollen from the IV needles. Rusty purred and contentedly fell asleep, exhausted from his ordeal in the box.

On that day, we knew our brave little Danica was still with us, that she still had the will to recover. She would soon return home to Rusty and her loving family. Danica had a long struggle ahead, but for now her grateful parents and grandmother watched the scene with misty eyes. We would always remember the day that Rusty, the tiny yellow tabby, brought joy and hope to The Children's Hospital.

Harmony

Kathleen Elliott-Gilroy

In the apex of my thumb
and forefinger

the six week old kitten
droops his head

as if this place is now
a sheltering womb

his body thrums
a soft toned purr—
no interludes—

steady assuredness
as if his stream of life
is finding its true course

the tone reverberates
across the bowl
of my cupped palm

and sifts its mantra
into my bones

so we are now co-species
humming positive energy
into the universe

Summer Dream

Jean Chapman Snow

Two Siamese drowse,
dreaming of twilight safaris in warm sands,
each a small still Sphinx
on its own sunwarmed concrete step.
Blue eyes closed, heads tilted against the sun,
their ears swivel at far-off sounds,
but it is too soon to yawn and stretch
for the evening hunt.

Below, unmoving and unseen,
a tiny satin ribbonsnake
hugs the warm riser of the bottom step
until a door softly clicks
and the snake vanishes in such a silent
quick
        silver
                slide
that not a whisker nor a chocolate ear
flicks. It is too soon.

Take-out Dinner

Barbara Ostrem

The inquisitive onlookers at the end of the dock were curiously intent on watching the fisherman a few yards away while he, happily absorbed in the task at hand, seemed oblivious to their scrutiny. He glanced briefly at their whiskered cheeks and went about cleaning the large trout he had fought hard to land just an hour ago.

He and his friend had looked forward to this jaunt to Loon Lake all during the work week. Ted had fished these familiar waters many times and was anxious to prove to Rob that it would be a great morning, trolling the great blue lake named for the black ducks with mournful calls that nested there. Rob had not caught a fish and was enduring the friendly jibes about his failure as an angler.

When they had loaded their gear in the rental boat earlier in the day, the owner had cautioned them to keep an eye on their catch if they planned on getting home with it. The onlookers were in fact a pair of newcomers, river otters who were skillfully practiced in the art of distraction and thievery, he told them, and they were quite adept at both.

That explained their quirky behavior: diving and rolling and popping their heads up frequently to be sure they were being seen. At least, one of them was. Stealthily, the larger of the duo glided quietly under the dock to a spot just beneath where Ted knelt, and with great precision snagged the tail of the prized trout and pulled it downward through the space between planks!

With his mouth agape, the knife still grasped in his hand, Ted looked with astonishment at the spot where his trout had just lain. Rob burst into laughter, and the dock owner grinned broadly. "Didn't I warn ya, young fella?" he said, then added, "Now ya see it, now ya don't!"

But worst of all was the sound of crunching and munching as the delighted otters dined on their catch just inches below the weathered planks.

Encounters with Crows

Ellaraine Lockie

The *caw-caw* from low in an acacia tree
grated like sandpaper
Too close and aggressive to be conversational
More like the threat of thunder
Or an adrenaline needle plunged into memory
of a black storm a foot from my face
Eyes as still as the storm's center
offset by slap of wings and flap of beak

The cause of a daily walk with weapons
An umbrella or baseball bat
and the armor of a wide-brimmed hat
Yet the pummeling from my own heart
The rock of dread so heavy and deep that Hitchcock
has buried his playground scene beneath it

These ghosts do not rest in peace
They peck away in want of recognition
for the job of nature's clean-up crew
For transforming death into life
They want awareness for black bigotry
and encroachment of orchards and fields
From those who hear the unnerving calls but not
the varied clicks, rattles and bell-like tones
Music ignored by those
who mistake the need for nest hair
as an act of aggression

One morning the sky blurs with half notes
Airwaves carry a cacophony of *caws*
In the oak tree hundreds of crows
hunch their shoulders with each cry
A sandpaper shield covering a baby fallen from its nest
And I feel the rock move in my chest
The *whoosh* of wings as Hitchcock's ghosts fly away

Handfuls of cat food litter the patio now
A plastic bag with brown curly hair protruding
from holes hangs from an oak tree
I sometimes sit in the back yard straining to hear
sounds that hint of childhood church bells
Like it was Easter Sunday

Note from a Cobalt Azure Butterfly

Carrie Ann Howell

Up north you found me insecure
On the brink of extinction you captured
Me. Awestruck by my natural azure
Color, then created expenditure.

Failing to exist,
You protected me and persist
I should not decease.
Oh! Me you did not deceive.

Though my kind is rare
My life, you did spare.
Placed me and a mate as suggested pair
For multiplication, we could share.

Not a matter, I am frail
Fragile and small as a thumbnail,
You observed me and did not fail,
Encage me in a see-through pail.

You kept me and provided deer weed
And plenty of delicious locoweed
Where we can breed
Oh Yes! And our young we feed.

Although our life is not very long
And we are not very strong
Yet! "We belong."
And you can hear our song.

Freed periodically from the pail of plastic
My first flight to find sugary nectar
I find a large yellow flower to peck
Then uncurl my snout to sip and enjoy.

Thousands of us were bred in captivity.
Then released! Captured! Rebred!
Once each year you let us go, the same time
I don't mind.

Back from nearly dead
Not us you overfed
Never even mislead
Then we are able to proceed

Though I miss my freedom
I thought I had in the wilderness
Among trees, bushes and others like me
You found me and the other three.

Out there where wild flowers
Grew, I was free
To flutter, fly, and sway
And even sip cool spring waters.

Oh! We would be not
To protect us four
If you were distraught
We would be no more.

Thank you conservationist,
And biologists
For going the distance
To preserve our existence

Sincerely Blue Azure Butterfly

For Creation, Benediction

Joan T. Doran

Bless all who leap, or run, or sidle
through the wooded glens, or rest
in burrows where they tend their young—
and all who fly upon earth's surging breath,
eye scanning for the merest
stirring of the grass, for shadow
near the water's surface,
for they are kin to one another,
and each other's sustenance.
Bless them in their infinite diversity,
their fur and scales, their feathers shining
in the sun, bless their sinuous passage
through the seas, bless them for thundering
across the veldt, and for
small passage over opening leaf.
Bless their roars and chatter,
upward-rising song and bellow,
those that sentinel the morning,
those that animate the night,
and bless us, their fellow creatures,
we who give them names.

Bless, too, those lovers of the world,
who, through their wonder in the other,
their delight of senses, mind, invention,
fuse the passions of the earth
to ecstacy of heaven, who, in giving selves
completely to another, are renewed.
Bless structures lovers build from trust,
bless gentleness, bless stumbling,
bless kindnesses, bless truthful words,
bless promises, whether kept or lost,
for both arise from the same hope,
bless hearts that transform all through love,
and give us, please, such hearts.

Bless those who clown,
who will not be ignored,
who throw their dignity
to heedless winds,
bless balls they throw into the air,
bless unconcern for falling down,
bless those who jumble into one
to separate as many, bless
how their colors blare and clash
in raucousness and impudence,
bless their silent painted mouths,
bless the rude sounds blurting
from their earth-bound bodies,
bless their outlandish dress
that mocks conformity's conceit,
bless the mirrors they hold up
for us to see ourselves in truth
and folly.

And for a moment may we dance
together on this throbbing fragment,
thankful that Creation somehow needs
Earth's wildly beating heart.

La Sabanilla de San Pasqual[1]

Rita Ries

a name conferred by Spanish soldiers in the 1700s
when they saw the poppies of California's shores.
Traveling inland, the brilliant carpet graced
the hills before them for twenty-five miles.
Civilization has now vanquished them to one area,
the Antelope Valley Reserve—
where antelopes no longer roam
but snakes lurk near pathways.

They flow over low Tahachapi hills
like rivers of orange gold.
Blossoms sway in the winds,
ripple like ponds in low spots, frame
Lupine, Red Stem Filaree and Cream Cups.
The California's state flower
exhibits its radiant performance art
for only a few weeks in the spring,
but catches one's breath at each vivid hill,
filling a soul to almost bursting.

Church being a long way off for a shepherd,
Saint Pascal communed with God
kneeling amidst Spain's fields of wildflowers.
I imagine him breathing in their silent beauty,
taking a long, reverent time, connecting
to his maker, his humble thanks so evident.
He probably made friends with rattlesnakes.

NOTE OF INTEREST: The most beautiful area of poppies was once called Rancho San Pasqual. Today it's known as Pasadena, Altadena, and Sierra Madre, California.

---

[1] The Altar-cloth of Saint Pascal

The Unexpected Guest and His Nocturnal Dip

John J. Brennan

Almost all veterinarians at one time or another are awakened in the middle of the night to care for a cat or dog hit by a car. Large animal vets are awakened more often for bovine dystocia cases (difficulty having a calf). Rarely, equine practitioners have to respond to birthing problems with mares. Mixed practitioners can expect all of the above problems, plus those cases that can be classed only as *bizarre*.

"Dr. Brennan, there's a horse in my swimming pool!"

Now that is bizarre. My client, Mr. Z, was totally unnerved and almost shouting into the telephone. I wasn't quick enough at 3 a.m. to respond, "It's okay, sir, they swim very well," but my brain did flash on with, "Is it your horse, and do you have a shallow end in your pool?"

The agitated caller replied *"No!"* and *"No!"*

By now, I'm really awake.

"Whose horse is it?"

"I don't know."

"Well, you must have neighbors who have horses. Find out if anyone is missing a horse and, by the way, do you know anyone who operates a tow truck? One with a sling hoist?"

Twenty minutes later, I'm on the scene, and I observe a very agitated equine making repeated attempts to climb out of his aquatic trap. My client reports that he has located the owner, and I stifle a large inward laugh as I'm told it belongs to Dr. Rowe's wife. *He'll owe me one for this one*, I muse. Dr. Rowe is a colleague who confines his practice to small animals. I usually take care of his wife's horses.

"Is she coming with a halter?"

"Yes."

"Have you contacted a tow truck?"

"Yes."

"With a sling hoist?"

"Yes."

"Well, then, all we can do is wait for a few minutes. Hopefully, Mrs. Rowe can quiet and assure her horse that he'll be okay without anyone getting hurt. I don't want to attempt to sedate the creature until we absolutely have to, if at all."

Dee Rowe rushed over through a hedgerow with a halter. I could see she was very frightened as I greeted her. "Good Morning, Dee. Try to calm yourself. Is Fred coming to help?" Fred Rowe, her husband, is a friend of mine and the colleague who barely tolerates his wife's equine passion.

"No, he's out of town," Dee replied.

"Well, then, Dee, you and I will have to halter your renegade runaway and control him with two lines, while our hoist truck lifts him out of the pool after we pass the sling under his belly."

We eventually accomplished all of the above with no injury to man or beast. When I checked a dripping wet equine, who felt very relieved, himself, to be on dry land, I found a few minor scrapes of little consequence.

Dee then marched him back home and made sure his stall was double-locked. I made my exit as dawn was breaking. I never did find out who paid for the tow truck and damage to the pool. My fee was paid by my client, the pool owner, and every once in a while I collect a chuckle, even a laugh, when we ask Dr. Fred about his wife's midnight swimming horse. I only wish I had called the local TV station to come along on the tow truck!

Horses usually swim very well and are fine if they're under control and able to enter and exit bodies of water via a gradual slope. In our area, the Saratoga Raceway, a racetrack for Standardbred racers—trotters and pacers who race with the cart and driver behind—has a therapeutic equine pool. This deep circular water tank has a built-in gradual runway ramp for easy in and out. Horses are exercised by swimming without pounding their legs and hooves on hard surfaces. It works very very well for many racehorses with lameness.

Dee and her horse recovered very well. My client's pool suffered a few scrapes. But Fred Rowe, DVM, will never be allowed to forget about his wife's floundering equine!

Watered Down Memories

Phyllis J. Seltzer

The water's heat penetrates my body, embracing me with healing kisses. I feel its deep soothing massage relaxing my muscles. Ahh… healing heaven! Glistening droplets streak the frosted glass door of the shower and jolt awake bits and pieces of long forgotten memories that seem to be reflected within their exquisite water art. Like shooting stars, past lived memories come alive as I gaze at the wet designs, wrapped securely in the water's warm, comforting hug.

I remember, as a little girl in the Bronx, lying in bed in my parents' apartment on Tryon Avenue after a frightening tonsillectomy. That was the bad news, but now it was time for the good news to begin. The antidote for the surgery was that I got to lie in their bed and receive the neighborhood guests who came to cheer me up. Best of all, we would get to eat ice cream out of dixie cups—more than one, they said. It would help my throat feel better.

The room was dark; the bed was big and made of dark wood. The Venetian blinds were drawn, and it seemed shadowy in the bedroom, but the ray of light would be the promised dixie cups, half chocolate and half vanilla. Junior, the bully from across the street, came to see me. I was only six and he was ten, so I was surprised to see him among the other people in the room. He said it was because I was just home from the hospital, but it wasn't really so—it was the ice cream he wanted. We found that out when he said goodbye after a while, and the ice cream left with him—all six treasured dixie cups, too. I am still disappointed, right here in the warm shower, even now at this advanced age.

The dripping water against the frosted door shines and sets off firefly lights and with it a new old memory, different from the Bedroom in the Bronx, with its shadows and dark thoughts of lost ice cream. This memory is sunny and bright, a crisp new day set out on blades of green grass and trees. There's a lake with a pool cribbed off within it for the younger children to swim in safely. We're in the Catskill Mountains of New York State. It's summertime, glorious time, away from the concrete and high rises of the Bronx—no crowds, no noise, just the sweet smell of fresh mountain air, and my three aunts and six cousins to play with all day. We share a huge stone house together with my brother and my mother. The dads come up on the weekends, after work, with treats like red pistachio nuts that stain my fingers all summer long, and baseballs and bats for the boys for their weekly games, and dolls or paper cutouts for the girls. We swim and sing songs and play checkers and cards all day and tell ghost stories at night. My family and I have the entire ground floor of the stone mansion, where each family has their own kitchen and bedrooms. Each morning, I'm lured to Aunt Lena's kitchen by the smell of her pineapple fritters, and I still smell them today.

Another large family rents the upper floor, and we all get along. Sydell, their cousin, suffers from cystic fibrosis and can't do as many things as the rest of us. And there's Billy Breakstone, with his fragile build, big dark eyes, and dark hair. We play board games each night with Sydell, and Billy and the boys practice basketball and running. We have no televisions sets, no email or computers—not even a telephone that I can remember in that big house, although there must be one somewhere. We're never bored and life is so good up here.

Of course, there are challenges, like the current of the lake that spills into the cribbed off pool. One of the boys serves as our lifeguard. One day, I find myself gulping mouthfuls of water while he's busy watching the pretty older girls. With each step I try to take into shallower water, I'm pulled two steps back, until I'm practically drowning. Then my father, arriving for the weekend, sees me and yells to him. Finally, I'm fished out, barely able to breathe. So there are challenges, I know, but by and large it's wonderful to be here.

But then the sound comes, the sound I still hear with great clarity. It's a sound I've never before or since heard. It's the sound of Billy Breakstone's head cracking open. The sound carries through all the laughter of the weekend baseball game we've all attended. No one recognizes the sound—the sound of terror—as my cousin Hank's bat splits Billie's head open. And when we do recognize it, the impact of it becomes a memory tattoo that can't be washed away.

That sound has left an indelible imprint, and it's here with me in my wet cocoon these sixty-five years later. Thankfully, Billy Breakstone survived and recovered, though I'm not sure my cousin Hank ever did. But out of all the red pistachio finger-stained and pineapple fritter summer delights of memory, for some unknown reason the sound of Billy's head cracking is what comes to me from within the water's shards of light, igniting bursts of memories as if brought to me on the backs of fireflies.

The water has run cold. I'm anxious to escape the cold embrace I no longer can bear to feel, and I open the shower door to leave.

Coming of Age
—for Mary

Eileen M. Ward

Cousined by our sister-mothers,
we youthful women
slipped softly that summer into Celtic mists,
gently wrapped in memories of your Irish childhood.

Our meeting erased the ocean separation of our lives,
and in those weeks
we pedaled boreens[1] over boggy ground
losing your Irish and my American ways
to become our mothers in their early years.

Each sister chose her way
between emigration or arranged marriage,
and we, their daughters, reaped
the bounty of their courage:
our options were boundless.

We slept on creaky iron beds
in our ancestral cottage,
then rose amid whispers
of early twentieth century days
when pungent peat smoke wafted upward
to swallow the ewer-frost
on too-early winter mornings.

Under Irish skies
ever likely to sparkle into double rainbows,
we met ourselves: spidery duplicates
of the women who shaped our lives.

Our laughter mingled
with the music of the sea,
that summer of my fifteenth year
when you were twenty-two.

---

[1] back roads

The Knot Hole

Anne McKenrick

Shortly after I had my house built, to give myself some privacy I had a fence installed around my property. The first thing I noticed was that there was a knot hole in one of the boards in the back yard, and that was a little annoying to me. It was a little larger than the size of a baseball and provided a perfect peek hole through which to spy. Fat lot of privacy that will afford me, I thought to myself. There wasn't really anything I could do about it—the fence was installed, and I could hardly ask the builder to replace one board because it had a knot hole—don't all fences have knot holes? I guess. I don't know much about wood, but it looked like the knotty pine I had seen in people's rec rooms and basements. I let it go, and it gradually became just part of the fence. Little did I know the many uses that would be found for that knot hole!

When my little granddaughter got big enough to play outside, the fence made the back yard a very safe place for her. One day, when she was about three, I noticed she was over by the knot hole, standing on a little piece of wood that she had pulled and tugged to get positioned just below the hole. Standing on it made her just tall enough to see through the knot hole. Lo and behold, there was another little girl on the other side of the fence, playing in her back yard.

"Grandma, Grandma, guess what! I found a friend through the knot hole."

Pretty soon, the two little girls were getting acquainted and sharing their toys through the knot hole in the fence.

One day, when we had baked cookies, Cheyanne asked, "Grandma, could we share our cookies through the knot hole with my friend?"

"I think that would be super, Chey," I told her. Soon she was outside shoving cookies through the hole.

Another day, they shared their lunch sandwiches through the hole. As the girls got older, not only did things get shared through the knot hole, they also discovered that it was great fun to throw stuff over the top of the fence. That began finding toys (and sometimes food) in my back yard that had been tossed over, and, of course, similar stuff in the other back yard.

The natural progression was for them to go around the fence and play in each other's back yard. We found that Payten was the same age as Cheyanne and in the same grade at school. Every time Cheyanne was at my house, she had to go immediately to Payten's or Payten came to our house. They spent nights and weekends at each other's homes and went on some trips together. They became best friends.

This past week, Cheyanne went camping for several days with Payten and her grandparents in their new motor home. In the middle of the afternoon on Wednesday, Cheyanne called to ask if she could come over to my house. When she came in, giant tears were rolling down her face.

"What's wrong, honey?" I asked, folding my arms around her.

"Payten's mom and dad are getting divorced, and Payten and Parker (her brother) and her mom are going to move. They're living with her sister now. Gram, she's my best friend, and now I won't see her anymore. Oh, Grandma, I met her through the knot hole when we were only three years old, and we've been best friends for eight years. We shared our toys through the knot hole and our lunches."

I hugged her and consoled her and reminded her of her first good friend, Carleigh. They met when they were one and were fast friends for two years. I said maybe someone would move next door who might have a little girl, and Cheyanne could introduce her to the knot hole.

I knew it wouldn't mean much to her, but I was thankful she had had the experience of a best friend for eight years. And, after she left, I thought back over the years and marveled how a little thing like a knot hole in my fence had played such an important part in our lives.

Winner: Best Non-fiction Contest

Blink

Tilya Gallay Helfield

It was snowing heavily the night Joan took me to see Harold. Her little Riley slipped and slid in the deep drifts, and the wipers worked furiously to keep the windshield clear. The heat inside the car magnified every whisper, as though we were entombed in a sound box, while outside the world dissolved behind a scrim of falling snow. Joan parked in the lot and we stamped through the deep drifts, but when I looked back, our footsteps had been covered without a trace.

The hospital corridor smelled of disinfectant and wet fur, and there were too many people in the elevator. When we got to Harold's room, Joan stopped, took a deep breath and pushed open the door. Harold's mother and his brother, Sol, were sitting in the corner. Harold lay on the bed. He knew me at once. His eyes lit up, first with surprise, then pleasure, then filled with tears.

I first saw Harold on a soft summer evening in June 1944. Joan and Ray and I had been sitting on our front verandah all day with our friends, watching while huge men in overalls wrestled heavy dark furniture into the empty house down the block. My best friend, Myrna, and I were hoping the new family had an eleven-year-old girl, like us. Joan and her friend, Marlene, wanted a girl too, but their age, nine. Ray and his friends, Stephen and Donnie, wanted another five-year-old boy.

At the supper table that night we listened to our parents discuss the new neighbours. "Pailishers," my father said. "Came over in '39, just before the war. Probably the last ones to get out." Polish Jews weren't as bad as Rumanian Jews, but both were a cut below our family, who were Litvaks from White Russia.

"They look as though they got off the boat yesterday," my mother said, her nose wrinkling with disdain. "Those clothes! And that furniture!" She and my father were Canadian born and bred, which was the best pedigree of all.

Harold appeared soon after supper. He scuffed down the street, pretending not to notice us, kicking imaginary stones at the curb. Joan and Ray and I and half a dozen neighbourhood kids sat on our front steps and watched him from the corners of our eyes. He shuffled past our house, ignoring our whispers. Suddenly, he wheeled and strode purposefully toward us. When he got to our sidewalk he stopped, reached into his pocket and fished out a switchblade knife. All conversation halted as we stared in fascination at the forbidden weapon. He clicked it open and, with a backward flick of his wrist, flung it at the ground. It landed in the grass inches from Joan's sandaled foot and quivered, glinting in the glare of the setting sun. He pulled it out, stared at us defiantly and asked, "Anybody want a throw?"

Despite my mother's opinion, I thought he looked pretty much like every other boy on the block, in khaki shorts, cotton shirt, and sandals. But there was a foreign look about his hair, which was long and cut straight all around, a marked difference from the G.I brushcuts the other boys had.

"Hey, Soupbowl," they'd holler, just to get a rise out of him. He'd wade into their midst, bony elbows and knees gouging, his hair streaming into his hot red face, and ultimately their taunts settled into a formulaic baiting which held considerable respect and even a little affection. I admired the way he stood up to them. When I walked past them, they hollered, "Hi, Cookie," and when I turned around, they jeered, "Not you, dog biscuit," until my face burned with shame.

Harold was Joan's age, with two brothers and a sister who were all much older. It must have been like having five parents constantly scolding, nagging, and giving him orders, but he ignored them when he could and obeyed them defiantly when he had no choice.

During the long hot summer days, he and the other boys played a game in the street in front of our house called "roll-the-bat," which was a complete misnomer. The batter hit the ball in the air and, while the other boys ran to catch it, he laid the bat down on the road. If one of the fielders caught the ball before the first bounce, he moved to the middle of the road, where the street was smooth, and rolled the ball toward the bat. If it missed the bat, or it hit the bat and bounced up and the batter caught it, he got another turn. If the batter didn't catch it, the kid who rolled the ball got a turn at bat. It was a pretty stupid game with rules that were apparently open to widely varied interpretation. Naturally, this generated frequent arguments in which Harold usually prevailed due to his persistence and his loud shrill voice, with which he protested every unfavourable decision.

Joan and I read or played dolls on our front verandah. Sometimes, when there weren't any boys around, Harold insisted on playing with us. We hated his games, especially one he called "concentration camp," in which he lit forbidden matches, set our dolls on fire and buried them in the gravel driveway beside our house. After supper, we all joined forces to play hide-and-seek until the wartime curfew snuffed the street lights, and we scurried for home past houses now strangely menacing in the sudden darkness.

Harold's family were Orthodox Jews who went to synagogue every Saturday morning. "Professional Jews," my mother sniffed. Like many of our Jewish neighbours, we went to synagogue only three times a year on the High Holy days, or when we were invited to a Bar Mitzvah. On Saturdays, we watched Harold trudge down the street wearing a dark suit with long trousers flapping against his thin ankles and a fedora that would have fallen over his eyes if his ears hadn't held it up. After synagogue, his father tried to make him spend the Sabbath quietly at home with the rest of the family, not cooking, driving, or turning on lights. Instead, Harold got filthy playing football with the other boys in the street in front of our house, while his horrified mother stood on their verandah wringing her hands and calling him to come home.

He had a pretty pretentious name for such a skinny little Jewish kid. It reminded me of the Battle of Hastings (we were studying British history in school) but the idea of Harold sharing the same name with royalty was ridiculous. It was never "Harry" or "Hal," always "Harold." Even so, it might not have caused much comment if it hadn't been for his mother's Yiddish accent. No matter what time of the day or night he was wanted, she would come out on their front verandah, fold her fat arms across her huge bosom, throw her head back and bellow his name. Dropping the initial H, she began with a monumental growl, rolling the V sound at the back of her throat, then swallowed the final letters in a single atavistic howl:

"AAAAARRRRRuldt!"

It was amazing to hear the varying inflections of love, pride, exasperation, and urgency that she could inject into that name. His entire family often joined the chorus: "AAAARRRRRuldt! AAAARRRRRuldt!" until the call was taken up by everyone else within earshot, so that Harold, when he finally heeded it, trudged reluctantly home with his name ringing in his ears.

Once he lost his patience and screamed, "Shut up, Ma. Shut up all of you—shut the Goddamn hell up!" There was a sudden, eerie silence as everyone, children and parents alike, all stopped, aghast that Harold had taken the name of the Lord in vain, and on the Sabbath, yet! Harold's brother, Sol, red-faced with shame, swooped down and carried him home on his hip like a football, while Harold shrieked and his arms and legs waved impotently in the air. It was pretty embarrassing to see him subjected to that kind of public humiliation. I was glad that my parents were so much more liberal.

Harold gave his parents more than one anxious moment. That summer, on a hot Sunday in July, the Lipshitzes took Joan and me to Brighton Beach on the Ottawa River. My mother was preoccupied with a rummage sale for her Hadassah group and was glad to have us taken off her hands for an afternoon. We often begged her to take us to the beach, but she always refused.

"Your father's away on another business trip, and I certainly can't manage all of you by myself. Besides, I'm much too busy to sit on a beach all day, browning like a chicken!" She was very proud of her pale redhead's complexion and thought tanned skin and freckles vulgar.

We drove in Mr. Lipshitz's black Ford—Harold, Joan, and I in the back and his parents in the front. Mrs. Lipshitz fussed continuously, balancing a huge straw picnic hamper in her lap, pulling her tight skirt down over her fat knees and snatching at the wisps of damp hair that whipped from her topknot in the wind of the open car window. She was a short woman with rolls of fat that bulged as though she were made of balloons twisted together, and she had a large nose and suspiciously black hair that she wore twisted into a bun on top of her head.

"Just like Mrs. Katzenjammer in the comics," I whispered to Joan, giggling behind my hands.

Throughout the hour-long hot dusty drive to the beach, I cringed with embarrassment as Mrs. Lipshitz directed a constant stream of admonition and invective at us, her husband, and every other driver on the road. "Kinder, be qviet! Papa, you are going too fast, already! Vatch out for that red car!" and leaning out the open window, "You! In the fency automobile! You are going to a fire, maybe?"

At last we arrived and, after several minutes' discussion about where and how to park the car, we filed through the clanking turnstile and went to change into our bathing suits. Joan and I giggled when Mr. Lipshitz emerged from the men's bathhouse in knee-length black trunks and a striped undershirt. Harold wore a pair of trunks that would take him years to grow into, and his shoulder blades stuck out in back like wings.

Mrs. Lipshitz didn't change. Exhausted by her efforts in getting us there safely, she settled herself under the yellow umbrella, unfastened her garters and, with a contented grunt, rolled down her stockings and planted her calloused toes in the sand. I couldn't help staring at her heavy legs, which were covered with long black hairs. My mother shaved the blond fuzz on her legs and under her arms every morning in the shower.

"Nu, kinder. Now you may go in the vater. But not too deep, remember. Not higher than the knees or you come right away out."

"Aw, Ma, fercornssake," Harold cried.

"It's my last vord."

Joan and I rolled our eyes at each other. Harold muttered his way down to the water, kicking up little eddies of sand in front of him. We paddled for about an hour before we were called for lunch.

Mrs. Lipshitz opened the picnic hamper and pulled out piles of packages wrapped in wax paper—huge portions of chicken legs, brisket and corned beef, rolls of salami, mounds of potato salad and sauerkraut, dill pickles and kasha, enough to feed the entire Russian army, my mother would have said. Mrs L. poured overflowing mugs of lemonade and iced tea, all the while keeping up a constant commentary:

"Papa, have another polka. 'Arold, sveetheart, let me vipe your chin. Nu, kinder. Ess! Ess! Ve have plenty! Ach! These girls! So skinny! They eat notting!"

After lunch, Mr. Lipshitz burped appreciatively and shooed us away like flies. "Go. Play in the sand."

"We'll go back in the water," Harold said.

"Liebschen. Not after such a heavy meal. Vait two hours," Mrs Lipshitz said.

"Ma, fer cryin' out loud, it's only up to my knees!"

"You'll get a cramp!"

"Where, in my ankle? Geez, at least make it a hour! Ma!"

He wheedled. He screamed with rage. It was no use. Joan and I shrugged. Even Harold seemed resigned. The Lipshitzes dozed. Suddenly, Harold was gone. Mrs. Lipshitz ran frantically up and down the beach, her hair streaming down her hot neck. "Ze river!" she shrieked, and there was Harold, swimming furiously.

Mr. Lipshitz ran toward the water. "'Arold! Come right away out! 'Arold! You hear? You vant I should come in after you? Out!" Harold ignored him. Mr. Lipshitz started to wade into the water. Harold went out deeper. His father followed, pleading, "'Arold! Sveetheart! Be a good boy. Come to Papa!"

Harold's head was now a small brown cork, bobbing in the middle of the river. A crowd gathered, pointing at the red rescue boat that knifed toward him. Joan and I stood under the lonely umbrella, clutching each other in terror.

"Will he drown?" she asked. Her teeth were chattering.

"Don't be so stupid," I yelled, furious that she had put my own fears into words. At last the crowd parted, and Harold marched up the beach toward us. My knees shook with relief.

"Didja see me swim?" he demanded. "Didja see how far out I went?" We nodded dumbly. "Didja see the lifeguards come after me? Neat, eh?"

"You were a stupid jerk," I yelled. "Your mother's going to kill you."

Instead, his mother ran up, sobbing, "My baby!" and wrapped a towel around him and covered his face with kisses, completely oblivious to the gaping crowd.

Harold threw the towel on the ground and pushed her away. "Ma, willya cut it out? I don't need it or you or nobody!" he shrieked and ducked under her outstretched arms, charged through the crowd and disappeared into the bathhouse.

On the Jewish holidays, the Lipshitzes adhered to Orthodox Jewish practice. But in secular matters, they tried to behave like their less religious neighbours. So Harold went to school in tweed breeches with leather knee patches, his pockets bulging with slingshot ammunition, balls, baseball cards, sticky coins and keys, and his precious knife, and he played hockey and baseball just like all the other boys. And at the beginning of August he announced that, just like every other kid on the block, he was going to have a birthday party, and we were all invited.

I begged my mother for a new party dress for the occasion. She was reluctant, but had to give in when she saw there was no more hem to let down on my old one. We shopped all Saturday afternoon and finally settled on something we both hated —a white polished cotton covered with huge red and purple roses.

"It looks like a bedspread!" I wailed.

"A most impractical fabric," my mother agreed. "But the price is right. I doubt that material will wash well, and I'm certainly not going to pay good money to have it dry cleaned, so you'd better not spill anything on it."

The party was set out in Harold's back yard on a long picnic table augmented by two smaller tables placed end to end to accommodate the huge quantities of sandwiches, cookies, chocolate ice cream, candy, and cake laid out on them. I was relieved to see that they were serving the usual birthday party fare, Mello-roll ice cream and a proper birthday cake from Woolworth's, complete with little tin favours wrapped in wax paper, just like our mothers served at our parties. Not a verenica or halishka in sight. The only wrong note was that the tables were covered with starched white linen tablecloths instead of the smart plastic place mats my mother always used outdoors.

Mr. Lipshiz organized endless rounds of Pin the Tail on the Donkey, Hide the Thimble and other stupid baby games, instead of the magic shows and home movies our fathers arranged at our parties. Harold didn't seem to notice our disgust. He joined enthusiastically in all the games until his mother called us to the table.

I sat down, but refused to put on the silly party hat Harold handed me. Despite my protests, he grabbed a pointed dunce cap, put it on my head and tried to fix the elastic under my chin. I ducked away from him and the hat flew off, knocking over my glass and spilling chocolate milk all over my dress. Everyone stared at me and, to my horror, I felt tears filling my eyes.

Mrs. Lipshitz smothered me against her huge breast. "There, there, dolling, don't cry," she said.

"My mother will kill me," I moaned.

"Kill? For a dress?" she asked, astounded. She grabbed my hand and pulled me into the kitchen, where she sat me down and handed me a plate of cookies still warm from the oven. "Don't vorry, leibschen. I make it gut like new, nu?" She laughed at her own joke as she whisked off my dress and wrapped me in a cotton housedress she took from a peg behind the door. Then she began to dab at my dress with a clean cloth soaked with soda water. When the stain was gone, she plugged in the iron, spat on its gleaming bottom until it sizzled and ironed my dress dry. She held it up to the light and said with satisfaction, "You see? Mama vill never know." She helped me put the dress back on, fussing with the collar until it sat just right, then led me back outside before the cake was served. My mother would have given the dress to the maid to clean and iron and, after a good scolding, she would have sent me to my room without supper.

At last, the birthday candles were blown out and the final verse of "For He's a Jolly Good Fellow" sung. We all got up to leave.

Suddenly, Mr. Lipshitz appeared at the top of the summer-kitchen steps, his bald head gleaming with exertion. He had taken off his jacket, and his blue shirt had dark stains under his armpits. He held up a Canadian flag. "Before ve go, ve sing to our country, yah?" Mortified, we watched him snap to attention and begin to sing "God Save the King" while his entire family stood and joined in. We were stunned at first to silence, then to embarrassed snickers. But, gradually, stung by Harold's accusing glare to an unaccustomed show of patriotism, we all joined in sheepishly, echoing the words Harold's shrill voice piped with such defiant clarity. It was wartime, after all, even though they weren't real Canadians, like us.

Harold's sister Esther was married that September. For several weeks beforehand, Harold let us into his house, which was cool and dim and smelled faintly of cabbage, and up the bare wooden stairs to Esther's bedroom to show us her trousseau. The gleaming satin wedding dress, tulle veil, and white satin shoes were duplicated in the chiffonier mirror like twin ghost brides. He proudly showed us boxes of satin and lace, which spilled from the shelves and drawers, and piles of wedding gifts arrayed on the big oak table in the dining room. He led the tour often in the weeks before the wedding, bursting with pride because he had a sister old enough to get married.

My parents, Joan, and I were invited to the wedding. Mr. Lipshitz was particularly grateful to my father for buying the liquor with his ration coupons. They carried out their transactions in our vestibule, Dad handing over the heavy brown paper bags and Mr. Lipshitz carefully counting out the money from a black leather purse. He shook my father's hand vigorously after each transaction and thanked him effusively, while my father assured him it was no trouble, no trouble at all. But Mr. Lipshitz insisted that my father was doing him a great favour and promised solemnly, "For your daughter's vedding and your son's Bar Mitzvah, you can count on me," and I remember my father saying soberly, "I hope the war will be over long before then."

Esther's wedding was held in the King Edward Street synagogue with its white onion-domed roof. Inside, delicately carved pillars soared to the vaulted ceiling from which etched glass lanterns swung imperceptibly on chains almost too fragile to support them. I had never sat downstairs before. During High Holy Day services, only the men and boys were allowed there, and I had to go upstairs with Joan and my mother to the women's balcony and peer through the railing at the service below.

The wedding took place in the late afternoon. I remember the stilted one-step to the sweet strains of the violin and the pop like a pistol shot when her new husband smashed the glass. I can still picture the stained glass windows as they filtered shafts of kaleidoscopic light in which the dust motes danced like diamonds.

I sat between my parents during the ceremony while my mother delivered an ongoing critique of the proceedings in a stage whisper over my head to my father. "I can't believe it! The mother of the bride in a floor-length gown at this hour of the day! So inappropriate!" She shuddered delicately. "And lilies in the bride's bouquet! Roses would have been so much more suitable!" But I was seduced by the silken swish of the bridesmaids' dresses and the hot sweet scent of stephanotis and candle wax and the women's perfume.

Harold was an usher. He fidgeted throughout the ceremony, pulling at his shirt collar and shuffling his shoes while his mother blinked her eyes furiously at him to stop. At the reception afterwards in the synagogue basement he was everywhere, stepping on toes, bumping into dancers, and elbowing his way to the buffet table. Joan and I stared, fascinated, as he crammed food into his mouth and drank great gulps of schnapps when he thought his father wasn't looking. He brought us heaping plates of food and glasses of wine until the small room became hot and heavy with hora music. When my mother finally collected us to go home, we waded heavy-legged through waves of sound to the door.

"The girls are drunk!" she exclaimed to my father. "Imagine offering liquor to children! It'll be double doses of ipecac for you two the minute we get home!" As we left, my last glimpse was of Harold, coat off, collar and tie askew, whirling with Esther in the center of a laughing, clapping family circle, while her gauzy tulle veil enveloped him like a cocoon.

I saw Harold rarely after that. We moved to my mother's dream house in Rockcliffe Park just before I went to college, married, and settled in Montreal. I heard about Harold now and then from Joan, who married and settled in Ottawa. Harold was an engineer, working in a construction firm, married, with two children. I was surprised to hear that he had settled down at such a young age. I always thought he'd take advantage of the independence he'd been fighting for all his life and take time off to see the world. Then Joan wrote that Harold had been rushed to the hospital after having a stroke. He was twenty-eight years old.

Harold opened a mouth full of rotting teeth and uttered a wailing moan that bubbled in his helpless throat until he choked, and Sol ran to call a nurse to put a suction tube down his throat.

Sol explained, "He needs so much medical care, the nurses don't even have time to brush his teeth. He can't move anything but one hand and his eyes. He's completely helpless. We have to cut little bits of food and poke them down his throat because he can't swallow properly."

The nurse finished and left the room. "Esther comes most mornings, and I come every evening. My mother is here nearly all the time." I didn't ask about Harold's wife. Joan had told me she'd taken the children and moved back to Montreal.

Mrs. Lipshitz jumped up and went over to the window ledge, which was piled with boxes, tins, and paper bags. She put a piece of cake on a paper plate. "Liebschen," she coaxed, "have a little cake. Such a nice cake, I baked myself this morning, fresh." Harold moaned and blinked his eyes.

"He doesn't want any now, Ma. Maybe later," Sol told her.

"A drink. Maybe a nice glass tea." Harold blinked again. She sighed and started to plump up the pillows. Harold groaned.

"Ma, leave him alone for a minute. Let him talk to his visitors," Sol begged. He motioned for me to sit down beside the bed while he explained what to do. It was long before the age of computers, so he'd posted the alphabet on the wall, divided into three sections. When Harold wanted to talk, he pressed your hand once, twice or three times to indicate the first, second or third section of the alphabet. Then you named, in order, the letters in that section. When you hit the one he wanted, he pressed your hand. The trouble was that his reactions were slow and sometimes you went past the letter he wanted before he could react. When you weren't sure you'd got it right, you asked him, and he blinked his eyes once for "yes" and twice for "no."

Then I tried. I took Harold's boneless hand in mine, straining to catch its faint response. We remembered Besserer Street and the time Colonel MacMillan sicced his dog on him when he caught him stealing apples from his yard.

"Do you remember how you swam into the middle of the river at Brighton Beach?" I asked. He blinked. "And how you wouldn't come out and the life guards had to send a boat out to rescue you?" He laughed, great, racking wheezes that jerked his body in terrible spasms.

A bell rang, signalling the end of visiting hours. Harold moaned when I got up. The sack attached to his catheter began to leak its contents onto the floor, and Sol covered the mess with paper towels. Harold's choking cries followed us down the hall to the elevator.

The next day, on my way back to Montreal, I stopped at the florist's and ordered a gift to be sent to his hospital room. It was a miniature Chinese garden in a shallow green bowl, with tiny china children playing beside a china river that wound its way through miniature ivy and cacti under a china apple tree in a perfect little world of their own.

The florist assured me it would last a long, long time.

Ruby Slippers

Bernadette Blue

We grew up Kansas sisters
Playing over the rainbow games
Friends following the yellow brick roads
Of our dreams.
Mine were ordinary it seems—
Growing zucchini,
And children
In the back yard.
But when she clicked her ruby slippers
She disappeared to Berkley,
Leaving me with decades of Christmas card envy—
Tales of life among the Inuit, conversations with gurus,
And studies in the I Ching.

Last year I found her in the toothpaste aisle,
Beaming underneath the neon lights.
She asked me how I was, and I smiled
My ordinary smile.
She wondered if I watched the skies.
Gateways were opening, she said.
She was going on a journey—
The planet Pleiades was waiting.
And so she wished me well
And disappeared
With those ruby slippers still intact,
Leaving me to think of her in Oz.

Now I stand alone with this Kansas mourning,
Staring into my kitchen pantry.
And I close my eyes in her memory
And click my heels three times.

Second Runner-up: Best Non-fiction Contest

Mobius Strip

Janet K. Thompson

I have had two longtime friends whose lives have been mighty different. Their contrasting burdens and blessings intrigued me and influenced my life. Jane is the first of my dearest old friends, whose forty-three moves led to her precarious life.

By the time Jane was in the middle of high school, she had already moved about a dozen times. Being older each time made it hard for her to find new friends. At first terribly shy and trying to fit in, over the years she became more of a showoff. After spending all of her first year money in just the first quarter, she dropped out of college. She had goofed off a lot, taking easy courses (Ceramics, Basket Weaving, Current World Problems, plus Cheerleading) and joined a sorority. She needed to leave time for all her extracurricular pursuits. At her first serious job, she earned only fifty cents an hour and, typically for the times, worked a half-day on Saturday.

Polio knocked her off her feet when she was twenty-one. She was crippled from the waist down. From the onset and through the start of her recovery, she was quarantined. Friends and neighbors who stopped visiting never returned after she recovered. Her vanity made it too humiliating to have anyone help her walk again.

Even before she was well, she married the only fellow who didn't mind her disability, just to get out of the house and away from her mother, who hovered over her in her illness. Few agreeable birth control methods were available in 1951, so three children arrived in the first four years of marriage. Family and friends had to pick up and carry the children for her while they were "in arms," because she wasn't strong enough to do so. Playing on the floor with them was always impossible, plus she could never chase after them when necessary. So she yelled a lot.

When she was twenty-six, her children were only two, three, and four. She and her husband had to file for bankruptcy when the family business failed. Within the next year her mother-in-law died of cancer and her father-in-law skipped town, leaving her and her husband with his two teenage sisters to care for. Her own family fell apart, too, from divorce and moves to other states.

In those years, because of existing bankruptcy laws, the family lost everything but a stove. From a beautiful new house, the six of them had to move to a crowded, tiny, damp, and dreary basement apartment, displacing a feisty and inquisitive mouse. Jane found a decent job, but her husband had to take a job where weekly wage garnishments swallowed his meager paycheck. To get decent work, her husband finally was forced to leave town; so the family moved yet again.

She divorced at age thirty-five, when the children were eleven, twelve, and thirteen. Two days later, her ex-husband married again to a woman with three younger children. Until her kids were grown and out of school, Jane received only one month's child support of $50.00 apiece. While she always worked full-time, her gas-guzzling, used car broke down regularly.

One day in the late 1970s, her father, a longtime alcoholic, was found in the gutter on a busy city boulevard. The next day, his disgusted wife dumped him on Jane's porch to live with her and her teenagers. It was a terrible arrangement, resulting in family in-fighting. She eventually succeeded in having her dad legally and involuntarily committed to an institution.

After the case wound its way through the courts, she found her seventh grader and her tenth grader dealing drugs in the junior high. No one admitted to these kinds of problems in those years, so after receiving no help from their father, she reluctantly had the two kids picked up and hauled off to juvenile hall. After three years, her boss fired her from what had become her "dream job."

When Jane was forty-seven, her dear forty-two-year-old brother died of alcoholism, and less than a year later her darling seventeen-year-old niece died of leukemia. Following more deaths and family and work troubles, Jane suffered a major depression at age fifty-five. Desperate, she went for treatment to a therapist, who explained that, in her last two years, she had undergone at least thirteen major events, which were likely to drive anyone "over the edge."

Single for twenty-two years, she risked marrying again and, after thirteen months, she gave up by divorcing again. Jane, the rolling stone, has moved 43 times.

MOBIUS STRIP

My second dear friend's name is Lee, and I would describe hers as a charmed life.

Until sixth grade, Lee attended a private girl's boarding school. It was upscale, having only a handful of students. As well as the regular curriculum, she was taught French, Spanish, Dancing, Piano, Art, and Etiquette. Discipline was firm, but she loved having several live-in "sisters." When she transferred to a public junior high, she was two years ahead of her grade level. She loved her studies, and in high school she took part in many extracurricular events. She was "a joiner," you might say.

Her first job netted her only about $100.00 a month, and she had to work on Saturdays, too. Her CPA-Attorney boss and his wife were childless and treated her as they might treat their own daughter. She was an eager learner, who willingly took responsibility, and they were excellent teachers. Eventually, they paid for her to attend university to take advanced accounting and law courses. She had a built-in tutor, since she roomed with the boss's wife, who was finishing her law degree.

Lee married a student who was starting his senior year of college. Because she had always been curious, she learned from typing his papers and asking questions. She and her husband later had a son and two daughters.

After a year spent as an officer's wife in the Air Force, she continued working and gained more experience in accounting, mostly in the construction and oil businesses. She loved small business, and later Lee became a self-employed accountant, builder, landlord, and a restorer of Victorian homes. For twenty years she had a wide variety of accounting clients, learning a great deal from each of them.

Lee always sought out folks who were more educated than she was, those who had savvy and were winners. She developed associations with business people, clubs, organizations, and churches. She learned to take risks, and she often volunteered. More importantly, as she got older, she learned to ask for help when she needed it.

A mother who had business moxie and who loved all things cultural influenced and inspired Lee. Her grandfather was a political junkie, and she inherited some of those interests. Her aunt and uncle were just like another set of parents, "salt of the earth," you might say. She appreciated and received recognition for some of her efforts. She learned to "give back" for her blessings.

No question, Lee has lived a charmed life.

∽

Put a "T" on Jane, and it becomes Janet. My middle name is Lee. Both of these women are me.

Back in 2007, Iola Barbee, a writer's group friend of mine, wrote a poem titled "Mobius Strip."[1] This is the last stanza:

> To travel through time—that would be a trip.
> Is time just a temporal Mobius strip?
> Perhaps time is a path whose goal is unknown.
> We must take it and walk it, and make it our own.

---

[1] Mobius Strip: "Because of the twist, the inner and outer surface is always the same side."

A Haunting Dream of Angels

Seretta Martin

In the nun's study, I flip
decades of pages, setting angels free.

Some pliant, others stone, awaken
after centuries, not knowing how long ago
it was that they smiled or fanned a wing.

Time jolts sleepers from ledges
of ancient architecture.

The archangel of sandstone, unaware
of missing parts, doesn't feel
his eroded cheek lost to trade winds,

nor does he know, while asleep,
other angels waltzed in his shadows.

Angels' lives were once like ours.

Winner: Best Poetry Contest

Evolution

Ellaraine Lockie

Even Casanova's poetic account
of what happened under Maria Maddalena's habit
Skirts up and her holding a rosary
His hunger for one of Christ's brides

Can't keep me from glancing at the bedroom
window between every page-turn at 2:00 a.m.
Watching for the serial killer who governs the media
A monarchal ghost marching
his reign of terror across my back patio

What I hear is not the rustle of pyracantha
against glass but last summer's haunt
of wildebeest screams in a Masai Mara night
The last hour of life as a hyena pulls out the entrails
Slow and messy like the suck
of spaghetti one strand at a time
And I give-in to the inevitability of it all

The need of a hawk to systematically pull feathers
from a sparrow before eating it alive
Or a kea to attach itself to the back
of a sheep and hammer beak to kidneys

 A deviant rabbit that eats her own young
The pyromaniac and pedophile
The priests who ministered the slow crush
of Maria's foot in a Spanish iron boot

I surrender to dichotomy
To the world and the obscure wisdom of its creator
Throw in my gun and ammunition
And with arms over head
walk into that place of peace in dreams
Where maybe Casanova waits

Conifer Resurrected

Evelyn Buretta

I marvel at you, my chunk of conifer,
the Big Bang throwing a speck, a seed.
You thrived, watched mammals and reptiles
before being uprooted and tossed,
your body buried in the Triassic Period,
blanketed for millions of years
by volcanic ash, mud, and an ocean.
You rose from receded waters
when the wind whipped over parched land.
Your crystallized bark retains its texture,
while the machine-polished side
with chocolate and crimson swirls
beams back my reflection.
A spirit radiates behind that looking glass.
You, a sliver of Eden.

Outward Bound

Lolene McFall

Life on this planet is good, some say,
And favored by the sun. True. Yet
I would make one joyous leap into infinity,
Arch into tumultuous, delicious foreverness,

Embrace All wholly, submerge in That,
Like a fluffy burrowing owl-et.
Then, gravity defied, emerge new!
An aerial-terrestrial being.

Leave behind like moldering cheese,
Slices of life that reek of tragedy;
The travesty of wanton ways
And wayward squandering of earthly splendors.

Earth-life once seemed good,
Blessed by the sun indeed,
Yet I would stroll among *all* the stars,
Reside with Love in forever-infinity.

Strategems

Neal Wilgus

I was pretending to read the bulletin board when a semi-senior officio suddenly appeared at my elbow. I thought I was nailed then and there, but she only gave me a slip of plastic and said, "Top security meeting at 07 hours, Compac 23. Be early." I nodded like I knew what I was doing and she went away.

When I'd signed up on SS Fornax out of Aldebaran 17 two months earlier, I was fropped out and didn't know what I was doing. Cerbus Corporation didn't either, of course, and the personnel on the Fornax mainly went through the motions, passing me on through the bureaucratic hurdles, validating my fraudulent documents and issuing more documents, uniforms, equipment, a new identity I made up on the spot. My name was now Humberto ("Bert") Del Fonzio, which seemed lacking to me when I sobered up, but passed muster anyway.

Once I was established as Bert Fonzio, Junior Officio, I was free to roam the Fornax pretty much at will, and since I'd managed to avoid any specific assignment, I was able to pretend I had some actual duties and knew what I was doing. Hence, my scrupulous reading of bulletin boards, manuals, memoranda, and whatever other pers came my way. I knew instinctively that you didn't have to know what you were doing as long as you looked like you did. It worked, of course.

The Fornax is a big starship, so it took me almost an hour to find Compac 23, a secured conference room in the upper level. I flashed the plastic, was passed through, and took a seat all alone at the conference table. I was pretending to read the notes of the last meeting when the semisenior came in, gave me a puzzled look, then waved and sat beside me.

"Glad you got here early," she said. "Makes us look good."

I nodded and shook her offered hand. "Bert," I said.

"Fet," she said. "Short for Lafetorina, of course."

I saw on her ID badge that she was Mid-Officio Gardanzio and figured she must be my boss. She didn't seem to notice I had no ID badge. She did notice the notes I was looking at and asked if I was on top of things. I said, "Absolutely," and she smiled and started to ask a question I would have been unable to answer, but at that moment two senior officios came in, and we stood and saluted. They were followed by various shades of flunkies, and soon the compac began to fill with other officios, other flunkies. I shook a lot of hands, of course.

Presently, the Commanding Officio came in, a stern-looking grey-haired man with a bushy black mustache and an incredible Senior Assistant Officio named Tammie. There was sudden silence in the compac, then the subdued shuffling of chairs and taking of seats. CO Tator cleared his throat and studied his notes for dramatic effect before looking around at the assembled officios and flunkios.

"Senior Officio Tambina O'Sullivan will fill you all in," the CO abruptly said. Then he sat back and watched intently, his importance established, his work done.

Officio O'Sullivan gave us all a warm smile, then turned deadly serious.

"War," she said, "has broken out between Cerbus Corp and Korpus Intergalactus, and we are now on Red Alert, the highest security condition. Korpus ships have attacked three of our warships and the colony on Fabrique, where a dispute over territory has long raged. Their false claims in the region have been soundly defeated in court, but now it seems we must also defeat them in battle."

At which point my eyes glazed over and I fell into a light sleep. I've managed, over the years, to do this while maintaining the appearance of being alert and interested. It's not that difficult, believe me.

I woke to the touch of Fet's hand on my arm and her warm "Congratulations" in my ear. "Oh yes," I managed, "it's quite an honor."

"You're too modest." She smiled at me. "The position you've inherited due to the unfortunate death of Sub-Commander Ajax puts you right in line to make the final decision in this so important war. You might well move into a slot of Vice Commander in Charge." She spoke close to my ear and may have tongued me.

Of course, I had to shake hands with CO Tator and all the lovely flunkoids, which gave me time to realise that I was now in serious trouble.

Me as Sub-Commander? Me making decisions about war and peace, about battles and ships and weapons and bombs and other stuff I knew nothing about? Come on, I told myself, this must be some strange dream or a hoax played on me by people I didn't even know.

But as I shook all those hands and patted all those backs and mouthed all those platitudes, I began to realize I might just pull this thing off. I didn't know a hell of a lot about military history or history in general, but I had the gut feeling that neither did the military men or historians, for that matter. Smile and be agreeable was my plan and look for an escape route if one should open up.

And then there was Fet, who stayed by my side, introducing me to Important Persons and speaking up when an embarassing question was asked. Technically speaking, she was still my superior officer...maybe...I really didn't know. But the more we worked the crowd side by side, the more it didn't matter, especially when our hands happened to touch.

After a lengthy planning session of which I understood little, Fet and I escaped to her office and the one next to it, which was now mine. I wasn't sure what I'd do with it, but I went through the motions, inspecting and approving each file cabinet and bookcase I'd never use. Loved the desk and compucent.

I hadn't expected to be invited to Fet's quarters for a meal and to get acquainted, but quickly agreed when she suggested it. She showed me the way to her rooms on level seven, stopping briefly at number 713, my new digs, before bringing us to her place, number 711. It was cool, comfortable, artistically decorated, with music that appealed to me and lots of old-fashioned books on old-fashioned shelves.

We made ourselves comfortable, shared some wine, and chatted about trivia as if there was no war looming on the horizon. I wondered how in the hell I was going to handle a leadership role in a military world I knew nothing about, but I decided not to worry about it. Fet laughed at my jokes, and I chuckled at hers, and then she ordered up some food and set an old-fashioned table for us.

During the meal we touched lightly on the standoff between Cerbus Corp and Korpus Intergalactus without getting into technical details—fortunately, for me, since I knew no details of any kind. Over dessert, Fet briefed me on some of the relevant history, the rivalry between the two giants, and what was at stake in the coming confrontation, and I pretended interest and concern. The trouble was, I couldn't tell Cerbus and Korpus apart.

Then we moved back to the living room, and she suggested we indulge in some frop, to which I readily agreed. Finally, something I knew something about. She kicked her shoes off and suggested I do the same.

With thoughts of war and strategy behind us, we moved into the more personal realm. She told me of her childhood on the Fabrique colony, the hardships her family had to endure there on a planet hostile to human life, even after it had been terraformed to suppress the native life forms. Her struggle to get an education and a position in Cerbus was long and detailed, and I fell back on my talent for seeming to listen and be interested while I mindlessly admired her stunning beauty.

Then it was time for my story, and I began making up incidents and adventures I'd read about or heard of, hoping I wasn't too obvious in my plagiarisms. Perhaps I went too far in claiming to have been born on Mars seventy years ago, but she didn't even blink and might not have been listening. Anyway, by now we were engaged in the ancient game called footsie.

We woke early, took a shower and had a light breakfast, and then she sat me down and turned deadly serious. "I'm on to you," she said, "and you've obviously been lying all along. I don't need to check the records to know you're not what you pretend to be. Your ridiculous life story last night alone was enough to give you away. Do you take me for a fool?"

I did my best to confuse the issue, to explain that I'd over-fropped and didn't know what I was saying. Besides, I said, we were obviously trying to impress each other, and perhaps I got carried away. And look where it took us.

"I don't buy it," Fet told me. "It's been obvious to me all along that you're not what you seem. And now that you're Sub-Commander, you're in a position to influence the whole course of the war. I've strung you along thus far in order to find out what you're really up to."

Again I fell back on my old reliable routines—you've got me all wrong, I really am what I am, I may have exaggerated a bit, but who doesn't? And did she really think I could reach the level I'd achieved by simply lying and bloviating? Surely, she couldn't believe that.

"The reason I believe it," Fet said, "is that I think you are, in reality, a spy for Korpus Intergalactus. No, don't deny it. Why else would you work so hard to advance to the position you're now in? Obviously, you now possess information that Korpus must have and will kill to get its hands on. A final showdown is coming soon, and you are in a position to make a difference either way."

How could she jump to such a preposterous conclusion? I asked. She had no evidence; she had no proof. If she knew what I really was she'd be shocked, all right, but I was far from being what she thought I was. What—me, a spy?

Fet gave me a quirky smile and rubbed my foot. "Spy vs. spy," she said.

I had to think about that for a moment while she sat back and continued to smile. Finally, she said, "I would have thought you'd have figured it out by now. Yes, Bert, it's true—I too am a spy for Korpus Intergalactus. I was sent here specifically to find someone like you and help your work in any way I can."

I laughed and kissed her, saying I was just drawing her out. I knew all along what she was up to. Now we had to make plans, to figure out how we could best aid the Korpus cause.

I don't panic easily, but now I was really in the hot seat and was, let's say, uncomfortable. Should I turn Fet in to the Cerbus authorities or just play along? If I threw her to the wolves, they might begin to sniff me out, too, and that couldn't be good. If I went along with Fet, there was no telling where it might end up. What to do?

"Here's what we should do," Fet told me. "I've made arrangements for us to escape from this ship and make our way to an outpost on Gamplex III, where Korpus has a contact who can get us back home. I've obtained new identity records for both of us. I'll go as a diplomatic officio to the Gamplex Council. You'll be a group laborer, so we won't travel together, alas."

I pretended to think it over, but knew instantly that the escape plan was the best way out. What came after that, who knew? But at least we'd be out of our present dilemma. I almost dozed off at this point, but snapped back in time to agree that her escape plan was just what was needed.

We spent the rest of the day and the following week in endless meetings, where I was forced to repeat what everyone else had just said, take bogus notes, and sign documents whose contents I was completely ignorant of. Fet was there to help, and somehow we got through the ordeal without raising any suspicions. And through it all we indulged in footsie whenever the opportunity arose.

Then came the day of our escape, and Fet asked, "Do you have all the information ready for Korpus? I hope it's well concealed." I assured her I had everything under control and tapped my forehead suggestively.

Soon we had shed our old identities like snakes shedding skin and assumed new roles. This required us to split up, of course, and we went our separate ways, looking forward to reuniting when we reached Gamplex III. I constantly scanned, however, for some alternate route that might allow me to escape the escape.

I was with a gang of laborers about to enter the transport ship when I saw Fet and other diplomats being processed for departure. That's why I was able to see when she was taken aside for questioning, and then taken into custody. They actually handcuffed her and stripped away her fake officio ensigna, seizing her briefcase, her suitcase, her mission to Korpus.

When they led her away, she passed not far from where I stood, but to her credit she never even glanced in my direction. She was a totally dedicated soldier, who truly believed in what she was doing. I admired that and knew down deep I was going to miss her.

Then the labor gang began to move forward, and I moved on into the ship, giving a last glance over my shoulder and wiping away a tear.

Once I was safe on Gamplex III, I shed the laborer skin in turn and dressed as inconspicuously as possible. I had no idea where I was going or what to do next, but that wasn't a new feeling, and I was sure I'd deal with it somehow. New opportunities came along all the time, and I knew where to begin.

So I spent the first few minutes of my newfound freedom pretending to read the bulletin board.

Kilroy Was Here

Bill Alewyn

Long Beach Man Fires on UFO

(AP) "I saw something big hovering over the storage yard and I shot it," Kilroy Wagner told police investigators responding to his 3:00 a.m. call involving an unidentified flying object that allegedly appeared over the premises Tuesday morning.

Wagner, a Burns Agency security guard who works at Grant Implements International in Wilmington, told police he fired six bullets from his .38 service revolver when the UFO failed to respond to his verbal commands. "At least five of them bullets struck the saucer amidships," Wagner said. "I know 'cause I picked up the spent rounds." Wagner then showed reporters one of the smashed lead bullets.

"I know this sounds crazy and it is but I never saw anything like this before and, believe me, I've seen it all. I'm a USN veteran who's been to Shanghai and Macao and everywhere in between, but what I saw last night was a genuine flying saucer, there's no other explanation for it."

According to Wagner the saucer "was silver-blue in color and was over fifty feet across. It made no sound and was five times faster than a Blue Angel jet."

Wagner directed reporters to a scorched concrete slab and a blackened ring approximately fifteen feet in diameter where the saucer allegedly hovered for several minutes. "Explain that," he said, pointing to a similarly scorched peace symbol etched into the concrete.

"After I opened fire on the saucer, it just took off vertically for about a thousand feet and then it disappeared over the harbor."

As yet no eyewitnesses have come forward to corroborate Wagner's sighting.

According to Jesse Villanova, Wagner's immediate supervisor, "Wagner is an excellent employee, very reliable, very steady. I've never had problems with him professionally and he's worked for Burns Security Agency for twenty years."

I read this story when it first appeared on the front page Metro section of the *Long Beach Press-Telegram* way back in 1969, the same year President Nixon implemented troop withdrawals from Vietnam and Armstrong and Aldrin walked on the moon. Wagner soon confessed under pressure from authorities that his UFO sighting had been an elaborate hoax. Consequently, Wagner, who was sixty-three years old at the time, was dismissed from Burns Security for "irresponsible conduct while in performance of his duties." What did the old prankster expect? He was near retirement age, anyway.

All of this happened when I was new to the agency, just a couple years out of college, in fact, and far less callous than I am today. I worked for the National UFO Research Center branch of the NSA out of our regional office in Los Angeles at the time and, believe me, the job wasn't nearly so covert or hush-hush as it all sounds. Don't get me wrong; everyone at NUFORC takes every alleged UFO sighting seriously until proven otherwise, or say we do, and case number 08-04-7221, a.k.a. Kilroy Wagner of 1729 Belmont Street in Long Beach, California, was no different.

Rest assured, this particular case has been officially closed for decades. I'm happily retired now, but back in the day I did my job earnestly and conscientiously, as expected. Don't ask me about Roswell or some of the other high profile investigations we've been involved with over the years. And, just for the record, Roswell was before my time. Besides, I was just a low echelon point man on these investigations. Statistically, 99.7% of the time UFO sightings are easily explained: low flying aircraft, lost geese, swamp gas, weather balloons, too much beer on a Saturday night. And sometimes, for whatever reasons, some people have a need to make up stories as much as the rest of us have the need to hear them. As for the remaining .3% of the cases, if for any reason a sighting cannot be easily explained, then the Propeller Head and Slide Rule Wizards are called into play.

My job as initial UFO investigator was to winnow the wheat from the chaff. Something like the anonymous insurance agent you first talk to over the telephone after a routine non-injury accident. I could immediately tell from the newspaper article that Kilroy Wagner fell into that 99.7 percentile, more chaff for the files, another open and shut case.

First, I interviewed over the phone several of Wagner's neighbors, hoping to arrive at some kind of character profile. Strictly s.o.p. and nothing out of the ordinary, just the usual "quiet good neighbor" routine everyone now associates with pedophiles and the unlikeliest of serial killers. Wagner was a retired USN Chief Petty Officer, a veteran of the War in the Pacific, I learned from one neighbor; a widower who kept to himself, I heard from another. After a couple of these preliminary phone conversations, I decided it was time to speak directly to Wagner.

His residence on Belmont turned out to be one of those rundown little courtyard apartments that were architecturally popular back in the twenties and thirties. The courtyard came complete with an adobe brick archway and a concrete walkway that led to each attached bungalow. There were a few stubborn weeds growing between the expansion cracks of those walkways.

"Mr. Wagner?" I asked. "Kilroy Wagner?" With a name like Kilroy and a World War II veteran to boot, who wouldn't suspect a hoax?

"Am I in hot water with the brass in Washington?" he said with a genuine look of concern when I showed him my NSA ID and asked whether he would be willing to answer a few personal questions.

"A serious hoax has been perpetrated upon the American people." I probably sounded more governmental than I needed to, considering the look of pained anxiety he wore on his face. "However, nobody's pressing charges and the damage has already been done—I heard about Burns Security letting you go."

"The ungrateful bastards." He widened the door to his living room and ushered me inside. "I worked for them bums almost as long as I've been in the Navy."

I liked former Chief Petty Officer Wagner right from the start and thought I detected a distant Brooklyn accent somewhere beyond the apprehension and indignation. I followed him to a big green sofa that dominated the rest of the room and sat down while he took a nearby chair. Both pieces of furniture faced a large TV. Wagner, I noticed, still walked with that old seaman's swagger. He was built like a buoy with tattooed arms and reminded me of a profane and now deceased uncle, a veteran of World War I and always a favorite of mine, who once owned a bar in downtown Seattle.

"You want a beer or something, Ensign?" he asked, still uncomfortable with my appearance on his doorstep.

"I'll have what you're having." For starters I wanted to put the old guy at ease. While he dug around in the kitchen, I used the opportunity to check out the living room, including the framed black and white photographs on the wall behind me. USN ships mostly. The one of a pretty blonde woman who posed for a picture with a younger and happier Wagner immediately caught my attention. She was laughing and looked exactly like Ginger Rogers, the movie star.

Wagner returned from the kitchen with two bottles of German beer and a box of vanilla wafers. "That's my wife, Betty, ain't she a lot of somethin'?" He took two porcelain beer steins off the faux fireplace mantel and poured the beers into the steins. "She's gone now, the cancer took her quick, but look at that big smile. Don't she look like Ginger Rogers in that picture?"

I said she did and took a foamy sip from my stein. The beer was cold and tasted the way you'd expect a good German beer to taste poured into a Munich stein. I dipped my hand into the vanilla wafers, which, after the beer, were disappointing: stale and brittle. Mr. Wagner, I figured, hadn't entertained many guests lately.

I took out a small brown notebook and pen and asked my first question after Wagner finally settled back into his big chair. "We're mainly interested in how you concocted the hoax," I said. "The bullets, for instance. Very persuasive evidence."

"That part was a snap." He was beginning to relax a little now, and that made my job easier. "They got a three-inch thick sheet of titanium back at the yard, the kind the Navy puts on them new nuclear submarines. I just took my Colt revolver and fired six rounds into that plate and let physics at eight hundred feet per second do the work. Flattened them .38 lead slugs down to the size of a couple a nickels." Wagner stretched out his legs where he sat and dug into his pants pocket. A second later, he pulled out one of the disfigured bullets, which he dutifully turned over to me.

"You can keep that one," he said. "For evidence or a souvenir, if you like. I got three more just like it. The police kept one for their evidence, and I never did find the sixth slug."

I dropped the deformed bullet into my coat pocket. "And what about that perfect scorched circle the police found in the concrete. How did you manage that one?"

"With an i-bolt screwed into a forty-pound lead weight. I just measured and tied seven and a half feet of chalk line to the i-bolt and drew a circle on the concrete, then I scorched the circle with an acetylene torch and stowed my gear away."

"What about the peace symbol they found inside the circle?"

"Same thing," he said. "I just used a shorter string to trace a smaller circle."

"No, I mean why did you burn an international peace symbol into the concrete to begin with? Not exactly what most folks associate with aliens. Were you making some kind of statement for world peace?"

"I wouldn't go so far as to call it that," he said. "Mostly, I just figured it was somethin' flyin' saucer men would leave behind as a warning to earth people, bein' that they're supposed to be smarter than us and all."

"Are you a pacifist, Mr. Wagner?"

"Ensign, do I *look* like a pacifist?" he asked, a challenge to my alleged authority in his voice. "Listen, I just wanted to play a funny joke. How was I to know the cops would take a sample of that scorched concrete back to their lab, and then know I used an acetylene torch?"

"If they hadn't, the lab people I work for would have, Mr. Wagner," I said. "They're very thorough."

"And I thought I was, you know, bein' thorough."

"What do you mean?"

"Take a closer look at the flattened head of that souvenir I gave you."

I pulled out the bullet. Sure enough, stamped into the mashed nose of that .38 slug was another peace symbol—☮—this one no bigger than ¼-inch in diameter. If nothing else, one had to admire the craftsmanship and precision of Wagner's work. "And how did you manage this one?" I asked.

"It wasn't hard," he said. "Back in the Navy I was a machinist mate before I worked my way up to CPO. In my spare time at work I made a punch small enough to fit—and the lead in them bullets is soft enough."

"Quite an elaborate hoax, Mr. Wagner."

The ex-CPO shrugged aside my tacit compliment. "But, like you said, the police saw through my joke quick enough."

"And, again, I have to ask…why the peace motif?"

"You ever been to war, Ensign?"

"Not even close."

"It ain't somethin' you quickly forget, that's for sure, and it ain't somethin' you want to pass on to your kids, either."

I reminded him about what he said about not looking like a pacifist.

Wagner's next shrug was bigger than his first one. "These kids today, the ones protestin' against the war, I ain't sayin' they're exactly right, and I ain't sayin' they're exactly wrong, you know what I'm sayin'?"

"I think I do," I said. "In any case, you're a very creative individual, Mr. Wagner."

The first of several smiles flashed across his worried face. "My wife, Betty, always said I had a knack for these things—pranks and practical jokes, that's what she called 'em. I played my first one back when I was sixteen and still on the farm. Dressed up an old scarecrow we kept in the garden in my old clothes and tied a hangman's noose around him, then tossed him from the hayloft, likely scared my mother half to death."

"Very inventive, Mr. Wagner, for a sixteen-year old kid."

"'Bout a year later I left the farm for good." He smiled at me again and said, "You can call me Kilroy or just Chief."

"Okay, Chief. Just one more question, please, and then I'll get out of your hair."

He smiled again, but this time I got the impression he thought I'd been making fun of him. "Listen, Ensign, I'm retired now, I got all the time in the world. So what's your last question?"

"Why did you do it?"

He'd been expecting that one, my parting shot. "Like I told the police and that newspaper man last week, I just wanted to see if I could get away with it. You see, it gets a little lonesome down there all alone on my watch. I guess you could say I got bored."

I set down my pen and notebook after that. "Don't bullshit me, Chief. I want the truth."

"Sometimes the truth ain't enough for guys like you."

"Try me," I said.

"Okay," he said. "You investigate guys like me for a living, you tell me why I did it, then we'll compare notes. I mean you must have some kind of theory on guys like me."

"I do, not that my theory matters much," I said. "Now tell me."

"You first," he said. "I know you probably won't believe me, but I really do feel bad that I lied."

I believed him. Why shouldn't I? A man who goes to all the trouble of stamping a peace symbol onto an alleged UFO-flattened bullet deserves the benefit of my doubts. "First of all, these aren't lies exactly," I said, coming at it obliquely. "I think most of us, probably all of us at one time or another, have this inner need, a hunger really, for new stories. I'm one of those people myself."

"Go on," he said, conducting the interview now. I didn't care one way or another about that; after all, getting Wagner to lead was just another way of getting him to let down his defenses and maybe talk more about himself.

"And some of us," I said, "you, Chief, for instance, have this compulsive desire to make up those stories."

"That's me, all right," Wagner said with a giant grin. "Only my wife, Betty, used to tell me I was a natural born liar. Used to tell stories back in the Navy, real whoppers, too, but don't ask me where they all come from—I don't even know myself."

"I think it's a little more complicated than that," I said. "I think for some of us it's been hard-wired into our brains since before we were born to tell stories around the campfire. Part of our collective ancestral heritage, I mean. Once it was ghosts or flying dragons or winged leprechauns. Today, it's the Cold War and UFOs on television, but don't ask me why. Maybe all these stories are just a way of coping with a world we no longer understand."

Wagner seemed altogether relieved by my opinions. "So you're saying I ain't really a criminal?"

"Hardly a criminal," I said, pocketing my notebook. "But, if I may make a suggestion, the next time you feel the urge to share a whopper, Chief, sit down at your typewriter instead of calling the local newspaper."

"I ain't much of a writer, never had the education," he said. "Been in the Navy since I was a kid, destroyers mostly. I was in the Pacific during World War II."

"You must have seen plenty of action," I said. "Plenty of stories, too."

"A real friggin' mess," the ex-C.P.O. said with a dismissive shrug. "Enough whoppers to last my lifetime. I was on the USS Laffey off Okinawa, maybe that don't mean squat now."

Wagner clammed up tight after that, and I knew from interviews with previous veterans that only one thing was certain now: no matter how hard I pressed him, Wagner wasn't going to elaborate anytime soon about his personal war experiences. Just like my Uncle Phil, the one who owned a bar back in Seattle. That's when I knew my interview with Kilroy Wagner had come to its practical end.

I stood up and shook the Chief's stubby, callused hand. Only then did I notice the two missing fingers on his right hand.

"I'm sure glad I'm not in any trouble here," he said. "My wife, Betty, would never approve of the prank I done."

"How long have you been a widower, Chief?"

"Eleven years come the first of April." Wagner's eyes veered to the eight by ten photograph on the wall. "My Betty was the best thing that ever happened to me. She kept me on compass, if you know what I mean."

I said I did, although maybe I didn't, really. Life, after all, is always more complicated than we think.

Wagner walked me to the door. "You still want to know why I did it?" he asked, wrestling with himself. "No notebooks and off the record?"

"Strictly off the record."

"I'm sixty-three years old, you unnerstand, and I ain't gonna be around forever, so maybe instead of a prank I just wanted, in my own way, to do something for everyone."

"That's a little vague, isn't it?"

"You know what I mean," he said. "About them peace symbols. Betty and me, we had a baby once, a boy, but he dint live past six months. He'd be nineteen years old this month, that would make him eligible for the draft today."

"I think I understand, Chief."

"So okay, I say, and I ain't in any hot water with the brass?"

"Just don't do it again," I said, as officially as possible. "Anyway, just to let you know, I'll be talking to a couple of your neighbors, strictly routine."

"I got nothin' to hide, Captain." Apparently, on the strength of our interview I'd been promoted from ensign.

He smiled at me one last time before he closed the door between us. That would have been the satisfactory conclusion to case number 08-04-7221 if I hadn't knocked on the door of Thelma Hollenbach, Wagner's landlady, that same afternoon. I had telephoned Mrs. Hollenbach earlier but she wasn't home.

On the other side of the door a pair of yapping and as yet unidentified canines exploded in kinetic frenzy at the sound of my first knock. A moment later the door opened and, NSA shield in hand, I introduced myself.

"You're that flying saucer man who's been talking to all my tenants," Thelma said. She stood around 5 feet 3 inches and must have weighed 250 pounds. Two identical Pekinese danced in tight circles around her dangerously swollen ankles. I've never liked little dogs as a rule and these two were by no means exceptions. Bulging brown eyes. Bad little teeth. They looked like miniature versions of Bette Davis minus the dental work and just as temperamental.

"Don't mind Charlie Chan and Number One Son," she assured me. "So you might as well come inside."

She led me to her sofa while she chose a dull orange reclining chair that was peeling away bits of aging vinyl. Those two Chinese curs, Charlie Chan and Number One Son, gradually calmed down, although every ten or fifteen seconds one of their probing pink tongues darted from an arrogant mashed-in face. Aside from the dogs, Thelma lived alone, just like her imaginative tenant in number twelve. Unlike Mr. Wagner, however, she did not offer me a beer or any stale vanilla wafers, and I felt shortchanged or as if, in some way, I had failed the Thelma Hollenbach test. There was an ornately lidded jar filled with an assortment of wrapped candies on the little round table within reach of her recliner. I wasn't offered any of those, either.

"I guess you want to hear about Mr. Wagner, our new celebrity," she said, friendly enough. "What do you want to know?"

Once again, my Parker and little brown notebook came out. "Is there anything you can tell me about him? For the record, I mean. Has he ever done anything like this before?"

"Not to my understanding, and I always make it my understanding to know my tenants," Thelma said. "Mr. Wagner always pays his rent on time, too. He's a good tenant, no loud TV or hi-fi stuff, doesn't go out much or have many visitors. He sticks to himself. No, this whole flying saucer business is news to me, and I should know."

"How long has he lived here?"

"Ever since he got out of the Navy in March of 1946, and I've got the rent records to prove it."

"And it's always been just Mr. Wagner and his wife, up until the time she passed away?"

My question seemed to come as a complete surprise to Thelma Hollenbach. "Wife? Is that what that old liar told you?" A reprimanding tone to her voice now, plus something else: personal disappointment. "Kilroy's been a confirmed bachelor all the years I've known him. And I don't allow overnight guests to sleep over—if you know what I mean."

"He told me he was married. I even saw the photograph of his wife on the wall, the one who looks like Ginger Rogers."

"*Mister*," Thelma intoned with an emerging superiority calculated to put me in my place, "you should take a closer look at that photograph—that *was* Ginger Rogers. He tried to play that same joke on me once, too—only maybe I ain't as gullible as you. What top secret government agency did you say you work for again?"

"The NSA," I told her, putting away my notebook and pen.

"Figures," she said. "Listen, there's nothing wrong with that man a little overdue feminine attention wouldn't fix. Believe me, I know. I've been baking that man cherry strudel and sewing on his buttons for twenty years. And what do I get? Lies, lies, and more lies. Now it's UFOs."

You and me both, Thelma. But, unlike bitter Thelma, I expected to get lied to in my line of work. And he'd warned me about himself, too. Mr. Wagner was no novitiate when it came to telling whoppers. In any case, my personal curiosity now aroused, I later double-checked his marital status. Thelma Hollenbach was right. Kilroy Wagner had never been married.

I rose from the spongy sofa and thanked Thelma for her patience and her time. Then I handed her one of my business cards with my name and office phone number. "Don't hesitate to call me if anything out of the ordinary occurs regarding Mr. Wagner."

That would have been the end of it too if, about three weeks later, I hadn't received a telephone call from Wagner himself, profusely apologizing once again for all the trouble and inconvenience he'd caused everyone. Truth of the matter is, I think he was lonely and just wanted to talk, and maybe that's why I didn't mention my conversation with Thelma Hollenbach or bring up the alleged Betty Wagner or their imaginary son. Also, by then I'd done a little more homework on case number 08-04-7221, and what I had learned gave me additional pause.

C.P.O. Kilroy Wagner had indeed been aboard the USS Laffey off Okinawa, that much was true. He had also been the recipient of the Navy Cross for heroism on the morning of May 11, 1945, when the Laffey was struck and seriously damaged by two kamikaze Zeroes. Despite his wounds, Wagner, the sole survivor of a 40mm anti-aircraft gun mount, singlehandedly brought down a third, and then a fourth and final Japanese Zero. These are the kinds of things you learn while working for the NUFORC branch of the NSA, and it made me a little sad to think that being a genuine war hero somehow wasn't quite good enough for the Kilroy Wagners of this world. For inexplicable, yet all too necessary reasons of their own, maybe, some of these guys need to tell stories, too. Or, being that we all originate from the same human paradox, did it even matter whether he was an elaborate prankster or a pathological liar? I think sometimes, when we're not careful, we just get caught up in the minutiae of the mystery. Working for the NUFORC of the NSA, I know I sometimes did. In any case, the more I learned about case number 08-04-7221, the less it seemed I really knew 08-04-7221 at all.

All I knew was that I felt both anger towards and a strange sense of affinity for that lonely old whopper-meister on the other end of the line. Perhaps because, in another lifetime maybe, we once sat around the same campfire and told stories of our own. What I mean is, maybe in our own mutual ways, he needed me as much as I needed him. You see, I wasn't bullshitting Wagner when I told him about my theory. I believe stories are connected to our private hopes and fears and dreams, and maybe we need those stories as a way to explain all the inexplicable mysteries in our lives.

I didn't tell Wagner any of this over the phone. Instead, I just stared at a mashed .38 slug with a curious miniature peace symbol stamped on its face, the one I kept in my ashtray, while I listened to his apologetic words on the other end of the line. I was about to ask Wagner if he wanted to go out for a beer when another incoming call distracted me. This one turned out to be another all-too-explicable UFO sighting, from Graver's Mill, New Jersey, no less, and when it was over I vaguely regretted having cut Wagner's conversation short.

About a week later, I received another phone call. This time from Thelma Hollenbach. Thelma sounded all too frantic with worry over the telephone, just like her hypermetabolic charges barking in the background.

"It's about poor Mr. Wagner," she said. "You better come down here right away."

"What happened?" I asked, reaching for my pen.

"He's...disappeared, that's what happened."

"Is this UFO-related?"

"You're the expert," she said with just the right amount of skepticism returning to her voice. "I think you better drive on back to Long Beach and see for yourself."

I did. She met me outside the courtyard and opened the door to number twelve with her key. "I knew something was wrong when the rents were due, and I hadn't heard from him. So I waited until Monday, but there was still no check. The next day, I knocked on his door and, again, there was no answer. That's when I used my passkey and saw what I saw with my own two eyes."

We entered the living room, which was exactly the same as the day I saw it, with the same German beer steins on the mantel, the same old photographs of the USS Laffey and Ginger Rogers on the wall. I would have bet that same box of stale vanilla wafers was still in the kitchen cupboard, too.

"Nothing's been touched or taken as far as I can see," she said. "And the door was locked from the inside."

"Maybe he's on vacation," I said.

"I haven't touched a thing. His wallet and all his keys are still on the nightstand. You can check for yourself." Thelma waddled down the short hallway to the bedroom. "What I want to show you is in here."

I followed her into the bedroom. There, my eyes immediately focused on the cinderblock wall above the perfectly made bed, and the strange words…

ABDUCKED BY A SAUCER MAN!
Kilroy

…chiseled into precise five-inch block letters as though they had been burned into the concrete by a laser beam. "Now, how the hell do you suppose he managed that?" I whispered.

"Saucer man, hell!" Thelma cursed with twenty years of unrequited cherry strudel in her voice. "That man won't be getting his security deposit back."

In parting, I gave her another one of my business cards, this one with my home telephone number on it, and told her to call me day or night, just as soon as she heard from Mr. Wagner. But, as far as I know, she never did.

Forty years have come and gone. I never expected to nor did I ever hear from Kilroy Wagner or Thelma Hollenbach again. They're both dead now,

I'm sure, but now that the years have long passed, I would like to believe with something more than a wishful grain of invention on my part that, somewhere, the final installment of Kilroy's story has been satisfactorily explained. If not around a friendly campfire, then at a neighborhood bar, or maybe in the living room of an empathetic landlady, where her enigmatic but not so distant tenant always paid his rent on time.

On the Lip of Summer

Irma Sheppard

                                                                         we savor
the crunchy sweetness of golden grapes from our vine,
celebrate the shifting of sun from south to north.
It is, of course, the earth that tilts, but
                                                                        there are stories
of a time the sun stood still, and it was daydayday
on one side, night on the other, dusk in between—
on the lip of summer, what could be worse?
                                                       People talked
to each other of these days and nights they couldn't forget,
told their children and children's children. In time someone
wrote it all down. Now it's seen as a myth—
                                                          something
that doesn't happen anymore, and maybe never
did—just a story primitives made up to explain
their world—people unschooled in telescopes,
                                                             tree rings
and trigonometry. Stories they made up on the lip
of summer to occupy and to instruct their young
in ways of correct belief and attitude,
                                                             to ensure
correct behavior—keep a tribe intact, a village
viable. Villages these days are fractured, even
neighborhoods are not what they want to be,
                                                      with freeways
barging through. Now archeologists pick through shards
to piece together what the ancients made, what they wore,
what they ate and threw away. We have
                                                   rangers to police
their deserted villages, guides to instruct us,
on the lip of summer, what to think and believe
about those long gone. When an artifact
                                                           doesn't fit
their theory, I've heard them say, well, it must have had
some religious significance—the artifact relegated
to the mythical dustbin—elevated and dismissed
                                                  in the same phrase.

Dynamite

Andrew J. Hogan

Franz left his writing ramada at two o'clock and entered the library to report on the day's progress with his novel. Harold was sitting at his desk with Hugh Norris, a Papago Indian Reservation deputy sheriff; they were examining a large document. They turned toward Franz, looking concerned. Harold grabbed the copy of the *Tucson Daily Citizen* from the other side of the desk and covered the document.

"Are you finished for the day, Franz?" Harold said.

"It's two o'clock. I always finish at two o'clock," Franz said.

"Would it be too much to hope that you would be inspired to write past your deadline once in a while?" Harold said.

"Yes, it would."

Harold looked at Hugh Norris and back to Franz. "Well, all right then. I'll see you at dinner."

Something was wrong. Harold never passed up a chance to lecture Franz on his writing efforts. Franz was a fanatic about the craft of writing, but he had never been able to complete any of his three novels. Only a quarter of his short stories and novellas had been published, in spite of his friend, Max Brod, constantly nagging him to submit them. In only six weeks Franz was scheduled to return to Prague, and his American novel, mundanely titled *Amerika*, was only half finished, notwithstanding Harold's incessant nagging.

Harold showed no sympathy for Franz's literary struggle. He wrote effortlessly, following an almost industrial writing routine: up at dawn, write for an hour or two before breakfast, and then for two or three hours before lunch. He could produce hundreds of pages of published text in a year, starting with a sixty-page synopsis, followed by a first, second, and then a final draft. Unlike Franz, Harold never seemed bothered by a lack of inspiration or any insecurity about the quality of what he had written.

Harold and Hugh continued to stare at Franz, waiting for him to leave. Franz closed the door slowly. The newspaper rustled off the document, and a conversation began in whispers.

Franz had been sent to live with Harold six months ago, on orders from his publisher in Berlin and his doctor back in Prague. Harold had cured himself of consumption by writing outdoors in the blazing heat of the Imperial Valley—and in the process produced a novel that sold nine million copies before the Great War. Franz couldn't afford the extravagant rates at Magic Mountain sanatoria, like Davos or Arosa, to fight his rapidly progressing consumption. Moreover, he was at risk of defaulting on the advances provided by his publisher for his "American" novel, a modernized and literary version of a still immensely popular Karl May western. Who better to revitalize Franz's failing health and launch his literary career than the retired minister who became America's bestselling author, Harold Bell Wright?

When the train brought Franz to Tucson last April, he thought God surely created Tucson as a prototype for Hell. Never had he experienced heat like this before, and April was only the beginning. All summer, Harold pushed Franz outside into the furnace of daylight. "The heat, the dryness, and the sun will cure your consumption, if you persevere," Harold told him.

Harold built a canopy of sticks outside the southeast corner of his Cross Anchor Ranch house and set up a writing table there for Franz. Harold expected Franz to be up with the sunlight to write for an hour and a half before breakfast. Now, in the shorter and cooler October days, Franz was permitted to enjoy his morning tea and eat breakfast before going out to his writing ramada at six-thirty.

In Prague, Franz rose at seven-thirty, summer and winter. After a light breakfast of tea and toast, he walked to work at the insurance agency at nine. At home, Franz did all of his writing from dusk to midnight—*Writing is a deeper sleep than death. Just as one wouldn't pull a corpse from its grave, I can't be dragged from my desk at night*

Harold fed Franz like a calf being fattened for slaughter. Breakfast consisted of eggs, some kind of strange sausage called a chorizo, beans and rice, a corn patty called a tortilla, with a large saucer of coffee and milk mixed together with plenty of sugar. Lunch and dinner were served in even larger portions with chicken or beef, beans, rice, tortillas, fruit, and a strange liquid made from rice flour called horchata. For the first three months Franz was so exhausted trying to digest all the food being forced upon him he barely had the energy to write. Most mornings, he sat at his writing table, sweating, and napped until the next meal.

Every Saturday, Harold would drag Franz on an expedition. Even though he carried two canteens, Franz was constantly thirsty under the shade of the ridiculous wide-brimmed hat Harold called a sombrero. They walked or, more dangerously, rode on horses through miles of cactus and desiccated bushes just to see some small watering hole that harbored a rare toad or to climb to a mountain vista that looked exactly like the vista from Franz's guest bedroom. Franz realized now how much he had idealized the America he knew only from Karl May's westerns. Franz thought how naive he'd been writing his vignette, *The Wish to Be a Red Indian:*

> *If one were only an Indian, instantly alert, and on a racing horse, leaning against the wind, kept on quivering jerkily over the quivering ground, until one shed one's spurs, for they needed no spurs, threw away the reins, for they needed no reins, and hardly saw that the land before one was smoothly shorn heath when horse's neck and head would be already gone.*

Franz frequently attempted to feign illness, but Harold was too knowledgeable about the disease. When Harold didn't see blood on Franz's handkerchief and noted the color in his cheeks, he insisted Franz keep going. Davos, Arosa, even the nearby Desert Sanatorium, all insisted on heavy eating for their consumption patients, but, contrary to Harold's regimen, they combined this with extensive, prescribed rest, even to the point of limiting conversations between patients. Harold's prescription for Franz sounded like a sermon he might have given before his retirement from the ministry: "Cure comes from the patient's own efforts to overcome his affliction."

For the last two weeks, Harold had been meeting regularly with Hugh Norris, who, besides being a deputy sheriff at San Xavier mission, was a widely used local interpreter on the Papago Indian Reservation. Harold had enlisted his help as a guide for trips he made to collect Indian legends for a book he was preparing with the help of an artist at the University of Arizona.

Until recently, Harold had been very open with Franz about the Indian legends project. Franz learned quickly to encourage Harold to undertake more field trips, because these required Harold and Hugh to ride to distant parts of the reservation, collecting stories from tribal elders and shamans. During these periods Franz could work at his own pace, on his own schedule, out from under Harold's thumb.

During Harold's absences Franz took a few days off to roam around Tucson. One Saturday, he attended religious services at the Temple Emanu-El on Stone Avenue. After the services Rabbi Bilgray introduced Franz to some of the local business leaders, which earned him a tour of Steinfeld's Department Store and lunch with the owner a couple of days later. Of course, when Harold returned from the reservation field trip, Franz had to pay the price.

"You have nothing to show for the time I was away," Harold said.

"I was doing background research here in the library," Franz said. "Isn't that what you do?"

Harold spent a great deal of effort understanding the physical environment in which his stories were set. His bestseller, *The Winning of Barbara Worth*, was set in the Imperial Valley, where he lived while he wrote it. For his second-to-last book, *When a Man is a Man*, he spent several months living on a cattle ranch next to Granite Mountain, near Prescott. For his latest novel-in-progress, *The Mine with the Iron Door*, he lived in a tent for several weeks in the area north of Tucson known as Oracle while writing the novel's sixty-page synopsis. His care in understanding the places in which his stories were set produced his best writing.

Harold stood up and leaned over his desk toward Franz. "That's different. Once I start writing, the research is over. It's just an excuse to procrastinate instead of getting the job done. You can fix any problems with details once you start editing the second draft."

"Not everyone writes the same way," Franz said.

"Well, if you expect to be the next Karl May, you need to model your writing efforts after someone who actually gets his books published," Harold said. "That's why your publisher sent you here, isn't it?"

"I came primarily for my health," Franz said. That wasn't really true; it was the publisher who paid his way here.

The next morning, Harold was called to town for some kind of emergency at the Adams Street Mission, which ministered to the needs of Tentville, Tucson's large tuberculosis colony. Franz went to his writing ramada after breakfast, but an unexpected shower drove him into the library to complete his morning writing duties. Hugh Norris had come to meet with Harold and was left in the library with Franz until Harold returned. Eager for an excuse to avoid his writing assignment, Franz quizzed Hugh about Harold's secretive project.

"Hugh, I asked Harold the other day about this town named Oracle, where he is setting his new novel. He said you might know if Apaches ever lived up there. In the books of Karl May, who is as famous a novelist in Germany as Harold is here in America, Apaches are noble savages and much admired."

Hugh was stingy with his facial expressions, but Franz almost saw a frown.

"The San Carlos Apaches made fall camps near Oracle for the harvest of the acorn, but they farmed corn along the San Pedro River in the summer," Hugh said. "The Desert People lived mostly in peace with them. The Chiricahua Apaches who lived east of here were raiders and thieves even before the Spanish came here."

"The Papagos didn't fight against the Spanish and Mexicans?"

"No, the Spanish, and later the Mexicans, protected us from the Chiricahuas. The Spanish brought horses to carry our burdens, and we spent the winters near Tucson, farming the wheat and fava beans the Spanish gave us. Before that, we roamed the mountains during the winter, gathering acorns and pine nuts. The Chiricahuas would raid our camps."

"The Spanish didn't oppress you? Make you work for them?" Franz said.

"We worked to support the Church, but they gave us a better religion than we had before," Hugh said. "Those who didn't want to work in the Church fields or in the Mine could move back to the desert, where no one would bother them."

"What mine?" Franz said.

"The Mine with the Iron Door."

"That's the title of Harold's book," Franz said.

"Yes, white men like stories of lost treasure," Hugh said. "Many books will be sold. Many foolish men will come here to find gold."

"Karl May wrote two novels about lost treasure, *The Treasure of Nugget Mountain* and *The Treasure of Silver Lake*. They were very popular," Franz said. "Do you know the location of the lost mine?"

"The location of the mine was lost after the Jesuits were suppressed by Pope Clement more than a century and a half ago," Hugh said. "My people had no use for gold. By the time the Dominicans arrived to replace the Jesuits, all those who knew the location of the mine were dead."

"It's hard to believe that the secret location of such a treasure could be forgotten."

"The Desert People could never have benefited from such treasure," Hugh said. "It could only invite the greed of white men."

"That's what Winnetou would have said."

"Winnetou?"

"The Apache Knight in *The Treasure of Nugget Mountain* and a dozen other Karl May novels." Franz said.

"Just because an Apache said it, doesn't mean it's not true."

"I didn't mean that…" Franz said. "What about the map you and Harold were looking at yesterday? Does that show where the mine might have been?"

"Henry Yao, who runs the Chinese grocery on Pennington and Church, sells these to tourists and other gullible people for $5," Hugh said. "He soaks the map in oolong tea, and then bakes it to make it look old."

"That's why you and Harold were studying it? Because it a fake?"

"It's a good map, except for the false location of the Mine," Hugh said. "We use it to plan our trips."

The library door opened and Harold hurried in, somewhat flushed. "Sorry to keep you waiting, Hugh. There was another suicide in Tentville. They're worried about imitators. I gave some money for a community dinner, to get people out of their cabins, maybe cheer them up a little."

Harold gave Franz a truant officer's look.

"It was raining. I came inside to write, but then Hugh and I got talking."

"Well, it's cleared off now," Harold said, looking at his watch. "And there's still an hour before lunch."

Franz picked up his papers. He closed the door slowly again. Hugh was telling Harold of his questions about the map.

During the month before Thanksgiving, Harold and Hugh met regularly. Franz could tell they were planning some kind of trek from the supply lists he found on Harold's desk and the letters Harold wrote arranging for pack mules and relief horses. Hugh was putting together a team of guides and packers from the members of his tribe. From the conversations Franz was able to overhear, the composition of the team seemed to be the most difficult detail to finalize. Each week, Hugh would bring Harold information on the last week's candidates, leading to the removal of most or all of them. Finally, by Thanksgiving they had settled on a list of only five packers, two less than Hugh had been arguing for, but he had run out of candidates to present to Harold.

Franz heard cars pulling into the turnaround at the entrance to Harold's house and knew the guests were arriving for Harold's Thanksgiving dinner party. Harold and his wife, Winnie, had been planning the party for weeks; it was a major social event in Tucson's literary and artistic community. In addition to the Provost of the University of Arizona and several deans, the mayor, and some councilmen, the guest list boasted a prominent local architect and his chief assistant, a woman who was the real talent in the firm, Harold said, and primarily responsible for the design of the Desert Sanatorium. Also invited was the artist, Catherine Kitt, Harold's collaborator on the Indian legends book, and her husband, William, chief of the pulmonary ward at St. Mary's Hospital, where Harold received his tuberculosis treatments. Franz preferred the physicians at Whitwell Hospital because Harold had no relations with them.

After introductions and the usual pleasantries, Franz found himself seated with Harold at the head of the table, next to Dr. Kitt.

"Harold tells me the work on your novel about America is progressing satisfactorily, Franz." This assessment was a surprise to Franz. "Why did you decide to write a novel set in America?"

"My publisher agreed to publish my more experimental novels, *The Trial* and *The Castle*, if I would write a popular novel in the style of Karl May's Winnetou western adventures. May was as popular in Germany as Harold is here in America. He has been dead for a decade, but is still selling well in German-speaking countries. My publisher believes the public is ready for some new material."

"So you came here to research your novel, the way Karl May did?" Dr. Kitt said.

"May wrote all of his Westerns before he ever set foot in North America. Four years before he died, he traveled as far west as Buffalo," Franz said.

"Before my publisher sent me to America, I had read the autobiography of Benjamin Franklin and the writings of Walt Whitman. My image of Americans was that they were all healthy and optimistic. However, my experiences here made me realize my original novel was based on misconceptions and myths about America. My new work will be much more realistic."

"And have you found our climate beneficial to your writing?" Dr. Kitt said.

"At first, I found that, after a day of eating and exercising with Harold, I had little energy left for writing. I have now accommodated my writing to Harold's morning schedule," Franz said. "I am hoping he will take me on one of his expeditions, perhaps the one he is making next week."

"Katherine didn't tell me you were planning another tour of the reservation to collect Papago legends," Dr. Kitt said to Harold.

"Oh, this trip is for my novel, actually," Harold said.

"I thought you had already done the background trip for *The Mine with the Iron Door*?" Franz said.

"Well, some questions have arisen that I need to resolve before I can finish the novel," Harold said.

"I thought you told me those kinds of details could wait until the editing of the second draft?" Franz said.

"This issue is major enough to change the course of the novel. I may go back and revise the original synopsis." Harold turned to Dr. Kitt. "I don't like to talk about my work in such a preliminary state."

Doctor Kitt laughed, so as to soften the pointedness of Harold's remark. "Perhaps the next time, Franz, you will have the pleasure of sleeping on the ground, eating food cooked over a campfire, and picking burrs out of your clothing at night."

Franz laughed. "I think you left out the pleasures of the saddle sores, like those I acquire on Harold's day trips up Sabino Creek." Franz coughed. There was blood on his handkerchief.

Doctor Kitt looked at Harold, and then said, "Tell me about your novel, Franz."

Shortly after Thanksgiving, Harold, Hugh, and the team of five packers set off on the expedition to Oracle on the other side of the Santa Catalina Mountains. Franz had read in the recent obituary of Tucson's Catholic bishop that he frequently visited the Kannally Ranch in Oracle to escape Tucson's summer heat. Harold clearly didn't need mules, guides, and packers to visit Oracle.

When Harold left, he locked the door to his study, but Winnie kept a set of keys on a peg in the kitchen. The next Sunday, while Winnie and her three sons were at church, Franz borrowed the keys and entered Harold's study. It took some time, but Franz found the key to Harold's desk and began looking for a locked box or secret compartment where the map might be hidden.

Before the secretive Oracle expedition, Franz avoided Harold except for the obligatory report on his writing day, but now, to discover what Harold was up to, Franz had been interrupting Harold in his office on random occasions. Last week, he had caught Harold tracing something onto a large piece of paper; Franz was almost certain Harold had left the original map behind.

The folder containing Harold's latest drafts of *The Mine with the Iron Door* was sitting on top of the desk. Franz opened it and read where the noble savage, Natachee, was telling a young miner why he and his fellow Indians had no interest in locating the lost mine:

> *Could I, with this gold, restore to my people the homeland of their fathers? Could I destroy your cities, your government, your laws, and all the institutions of your civilization that you have built up in this, the land that you have taken by force and treachery from my people? Could I, Natachee, with this gold bring back the forests you have cut down, the streams you have dried up or poisoned, the lands you have made desolate? Could I bring back the antelope, the deer, and all the life that the white man has destroyed?*

After half an hour, Franz found the release for the hidden compartment in the bottom kickboard of the Fred Macey roll-top desk and carefully removed the map. **La Tabula de la Pimeria Alta en la Vecinidad del Presidio de San Augustin de Tucson** was written across the top. The paper was old and stained, with a tear in the center where it had been folded too many times. The edges were ragged, and the bottom right corner was missing.

Franz recognized a few of the map's landmarks: the Santa Cruz River and its tributary, the Rillito River fed by streams from the Santa Catalina Mountains. The map showed no roads going north between the Catalina and Tortolita Mountains, only a wash that broke into a Y twenty miles north of its confluence with the Santa Cruz River, the right branch leading into the Santa Catalina Mountains and the left into the Tortolita Mountains. Off the right branch of the Y was a drawing of a door with a handle set into the side of a hill.

So, Franz thought, Harold does know the likely whereabouts of the Mine with the Iron Door. His secret trip has the purpose of discovering the Mine. In real life, Harold is a treasure hunter, just like the ones he disparaged in his novel. Such a hypocrite!

Lately, Harold had been complaining about his publisher and was negotiating a switch to D. Appleton & Co. Over the last decade, Harold's novel sales had gradually declined from over 1.6 million for the *Winning of Barbara Worth* to only 450,000 for *Helen of the Old House*. Revealing the whereabouts of the old Jesuit mine would be the perfect publicity stunt for the new novel, whether or not there was any treasure to be found.

The next Saturday, after services at Temple Emanu-El, Franz walked over to Yao's grocery and bought a map to the Mine with the Iron Door. When folded, it resembled Harold's map, complete with tears and creases. The next day, while Winnie and the boys were at Sunday services, Franz entered Harold's library and switched the maps. He took the original back to his room and hid it inside the lining of the suitcase he was packing for his return trip to Prague next week. With any luck, Harold wouldn't discover the switch until after Franz had left for Prague.

Harold and his expedition returned late on Thursday. Hugh and the five packers set up camp inside the barn that housed Harold's Packard Deluxe Roadster and the tools and equipment used on Cross Anchor Ranch. The next morning, Harold and Winnie put out an enormous breakfast for the expedition team. Franz was invited to attend. He questioned several of the packers about the trip, but their English was so elementary that he learned nothing.

After thanking the team as a group, Harold went to each man individually, shaking his hand and giving him an envelope. The men smiled pleasantly when Harold shook their hands, but they grinned widely as Harold moved to the next man and each had a chance to open his envelope.

Hugh stayed behind after the other packers had left. He and Harold went to the patio around the corner from Franz's writing ramada. Franz went quickly into the house and grabbed his writing materials. Soon, he was scribbling away at his desk. Once he was certain the coast was clear, he crept along the wall to the corner of the house, around which Harold and Hugh were talking.

"What do you want me to do with the rest of the dynamite?" Hugh said. "It's not safe to leave it lying around, especially in the summer heat; some of it's started to weep."

"I don't want to explode it around here. Nobody should know I have the stuff; it'll raise suspicions," Harold said. "That's why I had Benito Salvatierra sneak the dynamite out of the old Duarte Mine."

"Well, it's going to be more difficult to get rid of it around here," Hugh said. "If we had used all of it in the Cañada de Oro, we wouldn't have this problem."

"Then it would have looked like someone had been blasting up there," Harold said. "We might as well put a flag over the mine door. Now it looks like just another rock slide. Once the seven of us are gone and the map is destroyed, the mine will never be discovered."

"I'll take the dynamite over to Redington Pass," Hugh said. "I can drop it in the West Spring Tank. It will break down there, and no one will ever find it."

Franz slumped down alongside the wall. He'd assumed Harold was a hypocrite, that all the preaching in his new novel about the evils of treasure hunting was just popular malarkey to help sell the book to a gullible public. Now, Franz had to work out a plan to get the map back into its secret compartment in the desk before Harold attempted to destroy it.

Hugh said goodbye to Harold, who rose from his chair and started back into the house. Franz quickly gathered up his writing materials. Harold turned down the hall toward the library; Franz followed. Harold was about to shut the library door when Franz stepped in.

"Harold, I am at a crucial impasse in my novel. I need to use the books in your library to overcome it," Franz said.

"What's the problem?" Harold said. "Maybe I can solve it for you."

"No, I need to do this on my own," Franz said. "You've often told me that, to develop, a writer needs to confront his own challenges." Harold had never told him that, but it was the kind of self-reliance advice he was disposed to give.

"Oh, all right," Harold said. "I should probably check in at the Adams Street Mission to see how things are going since I left town."

"I will only need a couple of hours," Franz said. "If you could ask Winnie not to disturb me."

"Fine." Harold shrugged and left.

Ten minutes later, Franz saw a cloud of dust from the Packard float past the library window. Harold was on his way to Tentville, and Franz was on his way to his suitcase.

[Author's Note: The farthest west Franz Kafka traveled in his lifetime was to Berlin.]

Computers are a Good Thing

Nik Grant

Professor Friedkin cast a hurried look at the dignitaries waiting restlessly in the other room, then pushed open the door and made his way to the large window that looked into the heart of the machine. The room quieted as he smiled and raised his hands. "We're ready to go, ladies and gentlemen!"

"Professor." The Vice President of the United States spoke in a calm and authoritative voice. "Why the delay? Why weren't you ready on schedule?"

Ah, thought the professor, the politician distancing himself in case anything goes wrong. But first to take the credit. Outwardly, the professor jammed his hands into his jacket pockets and nodded enthusiastically. "Yes, yes, my apologies, ladies and gentlemen. As you have had ample time to read the handout, you will know this is the first computer of its kind, without precedent! We did not wish to switch it on only to find someone had forgotten to plug it in! That's all it was, a last minute check for each of us on the project to inspect for the last time." He looked around the room, beaming, and saw hands raised. "Ah, good—questions." He nodded. "Just a few—could I—yes, let's start with you."

"Sir, your field is not computers, it's history theory. Could you explain your role in this? And why haven't we heard of this project before, if it is the big breakthrough you seem to think?"

"Very good questions!" Friedkin's eyes twinkled, alerting those nearest in the audience that they were in the presence of an academic who liked the sound of his own voice. "I am by trade what is termed a psycho-historian; I research historical trends. I couple mass psychology with the study of external events, which then allows me to make behavioral predictions.

"As you know, computers are ideal for sifting through large amounts of data. With this, however," he indicated the vast machine behind him, "we hand off behavioral predictions."

"So you'll be out of a job!" called someone.

Professor Friedkin smiled indulgently. "For years, my qualifications as a human being gave me the edge on evaluating computer data. It's now time for me to step aside and not impede progress. It was inevitable; this...system...is much more capable of contributing to the future of humankind."

"You just now called it 'this system'," interrupted a statuesque, curly-haired blonde. "Why not The Friedkin Computer?"

His eyes flicked approvingly over her figure and stopped at her wide earnest eyes. "Thank you, but for mankind to best benefit, we must forego pleasures of the ego and acknowledge the greater power of a neutral evaluation. Our earlier implementations of this system were merely data-gathering parts sending their thirsty tendrils into the networked world. This final part is the Brain. When our extraordinarily patient Vice President here finally pulls the switch, we will enter a new age. Not so much a Ghost in the Machine, more a Conscience in the Machine."

"Or Guardian?" offered the Vice President.

Professor Friedkin was impressed. "The very essence, Mr. Vice President."

He positioned the admittedly photogenic Vice President in front of a rather ostentatious lever, which to Friedkin's playful mind brought an image of that life-giving laboratory of Dr. Frankenstein.

"Ladies and Gentlemen, what we have on the other side of this glass is a self-repairing, self-replicating, self-improving machine. And when the lever is pulled, we add Self-Awareness. One of its early tasks is to recreate itself in a more efficient design. Yes, it can physically rebuild itself in any location it chooses. More efficient and less vulnerable that way."

"What about sabotage?"

The Professor's lips pressed tightly. "The system will prevent it." His face returned to its smile. "Its Prime Directive is to serve mankind. It knows it can't do that if it is destroyed." He nodded to a raised hand, which Friedkin recognized as belonging to the Japanese Ambassador.

"Would it be possible to tell us what the function of this computer is other than its self-preservation?"

"Ah..." Professor Friedkin smiled at the gentle rebuke. "Throughout history, we humans have struggled to improve ourselves, to make life better for our children. This system identifies and promotes the best interests of humankind. In short, this system is designed to optimize solving and fixing

COMPUTERS ARE A GOOD THING

all mankind's problems. Ladies and gentlemen, without this system we cannot survive!

"No longer is the computer-connected world, with its vast resources, the sole domain of government secret access. The Vice President is here because he sees the limits of governmental bureaucracy. Without secrets, we can now open ourselves to our true potential."

"If the government is so dysfunctional, how will The Guardian's recommendations be implemented?"

Friedkin nodded to the Vice President, who took his cue and wrapped his hand around the lever. "Pyschology. Think: what could possibly overcome our differences and cause us to work towards a common cause? Even I can think of one thing: suppose we had to engage a common threat from outer space?"

A sudden murmur filled the room, which Friedkin cut off with a congenial smile. "Yes, yes, I'm sure you all have many excellent questions, but I'm sorry, ladies and gentlemen, we've run out of time. Mr. Vice President? Shall we?"

The Vice President smoothly took command. "As Vice President, it gives me great pleasure to inaugurate this giant leap for mankind. I begin the countdown to a new and improved world. *Three. Two. One. Now!* Ladies and gentlemen, The Guardian!" With those fateful words, the Vice President slid the switch.

A low thrum filled the air. A thought flashed into Friedkin's mind, which he suppressed quickly, almost as if he feared the computer could read his thoughts. If The Guardian saw humans as the problem, to what lengths would it go to resolve it? If we do not shape up, he thought, it *must* take control over us.

The gods peered down at the small blue planet.

"Ron-el, it appears that your investigation into free will has shown that it cannot work. By implementing this Guardian, your earthlings have contravened the free will parameters of your own guidelines. I'm afraid the council must cancel your little experiment."

"Yes," agreed Ron-el with a sigh. "You've been right all along, Jeen-al. I don't know why it's taken me so long to see this." He laughed bleakly. "Four billion earth years down the drain." He addressed the group.

"I admit I was wrong. I had thought that sentience with free will would be the most efficient way to auger prosperity, peace, and harmony. Yet, as many of you who are wiser have foretold, this has only yielded disaster, pettiness, greed, wholesale economic disaster, wars… When humans first came into existence, their destructive impulses were limited in effect. I was certain that successive generations would learn. But as they journeyed from their caves, human strife was merely amplified by the systems they created. Reluctantly, I have come to the conclusion that free will inevitably leads to two choices: denial of freedom, or self-destruction. It is time to terminate the experiment."

The council watched in interest as Ron-el prepared to re-integrate the planet with its primitive gaseous beginning. There was a brief pause while Ron-el concentrated, then a peculiar low hum filled the great hall.

"What just happened?" asked a junior councilor.

Ron-el looked confused.

Jeen-al spoke up sharply. "Ron-el, your planet still exists!"

A murmur spread round the chambers.

Then a look of understanding passed over Jeen-al's face. "It would appear that Ron-el's Guardian is anxious not to be terminated," she said mildly. "We have underestimated the powers of these humans and their creations. Perhaps if we all focus our powers to extinguish this planet…?"

There was assent from the council.

"All right, then," said Jeen-al. "At the count of three. One. Two. Three. *Now!*"

The council winked out of existence.

The Gormley Curse

Richard O'Donnell

The town of Ballybourne in the west of Ireland sits in a hollow framed by low hills and coursed by running streams. The town itself is best described as unprepossessing. It boasts no ancient abbeys, no castle ruins or stately mansions, nor has it any historic sites of the sort that usually draw visitors. But that made little difference to the stream of tourists wending farther west to fish the salmon-rich Lakes of Killarney or visit the Ring of Kerry. Ballybourne, touted by the Irish Board of Trade as the archetypal Irish village, with its scattered crofts, thatched cottages, shops featuring authentic local handcrafts, and a colorful native pub, was deemed worthy of a stopover and a look. Ballybourne, in short, exuded the aura of an age when people lived off the land and went their way undisturbed by time or circumstances. But Ballybourne was no mere stopover for Adrian Loverly, a cultural anthropologist from Oxford, who was amassing data for a doctoral thesis on Irish culture and folklore.

For three days, the locals had observed Loverly walking the countryside, snapping photos of cottages and chatting up their occupants, whose words he scrupulously set down in a notebook that he carried about in a shoulder bag. The cottagers were unfailingly polite and provided him with no end of idle gossip and family anecdotes, but they came up short in the folklore department. By the end of the third day, after cataloging a detailed description of the Gallagher family's genealogy and little else, he chucked it in early and repaired to the local pub.

Curran's—the only identifier above the window—was what was know as a snug, though Loverly thought cramped was more the word wanted. It appeared that the pub was intentionally built narrow so as to shorten the distance its patrons would have to traverse to reach the bar from their tables against the wall. A door at the far end of the pub opened onto a back yard and supplied most of the lighting for the otherwise dim interior. The design, on the whole, was altogether efficient, although the light that glared through the back doorway left Loverly with the unsettling sense of staring down a railroad tunnel toward an uncertain fate. He paused a moment inside the entrance till his eyes adjusted, then approached the bar and requested a bracing glass of gin and bitters.

"Hold on there, Hugh," a voice called to the publican. "See that drink is put on me tab. A man that has spent as much time as the gentleman in learnin' about the people of Ballybourne deserves a complimentary glass as befits a guest of the nation."

"Right you are, Jack, and done it is," Hugh answered.

"Grab your glass and join me," the man said to Loverly. "Perhaps I can be of service in your research. There's few who know Ballybourne as well as I. Am I not right, Derry?" he asked of a man at a neighboring table. The man, a looming figure in a well-cut suit topped by a bowler, mumbled, "Right you are," and returned to his drink.

"There ye have it," the man said. "The word of Derry Connors is as all the reference ye could want."

Loverly judged the man across the table to be in his mid-fifties and sturdily built, though not on the order of Derry Connors, nor was he togged up like him. He wore rough workman's brogues, corduroy trousers gone shiny at the knees, a turtleneck sweater beneath an old wool jacket, and a flat tweed cap that clung desperately to the side of his head, exposing a tangle of gray hair opposite. He was clearly not of the gentry, which for Loverly was all to the good, as he surmised that he might finally have found his man.

"Jack Gormley," the man said as he extended his hand. "And you would be Mr. Adrian Loverly, the English gentleman we've been hearing about, asking after the local history."

"Quite," Loverly replied. "I've learned a good deal about local genealogy—and all very interesting, mind you—but what I'm really grasping for is some authentic Irish folklore. You see, I'm writing a book that I've titled *Fable and Fantasy: The Lure of the Lore of Old Ireland*. Clever, wouldn't you say?"

"Beautiful beyond question," said Gormley. "Couldn't have worded it better meself."

"Well, what I need to flesh it out are tales of hauntings, eerie happenings, curses, and all that ruddy rubbish."

THE GORMLEY CURSE

"Then Jack Gormley's your man," he stated, "known far and wide as the seanachie of Ballybourne. But if it's banshees and leprechauns ye're after, ye can forget it. We save them tales for the tourists, so's they don't go home disappointed. Ye'll get none of that from me. But if it's curses you want, I've got the genuine goods. Didn't it happen to my own family, generations back? Everyone in Ballybourne knows the tale, but none can tell it with the authenticity of a man who still struggles under the Gormley Curse."

Loverly fetched his notebook and on a clean page scribbled the heading, "The Gormley Curse." Gormley meanwhile signaled Hugh for another round, giving a wink and a nod toward Loverly to indicate who would be paying. When the drinks were brought round, Gormley took a sustaining draft and commenced.

"It all started with a wondrous pig," he began.

Loverly's head shot up. He was expecting a tale a tad more exotic.

"Hear me out," Gormley cautioned, "for this was no ordinary pig. It was my great-grandfather Owen who was first introduced to the creature. At the time, Owen farmed a croft at the nether edge of Ballybourne, hard by the River Fergus. Ye can't see it from here, but ye can take my word for it. Anyhow, he was tillin' in the field one day when a voice behind him says, 'Good mornin' to you, sir.' Nearly scared him out of his boots. When he turned around, there was the oddest man he'd ever laid eyes on. He was a handsome man, with broad shoulders and a deep chest, holding aloft a stout blackthorn in a friendly salute. Owen could see at a glance that this was no local. He wore a well-cut suit the color of a ripened chestnut and fancied a brilliant orange cravat at his throat. Toppin' the rig was a brown bowler made of beaver, no less—a man of means, without question. But what was odd was not his getup, but his stature. The man was no more than a hop-o'-me-thumb. From the waist up he had the figure of a man six feet and more, yet he stood no more than four-and-a-half feet, countin' his boots. His legs, Owen later said, were that short 'twas all they could do to reach from his arse to his ankles. And that wasn't the half of it, for in his left hand he clutched a braided leash attached to a strappin' fine pig as white as a new potato.

"Owen may have been naught but a poor farmer, but he was a man of uncommon sense, and it didn't take long to ask himself, 'Now what in the world would a man of his cut be doin' standin' ankle deep in the middle of a tilled field, holdin' onto a pig?'"

"Owen asked that, did he?" asked Loverly.

"Amn't I tellin' ye so?" Gormley shot back. "Inscribed in Gormley lore them words are—handed down from generation to generation."

"Just trying to be precise," Loverly apologized as he quickly transferred the words to his notebook.

"If I may continue," said Gormley. "It was then that Owen asked, 'May I help you, sir?' And the hop-o'-me-thumb replies, 'It is I that am here to help you. I've arrived on a mission of good will. I've trod the length of Ballybourne askin' who is the man most desarvin' of a helpin' hand, and they all speak your name. Poor Owen hasn't a thing goin' for him, they say. He's got a sour piece of land, he can't farm, and he has neither wit nor talent for anythin' else. His wife is a rag of the woman he married, and his children are so thin they couldn't cast a shadow if they all scrunched together.'

"Owen's eyes filled, and the poor sod says, 'Wasn't that kind of them.' And with that, the little man holds out the leash and says, 'The pig is yours, sir.'

"Owen, of course, was expectin' somethin' ye could lay on the bar for services rendered, and a pig wasn't quite the thing. 'I see your disappointment,' says the wee fellow. 'Let me assure you that this is no ordinary pig, for he carries within him the blessings of good fortune to any who tend him and see that he doesn't end up on the spit. I myself am a perfect example of the benevolence of this noble swine. I was not always the man you see before you—indeed not. A year ago, I stood as ye do now, a man with neither fortune nor prospects nor education. Today, I possess all three, thanks to my friend here. There was only one condition laid on me by the man who presented me with the pig. As soon as my fortune was assured, I was to pass the pig on to the next worthy fellow or lose all I had gained. And so I hand over to ye the source of all that I am now, and may good fortune find ye, as I know it will. But, as I mentioned before, ye must treat the pig kindly, else no luck will attend ye and such good fortune as ye do receive will be snatched away. Am I clear on this point?'

"Owen nodded as he took hold of the leash. The wee fellow touched the brim of his bowler with his blackthorn and, with a wink, turned about and strode away, rollin' on his stubby legs like a ship wallowin' in the waves. Owen looked down at his new friend, then raised his head to thank the man and ask his name, but he was gone that fast and nowhere to be seen. I needn't tell ye that when Owen presented the pig to his wife, Maeve, and told her the strange tale, her eyes lit up and her mouth watered.

"But if the Gormleys were expectin' somethin' marvelous to happen on the morrow, they were sore disappointed. As the days passed, it seemed that a cruel joke had been played on them, and that the pig was no more than just that. And every evenin' as they sat down to their customary supper of watery broth and potatoes, Owen's wife grew grimmer at the thought that she had married an old fool who couldn't provide so much as a morsel of meat for the broth.

"Are ye gettin' all this down?" Gormley asked Loverly.

"Indeed, I am," he replied, scratching rapidly.

"Well, pay attention," warned Gormley, "for now comes the interestin' part."

"Interesting part," Loverly repeated as he jotted down the words.

"Never mind that," Gormley interrupted. "Only write down what follows, and here it comes. A week to the day since the arrival of the pig, Owen Gormley was returnin' from the field for supper when a delicious scent risin' from the cottage seized him. He smiled as he inhaled the aroma and wondered how long it had been since he'd eaten roast pork. That fast, he made the connection and ran into the cottage in a panic in time to see Maeve bastin' the remains of his one great hope. The poor man was utterly destroyed and could barely touch a morsel of the food when they sat down to supper.

"But not Maeve. 'If ye're not goin' to finish that, then pass it here,' she said, pointin' her fork at the untouched meat on his plate. Finishin' that, she licked her fingers, wiped her plate with a crust of bread, and belched heartily. Then, lookin' at poor Owen, she says, 'Did it not occur to ye that the only miracle this pig could work was to keep us from starvin'?'

"Owen went to bed hungry, as usual, tastin' nothing on his tongue but his own bile, and the next day went back to his fields sadly. About midday, he was still tillin' and rakin' up rocks when Maeve comes runnin' up, waving an envelope and yelling, 'We have mail.'

"Now mail was somethin' the Gormleys rarely received, and on the occasions that they did, it was usually bad news. All the same, Owen promptly opened the envelope and removed its contents. It was a letter from his older brother, Liam, who had dropped from sight when he migrated to America years before. Accordin' to his letter, Liam had prospered in the building trades, now had his own company, and was prepared to stand as sponsor to his younger brother and his family if they chose to follow him to America. If Owen agreed, he was to let him know, and he would send money to pay the family's passage. Owen had dreamed of nothing but migratin' since Liam had left, and now, out of the blue, his dream lay in his hands: passage to America and the promise of a prosperous new life. Maeve was ecstatic, to say the least. 'We'll celebrate,' she said. 'Run down to the widda McGreavey that runs the shebeen and fetch some poteen. We'll toast the pig proper for our good fortune.'

"The pig! It struck Owen with the force of a mallet as he recalled the warnin' the wee man had given him should anything bad befall the pig. 'Twas scarcely a week after Owen mailed a letter to Liam acceptin' his offer when another letter arrived from the States. Owen stared at it with trepidation, for he knew it was too soon for a response to his own letter. It was Maeve who opened and read it. It was from Liam, informing them that his business had failed suddenly, leavin' him with staggering debts, and that he would be unable to keep his promise of passage to America for the time bein'. He was deeply remorseful. Sincerely, et cetera.

"Owen remained silent for what seemed an eternity to Maeve. Finally, without lookin' at her, he asked, 'What is the date of the letter?'

"'The twentieth of the month,' she answered.

"With that, Owen turned and stared into her eyes. 'And what day was it you slaughtered the pig?' Maeve thought a minute, then the color drained from her already wan face, for it was the very day."

"Is that a fact?" Loverly asked incredulously.

"Haven't I said so?" Gormley answered. "The Owen Gormleys never had a day's luck since that date, nor have any of their descendants," he added. "And the curse always follows the same pattern—good luck is offered with one hand and snatched back with the other. Insidious is what it is. Oh, I could tell you tales of fortunes made and lost in the blink of an eye. But first, let's have a refill. My mouth is that dry from talkin' that my tongue is clickin' like a cast-yer-net."

A pint of stout and a gin and bitters arrived; after downing half of the pint at a swallow, Gormley resumed his tale.

"Consider my grand uncle Doyle—a classic example," he continued. "The man was holding the winning ticket to the Grand National back in '38 as he listened to the race on the wireless in this very pub. The horse was

Garryowen, odds of five to one and leading by two lengths on the homestretch, with Frankie McPhillip, one of the best jockeys in the game, whipping him on. Doyle had pawned and mortgaged everything he owned to bet on the horse, and here it was well ahead of the field. Then, with not a furlong to the finish line, doesn't McPhillip tumble from the saddle, dead of a heart attack, as they later said. Garryowen, stalwart steed that he was, soldiered on and crossed the finish line still leading by two lengths. Doyle was, in that instant, the wealthiest man in Ballybourne, if not the entire county. 'Drinks for the house,' he declared. Every man in the pub raced to the bar and was soon hoistin' a pint of Arthur Guinness's best to cheer the good fortune of their benefactor, Doyle Gormley. Doyle was that elated that he ordered a second round. The members of the house cheered again as they put in their orders. But the cheerin' died when a track spokesman came back on the wireless, announcing that Garryowen was disqualified for finishing the race riderless, an undisputed violation of Grand National rules. With that, Tom Curran, Hugh's grandfather, who was then mannin' the taps, wrote something down on a slip of paper and passed it to Doyle. The man looked at it and slumped to the floor."

Here Gormley paused for another restorative sip of stout.

"What was written on the paper?" Loverly asked anxiously.

"The final blow it was, the unkindest cut of all," replied Gormley, after wiping his lips. "It was the tab for two rounds for the house. Doyle was ruined, utterly, and for years thereafter he could be seen wanderin' the streets of Ballybourne, mutterin' over and over, 'Five to one and two lengths ahead.'"

"A tragedy," Loverly said.

"Shakespearean," Gormley added.

Loverly drained the last of his gin and bitters and folded his notebook. "This has all been exemplary," he said. "The very thing I needed. I hate to dash off, but I should like to transcribe my notes lest I forget anything."

"Think nothin' of it," Gormley said with a wave of his hand. "Always glad to aid a gentleman and a scholar. But before you leave, might I ask for some slight remuneration for my time and assistance? A mere matter of professional courtesy to the seanachie of Ballybourne, you understand."

Loverly took a five-pound note from his wallet and laid it on the table. Gormley eyed the bill and wrinkled his nose. "A tale from a genuine seanachie is worth two of them things at the least," said Gormley, at which Loverly added another fiver. "And didn't I tell ye two of them tales, about

Owen and Doyle?" he added, at which Loverly produced two more from his thinning wallet. "My gratitude is boundless," Gormley said, as Loverly rose to leave. "And see you settle the tab with Hugh on your way out." It was the first that Loverly was aware he owed as much as a farthing for the drinks.

"Might I pose a question?" Loverly asked Hugh as he pulled out his wallet. "The man Gormley referred to himself as a seanachie. Could you define that for me?"

"Is that how the old devil's now selling himself?" Hugh asked, as he shook his head. "The seanachie of old," he explained, "was a traveling storyteller, the living repository of Ireland's history and folklore and a man widely welcomed wherever he stopped. Jack Gormley's no seanachie, I can tell you. Blatherskite is more the word—a cadger, a blowhard, and a praiser of his own pretensions."

"Are you suggesting, then, that Mr. Gormley is not to be trusted?"

"Let me lay it on the bar for you," Hugh answered. "Jack Gormley is the largest liar east of the Shannon and west of the Liffey. If there's a word of truth in anything he says, you can be certain it's an oversight."

"Oh, dear," Loverly moaned. "It would appear that I've reached another dead end in my research, and a costly one at that."

"Not entirely," Hugh replied. "Stop by the grade school tomorrow and ask after a history teacher named Kieron Adare. The man descends from a long line of seanachies and has all the old tales down by heart—gives public readings at the school the year round."

"Marvelous!" Loverly exclaimed. "You've saved my day. I'll see this Mr. Adare first thing tomorrow. And what is my tab, good man?"

"It's on the house," said the publican. "I suspect you've been tapped enough by Gormley and his crony."

Loverly stepped outside and winced, blinded by the waning sunlight like a man emerging from a cave. He also felt terribly fragile, the result no doubt of the three gin and bitters, and needed to sit for a while on a chair outside the pub.

Inside Curran's, the large man called Derry turned to Gormley. "How many spondoolicks did he part with?" he asked.

Gormley arrayed the pound notes on the table. "Well played, Jack," the man said, "but next time, leave me out of Owen's story. It was a rare chance you took, what with me sitting right here."

"My apologies, Derry. It was an inspiration of the moment that wouldn't be denied. It won't be repeated."

"That's for certain. The pig parable is getting threadbare, to my thinking. I'm working on a new one about the Widow McGreavey. In this one, she observes wondrous results when she slips a saucer of poteen to a stray dog that comes round to her shebeen and next tries it on herself. I'm still working out the details, but, trust me, the tourists will love it." He then reached across to Gormley's table and removed two of the fivers. "I'll take my leave by the alley," he said. "It wouldn't do to encounter our Oxford don out front, though I expect he's well gone." He collected a stout blackthorn from the chair beside him and proceeded toward the rear of the pub. Halfway to the door, he turned and called to Hugh.

"Drinks for the house, Hugh, but nothing hard, do you mind, as Jack here is paying." He stepped through the back door, laughing, and dissolved into the glare of the sunlight amid loud cheering and stomping of brogans as patrons rushed to the bar with their orders.

Out front, Adrian Loverly was musing on the unexpected turn in his fortunes. He now saw his book as a collaborative effort, told in the words of Kieron Adare, an authentic latter-day seanachie. His colleagues might even crown it as a seminal work in the field of cultural anthropology.

Adrian Loverly was riding high when he was jolted by the sound of raucous cheering emanating from Curran's. He looked up quickly, and as he did he spied a curious man emerge from a nearby alley and strut briskly off with a rolling gait. The man was large, well dressed, wearing a bowler hat, and clutching a blackthorn. But the curious thing about him was the stretch of his legs, scarcely enough to reach from his arse to his ankles. (He'd heard that description somewhere, but couldn't quite place it. Perhaps it would come to him when he felt less fragile.)

As the cobwebs cleared, he rose, enlivened by the prospect of the fame that his book would bring, and strode purposefully up the street. He had even struck upon the perfect title for the new book: *Tales Told by a Turf Fire: A Seanachie Speaks.* "Spot on," he thought.

Prolonged laughter from the pub, now fading with each step, trailed raggedly in his wake. He smiled as he shook his head.

"Extraordinary people," he said. "Most extraordinary."

Pinball

Esther Brudo

the pinball machine
waits for a nickel
then lights up
beeps, rings, chimes
the whole store gets happy

customers move closer to watch
uncle jack sits on his stool
behind the counter
next to the cash register
smiling

louie is playing it careful
pulls back just so far
knocks out the ball
sways, hits the machine on the sides
grunts, moans

we hope he gets a free game
or will put in another nickel
or Charley watching behind him
will step up and play

on this dark winter night
chill air blows in when the door opens
no one wants to leave the hearth
the cheerful flickering lights of
the pinball machine

Skinny Post

Buck Dopp

POP! The patrons of Dillon's Pool Hall had just witnessed a pool shoot-out won by the now legendary Skinny Post. The bar erupted with a spontaneous gasp, and then everyone started clapping.

"He did it!" one man yelled out as the din of excitement rose to a clamor.

Skinny wasn't known for his billiard expertise, but for his thin frame, which stood out even more because of the way he dressed. Skinny liked to say he was an "eclectic dresser," which really meant he slapped on that rail-thin body anything that happened to be clean and nearby. Well, it really just had to be nearby. The other notable feature of Post's appearance was a black cowboy hat, tilted back slightly so the brim wouldn't obstruct his view of the pool table.

Skinny had made it to the finals of the Sunday pool tournament, where he faced Buddy Barbarossa, one of the top players, for the championship trophy. Buddy was as fat as Skinny was slim, and one could tell there were very few foods that Buddy didn't like. He had so much fat there were two stories to his stomach, one above the belt and another abundant bulge below it. The two protrusions jiggled in unison when he made shots. Newcomers were instructed not to stare too long at Buddy's stomach because he was a little sensitive about it. Rumor had it that Buddy had even put some hurt on someone a little too fascinated with his physical profile. The experienced "Buddy watchers" would always sneak a good look at his abdomen when Buddy was bending over the pool table, aiming his next shot. If you were lucky enough to be seated behind him, you also got a panoramic view of Buddy's big butt, which could have had its own zip code. His butt-crack, always showing, looked like the southern rim of the Grand Canyon.

Buddy had a ring in one ear and the tattoo of a dragon on his left forearm. His long black hair, cut into a mullet, arched over his back. His mustache and goatee were so sparse they almost didn't qualify as facial hair, yet he never seemed to have a clean shave. Buddy always smelled like onions.

Some guys assumed he usually ate a big sandwich prior to making his entrance to Dillon's, because he never ate while playing pool.

To be sure, Buddy was an excellent pool player and could make most shots with the best of them. He usually played in the finals of the tournaments and drank beer throughout. His fans said that Buddy seemed to get better with each beer he downed.

As the referee racked the balls for the championship game, Buddy eyed Skinny the way an eagle might scout a rabbit as his next prey in the open field. That look in his eye told the bystanders that Buddy didn't just want to win; he wanted to *crush the little twerp.*

Skinny tried not to look directly at Buddy or at the crowd settling in around their tables, ordering another round so they wouldn't miss any action. Skinny started scraping his blue block of chalk over the tip of his cue in short, rapid movements. He would need to have the game of his life, because Buddy had been unstoppable all day.

Buddy broke the colorful triangle of balls with a crashing sound, and they exploded in all directions. *Thunk!* The four-ball disappeared in the side pocket. Buddy then sank the two, five, and six before finally missing the three.

"Okay, Skinny, you've got stripes, little man!" Buddy's tone betrayed his intense emotion.

Skinny proceeded to run the table, sinking every striped ball except the 15, which he nearly made as well. Everyone groaned, because Buddy was known as a finisher, and if you didn't take advantage of an early lead, Buddy would make you pay.

Skinny called a double bank in the corner pocket, and the ball did exactly what Skinny said it would do. He made the shot look so easy, in fact, that everyone exhaled at the same time. Then all went silent. You could have heard a napkin hit the floor. All that was left now was to sink the eight ball. Skinny grabbed the chalk and stroked the tip. He might never get another chance to beat Buddy Barbarossa, so he had to make this shot count. What would make this shot so difficult was how easy it was. Pool players know that the easy shots are the hardest. He had to block everything out, including the sight of Buddy, who had moved to his right side as if to put a hex on Skinny's winning shot.

Skinny took a deep breath, then bent over the table. He pulled back the cue, then gave the white ball a gentle tap. It rolled toward the eight ball and hit it, sending the black ball slowly toward the pocket. As the eight ball neared the pocket, it began to slow down and appeared to teeter on the edge, reluctant to go in.

At that precise moment, Buddy Barbarossa farted. Everyone burst out laughing.

It wasn't your run-of-the-mill fart, either. This was a fart that had repercussions! Buddy never did anything half-assed. The window shades behind Buddy began fluttering as the sudden gust of wind woke them from their slumber. The lights seemed to flicker on and off. An odor began to permeate the bar, blocking out the smell of beer, replacing it with the smell of onions.

Probably because of Newton's Third Law of Motion—there had to be an equal and opposite reaction—the eight ball dropped into the pocket. Skinny Post was declared the winner. Buddy shook his head in disgust, and all the patrons grabbed their beer-filled mugs and headed outside for a much needed breath of fresh air.

"It's Not the Same!"

Alice Correll

Oh, I remember the Dixieland Jazz
The Swing bands during wartime
The famous cowboys, guitar in hand
We all loved the leader of the band.

The Ragtime music with the rolling hand
Then Jitterbug came after Swing
Square dance and the graceful Waltz
Also Boogie Woogie with Rock and Roll

Now we live in Country Western time
The Salsa or Lyrical Waltz
Hip Hop and Break dancing
Covered by the Rap and Hard Rock.

Music and dance have moved on…
As many other of our daily events even
the Outhouse, two holer and half-
moon on the door. Then a man named Krapper
added a room with a white stool, running water
and electricity.

What next?

Gotta Go

Susan Thompson

My urge to travel is surpassed only by my urge for lavatory facilities. I consider myself the President and CEO of TBA (Tiny Bladders of America) due to my inability to pass a restroom without paying a visit. Verification of these statements is available in the form of about a dozen photographs my dear husband has taken of me emerging from various public facilities. He thoughtfully hangs this photo collage in our bathroom. Increasing travel in recent years has broadened my knowledge about the varieties of accommodations available. I present for your edification some of my porcelain adventures, apologizing, somewhat lamely, to my male readers, as they do have an advantage in these matters.

The public bathrooms with which I am most familiar are those here in the United States, where technology abounds. Automation has taken over the provinces of flushing, as well as the dispensing of water, soap, towels, and the hurricane hand dryers. There is also a proliferation of toilet seat-shaped sanitation devices, frequently offered in connection with automatic toilets that have sensors to note your movement and flush when they "think" you are done. Often, the sensor reads movement while one tries to unfold the tissue and arrange it on the seat, so that the tissue is flushed down before it has a chance to be of service. Equally frustrating is the sleepy sensor that resists all flailing and gesturing, refusing to flush at all. How does one gracefully exit if there is a waiting line? And there's always a waiting line for ladies. And then there was that friendly toilet at Logan airport that greeted me with a flush of welcome when I opened the stall door.

Another major peeve is the placement of paper towel dispensers so high up on the wall that the water on your hands drips down your sleeve while you are cranking out the towel. It's a bit easier to avoid the dampness if there is an electronic sensor that you can activate with a quick upward pass. Sideways works best. Just pretend you are waving a magic wand. "Abracadabra" may or may not help.

I found many challenges in European toilet facilities. Often these are pay toilets, with friendly service people who smile as you drop your coin in the basket and offer you tissue paper to be used for wiping. It is nothing like the soft stuff we are used to, but is really more like wrapping paper. Hint: Always carry Kleenex in your purse. At least these pay facilities are usually equipped with real toilets, not the hole in the ground variety where you have to squat, gathering up your slacks or skirt as best you can so as not to dampen your wardrobe. Hint: There is now a new product available, a disposable cardboard cone to allow us females to pee standing up. I am not making this up. They are available by catalogue, under the heading, "Tame the toilets of the world."

Let me tell you about my adventure in a public restroom in Provence. Conveniently located within the stone wall of the small town, it was a "one holer," with no functional light. Numerous cracks in the ancient wall structure provided the limited light available. I precariously hung my purse around my neck to free both hands for the strip and crouch maneuver. Hint: Leave your purse outside with your travel companion. There must have been some kind of sensor because just as I had found the footpads and lowered myself into position, water came cascading into the crevasse below me. Fearing a complete deluge, I hastily gathered up my trousers, zipping only when I was at the exit door, and went in search of another alternative, my purse thumping on my chest.

In Paris I found a small, self-contained, self-cleaning, stand-alone toilet right on one of the major streets. It looks like a pregnant phone booth, without windows. I later learned these are somewhat affectionately known as pissoirs. Upon insertion of the proper coin, the door slides open, and I step into a neat, sparkling, metallically clean toilet room. The flusher is automatic, as are the sink water, soap, and the total cleanup of the entire cubicle upon my departure. This is the one that should win the "Loo of the Year" award.

Yes, my friends, there *is* a "Loo of the Year" award, and for several years it went to the loo at Edinburgh Castle. They have huge plaques out front to prove it. The amenities include: fresh flowers for decoration, Scottish dance music piped in, protective tissues for the seat, pleasantly fragrant and easily dispensed soap, choice of towels or hand dryers, and, best of all, plenty of stalls, so there is no waiting, Ladies!

HERE TO STAY

Jacqueline Hill

these women were shakin their hips and laughin,
rocking side to side
bouncing up and down
throwing hands high.
joy was circulating,
tapping first one, then another,
percolating a raucous good time.
peace flowed like wafting incense, healing spirits.
rhythms attached themselves to feet, electrifying souls.
these women celebrated this one moment,
no lost sons, no bitter defeats, no songs of sorrow.
just rising to give thanks and praise one more time.
these women are here to stay.

Called Home

Jacqueline Hill

From the time I was a college student, learning of my African heritage became my cultural reclamation project. Before then, I had never experienced positive images about the "dark continent." During my senior year at college, I enrolled in an African history class that thrust me into a lifelong yearning for more. I investigated the classical African civilizations and read great African literature. I amassed artifacts and heaps of photography albums showcasing the diverse people and the majestic geography of Africa. Yet the most important link, a journey to Africa, eluded my grasp.

In early 2003, my good friend Nadira announced, "The IABYT (International Association of Black Yoga Teachers) is traveling to Ghana. I'm going."

"I'm going, too," I declared. Where would I get the money? How would I get time off from work? What about my fear of flying? In spite of my questions, I began the necessary preparations.

When I reached JFK Airport, I acquainted myself with my travel group, although my normal preflight nerves knotted my stomach. The New York City to Amsterdam flight was crowded and uncomfortable. Amsterdam welcomed us with darkness and frigid cold. As African men and women began to board and fill the flight to Accra, my spirits lifted. While the airplane bounced and bumped for seven interminable hours, I noted the progress across the Mediterranean and down the west coast of Africa as charted on the monitor. I reflected, "If my ancestors could survive Middle Passage, surely I can weather this turbulence." At the seventh hour, the stars and the moon lit the brilliant blackness of Accra's sky. My tense body relaxed, and I gazed out of the window with a wonderful expectancy. Africa.

I awake in Ghana, West Africa, 8° north of the equator and 2° west. A lizard in the window tells me to rise. As I walk from my bungalow to the road, rolling lush green hills and steamy sunshine salute me. Across the road, a baby goat scurries while two small boys with water pails perched atop their heads emerge from a small cluster of trees. A grand promenade of folks, cars, vans, bicycles, trucks, and mopeds passes as one woman sets up a stand with large burlap bags of rice and huge tubular yams. I nod and smile.

The ride to the beach the next day for a special rites of passage ceremony takes the group through Accra-Central and Kwame Nkrumah Circle. Between buildings, I glimpse the ocean, an ugly slate gray. As we approach the beach, I am astounded by the teeming masses of people—moving, jostling, striding, strolling, and dodging the endless sea of cars, vans, and buses. Goats abound, munch whatever grass they can find amid the trash and garbage strewn over the red dirt path adjacent to the road.

We gather at the shoreline and face our host, Rev. Sam, standing amidst gentle waves; then we move closer, snapping our cameras and posing for photos. Teenagers, young adults, and children gaze in wonder at us.

One by one, Rev. Sam beckons us to the water, pointing to the horizon. Some dance jubilantly while others raise their hands in praise. I walk slowly as he intones, "Welcome back, queen of Africa. You are home." I taste salt water splashing on my face, embrace the reverend, and exclaim, "Thank you! Thank you, Jesus! Thank you, Lord!" When I come to myself, I am back on the shore, embraced within a circle of smiling women. Returning to the ocean, I give silent thanks to God for this journey.

Tours and activities each day keep us busy. One day, as the group heads off to an excursion, I decide to explore on my own with a trip to the bank. I've promised to purchase some striking Ghanaian art from two brothers, and they arrive, indicating they'll follow me to the bank. Off I go, hailing a taxi to the nearest Barclays Bank, twenty minutes away.

Accra has a legion of taxis, and they drive like taxi drivers around the world. Bumper to bumper traffic engulfs us, and after twenty minutes we've made little progress to the main road toward the bank. After a detour on a bumpy, twisting dirt path through a bustling market, we maneuver back to the main highway to be greeted by even more morning traffic. Thirty minutes later, we arrive at the bank. I make my way upstairs to the foreign section, where I cash my traveler's checks for a mound of Ghanaian bills—1.3 million Cedis—that I carry in a black plastic bag. The return trip is fast and detour-free.

After a nap, I take a stroll and encounter Vee, who invites me to market with her. It is 85 degrees and 100% humidity, and Vee's little car has no air conditioning. She and I share stories about our families and her ideas on entrepreneurship. Finding a parking space is no easy task, but we discover one, and are on our way—with Vee's caution to "mind your bag." Inside a large three-story building that resembles a 1950's department store are narrow corridors crowded with people selling and buying, a whirlwind of activity. Displayed on shelves, in barrels, sitting in huge metal pots, and lying on pieces of cloth placed on the cement floor is an array of items: bottled water, baby carriages, live crabs, okra, yams, tomatoes, dried beans, and sacks of rice.

I struggle to keep up with Vee's fast pace, but keep her in sight. Watching her barter for the beautiful fabrics is a business lesson. Although I don't understand the verbal exchange, I get the body language, the nuance of an age-old haggle, skillfully orchestrated and performed. Then we quickly return to the car.

On Tuesday, a steamy morning, our travel group leaves for Tamale in northern Ghana. Most of us sleep for the first few hours while the bus rolls through Accra's outskirts. We waken to stalled traffic and the beautiful faces of Ghanaian women and children walking alongside the bus. We open the windows to buy delicious fresh plantain chips, steamed peanuts, green tangerines with syrupy sweet juice, and bananas.

This ride is a photographer's dream: children with smooth, coal black faces; thatched buildings in compounds surrounded by banana trees and tall grass; a constant stream of smoke from wood fires; men and women pacing purposefully and carrying tools, baskets, animals, and children. We pass by massive trucks full of logs and others bursting with cattle and goats. The road is rough and hole-pocked in spots, but the driving is skillful, and the forest serenely beautiful. The twelve-hour trip saps our strength, but we share snacks, drinks, music, and dance in the aisles. Roadside signs like *Sister Cee Rasta Do*, *Afterlife Art Services*, and *Magic Johnson Aids Project* are a storyboard of life in Ghana. At a military checkpoint, youthful soldiers with automatic weapons slung across their chests wave us through.

A clear voice wails the Muslim call to prayer, and I awake to another day in Africa. Sitting on a boulder near the road, I observe Tamale's day commence. Tamale, a city of bicycles and mopeds, is alive, a kaleidoscope of colors, patterns, and shapes: uniformed children striding and skipping, young girls with hijab-covered heads, a family of four on one bicycle, and the ubiquitous wizened goats. Although we spend the morning in Kukuo village, I am disappointed when the meeting with the chief and elders is postponed. After a trip to a marketplace, we revisit Kukuo to meet with the chief and the elders.

Muniru, our guide, leads us past the village entrance, past the school, past the baobab tree where earlier this morning babies were weighed and immunized, past the compound of red clay buildings with straw roofs, past the house where we had our pottery lesson to a clearing where we abruptly halt, and I notice a cluster of men seated in front of one building. Muniru provides a brief etiquette lesson for meeting the chief. After much discussion by the men, we are ushered to three long planked benches. Custom requires an official welcome because we have traveled a long way.

The chief's linguist indicates that traditions stipulate we share a palm nut, which he bites and passes to each of us. I bite, trying desperately not to gag from the bitter green taste. Behind us gather women, children with babies on their backs, a solemn teenager on a bicycle, and children in school uniforms. A goat bleats and a rooster wanders through. A naked toddler feeds a puppy.

The linguist indicates that the chief is ready to begin the dialogue. He knows we have come a long way. IABYT founder Krishna shares the love, awe, and honor that we feel at being home in Africa. Her sincerity inspires the men to listen intently, even before the interpreter speaks. As I listen and gaze at the scene around me, I know that I will soon cry. The interpreter speaks, and each man concentrates, smiling occasionally and nodding in agreement. The chief, eyes framed in dark sunglasses, leans back, appraising the assembly. First one tear, then another, drops on my cheeks.

The chief smiles and speaks as the elders and their linguists stand. The chief has decided that there will be ceremonies to honor this group who have returned. We rise and face the clearing as the others move toward its center. Three chickens are brought to the clearing. The chief kneels and is handed a gourd of palm wine; he spills some of the wine on the ground as a libation for the ancestors. The interpreter explains that there will now be a sacrifice to determine if the ancestors will accept us back to the village. If the bird flops on its back when decapitated, the ancestors have agreed. To ensure good odds, three chickens will be sacrificed.

An elder cuts the chicken's neck and spills the blood into the area where the libation was poured. Each chicken flops around and lands on its back.

Broad smiles abound. The elder and linguists sip from the gourd of palm wine and pass it until, one by one, we pour a bit into the dirt and drink without hesitation. I have left my camera on the bus, but these images are seared into my memory.

IABYT founder Krishna presents our gifts and we sing, "May the long time sun shine upon you, all love surround you, and the pure light within guide your way on." With the interpretation, the chief and elders are visibly moved, and my tears flow again. The chief hopes that we return, that we bring our children and grandchildren, and that we send pictures so that they can know our families. He rises and the visit is over. My smile reflects the joy of this unique experience.

The next day we experience Elmina Slave Castle. The minute we leave the bus, walk across the bridge, and enter this fortress overlooking the Atlantic, conversations cease. As I explore until the formal tour begins, my aimless steps find a courtyard of thick cobblestones, and I stare up at the peeling gray-white walls, wondering if my own ancestors—horrified and numb—entered here bound for slavery.

Finally, we shuffle through a small door and hear, "Bend down, take five steps, before standing again." The light in this dark, damp, and moldy tomb emanates from a two-foot window. "The door of no return" overlooks the ocean and rocks below, where ships once awaited Elmina's human cargo. I stoop, see the ocean and sense the absolute doom Africans experienced here. We hang around, standing quietly, crying, staring, and snapping photos.

This land that my ancestors left is under my feet, in my eyes, and resounds through my spirit. I can go home again.

Negotiating Culture

Tony Zurlo

As predictable as the muezzin's call to prayer,
I jog past arthritic skeletons silhouetted against
craggy cliffs on the horizon—Fulani tending
their boney cattle. Into a stiff north wind
I turn to face grains of sand blowing in
from dunes on the outskirts of town.

Stacked with food baskets, bicycles pass me
bouncing along the laterite road to market.
Pestles pound from compounds like muffled drums.
A festival of colors dip and nod before my eyes—
bright blues, yellows, greens, and reds;
blending in stripes, spirals, and polka dots.

A tiny girl blushes and smiles, then waves,
costume jewelry jingling on her chocolate arm.
Her powdered face and deep-brown eyes
break my stride. I want to sweep her up
into my arms and race her to a safe haven,
to carry her far away from her destiny.

Boys run alongside of me, their fists raised
in greeting: "Sannu Batuuree," they chime
in harmony. "Lafiya lau," I reply out of tune.
Sun-baked, mud-gray walls straight ahead
mark the limit for Westerners who dream.
I must focus on the moment, not history.

In this race, victory is measured in inches,
by a pivot or a kick in the sand, gestures
that silently negotiate culture. I bend down
to tie my shoe and somersault forward
to the foot of the medieval Muslim façade.
Children's laughter welcomes me.

A Fake Rolex

Carl W. Snow

The Jockey Club in the mid-1980's was a five-star restaurant on the Kowloon peninsula in Hong Kong. Dark, polished wood paneling with green baize-covered walls; heavy tables and cushioned green chairs with cloth napkins in polished brass (were they gold?) napkin rings. Large, framed oil portraits of winning race horses, their owners, and their jockeys lined the walls.

A forty-ish man and woman were dining with their twenty-year-old son, who was on summer break from college in California. They had come down from Tokyo, where they were stationed with the U.S. Navy. The steaks were superb, the potatoes and vegetables done to perfection. The Sommelier's suggestions of wines complemented the meal exquisitely. Coffee and brandy following the meal loosened their purse strings for generous tipping. They lingered long over the coffee, reluctant to end the perfect meal and leave these opulent surroundings.

As they finally exited the restaurant and turned toward the large boulevard that would lead them to the Wanchai ferry and back to the China Fleet Club—their hotel on this visit—their son reminded them of his quest on behalf of a college roommate for a "fake" Rolex watch. These were to be had cheaply in Hong Kong, and he was on the lookout for a vendor. His inquiries at watch shops and jewelry stores had met with polite laughter and assurance that they didn't deal in such things; perhaps he should ask a street vendor. But be careful, they warned, such people can be unsavory, to say the least.

Since he was pursuing a fake to begin with, he reasoned, they couldn't very well mislead him into paying for a real Rolex, so he wasn't too worried about the person's character. What was the worst that could happen?

As they strolled along the wide, well-lit sidewalk, a young Oriental man approached the son and said something to him in Chinese. When he explained that he didn't understand, the young man quickly asked in English if he were interested in buying a tailor-made leather jacket. No, the son replied, but did the man know where he might locate a fake Rolex watch?

The young Chinese man took a half-step backward and asked, "A *fake* Rolex watch?"

Yes, was the answer, something for about thirty dollars American.

"I show you, but maybe fitty-dollah 'merican," he said.

"Okay, fifty dollars for a 'Submariner,' but it has to be a good imitation."

"Yes, yes, berry good imitation; you can't tell, you be supprised not real," he assured and turned to walk up the street, beckoning the small group to follow him.

The son eagerly bounded after him; his parents, unwilling to leave him, reluctantly followed. At the corner, the man turned into a side street and hurried along to an alleyway, where he went in, springing back out almost immediately to make sure they were following. He impatiently motioned them to come into the alley.

"I don't know about this, son," the father said, "maybe we'd better—"

"Aw, come on, Dad, we'll just get the watch and go. What's the worst that can happen?"

With much trepidation they followed. Down the alley a short way, they came to a doorway into which the man led them. Inside the doorway, two thugs with shaved heads wearing "wife beater" undershirts, their shoulders and arms covered with tattoos, lounged against the far wall. Acknowledging the "leading man" and leering at his "guests," they watched closely as he led his charges to an open-grated elevator just big enough for four people. They packed in, their eyes wide as the elevator lurched from the ground floor, wheezing and groaning up three stories to the second floor. Two more shaved heads, more menacing than the two downstairs, leaned against the wall outside the elevator. They glared as the strange procession moved past them.

The son, obviously excited at the adventure and blissfully ignorant of any danger, turned to his parents and said, "See? Nothing to worry about." He seemed not to notice the murkiness, the reek of urine, the muffled scurrying of tiny feet as they followed their guide.

At the end of the hallway was a steel door that appeared to be armor-plated with rows of bolt-heads along its perimeter. A dim, shaded light bulb illuminated a small circle in front of the door. The young Chinese man approached the door and rapped softly in what seemed to be a coded pattern. A peep-hole opened and an eye appeared. Apparently recognizing the guide, the man inside opened the door a crack and further surveyed the curious group in the hall.

After a brief conversation in hushed Chinese, the door opened just enough to allow one person at a time to sidle in sideways. Inside the small room, four or five young men lounged on a worn sofa against the dingy beige wall to the right. If possible, they looked meaner and more ruthless than their compatriots in the hallway. Across from the door were windows with cloth shades drawn. Another larger room opened opposite the sofa and, though darkened, seemed to be stacked full with boxes or cases, presumably of watches.

Next to this doorway, a middle-aged man sat at a folding card table, counting money into a steel box. He was the obvious leader of whatever organization this was. Everyone waited in silence, watching him count. Finally, the older man rose and turned, displaying a black revolver tucked into his waistband at the small of his back. He asked the young "guide" something that was answered with much gesticulating toward the woman, her husband, and their son, who were all trying to look inoffensive and wishing nothing more than to escape unscathed (or even slightly scathed, but free).

Their guide turned and asked, "How many watches you want?"

"One," was the answer.

This set off a louder and more passionate discussion between the older man, the guide, and the men on the sofa. The argument became still more heated until, with obvious anger, one of the men on the sofa rose and slapped the guide on the back of the head, hard enough to buckle his knees. The tourist trio flinched, moving instinctively toward the door. Apparently, the thugs meant to sell in dealer quantities, and the youngster had incurred much displeasure by bringing customers to the "lair" for a single watch. The leader ordered a man from the sofa into the darkened room, and he presently returned with what looked very much like a Rolex Submariner.

Recovering his enthusiasm at the sight of the object of his mission, the son quickly counted out fifty American dollars—the older man was very clear in his stipulation that he wanted "green"— tucked the watch into his pocket, and the trio turned as one to the door. The leader emitted a raspy growl that turned into a laugh and, after a slight hesitation, the others joined in, including the young guide, chastened and apparently forgiven his indiscretion. The gang leader said to the tourists, in heavily accented English, "Enjoy you stay inna Hong Kong and enjoy you watch." A man leaped from the sofa and, with much clicking and clanging, opened the armored door. He bowed with a flourish and motioned for them to leave.

Without a word, all three hurried to the elevator and clanked and wheezed to the ground floor as the still-lurking loungers watched carefully. They scurried out into the alley and nearly ran to the street to retrace their steps to the main thoroughfare. Gaining the lighted sidewalk, the son said to his parents, "That wasn't so bad, was it? I can't believe I found the watch so easily! You just have to ask the right person."

They hurried all the way to the waterfront and didn't stop looking over their shoulders until the ferry, vibrating and humming loudly, pulled away from Kowloon to cross the harbor.

The son pulled the watch out and studied it for a moment before holding it up for his mother and father to see. "Notice how the second hand steps from number to number? A real Rolex would sweep smoothly around the dial."

Looking at the dial his father said, "We laid our lives on the line for a ROTEX."

His mother chimed in, "I just hope it's worth scaring us out of our wits in that gangster's den."

"How can I get it through customs when I get to Los Angeles?" the son mused.

His mother looked at him. "Just wear it," she said. "If someone asks, say your watch stopped, so you bought the cheapest thing you could find in Hong Kong."

The Salami Story

Howard Schuman

As a Peace Corps Volunteer in southern Thailand in the late 1960's, I was a bit of a celebrity. Because the Australian missionary residing there left soon after I arrived, I was the only Westerner living in the district capital, where I was an English teacher. It was he who told me at the end of our first and only conversation, "It's nice to have another white face in town." Needless to say, he was not missed.

I should more accurately say that I was a "postal celebrity," because for a period of time I received any mail in the entire province that had an address written in English. The Thai postal authorities could read the English alphabet, and you could even send telegrams in English, but none of the Post and Telegraph employees knew what any of the words meant. This enabled my closest Peace Corps neighbor, who lived about three hours away by train, to send me affable telegrams on occasion with messages such as "Screw you, Love Wayne."

In any case, because of my English language ability, my strange looks, and even stranger way of speaking Thai, any time something arrived at the post office from afar sent to Mis-is-ter Howaats, as I was called, it made news.

This phenomenon had its most dramatic example the day of "the package." I was informed at school that the post office delivery man was looking for me because a very important package had arrived. It was so important that he could not deliver it himself, and it required my personal signature to be witnessed by the postmaster. Now, normally my mail consisted of month-old *Time* and *Life* magazines sent by my mother, piles of mostly junk information sent from the Peace Corps office in Bangkok, and an occasional "aerogramme" from one of my friends or relatives. For those old enough to remember, these were blue envelopes one could write on, fold over in origami-like fashion, and mail anywhere in the world for a set price. They were also impossible to open without shredding at least one-third of the message contained inside, and your letter became more like a jigsaw puzzle when trying to reconstruct its contents.

So getting a package was special. Off I went at the end of the school day to retrieve my surprise. Along the way, at least three or four kids told me I had a package at the post office. (It was not a very big town.) And when I finally arrived, I was greeted by about a dozen residents, all mulling around the post office counter. After the showing of the latest Bruce Lee Kung Fu film from Hong Kong at the rickety movie house, this was the biggest entertainment available in our little community. The postmaster then solemnly presented me with an oblong carton about sixteen inches in length, postmarked NYC, and asked for my signature.

Now, I know I disappointed many when I did not open the carton in their presence, but took it home to see what it held. There, to my amazement, I found a kosher salami encrusted in green mold, having been sent by ship from none other than Katz's Delicatessen on the lower east side of Manhattan. For those of you who never experienced the ambiance of Katz's, it's one of those old world delis where each waiter has worked for at least fifty years, and when you place an order he is more likely than not to tell you, "Nah, it's not so good today." I think that scene in "When Harry Met Sally," where Meg Ryan proves to Billy Crystal that women really do know how to fake it, was filmed there.

I do remember seeing, when I was a kid—and have since returned to verify its existence—a long sign hanging from the ceiling in Katz's that says, "We will send a salami anywhere in the world!" And, no doubt, during one of their trips to this culinary landmark, my parents decided in 1969 to take advantage of their offer.

I was taken aback by all the green mold on my newfound treasure and already thinking, *Oh, what a waste*, when to my great surprise I was able to peel back the tight cellophane wrapping, smelled the salami, and determined it seemed okay. Salami, which is really highly salted and pickled meat, is the modern version of what medieval folks and sailors must have lived off of in pre-refrigeration days,

I proceededto take the lengthy conversation piece to my favorite coffee shop opposite the train station, which boasted a TV that got reception in Malay and English. (I watched the moon landing there and translated for the patrons.) They also had a fridge. I asked if I could store my exotic snack

THE SALAMI STORY

and have slices of it over time, along with the big bottle of Thai beer I treated myself to as often as possible. They kindly agreed, and I relished my kosher salami for a couple of weeks, bit by bit. The kids who lived with me, both Thai Muslim, refused to try the salami despite the fact that I told them it was "halal" (kosher). They didn't trust that bunch of New Yorkers who manufactured such strange meat.

Those two still live in southern Thailand, one a professor of English at a university, and the other a corrupt local politician and multi-level marketer in the same province where I once lived. The last time I saw them, a few years ago, they arrived in Bangkok to visit me, having traveled on the train up from the south. They carried with them an almost empty bottle of Johnnie Walker Black Label, most of which they had consumed on the train. Holding up the bottle and greeting me at the door of a friend's apartment, they half slurred, half shouted, "Welcome, Howard. You taught us everything we know!"

At the Supermarket the Other Day

Jean Marie Purcell

With no thought in my head of J. A. Prufrock
I bought a little colorful rock
that was labeled and looked like a peach.
I believed it would ripen as is nature's plot.
That turned out to be a reach!
I just got to watch it rot.

Thomas Stearns, Mr. Eliot, sir,
I urge you from your grave bestir
and part, however, your thinning hair.
Wear your trouser bottoms rolled—or not.
But to sate your taste for that peach, *don't* dare.
Consider instead a kumquat.

Second Runner-up: Best Fiction Contest

Food for Thought

Elisa Drachenberg

If there is one thing that stands out most, it's this: she has always been unwilling to accept my habits, to see them for what they are—simply charming. I am not pointing fingers here; she might even agree with me on this, but perhaps not today. That is because she lacks my unrelenting optimism and my gift for forgiveness. Going back to the incident on that Wednesday night—I only bring this up to put what happened in context; normally, I would not mention anything from the past—when I came home from work, I knew by the smell in the hallway that something was off. After all, it was Wednesday, not Thursday or Friday. But you wouldn't have been able to tell.

The other thing that struck me as odd was the photo. Someone had moved it from the entrance, where the sunlight could never reach it, to the wall opposite the window, directly under the skylight—the sunniest spot in the house. In this stark Arizona light, the photo was bound to fade within a month. And, tell me, what would be the sense of having a bleached-out picture of anyone, let alone of a person we all cherished and admired for her generosity, a person who would offer her last Dollar to help us, who made all this possible? All this being the imposing building on Gurley Street, right across the courthouse downtown. Actually, it's an entire three-story brick house, the historic Goodwin Building, lovingly restored to its old glory. Mother bought it for the three of us and had it renovated, which, by the way, took an entire year. She put in hardwood floors, mindful of her allergies. She selected all furniture and amazed us with her debonair taste. She had the painters tint the ceilings with a bright golden sheen that matched the gold in the red velvet wallpaper, just as she had envisioned it from the very beginning.

We were spoiled, I cannot call it anything else. Yes, spoiled. Everything, and I mean everything, was provided for us. Sheila never had to lift a finger.

Mother bought the blinds, the lamps, the kitchen and bathroom cabinets, the mirrors, the paintings, e-ve-ry-thing. Best of all, she did not bother us with the fastidious process of choosing; she never asked us to weigh options or reach decisions. She alone took on that agonizing process of selecting, ordering, returning, and arranging all the things that make a house a home. Our home. It took vast dedication and true vision.

And Sheila—she would tell you so herself—profoundly lacked visual imagination. She always fretted over color combinations, even with her clothes. Where she would call herself meticulous, I'd call her insecure. But what's in an adjective? Let's not argue about her limitations.

As I said, I am an optimist. I felt certain that things would work out, that Sheila would, eventually, see things my way, *our* way, really, since Mother felt the same. Let's be honest, Mother didn't ask much in return for all the money and energy she spent on her faithful restoration and decoration; in fact, she didn't ask for anything. All my kind, soft-spoken mother needed was a little looking after. Just a tiny bit, was that too much to ask? For crying out loud, just breakfast, a simple breakfast of Irish steel-cut oats, cooked twenty minutes in vanilla-flavored milk, with a dash of sea salt and an inch-piece of fresh gingerroot finely minced with one of the two choppers that Mother had provided for our kitchen: a white one for her ginger, a red one for Sheila's garlic.

Mother, blessed with an exceptional olfactory sense, could taste immediately if the garlic chopper had been used to cut up her ginger. She loathed garlic, just the smell of it made her gag. At her age, almost seventy-five, she needed to tend her delicate digestive system and not torment it further with pieces of garlic that persistently found their way into her porridge.

Sheila did her best, but she was clearly handicapped when it came to cleanliness. If I were not such an optimist, I would have despaired long ago. Sheila has 20-20 vision, but no eyes to detect a stray smidgen of garlic clinging to the blade of a chopper she should not have used in the first place. Somehow, Sheila kept confusing Mother's white ginger chopper with the red garlic chopper. Sheila's love for roasted garlic and caramelized onions—another food Mother's stomach revolted against—kept Mother from coming downstairs in the morning. But the elevator, installed during the renovation, greatly facilitated things. All Sheila had to do was pour the boiled porridge into a pre-heated bowl, sprinkle it with spicy Saigon cinnamon, add half a tablespoon of unsalted Irish butter, and take Mother's breakfast up to the third floor.

After moving to Gurley Street, Mother, generous to a fault, also shared her precious Villeroy and Boch china. "Everyone should own fine porcelain dishes," she said. I never could understand why Sheila questioned Mother's motives, but she did.

"She doesn't want to eat from our earthenware. It's too shabby for Madame." Sheila held up one of the delicate plates, pointing with a trembling finger. "And this wide golden rim…I am sure…is supposed to prevent me from heating food in the microwave."

At six in the morning, when Sheila rolled out of bed to prepare our breakfasts, I cheered her up with happy songs like "Always Look at the Bright Side" or "Happy Days Are Here Again." Sheila was definitely not a morning person. She probably would have slept until eight o'clock. But considering Mother's sensitive stomach, I really couldn't let Sheila sleep in. If she had been ambidextrous like I am, I could have set the alarm clock for later, however, besides having no green thumb, she was cursed with arthritic fingers. It always took her a while to peel and slice the ginger before chopping it. That's why I heartened her with my tunes. I couldn't change reality; I could only change her perception of it.

Don't get me wrong. I, of course, could and would have prepared my own breakfast if that had not caused Sheila to be even more aware of her clumsiness. She dropped knives and cut herself frequently. When she squeezed my orange juice, she winced. I didn't want to humiliate her by witnessing her ineptitude.

Once, when noting her trembling hands, Dr. Gallon had mumbled something about testing for Parkinson's disease. I always doubted his judgment. After all, Mother was twenty-five years older than Sheila, and, despite her high cholesterol, fit as a fiddle. Every day, she ambled around the Courthouse Plaza and had long conversations with her friends. There was no slur in her speech, no limp in her walk, no dragging of feet. Some might have called her obese, yet, with a smile on her lips and a friendly word for every poodle owner in town, she made her rounds.

Mother used to have poodles, but they died under inexplicable circumstances when she went to see her lawyers in Chicago. They, the poodles, stayed with us at the cottage, where we used to live before moving into this house, and Sheila fed them chicken livers, just as Mother had instructed her. But two days after Mother's return all four poodles—first the two white miniatures, then the large black male, and finally the golden darling of everyone—lingered on their down pillows, barely lifting their heads when called. There was none of the usual yapping that Sheila failed to see for what it was: happy communication. Sheila insisted they "communicated" far too much.

"You don't know how they terrorize me when you're off to work," she complained, mistaking their playful snapping and snarling for aggression. She claimed the dogs not only growled, but actually tried to bite her, making her scamper for cover. Personally, I think this was Sheila's way of disguising her frequent falls and stumbles. Anyway, the vet was unable to pinpoint the dogs' cause of death.

"The autopsy showed no signs of foul play," Mother told Sheila, clearing her of all wrongdoing. Mother never went on blaming anyone who couldn't be proven guilty. But she did continue walking around the square after breakfast, now dogless and grief-stricken, still greeting every dog by name, patting every poodle on the head, and offering a friendly word to each of their owners.

After a double espresso at the Coffee-Brewery next to the bookstore, she began shopping in the stores and galleries on Montezuma. She always found little gifts for everyone: a crystal paperweight to cheer up ailing Edna; a golden necklace for Ruth's ninetieth birthday; a turquoise bracelet to thank Doreen for painting such an attractive picture of Thumb Butte, in which— cleverly incorporated in the foreground—a tiny Mother-look-alike figure embraced a poodle; a sapphire tie pin for me.

On days when all items were marked down 50%, she also stopped at El Vicente's Thrift Store on Cortez. You'd be surprised what she kept finding there for Sheila. One time, Mother bought her a fine-looking Tiffany lamp adorned with intricate green peacocks. Granted, Sheila loathed anything green; still, the lamp was ideal for the dining room desk, where she paid the bills. Frankly, I thought it petty of her to point out that she'd seen the same lamp at Wal-Mart for $9.99 the year before or that she'd discovered a *Made-in-China* sticker on the switch when scrubbing off the "thrift-shop grime." Sheila never could appreciate Mother's gifts.

"It's the thought that counts," I told her, but Sheila only sneered.

"Ha, some thought."

"A lamp—good God, Sheila, it's a lamp! Let's not make this into an argument. You know Mother means well."

"No, I don't know that," she grumbled.

As you can see, Sheila was difficult to please. Too many things had happened in the distant past for her to be carefree now. But we won't go into that. The same way we won't talk about the knitted booties in pink and blue and white: for the baby girl, for the baby boy, and finally for something that decided to leave her womb before we even knew its sex. After that, Sheila stopped knitting. That was long before she developed arthritis.

And I could not help but forgive her; that's the kind of man I am. I forgave her for not bearing me any children. For being allergic to animals. For stumbling in embarrassing ways in the concert hall, when all eyes were upon us because we were late, always late, since Sheila needed much longer to reach the building than I.

After her husband's deadly accident, I took Sheila under my wing. And, no, I did not flap her to death, as she quickly demurred when I reminded her how truly lucky she was. I mean, there she was, living in a grand house—smartly renovated and decorated by Mother—and all she did was whine, always complaining she didn't have any leisure time.

"We go to the symphony."

"Your *mother* goes to the symphony. *We* accompany her."

"We are lucky the symphony comes up here from Phoenix."

"I don't like classical music."

"Only barbarians dislike the classics; even Hitler liked Wagner."

"See where that got us?" Sheila rolled her eyes. "Your mother has her strolls on the square, she goes shopping and visits her friends. I don't have time for friends. All I do is run errands, buy groceries, clean and cook...and cook and cook."

As if anyone could help it that Mother had allergies, or that downtown Prescott was dusty, or that wooden floors needed to be mopped every day. We couldn't expect Mother to hire one of the Mexican maids our neighbors employed. Money was not the issue—I mean, for $6 an hour they were quite reasonable—but Mother's Hummel figurines were much too valuable to be handled by some peasant girl who escaped her muddy village to come to this great nation that gave her the opportunity to work for people like us.

Honestly, how long could cleaning and cooking take? We were only talking about four meals a day, that's all. Freshly baked biscotti for tea. And, here again, if Sheila had simply joined Mother for coffee instead of carrying on with her herbal teas, that would've saved time. And I am convinced that she could've come to like porridge in the morning if she'd made an effort. More important: if Sheila had stopped insisting on being a vegetarian—merely because some "allergist" had diagnosed her with "animal-protein intolerance"—one undemanding lunch would have sufficed. If Sheila wanted to get by on vegetables, splendid, but it would have been ludicrous to ask Mother to give up her bison-burgers or salmon-filled ciabattas.

And dinner? Well, since Sheila, in her stubborn way, favored foods with garlic, onions, and jalapeno peppers—to which she added all kinds of bizarre spices that gave Mother and me instant heartburn—it could not be helped if she once more had to fix two meals. Certainly, it takes longer to fix two meals. Then again, how long does it take to make Swedish meatballs or marinated Philly steaks with crisp homefries or, on Fridays in May, halibut gently simmered in white wine, served with fingerling potatoes and white asparagus? Mother discovered the asparagus in a small Dutch-Indonesian toko in Phoenix, where Sheila usually bought her seasonings.

"Look, asparagus from Holland," Mother said, pointing to a bundle of spears.

"Michigan?"

"No, dear, from the Netherlands."

Ever since we traveled to Holland, Mother and I cherished the finer foods of that country: raw, salted herring, mayonnaise-covered French fries, and meaty croquettes. It was there that we first tasted juicy white asparagus with Bechamel sauce and cooked ham. Sheila had no appetite for any of those delicacies. And on the day we planned a trip to the Keukenhof—a Dutch park, where flowers surround you in unequaled beauty and abundance—Sheila feigned a headache, or had one, we won't go into that now. At any rate, she didn't want to accompany us to the fields of blooming tulips, freesias, and hyacinths, claiming that the overpowering smell would exacerbate her migraines. So, while we admired the colors of spring and inhaled the intoxicating fragrance of red, white, and blue hyacinths, Sheila visited the van Gogh museum, the Stedelijk and Rijksmuseum in Amsterdam. She ate a vegetarian rijsttafel and wound up in the bookstore de Slegte, where she bought more books than we could take home without paying a fortune for overweight.

I guess by now you must realize that Sheila had a way of making life difficult for herself. As I said, she insisted on living a meatless existence, which didn't bother us, as long as she didn't expect us to join her. Mother and I adored the smell and taste of everything lamb, pig, chicken, and cow: grilled lamb chops with rosemary glaze, slow-roasted ribs, chicken wings in honey-lime sauce or veal with Gorgonzola. Unfortunately, though, Sheila's insistence on being a vegetarian or vegan, or whatever they call someone like her, inevitably required the preparation of two dinners. And given Mother's sensitive stomach, freshly cooked, homemade meals—never that processed foodstuff—were crucial.

Some time back, when Sheila was in the hospital, we tried meals from the pizzeria next door. Let me just say they were awful; we couldn't wait for Sheila to come home. She might have complained a lot for someone so privileged, but her meals were scrumptious. If Sheila was one thing, she was a gifted cook. In fact, she was such a superb cook that Mother and I reluctantly accepted the ghastly odor her own concoctions generated in the house. We learned to ignore those awful wafts of garlicky lentil-curries, while savoring tender slices of leg of lamb in whiskey sauce served with sweet potato pie: an orgasmic palate-sensation. Yet nothing surpassed her beef Stroganoff.

Every morning following breakfast, I first took the elevator up for a quick visit to Mother on the third floor, then down to work on the second. Wednesday mornings were no different, except, while unlocking the office, I already anticipated the familiar aroma. We all did. Our entire legal four-leaf clover—Jorge Capdevila, the immigration guy; David Cramer, the divorce specialist; Jimmy Barton, the estate fixer; and I, the former tax lawyer—eagerly awaited the afternoon. All members of *Lucky Legality* knew the routine. Starting around three o'clock, we got our first whiff of Sheila's chicken soup: whole organic chicken, fresh celery, carrots, and peas and who knows what else Sheila dreamed up to make our mouths water.

By four o'clock the scent of her beef Stroganoff was seeping through the floorboards. If the chicken soup whetted our appetite, the beef Stroganoff triggered nostalgic cravings. The other lawyers clearly envied me, especially Jorge, our recently widowed colleague, who now ate at the food court in the mall.

"My wife was a fine cook, too. I miss home-cooked meals," he said with a forlorn smile. The moment I told Sheila, she decided that Jorge, who always worked late, might as well take our "leftovers" home.

At precisely 5:30 in the afternoon, as Sheila served us her steaming chicken soup with its thick round eyes of fat floating freely, I touched the silver cutlery, stroked the starched white linen, caressed the imported crystal wineglasses and joined Mother in a prayer. Shivering with desire, we dipped our spoons into the broth and savored satisfaction. Our eyes told Sheila all she needed to know: the soup was fabulous. Sometimes, when putting the plates in front of us, Sheila's hands shook quite violently. We never said a word about her spills; we didn't want to call attention to her shortcomings. Instead, we smiled benevolently, brought napkins to our lips, dabbed them slightly before raising our glasses, and chanted with the purest intentions: "To Sheila, the best cook in town, perhaps the state, possibly the entire nation."

I can't say that Sheila was appreciative of our praise.

"Yeah, yeah, yeah," she muttered, stumbling back into the kitchen and not returning until we were ready for our beef Stroganoff.

While we gorged, Sheila usually ate her food in the kitchen, but on Wednesdays she joined us for dessert: upside-down pineapple cake, our favorite. We drank coffee; she, green tea. The three of us silently enjoyed the cake, which was baked with egg-substitute, not as tasty as with real eggs. As I said, we gladly sacrificed for shaking Sheila. She, on the other hand, never accepted me as I am.

There was another point of contention. Sheila declined to limit her cooking skills to a few tried and true menus. She liked to experiment, wanted to create new and different combinations. Mother and I were much more conservative. We preferred to know in the morning what we would eat at night, and how it would taste. We figured that Sheila could employ her creative tendencies on her own dishes, ail seasoned with spices—from turmeric to lemongrass—we detested.

"In a world they cannot control, they want the predictability of my meals. They insist on the same food, at the same time, on the same days. It drives me insane," I once overheard Sheila tell someone on the phone. She quickly hung up when she noticed me standing in the doorway.

Every afternoon, at exactly five o'clock, I walked downstairs, unlocked the front door, went to the bathroom to wash up, took off my tie, changed shirts—white at the office, stripes at night—met Mother in the dining room at 5:15 and poured the martinis Sheila had prepared. Sheila never drank; she wasn't a Muslim or recovering alcoholic, she just didn't like alcohol, which worked out fine, her not joining us for drinks, since she obviously needed this period to put the finishing touches on our meal. Mother and I understood that and respected her alone time.

When I came home on the Wednesday in question—I just need to bring this up to let you see what happened, and why none of this could possibly be construed to be my fault—I immediately noticed that Mother's photo, taken when she was just sixteen, no longer hung in its usual spot.

The very first time she showed it to me, I commented on her mysterious smile. "I had just found out that I was pregnant with you," she said, and that same mysterious smile returned to her now no longer full lips. "I met your father at our usual hiding place in the park to tell him the news."

Actually, and I found this out in bits and pieces, Mother had brought along the camera, one of my father's many gifts, and encouraged him to photograph her in various stages of undress. Later, after all his customary fondling and probing, she took a few pictures of him: unbuckling his belt, lowering his trousers…sprawled on the grass. He was slow in understanding when she mentioned her plan to tell the Tribune, or his wife, or both that he had impregnated her, an innocent minor, a child really, who had trusted him and lost her virginity to the persuasive senator from Illinois, who at that moment happened to be in a tight race against a ruthless moralist—a young man, fast gaining in popularity, until, unexpectedly, allegations about the chap's sexual transgressions surfaced, which may or may not have been fabricated. Needless to say, the senator could ill afford a scandal of his own, much less one that could easily be proven to be true.

"I did it for you," Mother claimed. "If you take into account how wealthy his wife was, and how powerful he became after the election, which he won thanks to my silence, I think—no, I know—he got off easy. Considering that I had to raise you by myself here in the desert, in this dusty, windy three-horse town, in this unglamorous one-time capital, where gold miners and whores once drank themselves into a stupor, in this…but those were the conditions, and I signed the papers."

I had heard the story so many times, I could tell it myself. I could never figure out, though, what she meant by "I did it for you." Surely, she could not mean getting pregnant. Mother had a way of being vague when it suited her. So it came as no surprise that she never got around to revealing the identity of the grinning soldier whose photo I discovered in one of her drawers. "He vanished," she said, snatching the picture from my hands. I was seven then, anxiously aiming to recall the face of the somehow familiar-looking mystery man, who apparently had not made it home, but whom she still remembered with a surprisingly tender voice and misty eyes.

"I spared nothing to make you succeed," she would say, as only mothers can who are so clearly disappointed in their offspring. I did not make Harvard. I was lucky that the University of Guadalajara supplied me with something that could be interpreted as a law degree. And then there was the drinking and the accident and…but I digress.

First-time visitors to the house usually asked about the woman with the Mona Lisa smile. Mother's photo—I had it retouched and enlarged for her seventieth birthday and also selected the gold-colored, wooden frame that matched the antiqued mirror in the hallway—turned out to be a real icebreaker, and Sheila should have been pleased. She was not exactly outgoing, not much of a talker, either. She should have been grateful that Mother took over the conversation after the guests, mostly my clients, commented on her portrait.

"That's me," Mother would begin, leaving out the circumstances that had brought her to Arizona. She was much too classy to mention any of that. There was also the contract, still legally binding, even though the man in question had long since died. I knew enough about the law to be certain that his three surviving sons—one, a senator like his father; one, an advisor in the White House; one, the governor of Nevada—would not have welcomed the news of another sibling. Besides, Mother's generous monthly checks and the even more generous annual Christmas bonus, both so aptly negotiated long ago despite her very young age, would have ceased coming if she had ever exposed my father.

But no, Sheila loathed Mother's portrait in the entrance and hated living under the same roof with her. She preferred our cottage in Piñon Heights.

"If you want something truly eye-catching, why don't you hang one of my paintings in that spot?" she suggested with fluttering eyelids, fingertips pressed together to hide the tremor. Granted, at the cottage Sheila used to paint colorful things, abstracts, if you know what I mean. And the tremor of her hands actually added something special to the way her colors stuttered toward each other. Her paintings filled all walls. But to call her hobby art goes too far. Yes, in the past she sold some large canvases in galleries in Phoenix and Tucson and a few in Palm Springs, and yes, a few more to a prominent banker in Flagstaff, a commercial realtor in Florida, and a fund-manager in Las Vegas, who valued its "anguished appeal."

But by far her biggest client was Jorge—our second-floor immigration lawyer—probably because Mexicans have a different color appreciation. His parents had moved to Arizona half a century ago, and he claims to be an American, which technically he is, but his DNA is still Mexican, if there is such a thing as country-specific DNA. I mean, the fact that he appreciated Sheila's paintings enough to keep buying them should tell you a thing or two.

But back to that Wednesday. When I opened the front door, perspiring profusely and bone-weary from my trip to Scottsdale, where I had spent all day with an elderly couple who needed detailed advice on how best to camouflage their assets—a matter I cannot discuss here—perfidy engulfed me. Mother's portrait had been moved and placed directly under the skylight. Already it seemed sun-bleached. Her smile looked faded, the sparkle in her eyes subdued.

Not only my eyes registered betrayal. Today was beef-Stroganoff day, but my nose could not detect the enticing aroma, or, for that matter, any other smell of food. The mere thought of Sheila's dish—prepared with liberal amounts of vodka, wine, and sour cream—had made my mouth salivate on my way up from the Valley. And now nothing. Olfactory silence! Equally alarming was the complete lack of sound from the kitchen. And where the air-conditioning should have been silent, it now coughed blasts of icy air in my direction. The arctic cold coaxed immediate goose bumps into budding. As my brain strained to make sense of the eerie setting, my mouth grew dry, my legs wobbled, and acid flooded my stomach. All senses screamed calamity.

The thermostat indicated sixty-one degrees. I had spent roughly two hours in a traffic jam on I-17, repeatedly trying and unable to reach Sheila on my cell. It was long past six o'clock, and more than anything I needed a drink. Without washing up, I entered the dining room, somehow still expecting to see Mother in her usual armchair, sipping a martini.

And, fortunately, Mother was sitting there, right in front of the fireplace, which—another curious detail—was not burning. Mother didn't turn her head. The ice in the near empty pitcher on the side table had melted, despite the chilly temperature in the room. I filled a glass.

"What's going on?" I asked, gulping down my first tepid martini. No answer. I assumed Mother to be as appalled by Sheila's behavior as I was and went to place a kiss on her cheek, as I always did when she needed calming. She looked asleep: head tilted forward, triple chin resting on chest, mouth hanging open, hands folded around an empty glass in her lap, a smudge of rose-colored lipstick on its rim. When I kissed her, right below those once marvelous high cheekbones that had made my father swoon, I realized that her wig was slightly askew.

"Mother."

Silence.

"Mother!"

No reaction.

I knelt down to unclasp her fingers, meaning to check her pulse. Only then, after managing to take hold of one cold, limp hand, did I detect the plastic bottle on the rug, nestling innocently against the armchair, spilling blue tranquilizers.

I shook her shoulders. "Mother? Mother? Mother?" I wailed.

I might have dribbled. Other bodily fluids formed, gathered, sought outlets and converged: tears streamed, saliva trickled, snot escaped. A heavy drop tumbled and splashed on Mother's forehead. Suddenly, as if startled, she blinked and opened her eyes, tentatively displaying the same dreadfully faded look that I had glimpsed on her portrait in the hallway.

Her mouth opened wider, as if to scream, but only a moan emerged. Again, she tried, but I could only make out a rattling sound. With what seemed like an enormous effort, she pointed her chin toward the fireplace. And now I spotted it, pasted on the mantle, a pink piece of paper torn from Sheila's notebook. Her shaky handwriting, difficult to read under normal circumstances, now seemed impossible to decipher. When I finally did, I kept reading those three words over and over: *Adios and Goodbye*. She had not even signed the note.

Just for the record, I never could locate Sheila again, nor, for that matter, Jorge Capdevila. Mother confirmed that nothing was missing except some of Sheila's clothes. But the shock of abandonment and the constant stress of having to deal with the infinite number of incompetent, unreliable, and dishonest cooks and cleaners that the *Home-Sweet-Home* agency sent us finally took their toll. Only two months after Sheila's vicious desertion, Mother followed her four poodles to the land of no return.

After the funeral, I stopped at the cottage where Sheila and I had once lived. All walls were bare. Without warning, Sheila had retrieved every one of her paintings, deliberately hampering the intended sale of the place. As I told you in the beginning, unlike me, she was an unforgiving person, unwilling to love me as I am, and wouldn't you agree that it was a further sign of her utter disregard for me to leave another of her callous pink notes on the table. Four words this time: *Life with you sucked.*

Second Runner-up: Best Poetry Contest

We Deliver

William Killian

My phone number is one digit off
the neighborhood *Pizza Hut*.
We get lots of calls.
Tonight I didn't want to be nice,
I wanted to have some fun.

I'll take the order and not show up. No, no fun there.
We're being robbed, please call 911. Sick.
Try flirting? Get angry—*what the hell god damn number did you
dial* and slam the phone.
Or say *you are the lucky caller—
free pizza and Pepsi for a year!*

But I took the order, got the address,
went to *Pizza Hut*, placed the order,
went off to meet a happy family.

But I could hardly make it to the door,
walking around the patrol cars,
the armed officers in uniform,
all weeping and drunk.
I stood at the door. Their story rode like a black cloud
over my night of generosity. The drunkenness,
the feigned laughter, the scent of grief
pulled me into their darkness.

I wanted to tell them my fun idea,
now unimportant, not the time nor the place.
I tried to stop the tipping as broken man after broken man gave
up 10s, 20s, some 50s.

I tried to tell them, *the pizzas are free, no tipping please*,
but their weeping, cussing would not let them listen.

I cried when the puzzle became clear.
Their comrade in the Sheriff's Department
had young children in this home that he built.
The story goes that there were two sad souls
in a pickup truck
that hangs rifles in the back window—
their rifle wasn't hanging.

The deputy tried to talk the country boy down,
didn't want to hurt him, could have, would have,
but didn't want to, just wanted to help him
leave the dirt parking lot,
get him home to sleep it off.

The still desert had never heard such a sound.
Coyotes froze, crickets shut down, owls stared.
Dogs left the area in a flash.
The shot cracked a family wide open,
stopped three small children in their paths,
knocked a bunch of deputies to the ground.

I was sobbing, immobile, wondering why
I had answered the telephone…

This is how we do it sir,
when one of us goes down. We gather
at his house to be close, to remember.
You take this to cover the pizzas, your time,
and do something good with the rest.
You go now, drive careful, you hear?
We're watching you—
we don't ever want to have to phone your home.

A Blue Funk

Carol Poss

I'm in a blue funk! Don't know why,
don't really care. It doesn't feel good.
It doesn't feel fair. I want to be alone,
but I can't stand myself. I'm goin'
to the kitchen and raid the candy shelf,
eat six bars of chocolate and feel bad
all day long, turn on the stereo and
sing a sad blues song. Maybe it's the
humidity or the planets misaligned
or the barometric pressure or the
astrologic sign. Too tired to get mad,
too weary to shout, don't want to
analyze or figure it out. Don't try
to fix me or help me to fight it.
It's my pity-party and you're not
invited. I don't know why, don't
really care, it doesn't feel good.
It doesn't feel fair. Blues don't
last forever, at least that's what is
said, but for now forget it.
I'm goin' back to bed!

Windmills

Marlene Newman

In God We Rust

She thought she chose her battles. She thought that, if she were selective and critical, she could effect change and, perhaps, some small justice might prevail. But the system was constructed to wear one down. This was accomplished by the most subtle cruelty. If you fought the good fight with integrity and honor, the opposition smeared and distorted. If you defended, you were being unprofessional. If you spoke with the passion of conviction, you were emotional or, worse, unstable. You were double-bound, stymied and frustrated at every turn.

And, if you did nothing, you not only had to live with yourself, but you had to continue to accept the unacceptable. Take the parking ticket, for instance. The initial assault occurred when she left the post office. There it was, a ticket on the windshield, twelve minutes left on the meter, and a policeman walking away.

"Officer!" and, again, a little louder, "Officer!"

He continued toward the crossing.

She ran and called, reached within a foot or two and yelled, "There's time left on the meter…twelve minutes."

"Wrong meter," he mumbled, barely glancing back, not stopping.

"Come look at it. There's still time on the meter."

He neither stopped nor slowed down, but continued across the intersection and stepped inside the lobby of a nearby office building. On the other side of the street, she spotted another patrolman. Still hoping for justice, she repeated her story, this time adding a description of the officer's behavior.

"I'm sorry, we only do moving violations," the patrolman answered. "We have nothing to do with parking. That's the men in the white shirts."

"Come look at the meter, please."

He shrugged. "Sorry."

Pay the Ten Dollars

On Monday, lunchtime was spent waiting at a window marked Parking Violations. At her turn, she told her tale.

"You'll have to come when court is in session."

"I work. Isn't there anyone I can talk to?"

"You'll have to see the judge. You'll have to come when court is in session."

Tell It to the Judge

Thursday, 8 a.m. Police desk

"When can I see someone about this ticket?"

"Carlson…second door on the right."

"The lieutenant is on the phone. He'll be right with you."

And he was. This time her wait was brief. Again, she recited her story, this time adding, "It's not the ten dollars. It's the principal of the thing. I don't think this man should be allowed to issue summonses for cars that are legally parked."

"He's one of our best officers," was the reply.

"Well, what do I do now?"

"Come back at 9 and see if the ticket has come back from the computer. It looks like it's too soon, but if it's back you can see the judge."

A quick cup of coffee followed by some fierce heartburn and a return to the window marked Parking Violations.

"Is this ticket back from the computer? I'd like to see the judge."

The clerk took the ticket from her. "We don't have a computer here. Part II, last door on the right."

An assortment of people, about a baker's dozen, were already waiting for justice. They fidgeted in fits of mild to moderate agitation, restlessness, and boredom. The door at the right of the judge's bench would open from time to time. A clerk would enter, add some papers to the bench, and exit. Another clerk would then appear and call out names to establish who, in fact, was seated in the court room. An occasional lawyer would come in, walk through the swinging doors that separated the judge's domain from the public seating, and silently depart.

Still sitting...still waiting...still hoping the judge would soon be there. Another double bind. Should she wait? Should she go? Her husband was sure to be worried or, possibly, even angry. The ticket...they had taken the ticket away from her. Talk about the horns of a dilemma. A quick phone call. Leave a message on the answering machine. Let him know you're alive and well...and stupid. And know full well the many future opportunities that will occur for you to be reminded of your folly.

11:00 a.m.

Still sitting...still waiting, despite the assurance and reassurance of the kindly court clerk

11:18 a.m.

The judge has yet to enter, but only a few remain in their seats. The others have strangely disappeared. And now we are five...shades of Agatha Christie...would there soon be none?

Use the time to reflect, she thought, *to regroup, rethink...recover.*

The previous evening had been another painful experience, another frustration in a mounting series of losing battles for a just cause.

"Is there such a thing as emotional carnage? How does one measure the casualties? Who are the winners? What's it all about, Aaalllfeeee?"

Here Come the Judge

Judge Crater Presiding...

A truck driver told of stopping to help a blind man across the street, only to receive a summons for obstructing traffic from the officer who could have/should have assisted the sightless pedestrian.

A young mother was called to school in response to her child's medical emergency.

At last, her name was called. Her story told, the judge, with a patronizing smile, condescended to dismiss the ticket on the grounds that she had gone through so much to rectify the matter.

If she had won, why did she feel so defeated?

Two months later, she received a notice in the mail of an unpaid parking ticket, including late charges.

Invisible

Gloria Salas-Jennings

I change your babies, carry your groceries,
mop your bathrooms,
but you don't see me.

I rub hard,
my brown skin
yields thin mahogany ropes,

As I hope that just beyond this layer
is the alabaster skin
that will make me visible.

Would you see me then?

First Runner-up: Best Fiction Contest

Squeegee

R. E. Hayes

Some of Carlisle's seniors often wear too much clothing. Chicago in midsummer, yet their venerable brains no longer accurately control body temperature. Summer breezes could clobber them like January wind chills. Take Mrs. Addie Mae Starks, always in that big brown wool coat. She'd wear it trekking in the Gobi desert, Carlisle thought.

Maybe she's sewn money inside. He'd heard of old ladies pulling this maneuver, literally wearing a nest egg on their back. But with her gnarled arthritic hands, how would she ever thread a needle? Almost eighty, he guessed, but still sharp. Sharper than any double-latte-sipping MBA hotshot who wouldn't give him a second chance.

Even with a degree, they don't give a rat's ass, and my only brother's no better.

On the mornings when he picked her up, the response to his greeting was usually the same. "Fair-to-middling, young man, fair-to-middling." Then she'd pat her bosom on top of the brown coat, seeming obliged to convey an acceptable level of vigor. Of course, he had introduced himself, but apparently she preferred the generic "young man."

He put his arm out for her. She leaned her weight on him and stepped into the ambulette. He leaned in and fastened her seat belt. She seemed bemused that someone cared enough to fuss over her ancient body. Outside the vehicle, he lifted his feet, sliding them east and west on the hot pavement, giving her time to adjust or complain if something wasn't right.

Wayne Carlisle hustled around to the driver's side and jumped in. Checked the mirrors and eased away from Fellowship Nursing Home up to the light, then swung a left onto Fullerton Street. Thirty-five minutes to Dr. Rader's office through the city. Mrs. Starks had asked him to please not drive on the Kennedy Expressway. "Fast cars scare me."

He raised his right hand and positioned the rear-view mirror, then adjusted the air conditioner. "You're not too hot in this coat, are you?"

"I'm fine, thank you, young man, but I was wondering…"

Twice a week for three months, Carlisle had made this trip, listening to her stories, getting to know her. An ex-cop and ex-con, he wanted her to know precious little about him.

"Wondering?" he sang out, anticipating another chapter in her remarkable life. He guessed she found comfort in storytelling, bestowing the gift of her righteous past on a friendly white man. In high school, Carlisle hung out with wiggers: white kids awed by all things black. In college, he'd taken a course in post-reconstruction African-American history. He wasn't ignorant. He could relate.

"Yes. Just a-wondering why a nice-looking young feller like yourself would be doing this here piddly work, driving us old folks around. The one before had nothing on the ball, don't know why the church association gave him the job. What's his name…Lester? Yes, that's it, Lester. A trifling Negro, didn't last but two weeks. Calling me sister! I told him my Mama didn't give me no brothers who looked like him. Scared the wits out of me with his awful driving. You seem like a decent young man, so how come you doing this?"

Stopped for a crowded school bus, he watched with humorless detachment the kids waving and mugging in the back seat. *What can I say?* Again, he thought of Sandy, the family he'd disgraced and destroyed. She had pulled up stakes during the four years he was away. Lit out for Montana, Oregon, somewhere out west, taking Nick who'd be eleven now and Danny, nine.

She probably tells them daddy's dead.

They had dated since high school, so he appreciated the tenacious pull religion exerted, couldn't imagine Sandy ever considering taking him back. She'd packed up the Patsy Cline CDs, telling him (with Zoloft-induced composure) she might have explored marriage counseling, "even watching those raunchy, bend over DVDs," but she could not become a black bimbo, which he obviously preferred.

No words ever sound so resolute, so gut wrenching, so heart-piercingly final as the words, "It's too late," dripping from the chilled lips of a woman who once loved and cared for you, triggered by some thoughtless, penis-driven frolic on the side.

Five years ago on a muggy airless Saturday night, Carlisle shot a boozed-up black man while skulking around with Ginger, a half white, half black part-time lingerie model. During the trial for involuntary manslaughter, people said Howard Johnson (AKA Captain Serenade) used to clean car windshields for chump change, singing while he worked.

Singing when the slug crashed into the side of his unsuspecting gray wool head.

Witnesses testified Captain Serenade was clowning as usual, handling his wet squeegee like a pretend microphone, crooning in Ginger's face, shifting the tool from hand to hand à la Wayne Newton working a Vegas showroom. Water, a thimble full, splashed her navy suede sling-backs, and she exploded with curses. Carlisle stepped forward and smacked the vocal entertainer on the head with the flat barrel of his department issue Glock 9mm automatic. The shock of the thunderous eruption distressed the membrane surrounding every cell in Carlisle's body. It all happened so fast, he testified later. He intended the blow, but not the aftermath. So dark. He feared the liquored up old-timer was set to rap Ginger across her café au lait neck and shoulders with the dripping squeegee.

After the bus driver retracted the stop sign, Carlisle sucked in a deep breath and drove on, telling Mrs. Starks he was saving money for school.

"You ain't finished with school? What kinda school?" Amused astonishment resonated in her tone.

"What kind? Grad school," he said, gazing in the mirror into liquid brown eyes, realizing the intensity of her regard had ensnared him, that he would never apply.

"Yes, yes, that's why you been pestering me about the olden days. You whipper-snappers are something else!" She laughed, but it soon turned to wheezing.

"Are we okay back there?"

"Yes, I'm fine, thank you," she said, dabbing a white handkerchief to her temple.

They grew quiet. He listened to her breathing and decided it sounded normal for a woman her age. Dr. Rader's office was in the semi-upscale neighborhood of Wrigleyville, near Wrigley Field, up ahead a few blocks. Help her out of the ambulette, make sure the nurse was available, and then free coffee if any was left. On a typical day, he'd transport at least four seniors. Easy trip today, only Mrs. Starks on board.

"Mrs. Starks, let me ask you something," he said. "Suppose you were sitting in a Corvette on a gorgeous sunny day, minding your own business, waiting for someone. All of a sudden, the car's sliding, rolling backwards, what...what would you think?"

"What chew call it?" she asked. "A Carvette?"

He felt her eyes shifting, coming to rest on the back of his head, and a frisson of hope trilled his spine. "A Corvette, a sports car, a two-seater," he said, closing in on something, a prelude to knowledge that might inform his fractured soul.

Deceit runs in the family. Carlisle's brother, Magnus, owner of a small towing company, had recently told Carlisle he could not hire him, an ex-con, for "insurance reasons." Skinner, his only employee, specializes in seizing a parking violator's car, grappling the under frame with a formidable cast-iron hook, and thus guaranteeing a miserable experience for some luckless driver. Skinner had towed a Vette with an elderly woman inside. Claimed he never saw her.

Carlisle figured his disregard for the safety of the old woman stemmed from his desire to make a grubby buck, an act more contemptible than his own tragic mistake. That's what Mr. Mendoza called it, he reminded himself, grateful for the reassurance given by his new boss, who knew about the shooting from the newspapers and TV and hired him, anyway.

Carlisle guided the ambulette into the parking space reserved for loading and unloading, left the engine running, then jumped out to offer his strong arm.

"We'll finish this on the way back," he said, aware he sounded too anxious.

Forty-five minutes later, Carlisle returned for Mrs. Starks. While buckling her in, she asked, as if no time had passed, "What do you mean, rolling back?"

Really a sharp old gal, he said to himself, pleased she'd revived the subject. "Yes, right. What would you think? Suddenly rolling back, what would you think?" He smiled, picturing her spooned inside a Vette.

At length she spoke, slowly, measured. "First off, I'd look to find out if any white men was around. Mean white men. My mama raised me to be scared of them."

Again, his eyes found the mirror, and the sudden change was startling. Gone were the dignified and expressive wrinkles, replaced by notched and creased lines meandering randomly over her mahogany face. The lips had a severe set; nut hard eyes stared straight ahead as if considering past affronts by men who'd behaved badly toward her and those she loved.

She asked, "Was it mean white men setting this Carvette to rolling back?" A leathery brown hand rose slowly, shading her eyes. Seconds later, a cluster of puffy scud clouds trundled across the sky, cloaking her in slight shadows.

"Well, I guess so," Carlisle said, feeling his cheeks burn.

Behind prison walls, time is a menacing specter undermining captive existence minute by minute. No inmate is granted the benefit of a doubt. What does a convicted cop behind bars fear most, a shank in the back surrounded by great books or gruesome strangulation by pillowcase in the laundry room?

Like a baseball pitcher traded to a rival team who divulges secrets of his former team, Carlisle revealed to inmates insider tips the police don't want the public to know. He kept prison rapists at bay by connecting with feared white nationalist skinheads, proof that a caged man will do anything to survive.

Carlisle caught a break.

He had a BA degree, so officials scheduled him to work in the library, where he tutored reading. He checked out books on crime and death to read in the relative safety of his cell. Naively, he tackled Joyce's symbolism in "The Dead," hoping to discover how, in one twisted moment, he'd severed his connection with the everlasting trajectory of humanity, trying to defend a she-wolf.

Monks in "The Dead" have taken a vow of silence; they sleep in coffins to atone for the world's sins. Locked down at night, Carlisle thought about the depth of their faith. Not a spiritual man, he couldn't imagine going this far. Besides, how would they know if it worked?

Now, crossing Addison Avenue in slowed traffic, he pictured pine coffins lined up like army bunks in a squad bay. And in front of each, monks wearing brown sackcloth robes kneeled, praying to have the ground cut from under mean white men.

Mrs. Starks said, "West hell is all they deserve."

He figured she'd soon clarify the reference. Instead, she started again talking up her great-grandfather, how as a young boy he had picked cotton for the meanest overseer ever to walk upright on the Lord's earth.

"Picked cotton from can see in the morning to can't see at night," she said. "Then one day he just up and flew the coop. Ran into the Georgia woods. Gone two whole days before the dogs got ahold his scent and chased him up a big ole catalpa tree." She was a little girl when her mother told how the slave-catching patrols—*paddy rollers*—had dragged him down and beaten him brutally. Afterwards, her mother deliberately set out to put the fear in her only child, for her own good.

"Later, when he got to be sixteen or so, he escaped for good," she said with obvious pride. "Made it all the way to Ohio, a free State."

"Ohio."

"But many-a-time he'd sneak back over to Kentucky to help runaways get across the River Jordan to freedom."

"Jordan? You mean the Ohio river."

"That's right. And if it was all iced over, they could walk, pretty as you please. A slew of 'em kept on walking up to Canada. Yes, sir." She grew silent in a deeply warming way. "One day, he went back to help a low-down man who truly wasn't worth stink. Great-granddaddy fount out later he had the nicest wife and took to beating on her all the time."

She paused, gathering the coat with both hands, as if the effort of recalling this bleak era had blown up a chill wind. He sensed she'd told the story before, timing the pauses for effect. At least eighty-five, he guessed, trying to puzzle out when all this happened.

"Granddaddy just ached for this mean overseer to take up residence in west hell."

He eyed her in the mirror, rocking side-to-side like a one-woman gospel choir. He guessed a blithe spirit had taken her over. He had never touched Sandy in anger and wanted Mrs. Starks to know, considered saying this, as though it would help him gather the remnants of his shaken soul. He tamped down tears welling behind blinking eyes, couldn't let flow.

She went on. "Why, it's so horribly hot in west hell, the devil's helpers use *rubber* coffins to bounce in the really unforgivable souls. Bounces them straight on through regular hell, nonstop. Shoot! Even the devil don't want his helpers going into west hell."

She leaned back looking spent, slowly unbuttoning her coat, six brown quarter-size buttons.

"My, my, I've been talking and carrying on a blue streak. Don't know when I've run on so much. Talked myself clean out of breath."

He turned the wheel, easing through traffic, wanting the return trip to last longer. "I hope your great-grandfather got his wish."

She must have heard the smile percolating in his throat because she laughed with surprising vitality. "By and by, I suspect he did."

If he doubted it before, Carlisle was convinced the fib he'd once told regarding his churchgoing habits was unavoidable. The truth, now, would only disappoint, and truth, however righteous and noble, was no reason to hurt this gentle old lady.

Five blocks from the nursing home, she rustled the brown coat off. "I am feeling kinda warm in this coat, young man, wearing entirely too much fuffle." She placed the garment across her lap, gentle, as one would tend a sick cat.

"Good," he said. "Good for you."

Still crawling behind a green van, Carlisle's filled to distraction with upsurges of joy followed by pulsating remorse. Something's coming to him, the shape fuzzy and elusive, like trying to catch a revealing dream just after awakening. In a flash, his head snaps back. Alerting. He's following too close. Not enough time. All he can do now is brace for immediate collision. In the split second before impact, he pictures his dark past floating up, eclipsing the surreally inverted present. The beat cop investigating this routine fender-bender will soon move to the driver's side of the ambulette, reddish eyes beneath the visor narrowing to take everything in. He's wary. A spark of law enforcement acuity flickers like erratic nightclub neon.

It's inevitable, this smirking cop is about to unmask Carlisle, a convicted felon. "You took down that squeegee perp, you're the copper with the chocolate honey," he'll soon blurt out, rocking on the balls of his feet, scanning the driver's license. "You shoulda popped the ammo clip out before you smacked that mope," he says, referencing unauthorized police procedure for smacking an old wino's head—street justice—that the disgraced ex-officer obviously had not heeded.

The radio is not on, yet inside Carlisle's undefended center, he hears Patsy Cline imploring some jackleg to hurt her now and get it over if he has cheating on his mind. Again the silent monks appear, pious little men in brown, face up in wooden coffins. This time, Carlisle's lying beside them, lips moving but nothing comes out.

Mercifully, the collision occurred only in his roiled imagination. When the brakes slammed, the seat belt jerked tight, eliciting a mild grunt from

Mrs. Starks. Still turtling behind the green van, Carlisle wished he had ignored her qualms and taken the Kennedy Expressway.

"Sorry about that," he said, springing free from a wave of self-pity.

The van turned left and minutes later intermittent cloud cover broke. Once again, the rolling ambulette belonged to the sun, captured by its resplendence. Lustrous rays angled across Mrs. Starks, draping her oval face and upper torso like a gilded sash. From behind again came the rustle and swish of clothing. Genial, assuring sounds, as though from a friend speaking evenly in a difficult moment.

Tires humming, eyes on the road, he listened to her breathing and contemplated the right direction for bypassing west hell.

Curtain

William Killian

When I die
they will ruffle through my poetry
after someone says

did you know he wrote poems
to find one to bless my passing.
I hope it's not one I dressed up to sell,

I hope they use the one
that dismantled the moment,
the one that invaded cellular time

and exposed the lies and illusions
that make enemies necessary
and wars just

a fucking waste.
When I die
they will rush home from the cemetery

to their lists of things to do,
and I will be whispering
read slowly…your list is your poetry.

CONTRIBUTOR'S NOTES

This is the second appearance of BILL ALEWYN's fiction in *OASIS Journal*. His other short fiction has appeared in *LUX, Saguaro Speaks,* and other literary magazines. He came to Casa Grande, Arizona for the waters; he was misinformed. [301]

JOHN BARBEE: My wife, Iola, writer and teacher, always intended to write the story of our lives together, and raising our combined family of eight children. With her many projects she never got to it, so I, who almost flunked English in school, decided to learn to write in order to record our many stories. I joined the "Creative Writers of Menifee Valley," whose members have published a number of stories in *OASIS Journal*. Their weekly workshops have helped me a lot. So I advise others to join a good writers workshop. You will make some wonderful new friends. [59]

TABINDA BASHIR is a retired doctor; her husband, a retired engineer. Ten years ago, they emigrated from Pakistan to be with their computer engineer daughter, and settled here. After furnishing the condo, they had the inevitable culture shock. To fill her time, Tabinda opted for Creative Writing. She has had stories published in Pakistani magazines, in the *Moon Journal* here, won the Daily Herald Citizens' award, and has a chap book, "Turning Point." In the absence of a social circle, she tends to look inward. That is how "Bound" came into being. Some of her friends and patients are in there. [33]

HELEN BENSON: My poems are not autobiographical, but they are personal, as they filter my observations of and my reactions to the world around me. One of the old poets—I think it was Wordsworth—said, "Poetry is emotion remembered in tranquillity." Poets are not unique in these feelings; they just write them down. It seems the older one gets, the more one sees. It's like climbing a mountain; the higher the path, the greater the vista. [80, 122]

MARY H. BER IS a writer who has spent over fifty years in classroom teaching. Currently, she teaches at Pima Community College Northwest and in writing workshops. Her most popular workshop is called "Writing from the

Deep Heart," a combination of writing and Sufi meditation practices. She was a founding editor of Moon Journal Press and its editor-in-chief for fifteen years. Contact her at Maryhber@aol.com. [32]

JOEL BERMAN has published mystery novels, historical novels, short stories, medical texts, and humorous verse. He currently resides in southern California. "Cancer" is from his recent book of short stories, *Fifty-two Pieces* (Pennywyse Press, 2010). [217]

BOBBIE JEAN BISHOP: Earlier in my life, I wrote to survive that edge between the inner and the outer world. The edge today is not as raw as it used to be. Now I can breathe more deeply and explore with more serenity what asks to be expressed, engaging faculties of discernment that were once out of reach. I thank all avenues of publication through the years for including me in their journals and anthologies. [77, 214]

BERNADETTE BLUE grew up in various American communities throughout the rural Midwest. Many of her poems are an attempt to frame those disarmingly simple days of childhood and the lasting spells they cast. Today, she lives in Arizona with her husband. In addition to writing poetry, she compiles family genealogies. "Ruby Slippers" is her second poem to be published in *OASIS Journal*. [286]

SARAH BOLEK began her art education at the Chicago Art Institute as a teenager. After marrying, she pursued her interest in art, studying and exhibiting in South America, Europe, Mexico, and the United States. Her search for meaningful titles for her paintings led her to poetry, where she found that the two were "kindred spirits." At OASIS she began to explore her interest in poetry as a second language under the tutelage of their excellent teachers. Thank you, OASIS, for fostering the Art Spirit in all of us and showing us that it can endure as long as we live. [151]

JANE BORUSZEWSKI was born in Eastern Poland and deported to Siberia in 1940. While traveling by train after amnesty, she and her sister and brother were hospitalized with typhoid and separated from family. Jane was brought to East Africa in 1942, where she graduated from high school in Tengeru. After WWII she signed up for work in England, where she met and married her husband, Walt. They emigrated to America in 1950 and raised three daughters. Later, Jane graduated from Onondaga Community College with highest honors. Jane's novel, *Escape from Russia*, was published posthumously in 2010 by Pennywyse Press. [88]

JOHN J. BRENNAN is an 80-year-old retired Veterinarian. Throughout his veterinary years, his family urged him to write a book to tell others about the interesting incidents that made his career so wonderful. John met his wife during their last year at Cornell. Two of their children are also Cornellians. The non-Cornellian has practiced medicine in Ithaca for over 30 years. So far, two grandchildren are also Cornellians. So Cornell University and Ithaca, New York are very important locations for the Brennan family. John has lived in the town of Guilderland for 55 years. He established Guilderland Animal Hospital in 1955. [267]

ROBERT BROOKS was born in Cleveland, Ohio in 1927. He very much enjoys languages (foreign and domestic), literature, classical music, animals (wild and domestic), infants, and small children. At the neighborhood school where he tutors first-graders, he has had the thrill of discovering budding authors who still have their baby-teeth! Robert write memoirs because he believes that, to a large extent, we are what we remember. He hopes that, someday, the younger generation in his family will want to find out who he was. [235]

ESTHER BRUDO: The pinball machine in my Uncle Jack's American Delicatessen, I sensed even as a child, was his one way of having light-hearted fun during his long hours behind the counter. Much like the practice of darts in an English pub, it also united in pleasurable enterprise his small band of devoted customers. So I enjoyed writing this homage and am glad it was selected. As I write this, I see some parallels to my OASIS poetry class, where we have gathered year after year in the warmth and glow of poetry writing. [340]

EVELYN BURETTA returned from California to her Midwestern roots after completing careers in technical writing and the U.S. Army Reserve. "Rising From Ruins," one of her first poems, was published in the anthology *Tree Magic: Natures Antennas*, SunShine Press Publications, 2005. Her poetry has been published in *OASIS Journal 2007, 2008,* and *2009*. Writing inspirations come from her childhood experiences in rural southern Illinois in the '40s and '50s. Her current "No Small Gift" is such an example; others come from workshops and everyday surroundings. Evelyn resides in St. Louis, Missouri. [147, 293]

Through the years of a satisfying career, JACK CAMPBELL would occasionally write poetry for special days. When retirement loomed, his "well to go to" was overflowing, and he has not stopped writing. His joy still remains in the fulfillment he gets from birthing a new effort. Selling his work would probably be a high, but he doesn't dwell on it or need the money, which leaves him free to please himself, and not an editor. The writing must continue, as long as the well he goes to is "half full," and even if it's half empty! [97]

TRUDY CAMPBELL: Most importantly, I want to thank my precious Mom for never giving up on me or my creative talents. I also learned much from Judy

Reeves, Mary Harker, Arn Shein, and a small group of friends. I am retired from the public school system and feel strongly that the arts are vital for every child. For me, writing, painting, and taking photograhs are as necessary as breathing. My dear Joe has been there for me for over 35 years. This poem is in no way a lack of respect for my father. This is my first publication. [117]

SALLY CARPER: I have been attending the creative writing class at the Milwaukie Senior Center in Milwaukie, Oregon for several years. Our instructor is a constant source of inspiration, and I am so proud to be joined by several of my fellow classmates within these pages. "A Second Chance" is dedicated to the memory of my dear friend, Georgia, and Georgia's son, who strayed from life's path. Anyone who is blessed with a "second chance" needs to use it wisely. [203]

CAROL CHRISTIAN: My writing class is where I began seriously learning to write about my innermost feelings and ideas. I have created poems and stories since I was a child, but have grown up as a writer in my Wednesday Group. My husband, children, grandchildren, great-grandchild, and the rest of my family, plus my friends, teacher, writing classmates, and two cats have given me much inspiration. I'd like to thank them all for their love and encouragement. What a joyful and meaningful way to spend my retirement. [141, 161]

TERESA CIVELLO spent more than 35 years as a senior manager at NYC Medicaid and as a private consultant writing technical training manuals for healthcare providers. "And on the Seventh Day" is based on an actual event. Teresa divides her time between New York City and Albuquerque, New Mexico. She's a member of SouthWest Writers and has taken classes at Gotham Writers' in New York. [57]

ALICE R. CORRELL: I've been writing small stories and bits of poetry for years. A few years ago, I joined a Creative Writing class at the Senior Center in Milwaukie, Oregon, which I enjoyed so much that I started one at the resort in Yuma, Arizona, where I spend my winters. At one time I worked with Arizona Live Poets in Yuma. I grew up in Nebraska and South Dakota and taught there in rural schools for a few years, then went on vacation in Oregon and never returned. We ran a small town Movie Theatre there for many years. [344]

JOAN T. DORAN: When I retired some years ago as a social service agency director, I couldn't have imagined the major role that writing would come to play in my "Third Age." By now, I have written enough poems, essays, and family stories to fill several books, and some of them gratifyingly find their way into print. "For Creation, Benediction" is the result of a local poet's challenge to try to include "animals, lovers, and clowns" in one poem. How well this succeeds, I'm not sure, but it was great fun to write. [262]

ELISA DRACHENBERG: "Are your stories autobiographical?" My characters range from a food-obsessed lawyer, whose fascination with all things Mother might have delighted Freud, to a skinny, red-haired painter fearful of losing her talent, husband, and health; a clever little girl who gets caught in the tensions of post-war Germany's search for its missing soldiers; a son of an eminent Dutch writer who prefers soccer to literature; an accident-prone professor who loves motorcycles; a scientist with the uncanny ability to predict the devastation of a hurricane; a grandmother taking revenge on her annoying grand-kids...So the answer is a sonorous: yes. [363]

MARY ROSE DURFEE was born in 1916 and has lived her entire life in Central New York State. At age 94 she continues to live a happy, independent life, driving her friends to Bingo, doctor appointments, and social events. She loves writing about her life experiences. Her articles and stories have been published in local newspapers, but it is a special honor to be published in the *OASIS Journal* again. The idea for "The Price of Bubbles" came to her during some recent paving of her street, and the odor of tar brought memories of a time she will always remember. [231]

BUCK DOPP retired in 2009 from a 27-year career in the telecommunications industry. He and Stephanie, his wife of 35 years, relocated from the Philadelphia area to Lake Havasu City, Arizona. He decided to become serious about writing, joined the Havasu Writers Group, and has been writing short stories ever since. Buck and Stephanie regularly play pool in local tournaments and have enjoyed the camaraderie of their fellow pool players, who are all unique but share a common love for pool. They inspired him to write the story of "Skinny Post." [341]

MARGARET E. FRANCIS was born on July 4, 1923, in London, England. When the bombing of London started, her mother sent her to Rickinghall for safekeeping. There she met her husband, who had just come back from Dunkirk and was stationed at a small village close by. They were married in July, 1942. When he was shipped off to North Africa and Italy, she joined the WRNS (Women's Royal Naval Service) and worked on the Turing Bombe in the Enigma program. [92]

HELENA FREY: My story is one of those memories gleaned from the past. This is my third opportunity to be published in *OASIS Journal*. I again say "thank you" to the Scribes group sponsored by OASIS in Pittsburgh, Pennsylvania, and to our Moderator, Joan Zekas, for giving us the inspiration we need to write our stories. We have an open house in the spring and invite OASIS members in Pittsburgh to come and hear the stories and poems we've submitted to *OASIS Journal.* [181]

JIM FRISBIE and his wife, Rinya, are United Methodist Pastors living near Portland, Oregon. They have two grown sons. Jim has many outdoor interests, including backpacking, skiing, canoeing, working with horses, and building and flying his own airplane. The poem, "On Baldy," came out of their time living and working in Idaho. Jim describes his writing this way: "Poetry, for me, is an exercise in brevity…a good skill for a preacher to cultivate!" Jim has had poems published in *Alive Now*, local and national church publications, and the University of Wyoming annual anthology, *Hard Ground.* [153]

GINGER GALLOWAY: I believe writing may be considered a form of art therapy designed to promote the personal healing of those exposed to trauma. For instance, when I am troubled, and the words come tumbling out of my head and onto the paper, I am no longer a victim. Words…set me free! "Small Miracles" was not intended to be a political statement, rather to demonstrate the personal healing process of a very young operating room technician fresh out of school, enlightened by a vast new world of surgery…but also shocked by the horror she sees during an unforeseen emergency crisis. [223]

MARIE THERESE GASS, born in Canada, moved to the States in 1947 with her parents and siblings. She taught full high school plus adult education classes in various visual arts. Marie began writing seriously in 1990 and has been hooked ever since. Three of her books are currently available on amazon.com. In 2000, her husband sustained Traumatic Brain Injury, and Marie credits writing with getting her through the past 10 years of 24/7 caregiving. "Lullaby" is a true story. Marie may be reached at caregive@easystreet.net. [123]

KATHLEEN ELLIOTT GILROY: Even when I had a full time job as a special education teacher, I was a volunteer with animals: The Feral Cat Coalition in San Diego County, a foster parent for kittens (through the local Animal Care Facility), and an animal communicator/massage person (not just for felines). I have had several writings published, including with OASIS. The poem, "Harmony," came from an actual experience. I am grateful for my family, animals, friends, writing, nature, still being productive, and still learning. [255]

NATALIE GOTTLIEB is a retired psychotherapist and a practicing fine artist. Recently, she has added writing to her pool of creative expressions. Counseling people, painting them, or writing about their struggles all seem to mirror one another. Natalie strives to extract the hidden emotional kernel that stirs just beneath the surface and to translate that feeling into a painting, poem, or story. Her constant search for the unseen motivates her. She is deeply concerned with the human condition and how people's desires, disappointments, and triumphs affect their lives. Her own experience of a recent loss prompted her to write "Vigilant." [174]

NIK GRANT: "Computers Are a Good Thing" pays homage to my childhood reading during the Golden Age of Science Fiction, where I encountered the writings of Asimov, Bradbury, Clarke, and others. One day, our Escondido OASIS writing class instructor recounted a frustrating experience with his Freakin Computer. My "Computers Are a Good Thing" was nearly birthed right then, the germinator being The Friedkin Computer. [327]

FLORA GRATERON has been writing most of her life. Her stories and poems reflect the complexity and rewards of living among a Mexican-American family rich in culture and tradition. "Cosmo Dog" developed after a family discussion on putting a lifelong pet to rest. Flora's work has been published in *The Blue Guitar*, an arts and literary magazine of the Arizona Consortium for the Arts, and in *La Bloga*, a Flor y Canto speaking out on Immigration issues. She belongs to Sowing the Seeds, a women's writers group, and teaches English/Language Arts in the Sunnyside School District in Tucson, Arizona. [244]

DIANA GRIGGS is a transplant from England. This year she is published in *San Diega Poetry Annual* and finds Mary Harker's OASIS poetry class a constant source of inspiration and support. [121]

JOAN HARRIS: My English/Drama teacher picked the stage play I'd written as the best of my class. Unfortunately, although he encouraged me to keep writing, events in my life led me in another direction. It took an early retirement and an OASIS Creative Writing class to renew that passion. My short stories and poems mostly reflect real life events. However, the three screenplays I've written and the novel I've recently finished are fiction, as is my second novel. My latest challenge is helping a friend turn his series of short stories into a screenplay for a pilot of a possible TV series. [207]

R. E. HAYES was born in Chicago, joined the Marines after high school, and served four years as an infantry machine gunner. Formerly a federal labor lawyer, he was educated at Indiana University. Recent publishing credits include a story in the spring 2010 issue of *Evening Street Review* and one coming out in September in the *Crab Orchard Review*. "Squeegee" is based on two unrelated news items: an off-duty cop shot and killed a man under questionable circumstances and went to prison, and a tow truck operator towed a car with an elderly woman inside, probably scared out of her wits. [383]

When not writing in her lakeside home in Haliburton County, Ontario, TIINA HEATHCOCK has devoted her time to arranging events to mentor young writers and events to provide an opportunity for people from various forms of the arts to meet and perform together. Her first collection of poetry, *up North*, was published by Passion Among the Cacti Press in 2004. Her second collection, *afterimages*, came out in April 2005. She has also been published in *Quills*, and various anthologies, magazines, and newspapers. In the past, she was Writer in Residence for the Dorset Library. [118, 148]

TILYA GALLAY HELFIELD was born and raised in Ottawa, and now resides in Toronto. Her memoir, *Metaphors for Love*, is now being considered for publication by a Toronto publisher. Tilya's short stories and essays have appeared in *TV Guide*, *The Fiddlehead*, *Viewpoints*, and *Monday Morning*. An accomplished multi-media artist, she has participated in 12 solo and more than 75 juried group exhibitions in Canada, the U.S., Spain, Brazil, Japan and Korea, and has won several awards. Her work may be found in 27 public collections, in private collections in Canada, the U.S. and Europe and can be seen at www.tilyahelfield.com. [275]

JEANNE HENDERSON resides with her husband of forty-one years in San Marcos, California. She has a bachelor's degree in Language Arts and has been writing short stories, memoirs, and poetry for thirty years. "The Sandals" is her first submission for publication. The idea for the story was a prompt given in an OASIS creative writing class: "You are walking along and come upon a sandal." Of all the stories Jeanne has written, this is one of her favorites. [171]

JACQUELINE HILL: Born in Ohio, I am a Southern Californian, retired educator, now free to pursue my dream of publishing my writing. I have been seeing, dreaming, living, and writing poetry, stories, and essays for at least fifty years. I am a member of Writers Anonymous, a workshop sponsored through the UCLA Writing Project. "Here to Stay" and "Called Home" celebrate my connections to all of my families, whose stories inspire me. [347, 349]

MAURICE HIRSCH authored three poetry collections: *Taking Stock*, *Stares to Other Places*, and *Roots and Paths*. His work has appeared in *Untamed Ink* and *New Harvest: Jewish Writing in St. Louis, 1998-2005*. He and his wife live on a farm in Chesterfield, Missouri, where he rides Paso Fino horses. "Choosing Burial Plots" – I'm interested in how poets think about and deal with their own deaths. This is in no way morbid or depressing. While the basis of this poem occurred almost 20 years ago, it made an impression that lay dormant until I started to explore feelings around my 70th birthday. [142]

ANDREW HOGAN received his doctorate in development studies from the University of Wisconsin-Madison. Before retirement, he was a faculty member at SUNY Stony Brook, the University of Michigan, and Michigan

State University, where he taught medical ethics, health policy, and the social organization of medicine in the College of Human Medicine. Dr. Hogan published more than five dozen professional articles on health services research and health policy. "Dynamite" is his sixth published work of fiction and was prepared for the Advanced Fiction Workshop at Pima Community College, where he is a student of creative writing. [315]

THOMAS J. HUMPHREY: "Introspection" is from my unpublished short story collection, *The Reader's Buffet*. I usually write merely for fun, but "Introspection" is a fictionalized version of a personal experience. Most of my published works have been non-fiction, a book on computer programming and half a dozen magazine articles. My amateur screenplay, "The Stairwell," won second prize in a contest and was published. My short story, "The Exospatial Theory of Hellenic Origin," was published in a science fiction anthology. My first novel, "A Knight on Long Island," is unpublished, but I'm pushing it (argh, grunt, grunt). [163]

UNA NICHOLS HYNUM, most recently published in *A Year in Ink*, *Magee Park Anthology*, *OASIS Journal*, *San Diego Poetry Annual*, a finalist for James Hearst Poetry Prize, *The Writers Digest*, and *Margie*. [144, 210]

JANET IRVIN's work has appeared in a variety of print and online publications. Three of her stories have sold to *Alfred Hitchcock Mystery Magazine*, the most recent one in May, 2010. "Searching for Mr. Mistletoe" exists because a group of her students demanded that she write a tale that included all of them! She accepted the challenge, believing that to teach is also to do, and that rules re the number of characters, while generally admirable, must sometimes be circumvented. She changed the names of the students, but preserved, she hopes, their unique personalities. [21]

RUTH MOON KEMPHER has had her poetry and short prose appear in various publications since 1958, and has published other people's work through her Kings Estate Press in St. Augustine, Florida, since 1994. Retired from teaching in the English Department of the local community college, her latest collection of verse is *Visions and Aspirations of Sister Hilda H.* from Kindred Spirit Press. After years of living at the beach, she now lives in the woods in an old cracker house, with two dogs: Sadie, a long-legged hound, and Mister Frost, an emotional American Husky. [72, 73]

WILLIAM KILLIAN is an actor, poet, minister, and marriage and family therapist who loves the game of basketball. His most recent book of poetry, a journal of his work and life, is *All The Faces I Have Been: An Actor's Notebook* (Imago Press, 2010). Bill lives in Tucson, Arizona. [376, 391]

SHARON LAABS graduated with a degree in Music from Washington State University and taught in the public schools, later working in Group Sales. After retirement, she accidentally discovered writing poetry and has had great fun with it every since. Her work has appeared in the San Diego Poetry Annual 2009-10. "The Delightful Oblivion of Being Five" is written from memories of growing up in southern Idaho in the 1940's. [230]

KAY LESH is a professional counselor in Tucson and teaches Psychology for Pima Community College. She enjoys working, so has no plans to retire just yet. When work is no longer fun, it will be time to stop. Kay has written some professional articles and co-authored books on self-esteem and dealing with the psychological aspects of money. Her writing is changing as she ages, and she is moving into doing more personal essays and fiction. "Invisibility" is a look at one aspect of her own aging process. [139]

ELLARAINE LOCKIE writes poetry, nonfiction books, essays, and children's stories. She has received writing residencies at Centrum in Port Townsend, WA, and eleven Pushcart Prize nominations. She's been a recent recipient of the Lois Beebe Hayna Award, the One Page Poem Prize, the Elizabeth R. Curry Prize, the Writecorner Press Poetry Award, the Skysaje Poetry Prize, and the Dean Wagner Poetry Prize. Ellaraine has authored eight chapbooks, and the last one, *Red for the Funeral*, won the 2010 San Gabriel Valley Poetry Festival Chapbook Contest. She also serves as Poetry Editor for the lifestyles magazine, *Lilipoh*, and teaches poetry/writing workshops. [258, 292]

SUSE MARSH was born, raised, and educated in Germany in the beautiful Black Forest region. In 1961 fell in love with an American engineer while visiting the U.S. They were married in 1965 in Germany. Suse has three children and three grandchildren, and for them she decided to write her story on growing up in Germany. The Scribes group at OASIS inspires her. Suse still visits Germany yearly and feels fortunate to know two different countries and their cultures in depth and, most importantly, to have family and friends to make it home. [119]

MARTHA J. MARTIN is an 83-year-old new writer, recently retired for the third time after a sixty-five-year bookkeeping career. Upon joining the Menifee Writers Group in 2007, her first memoir/essay was "My Two True Loves," referring to numbers and words. Obviously, she followed her love of numbers during her working life. Now free to indulge in her love of words and seeking a Christmas theme to write about, this memory of "Christmas 1944" popped up in the middle of the night, accompanied by the rhyming words which begged to be written. [114]

SERETTA MARTIN, regional editor for the San Diego Poetry Annual, hosts the Barnes and Noble Poetry Series, La Mesa, and is a founding member of Haiku San Diego Society. Recent publishing credits include: *OASIS Journal 2007* and *2009*, *A Year in Ink Volumes I and III*, *Margie: The American Journal of Poetry*, Oberon Foundation, San Diego Poetry Annuals, *Tidepools*, St. Marks Religions Art Festivals, *The Best Of Border Voices*, and on-line journals *Web del Sol*, *Poetic Voices*, and *Muse Apprentice*. Her book, *Foreign Dust, Familiar Rain*, is available at barnesandnoble.com and amazon.com. (See wordsoup@juno.com, web.mac.com/serettamartin, haikusandiego.blogspot.com) [291]

MARILYN L. KISH MASON: My poem, "Witch Creek," appeared in *OASIS Journal 2009*. This year, I decided to submit a short story and was delighted when it was accepted. "Special Delivery" was written some time ago and many things have changed since then. My granddaughter has recovered, attended college, is working, and has a miracle child of her own. My poems appear in two books written by friends, on the Internet, and in four volumes of the International Library of Poetry. I enjoy the friendships I've made in Mary Harker's classes, where I feel I continue to grow as a poet. [253]

LOLENE McFALL: Being included in *OASIS Journal* for a third year is both a pleasure and a privilege. It's been a journey with Mary Harker's class at OASIS in San Diego, CA. Some poems develop slowly; others surprise and demand to be written. While driving, I passed a car carrying a large sign, *Life is Good*. Thoughts were quickly scrawled on a scrap of paper while waiting in traffic at every red light until I reached home. Two hours later, after some argument, the poem, "Outward Bound," had its final word. [294]

ANNE McKENRICK: I'm elated to have another story about my granddaughter and her best friend ("The Knot Hole") selected for *OASIS Journal 2010*. "Little Girls," about her and two of her friends, was published in *OASIS Journal 2009*. I've always loved to write, and my small weekly writing group takes precedence over most other activities in my life. My fellow students are observant, insightful, and contribute meaningfully to any finished product I achieve. Pat Arnold, who teaches creative writing in Milwaukie, Oregon, is a perceptive instructor. I'm grateful Pat pushes her students to the limit - and then some. [273]

Tucson writer/poet/geologist SUSAN CUMMINS MILLER, a research affiliate of the University of Arizona's Southwest Institute for Research on Women, penned the award-winning Frankie MacFarlane mystery novels *Death Assemblage*, *Detachment Fault*, *Quarry*, *Hoodoo*, and *Fracture* (in press, Texas Tech UP). She also edited *A Sweet, Separate Intimacy: Women Writers of the*

American Frontier, 1800-1922. Her poems have appeared in regional journals and anthologies, including *What Wildness Is This: Women Write about the Southwest, SandScript 2009, New Texas 2009,* and *Roundup! Western Writers of America Presents Great Stories of the West from Today's Leading Western Writers* (2010). [221]

TINA MORI: I can't remember a time when I did not have the urge to write down the dreams, stories, songs, and poems constantly rattling around in my head. Writing has always been a place to unwind from the daily pressures of work, raising three daughters as a single parent, and general survival. I've been told I have a trilogy of books inside me. I woke up one morning from a dream about my recently deceased mother and outlined them in detail. *Exit My Soul* will be written from the perspective of my mother, as she descends into the world of Alzheimer's. [175]

MICHAEL B. MOSSMAN was born in Alton, Illinois, served honorably with the U.S. Marine Corps in Vietnam, graduated from Southern Illinois University at Edwardsville, and received a Masters from the University of Oklahoma at Norman. Michael spent thirty-three years in the fields of Elementary and Special Education. Now retired, he spends his time writing stories and doing art. Michael's story, "The Last Letter," appeared in *OASIS Journal 2008.* He wrote "A Date to Remember" out of fondness for his college days, and in remembrance of the special way he met his wife. Michael and his wife live in Edwardsville, Illinois. [61]

ELEANOR WHITNEY NELSON has enjoyed a career as an exploration geologist traveling worldwide with her geologist husband, Frank. A longtime Tucson resident, she holds degrees in English and Geology. With numerous short works in print, she can be read in several anthologies, including *OASIS Journal, The Story Teller,* and *Chicken Soup for the Soul.* She often draws from her journals for her short stories, memoirs, poetry, and novels. "Why Disturb a Winner?" is a companion piece to "Rafting," last year's account of home ownership woes. Again, seat-of-the-pants ingenuity is called on, this time with the hope of rescuing a remodeling nightmare. [199]

MARLENE NEWMAN, mother of four, grandmother of two, has always found words and language fascinating. For many years, she shared her knowledge of reading, writing, and library skills as an elementary school teacher, a reading specialist, and a school librarian. Her book, *Myron's Magic Cow,* was published in 2005 by Barefoot Books. She was, indeed, ticketed for overtime parking the morning after she spoke up to protest an action by the Board of Education. The letter 'T' had fallen from a nameplate in the court room so that it read, "In God We _rust." [379]

KATHLEEN O'BRIEN began writing two years after the death of her husband. Her first poem, "Permission" (to be happy), came as she walked around a lake. She wrote "Acoustics of Autumn" reliving delight with her grandson. "A Bunch of Daffodils" expresses kinship felt with an old woman who loved beauty. Hobbies include reading, writing, poetry, dancing, gardening, volunteering for hospice. The mother of four grown children, "Nanny" to four grandsons, and former teacher, she's now an LPN working two days a week to pay for her love of travel (just returned from a two-week tour of Ireland and Scotland). [138, 228]

RICHARD O'DONNELL began writing fiction, a lifelong ambition, after a career as a business journalist, speechwriter, and publications editor. Although the two fields, fact and fiction, couldn't be more dissimilar, he says, his years of writing nonfiction taught him the virtues of accuracy, brevity, scrupulous editing, and letting a story speak for itself. "The Gormley Curse" marks his fourth published story in *OASIS Journal*. [331]

BARBARA OSTREM: At 75, having a story of mine accepted for publication is truly a thrill. My friend and I have taken creative writing at a local senior center for six years and have developed close friendships with several classmates. My beloved husband of 52 years was an avid fisherman, and "Take Out Dinner" is only one of many true experiences. Our two daughters, grandchildren, and great grandchildren are my life's blessings. I enjoy writing, lunching with book club friends, and the company of squirrels, wild birds, and the neighbors' cats in my back yard. [257]

DOROTHY PARCEL: "I am 82 years old and have been reading and writing all this time. I have been married to the same man for 65 years, and we have three kids. I guess all that gives a person a sense of humor or thoughts of homicide. I taught children and adults and, on the way, I learned that writers are the most interesting people to know." [239]

ANTHONY ADRIAN PINO teaches English at Ohlone College in Fremont, California and San Jose City College. His poetry and fiction have been published in *riverbabble, Tattoo Highway, Poets Against the War, A Day Without Art, Occam's Razor, Door Knobs and Body Paint*, and *OASIS Journal 2005*. He won the Jackie DeClerq Poetry Award and the Don Markos Poetry Award. One of his poems, "Concerto Pacifico," was honorably mentioned by the California Poetry Society, and another won the "Picture is Worth a Thousand Words" contest at *Tattoo Highway*. [86]

BARBARA PONOMAREFF is a retired child psychotherapist with published short stories in *Descant, (Ex)cite, Precipice, Artsforum*, and *Surfacing*. Her novella, *A Minor Genre*, was published in the arts magazine, *Artichoke*, and later as a chapbook. Some of her poetry can be found in professional publications. Lately, her work has been included in *Artsforum* and the anthology, *The Saving Bannister*. A number of poems were displayed alongside her abstract paintings in last year's *Word and Image* show. "Evening Light" was inspired by walks up to the next concession in the countryside close to her home in the greater Toronto area. [216]

CAROL POSS is happily retired and enjoying participating in OASIS programs, including the Writers' Group and the Person to Person Peer Support Group. She has published poems in *Voices along the River, Inkwell Echoes,* and *Lucidity*. The poem, "Night Train," was the result of an assignment in the Open Mike Poetry Venue with Poet Laureate Chris Crabtree, at Barnes and Noble Book Store. "A Blue Funk" was written from memories of being a working mother, raising six children, sharing with other women and, through it all, finding humor and learning to laugh at oneself. [87, 378]

DAVID RAY's writings focus on a number of leadings, ranging from lyric poems of love and grief to passionate protest and memoir. His memoir, *The Endless Search*, is a probing search of his early years, which have been described as "Dickensian, full of abuse and tragedy." To this work he brings the insights of a man who has studied his own history as both clinical and mystical reality, a celebration of survival. [155]

JUDY RAY's most recent book is *To Fly Without Wings: Poems* (Helicon Nine Editions, 2009). A review in *The Tucson Weekly* claims that in this book "Judy Ray manages a difficult balancing act between fearless autobiography and strict formalism." Other recent publications include the chapbooks *Fishing in Green Waters, Sleeping in the Larder: Poems of a Sussex Childhood*, and *Judy Ray: Greatest Hits 1974 – 2008*. More information is at www.davidraypoet. com/JudyRay. [189]

RITA RIES, busy retired lady, has been published several times in *OASIS Journal*. She loves to trek out to the poppy fields every spring. In April she introduced Sheila, a dear friend who has cancer, to the abundant blossoms, a truly memorable event for both. "La Sabanilla" is dedicated to this special friend. Rita continues in her two ongoing poetry classes, as she has for the past nine years. She is also publishing her first book of poetry this year in honor of her five children as a surprise! She also hopes for many more springs of Copa de Ora. [265]

ADRIENNE ROGERS: "Coming Upstate – the Immigrant Experience" is nonfiction about a transition from urban life to a more rural—though still in a city—existence, beginning in the early '60s. It adds on to "Voices," published as fiction in *OASIS Journal 2007*, which dealt with anxieties in preparation for a test with serious career implications. A dear friend—the inspiration for Milton Cohen in "Portrait of a Lady in Red" (*OASIS Journal 2008*)—who died recently always urged me to write about the "life stories" I told him. Perhaps they, too, will find their way into future editions of *OASIS Journal*. [185]

JUDITH K. ROSE was writing "The Quality of Light" the morning her friend, Neil Coleman, died. In 2007 they both had to move due to the 'Ellis Act', whereby an owner can evict all tenants by going out of the rental business. Judith now lives even closer to Santa Monica beach! She is working on a chapbook titled *Creation Myth Poems & A New Year Poem*, and is also planning a CD. Her poem published in *Sarah's Daughters Sing* was reprinted in *The Torah: A Women's Commentary*. She fulfilled a pre-natal dream by studying post-modern dance and choreography 1994-2000. [188]

ALBERT RUSSO, who has published worldwide over 65 books of poetry, fiction, and photography in English and in French, is the recipient of many awards, including The American Society of Writers Fiction Award, The British Diversity Short Story Award, several New York Poetry Forum Awards, Amelia Prose and Poetry awards, and the Prix Colette. His work has been translated into a dozen languages and broadcast by the World Service of the BBC. He was also a member of the 1996 jury for the prestigious Neustadt International Prize for Literature, which often leads to the Nobel Prize of Literature. [81]

GLORIA SALAS-JENNINGS serves as the Intergenerational Programs Coordinator at San Antonio OASIS. Additionally, she teaches Creative Writing Classes at OASIS. She facilitates the OASIS Writers Group, where she uses the power of words to inspire and motivate. She creates a passion in her students to put their creativity to work and to be free with their imagination. She writes about herself, her life, and the people who have made her the mujer—the woman—she is today. [382]

SUZANNE SCHMIDT is a writer, poet, teacher, and active member of the Writer's Circle of Durham Region and the Ontario Poetry Society. Her work is inspired by her loving mother's display of optimism and strength after given only two months to live, their incredible journey, and the special bond they shared. The short story presented in this book is an excerpt from her memoir, *Till We Meet Again*, and is only one of many hilarious lifelong adventures they shared. To read more of Suzanne's work, visit www.writingfromthesoulsuzanne.com. [129]

FREDERICK SCHUBERT was born in Albany, New York on November 11, 1931, and graduated from high school in 1949. In the fall of '51 he joined the Marine Corps, where he served in Korea and was discharged in 1954. He worked for Honeywell as a field tech rep for 39 years. He has been married to his wife, Claudette, for 54 years. They have two daughters. His poem resulted from attempts to explain to some of the younger generation what "Rushing the Growler" means. This is his first work to be published. [154]

HOWARD SCHUMAN has lived and worked in over 30 countries. He is an international human resources consultant who enjoys writing essays about his travels. He has authored two books, *Making It Abroad: The International Job Hunting Guide* (Wiley) and *Human Resources Toolkit for Financial Institutions in Developing Markets* (World Bank). Other recent essays by Howard include "Vietnam Volumes," "Lost Luggage," and "Liberia 2010." He lives in Eugene, Oregon with his wife and daughter, who join him on his travels whenever possible. [359]

CLARE SELGIN is an anthropologist by training and a freelance editor by profession. "Jamaica Romance" is her first published fiction, adapted from a full-length unpublished novel. [45]

PHYLLIS SELTZER: I've been published in various poetry anthologies and previously twice in *OASIS Journal*. I am thrilled to have my story selected for publication. I love writing both poetry and prose, and enjoy belonging to a very small group of poets who meet each week to write together. I am the very lucky Wife of David, Daughter of Pearl, Mother of Rebecca, Jeffrey, Elizabeth, and Susie, Grandmother of Sara, Lauren, Julie, Abigayle, and Jake. I enjoy painting and drawing as well as writing and am so grateful for this creative outlet. [269]

In private practice as a psychotherapist, IRMA SHEPPARD has lived in Tucson for the past twenty-seven years with her husband and a succession of cats. Living in the foothills next to the desert allows her to include snakes, scorpions, and tarantulas in the pool, coyote concerts, and strolling bobcats in her list of so-called cheap thrills. The challenge of saying much in the compressed forms of poetry continues to thrill and delight her. In 2000, she received the Martindale Literary Award. Her short stories and poems have been published in numerous journals across the country. [314]

FRANCES ("MITZIE") SKRBIN is 76, widowed, retired, and active in her church, AARP, and OASIS. She wrote the first two verses of "God Doesn't Make Mistakes" when her youngest son turned 21. She remembers how upset she was when she became pregnant for the sixth time, but that was before she knew what a blessing this child would be to everyone who knew him. When Michael was 29, he was diagnosed with stage 4 colon cancer. Determined to beat it, he fought valiantly for two years. The week before he died, she came across this poem and added the third verse. [227]

A native of Kansas City, CARL SNOW graduated from the University of Maryland and had a long career in the United States Navy. After retirement, he worked as Assistant Editor for *The Hook* magazine, and then as Production Editor for the *Topgun Journal* at the Navy Fighter Weapons School. When *Topgun* moved to Fallon, Nevada, Carl remained in San Diego, working as a Technical Writer, researching and writing manufacturing process documents for hi-tech electronics manufacturers. Carl retired for good in March of this year and lives with his dog, Rudy, in Valley Center, California. [355]

JEAN SNOW graduated from New York State College for Teachers, taught French, translated *Medieval Latin Literature*, later became a professional singer, teaching voice at home and at a private girls' school. In 1993, she wrote her first poem. The next year she won 1st and 2nd prizes at a Shakespeare Festival in Olympia, Washington for her sonnets. Jean has sold many articles and poems, and won other prizes. She was a columnist from 2000-2008 for her genealogy society's quarterly, and taught a writers' group since 2002. She's currently researching and working on a memoir, *The Day Before April*. [256]

STEVE SNYDER lives in Tucson and pursues literature, growth, and God. He began writing poetry and fiction as a teenager. Many of his poems and stories have been published or read on the radio. "Long Dark Night" is a theraputic poem written on the last day of 2009. It's one in a series of over three dozen poems, "The Karen Chronicles," an attempt to process the loss of the love of someone special. [78]

MARY LOU STAFFORD loves to write and has been keeping a journal for over forty years. Five years ago, she started making major changes in her life and began writing poetry in earnest. She's written close to fifty poems since then. "It All Comes Down to This" was written shortly before her father died. Born in Mallory, New York, he was surviving only on ice chips by the end. As they sat together, she saw so clearly the message that her poem conveys. Mary Lou lives in San Diego, California, and this is the first poem she has ever submitted for publication. [143]

ALBERT STUMPH was born near Indianapolis and attended schools in several States on his journey to ordination as a Roman Catholic priest. After resigning his priesthood in 1970, he married and took up a career in social services work. More recently, he has worked mowing lawns for his neighbors in the Chatham, New York area and building furniture in the winters for sale to the general public. He writes the occasional essay just for the fun of it. [248]

FRED K. TAYLOR is a painter and sculptor. A poetry award winner in an international contest sponsored by the Southwestern Society of Authors, he is a naval veteran of the Vietnam war, and owned and worked a farm in

Wisconsin before retiring with his wife, Faye, to Arizona. His most recent book of poetry and short fiction (illustrated) is *Ask No Questions* (Pennywyse Press, 2010). [211]

The 2003 death of a beautifully eccentric friend motivated JANET K. THOMPSON to write about Pearl. As more friends died, writing about them and living friends and relatives revealed the story of her own life. A boarding school survivor who moved 43 times, she experienced many life challenges, two marriages, and two divorces. She was a 1951 Polio epidemic victim, college dropout, office manager, and self-employed bookkeeper. In other incarnations, she was an historic property renovator, urban pioneer, slumlord, water well drilling and other construction companies' partner, financial winner and loser. "Mobius Strip" is the first chapter of Janet's memoirs. [287]

SUSAN C. THOMPSON began her career as an elementary school teacher and went on to focus on special education. The last 35 years of full-time employment she served special needs children in foster care. Now retired, she volunteers as a tutor at a nearby elementary school and works with Community Hospice. Her leisure time passions include opera, theatre, reading, writing, and exercising daily. "Gotta Go" is her first actual publication effort since her high school literary magazine. Her expertise in public toilets arises from the numerous trips she has taken abroad, including Canada, Australia, Ireland, Scotland, England, France, and Italy. [345]

MANUEL TORREZ, JR.: The idea for the poem, "She Was Lost in Time," comes from a time-proven truth, "watch what you wish for." The story, "The Panhandler," is an accumulation of personal experiences, hopes, and fears that I've tried to make plausible with the addition of a lot of imagination. When I write, I want the reader to say, "I have been there; I remember something like that; that could be me." [64, 65]

RUTH TURNER began writing less than ten years ago when, in pursuit of a new hobby, she enrolled in a creative writing class at her local senior center. She now attends a writing group with friends and fellow writers, where she receives her weekly dose of encouragement and inspiration. Her poem, "Mrs. Bumble Goes to Town," reflects the ambience and fond memories of when her children and grandchildren sat on her lap, enjoying a bit of whimsy while she read to them. [136]

BILL VALITUS, born in Chicago in 1930, is a retired mechanical engineer, who spends his time writing and bass fishing in Canyon Lake, California, where he lives. "The Pea Coat Fiasco" is an excerpt from his book, *Navy Daze*, an account of his stint in the U.S. Navy during the Korean conflict. He's currently working on a Science Fiction novel, while continually adding to his collection of satirical anecdotes. His ambition is to fish the headwaters of the Orinoco in Brazil, and he's presently seeking an agent or publisher to make his dream come true. He can be reached at bvalitus@hotmail.com. [103]

SHARON (REISS) VOELLER was born in Minnesota and moved to Portland, Oregon when she was five years old. Her father preceded the family to Portland to work in the shipyards in 1943. Her mother and brother came out a few months later, after her father found housing at University Homes for his family. Sharon graduated from Hillsboro High School and trained at IBM to be a keypunch operator. She worked at Portland General Electric for seven years, during which time she married her husband, Paul. They have four children and seven grandchildren. Her hobbies are Genealogy and Creative Writing. [238]

PAUL VOELLER was born and raised in Portland, Oregon. Thanks to God and his parents' influence, his life has been normal or better most of the time. Portland is a good place to live if you don't mind the rain ten months a year. If you ride a bicycle in the rain and don't have fenders, your lower extremities will get soaked in a hurry. Heavy rainfall helped produce big trees in the Northwest, which resulted in Roseburg being named the "Timber Capitol of the World," a place where several of his uncles owned and operated a saw mill. [215]

EILEEN M. WARD: Retired now from thirty-seven years as an educator in humanities and writing, I have begun pulling together my own thoughts and experiences creatively. "Coming of Age" is a recollection of my first visit, at age fifteen, to my parents' Irish roots, with my maternal cousin as my guide. Walking in ancestral footsteps generously illumines self-identity. [272]

JOHN RUSSELL WEBB is an artist and poet who shares his time between Fayetteville and Brantingham, New York. After retiring from a financial career in 1989, his interests turned to writing and acrylic painting. His first book of poems, *Good Evening Friends*, was published in 2007. The poem, "A Painted Clock," was inspired by a childhood memory of a neighborhood pawn shop, where he first encountered such a clock hanging over the doorway. John is a member of OASIS in Syracuse, New York. [202]

SARAH WELLEN is grateful to *OASIS Journal* for publishing her poems in 2004, 2007, and 2009. She has also been published in various newspapers, newsletters, and anthologies, and has won several poetry contests. Occasionally, she gives poetry readings. Her self-published book of poems, *Reflections*, came out in 2007. The poems published *OASIS Journal 2010* were written in the throes of grief. "The Bent Trunks" was written for her sister, who died at age 20 along with two friends in an auto accident; "onlyness" was written shortly after her husband's death. For Sarah, expressing her grief through poetry was a catharsis. [180, 206]

ANNE WHITLOCK, a retired teacher and systems analyst, enjoys poetry, cats, opera, and anything French. Her Maine Coon, "Baby," who inspired the poem "Chat with a Cat," and her calico, "Fuzzy," are an endless source of mischief and delight. She is grateful for Mary Harker's poetry class at OASIS and for the camaraderie of fellow writers. Although ambiguous about her feelings when she was an elementary school teacher, she absolutely adores teaching the adults in her OASIS French reading class, who share hours of fun reading "editions simplifiées" of writers like Pagnol, Daudet, Hugo, and everyone's favorite: the mysteries of Georges Simenon. [135, 252]

M. CLARK WILDE: Although I have written poetry for many years (see *OASIS Journal 2007*), "Confusion at Edgewater Memory Care" is the first prose piece I have had published. It is the result of a writing exercise in a class I've been enjoying since retirement. The story was inspired by my experience driving an older friend to visit his wife in a care facility. In order for Hershel to retain some of his own retirement funds, he had to divorce his wife. Hershel was heartbroken when her illness caused her to no longer recognize him. [133]

JOAN ELIZABETH ZEKAS: It's been my pleasure and my Joy to continue moderating the Scribes writing group at OASIS in Pittsburgh, Pennsylvania. And what a happy coincidence that my Haiku poems have been accepted for *OASIS Journal 2010*. This trimester our Pittsburgh program has an Asian theme and includes a Japanese tea ceremony, a Feng Shui session, and visits to local temples. My piece, "An Immigrant Life: Snapshots"(OASIS Journal 2008), developed a "life" of its own and ultimately became a DVD. It is now being used for teaching purposes. Blessedly, it also served to heal an old family rift. I am most grateful. [198]

TONY ZURLO's book, *The Mind Dancing*, recently won the award for the Outstanding Poetry Book published by a Peace Corps writer during 2009. His latest publications include two chapbooks: *Go Home Bones*, about the impact of war on loved ones, and *Quantum Chaos: Learning to Live with Cosmic Confusion*, about reflections on contemporary life. Tony's fiction, poetry, essays, and reviews have appeared in more than a hundred newspapers and journals. He has also published books on Vietnam, China, Hong Kong, Japan, Japanese Americans, West Africa, Algeria, Syria, and the United States Congress. [44, 354]

ORDER INFORMATION

Copies of *OASIS Journal 2008* through *2010* are available at:

www.amazon.com
www.barnesandnoble.com

Copies of *OASIS Journal* from previous years (2002-2007) may be ordered at a discount from the publisher at the address below as availability allows. Please enclose $10.00 for each book ordered, plus $3.00 shipping & handling for each order to be sent to one address.

Please make checks payable to Imago Press. Arizona residents add $0.91 sales tax for each book ordered.

Proceeds from the sale of this book go toward the production of next year's *OASIS Journal*. Ten per cent of the net proceeds are donated every year to The OASIS Institute. Your purchase will help us further the creative efforts of older adults. Thank you for your support.

Imago Press
3710 East Edison
Tucson AZ 85716

Breinigsville, PA USA
10 October 2010
246993BV00001B/4/P